Real-World Skin Solutions

The Nature, Nurture, and Science of Modern Skin Care

Ahmed Al-Qahtani, PhD

Publisher's Cataloging-in-Publication data

Al-Qahtani, Ahmed.

Real-world skin solutions: the nature, nurture, and science of modern skin care / Ahmed Al-Qahtani.

p. cm.

ISBN 978-0-9860498-0-4 (pbk.)
ISBN 978-0-9860498-1-1 (e-book)

Includes index.

1. Skin—Care and hygiene. 2. Cosmetics. 3. Beauty, Personal. 4. Skin—Diseases—Popular works. 5. Acne. 6. Aesthetics. 7. Dermatology. I. Title.

RL87 .A47 2014

616.5—dc23 2013954750

This publication contains the opinions and ideas of its author. It is intended to provide helpful and informative material on subjects addressed in the publication. It is sold with the understanding that the author is not engaged in rendering medical, health, or any other kind of personal professional services in the book. The reader should consult his or her medical, health, or other competent professional before adopting any of the suggestions in the book or drawing inferences from it.

The author specifically disclaims all responsibility for any liability, loss, or risk, personal or otherwise, that is incurred as a consequence, directly or indirectly, of the use or application of any of the contents of this book.

Printed and bound in the United States of America.

Contents

Acknowledgments

I would like to express the deepest appreciation and love for my parents. Without them, I would not be the person I am today. I will forever be indebted for all the sacrifices they made for me. I am thankful to my entire family for the support and encouragement I have received from them for my simple accomplishments.

I owe a great many thanks to all the teachers I encountered throughout my education. Each has taught me something that made me a better man.

I would like to thank my friends who have kept me in their thoughts and prayers even when I am not close. They have protected our friendship against time and distance.

Last, but not least, I would like to express my deepest gratitude to my country, the United Arab Emirates (UAE), and to H.H. Sheikh Zayed bin Sultan Al Nahyan, who encouraged me at a young age to pursue my education outside the borders of the UAE. I am fortunate to have been born in the UAE and I now have the opportunity to give back the insights gained through studying on four continents.

CHAPTER 1 Real-World Skin Solutions

The Nature, Nurture, and Science of Modern Skin Care

Human skin is a miracle. It is warm, soft, and amazingly rugged. Whether you have to deal with wrinkles and acne or wounds and burns, your skin has a remarkable capacity to protect and heal. Its blanket of protection keeps your organs and vessels safe, protects you from environmental hazards, and holds the form of all the things you are and all the things you are becoming. It tells you when there is something wrong on the outside and on the inside, so you can deal with health issues before they become big problems.

Our skin manufactures and secretes many beneficial substances, such as waxes and oils. These act as our bodies' natural waterproofing and as a barrier against germs, and they make our skin softer. Sweat glands in the skin produce sweat, which is made up mostly of water and a high concentration of sodium. This fluid moves toward your skin's surface through pores, ridding the body of wastes, and, in a stroke of genius, the natural evaporation of the water cools you down.

The entire operation of the skin is an organic, breathing miracle. It is a multilevel living system with nerves, blood, glands, sensory signals—an unbelievable number of activities all taking place at the same time. The old cells move up to the outer layers and are continuously replaced by a completely new formation of young cells. You manufacture a new batch of surface cells every month or so and lose millions of cells each day.

Yet, even though your skin is your largest organ, and one of the hardest-working organs, it is the organ people take most for granted and tend to know the least about. We suffer for its appearance, and we rub concoctions with mysterious ingredients into its surface. We try to promise it a youthful glow, and then fail to protect it properly with knowledge and care.

Part of the problem is not our skin's vulnerability, but our psychological vulnerability. We want to believe everything skin-care marketers tell us about their products. We want to believe that the signs of time and experience can be smoothed away with lotions. At the same time, we always suspect that we are being had, and we feel ashamed that we are so easily sucked in, even though the skin-care industry is so large—and the financial stakes have become so great—that the marketers work very hard to make it difficult for us to resist their products.

We live in a time when scientific and medical discoveries save and improve many lives. It is also true that these discoveries help us live longer and look younger. These are not promises for the future. This is knowledge we have and are using right now in the real world. Every piece of information and every opinion in this book sheds light on what is out there in today's global market, what products and techniques really work, how to find them, and how to bring all that learning together into a system that works for you.

Separating the truth of science and medicine from the scientific jargon as it is used in cosmetics market-speak is not an easy task. I wrote this book to make it easier.

I have dedicated my professional life to understanding the skin and teaching others about how it works. I have studied at the University of California, the Royal Melbourne Institute of Technology in Australia, the Royal College of Surgeons in Ireland, and the University of San Francisco. While working on my PhD in immunology, I focused on antibodies maturation and response in B lymphocytes.

My research led me to learn more about wounds and burns, during which time I explored the application of growth factors for healing wounded tissue and burns. These clinical dermatology studies taught me how to heal the skin. In my case, taking action has meant sharing my expertise and experience through this book.

I have seen how my own research has been misrepresented. Growth factors are signaling mechanisms that tell the cells when they have healing work to do in your skin. Naturally, this science has the potential to change skin-care outcomes in the same way it has improved the lives of so many burn patients.

Like many other recent discoveries, the term *growth factors* has been abused by the cosmetics industry to promote its products. All of us suffer when we are misinformed and allow ourselves to remain uneducated. With so many new cases of skin cancer being diagnosed every year, and with so many people trying every new antiaging product and procedure available, it has never been more urgent to provide clear and concise information about the skin and its care that everyone can understand.

The pace of technical, scientific, and medical advances has been so fast in our society that we are almost encouraged to give up understanding the tools and substances we use every day. If we experience a new and faster computer, we do not need to know how it works; however, when it comes to skin-care technology, we are talking about your health. The skin is a huge part of the basic operating system of life and beauty. It has a unique nature and it requires a special kind of nurturing from you. Science can help you in the nurturing of your skin, and I would like to tell you how.

The Naked Terms

The skin is a remarkably interesting and complex organ, but it is not too complex to understand. There are a few basic terms we need to define in order to get started. These terms form the basis for understanding how your skin works, its nature; how you should take care of it, its nurture; and the framework that scientific researchers and cosmetics marketers use to talk about it—the science of the skin.

You hear terms such as *collagen* and *elastin* in advertisements for skin-care products all the time, but manufacturers who produce these products rarely take the time to explain them. Here are some of the most popular dermatology terms and a brief definition for each one:

Collagen: Collagen is the protein that forms the primary component of connective tissues and is the principal structural protein in the skin. It supports the tendons that are responsible for attaching muscle to bone, and it is abundant in cartilage and bone. It also holds cells and tissue together in areas as diverse as the heart, bladder, and blood vessels. As we age, collagen production declines and its cell structure weakens, causing our bodies to begin to sag.

Dermis: The dermis is the skin's equivalent of a brain. All the skin's fibers, acids, blood vessels, nerves, glands, and hair follicles are contained in the dermis. It is the layer of skin located directly beneath the epidermis, or the uppermost layer of skin.

Elastin: Young people enjoy smooth, wrinkle-free skin because they have an abundance of elastin. This protein is responsible for preserving pliability and elasticity. When skin is stretched, poked, or pinched, it springs right back into shape. Factors such as the aging process and skin damage from environmental conditions cause elastin production to decrease. Unfortunately, that means human skin loses that smooth, wrinkle-free firmness as we age.

Epidermis: The epidermis is the outermost layer of the skin. It forms a type of protective shield that keeps all of us safe from infection, dehydration, sunburn, and other environmental factors. The majority of cells that make pigment, or skin color, are found in this layer of the skin as well.

Fibroblasts: Fibroblasts are the cells that generate connective tissue and the skin's collagen and elastin components.

Free radicals: Some of the skin's primary enemies are molecules called free radicals. Factors such as sun damage, air pollution, and smoking create free radicals that damage the DNA and destroy the skin's collagen and elastin, but, fortunately, we can limit the damage with the use of antioxidants.

Keratin: Keratin is a strong structural protein that makes up the epidermis. It is also a key structural component of nails and hair. Keratin keeps the skin hydrated by preventing evaporation of the body's water.

Melanin: Melanin is a pigment produced by cells called *melanocytes.* This pigment not only gives skin, eyes, and hair their color but it also protects us from the sun's damaging ultraviolet (UV) radiation.

Sebaceous glands: Sebaceous glands are the microscopic glands usually found next to the hair follicles in the dermis area of the skin. These are responsible for keeping the skin moisturized and waterproofed by secreting a fatty fluid called sebum, which includes wax, triglycerides, and fatty acids. Sebaceous ducts connect the gland to the hair follicle, and the secretions (as well as dead skin cells) then travel along the hair shaft to the surface of the skin.

T-zone: The T-zone is something you have probably heard of even if you are not a fan of late-night infomercials pushing skin products onto insomniac consumers. The T-zone got its name because the forehead, nose, and chin form the shape of a capital letter T. This area can produce more oil than any other part of your skin, which is why it is more likely to be a candidate for acne problems such as pimples and blackheads.

An Inspiration

For all of our lives, the epidermis is our signature whenever we meet anyone. My patients in the burn unit have shown me, and themselves, repeatedly what a great gift it is to enjoy our health. They have shown me how amazing our skin is and how it is not a chore, but a blessing, to be able to take good care of it.

As a scientist, I began to see skin as a true friend. Seeing the skin damaged or injured is heartrending. The despair of such great loss is deeply moving and led me to go back to the laboratories, where I did research to look closely at what science has to offer those of us who have suffered skin injuries, as well as those of us who seek to care for our skin with love and respect.

The more I dug into the data, the closer I came to understanding just what a remarkable age we live in. I began to see that I could use our newest knowledge of the skin to effect truly amazing results. The empathy one feels for people who have experienced severe skin trauma cannot be fully expressed in words, but those feelings inspired my deep desire to dedicate my life to giving people the gift of understanding their skin.

With this book, you are taking off on a fabulous voyage designed to put you in charge of caring for your skin. Your journey will take you around the amazing membrane of cells that is closer to you than anything else in the universe. It is time to begin your exploration of the nature, nurture, and science of modern skin care.

Take a moment to relax and consider your skin right now. While meditation is not a cure for any skin ailment, all activities that boost the immune system are also good for the skin's functions and appearance. If you showered too quickly this morning, you may not have taken the time to rub your skin lightly with your hands. This action alone is a simple form of care and protection. If you have any lumps, bumps, or other irregularities on the surface of your skin, your hands will find them, even if there is no redness, itching, or other signs of irritation. Your skin is your primary protector from the harshness of the world, and your first receptor to its pleasures. Gently thank your skin for all it does for you and try to appreciate how hard it works.

As you meditate on your skin, remember the last time you watched a baby entertain himself or herself. That baby you smiled at was still very much in contact with his or her own body as he or she began learning about being alive. We can all learn a great deal about how we are living as adults by watching children. Infants will lie on their backs and touch their hands, just feeling the miracle of their skin and the rest of their bodies for long periods of time. As we get older, many of us lose this intimacy with ourselves. Use this meditation time to try to regain that intimacy.

SECTION ONE

Science versus Snake Oil

The biggest challenges in navigating modern skin care will be overcome by understanding the scientific research and how it is used.

As a species, we have always been concerned about our appearance. This desire to be beautiful and attract beautiful mates inspired some of our first forays into experimentation and discovery. In the following chapters, you will explore how we moved from the stream bed to the laboratory and came to lose our way in market-speak. It is my hope that by understanding these origins, we can more easily separate the scientists from the snake-oil salespeople.

The history of cosmetics and skin care does not move smoothly from Cleopatra's milk baths and the Native Americans' "face paint" into our era of genetic research, the use of stem cells, and the discovery of growth factors. What history does tell us is that we have always been on this bumpy and crooked path, for exactly the same reasons, since the dawn of time. This section of the book tells the story of how modern skin care developed and how we arrived where we are right now.

CHAPTER 2

A Beautiful and Scientific Species

Our Ancestry and Cosmetics Science

Human beings have always sought to protect, treat, and adorn the skin. We are a species obsessed with the good health that beauty suggests. That obsession may just have inspired us to become the scientific species we certainly are today.

Archaeological digs have helped us uncover the evidence. Among our early historical finds are remnants of all sorts of treasures from nature's pharmacopeia, many of which are still in use today. These artifacts represent the beginnings of the science now used in the cosmetics industry. The first evidence we have of the use of pigments comes from the Middle Paleolithic Age, about 250,000 years ago. Use of iron oxides, such as the black, red, orange, and yellow hues of hematite and ocher, went on to be widely used in burial rituals, cave paintings, and often as body paint.

Early humans used nature's cosmetics and skin-care warehouse for soothing and adorning the skin. Honey, mineral and vegetable dyes, clay, ash, and animal fat meant that a huge range of fireside science was at play from the start.

That quest for healing with mud and herbs is also used by the other animals in their own form of primitive laboratory investigation. Likewise, the ability to ignite sexual urges is not unique to humans, but is the central activity of all living creatures. For example, the adornment with natural elements such as the brightly colored feathers on male birds hot-wires the reproductive engine of birds. The mating theater is one of the most amazing, wonderful phenomena on our planet, and modern cosmetics science is an extension of the original dance.

After millennia, when the use of pigments for ritual body painting began, you can imagine how the story of their use as cosmetics might have begun. A few women, bathing and having fun with their reflections in the water, teased their eyelids using charcoal from the firepit mixed with some fine streambed clay, and the first makeup arose. When the women returned to their encampment, the men's heads jerked around to check out this new look the women had adopted. The men probably failed to see exactly what had happened, but they were naturally swept away by their newfound attraction to the mysteries of the feminine. The women, naturally, did not miss a thing.

Soon, small rawhide bags full of the charcoal and porcelain clay mix were at their disposal all the time. When they wanted something from men, they applied the come-hither potion and their mates grew immediately more attentive.

The women at the streambed could have been some of the founders of the cosmetics industry, and its first scientists. Not only did they know how to use eye makeup to attract men's interest when they wanted to, they also learned about natural curatives for their babies. They used aloe vera to ease the pain of burns, charcoal to treat digestive ailments, and the hydrating magic of beeswax esters for the skin. The encampment was their laboratory, and they operated as their own chemists. The science of beautification in this tradition began and continued for thousands of years. "Marketing" was by word of mouth and straightforward: People had to stand by their products or receive the wrath of their cohorts first hand. The hype and obfuscation of today's marketing teams would have come to a quick, violent end if their products had not fulfilled their promises.

The foundations for what we call civilization began about ten thousand years ago, when sheep and goats were domesticated and wheat, barley, figs, and rice started to be cultivated in various areas of the world. Crop harvests, stored away after the growing season, were able to sustain large populations. Towns and cities with complex social hierarchies began to develop. The next phase of cosmetics science was launched as men and women of high social status frequently adorned their faces with elaborate markings.

Many ancient civilizations were famous for their legacies of grooming and beauty. Six thousand years ago, ancient Egyptians were using cosmetics created from copper, lead ore, ash, ocher, and malachite to give their eyes an almond shape that is now widely associated with the culture. They used galena, a toxic lead sulfide mix originally used to ward off eye infections, to make dark, glossy eye shadow and other cosmetics. Their makeup was so wildly popular that people carried the mixtures around in little decorative boxes. Making the complexion as fine, glistening, and lustrous as possible was a feat of chemistry, even in those early times. Cleopatra supposedly bathed in donkeys' milk to smooth her skin. However, the beauty legacy of the ancient Egyptians did not die out with the pharaohs. They also loved using the dark allure of kohl around the eyes and castor oil as a moisturizer. Both ingredients are still used today.

Early chemistry was not limited to the ancient Egyptians. At around 3000 BC, the Chinese began using natural products such as beeswax, gelatin, and egg whites to stain their fingernails. Red balsam, rose, and orchid petals crushed with alum were applied to the nails to create a pink or reddish color. Members of the Zhou dynasty (1046–256 BC) used gold and silver; later, royals wore red or black, whereas the lower classes were resigned to pale, more demure shades of color. In the fourth century BC, Grecian women painted their faces with white lead and ground mulberries to use as rouge. They also darkened their eyebrows with lampblack.

The ancient Romans used a variety of products that included substances such as rosewater, beeswax, and olive oil. They also used mud baths and treated pimples with edible ingredients such as barley flour and butter. They used a mixture of sheep fat and blood to create nail polish. Although many modern beauty-supply stores lean toward products with organic ingredients, it is fairly certain none of them use this exact recipe.

Cosmetics were not solely for females during the time of ancient Rome. Men of the era often dyed their hair blonde, and the wealthiest would sprinkle it with gold dust. North African, Indian, and Middle Eastern people used henna as a hair dye, as well as a way to paint intricate designs on their hands and feet.

Around 1500 BC citizens of Japan and China began using rice powder to tint their faces white. They also painted their teeth gold or black and shaved their eyebrows. Face whitening was not limited to the continent of Asia, though. Five hundred years after the Chinese and Japanese began the trend, the Greeks caught the movement and used white lead or chalk face powder in conjunction with ocher clay mixed with red iron as lipstick.

The Arabs perfected the art of distilling, and after the Crusades, rosewater and other perfumes were exported to European countries in huge amounts. Italy and France during the fourteenth and sixteenth centuries were the centers of cosmetics production. The height of fashion turned once again to hair in Elizabethan England, when the red-haired Queen Elizabeth was on the throne, and people began dying their hair red. Raw egg whites, powdered eggshell, borax, poppy seeds, and alum were applied directly to the skin in an attempt to obtain a paler, luminous complexion. However, cosmetics could still be dangerous. By the end of the 1500s, a combination of white lead and vinegar was used to lighten the complexion. The tanned skin tones of the lower orders who worked in the fields were definitely not desired.

In Europe, cosmetics science burgeoned and was transported to the Americas with the European settlers. During the nineteenth century, Queen Victoria frowned on painted faces, declaring them a vulgar impropriety suitable only for those performing in stage productions. Fortunately for actors everywhere, deadly combinations of lead and copper were replaced with zinc oxide–based face powders around this time.

The differences between marketing hype and the actual benefits of products remained closely entwined until around the middle 1800s, when the industrial age was well underway and manufacturers could remove themselves from the wrath of their clientele.

Question: A friend of mine from Pakistan treats scrapes and cuts with a paste made of turmeric rather than applying a bandage. She says it prevents infection and encourages healing. Does it?

Answer: Turmeric is a strong anti-inflammatory agent used by many cultures to treat wounds and injuries. It can also be mixed with salt and milk and taken orally to relieve the pain of a sore throat. Turmeric contains curcumin and belongs to the same family as ginger. Studies show it may help the immune system and liver function; there is also evidence that it can calm inflamed joints and regulate blood flow.

The Modern Cosmetics Laboratory Develops

The modern cosmetics industry began at the beginning of the twentieth century. Despite Queen Victoria's disapproval, the subtle application of cosmetics was widespread by 1900. With the death of Queen Victoria and her careful propriety, her wild son Edward took the throne. King Edward VII was a renowned playboy well into old age, and it was during his reign that the production of cosmetics became a booming part of global commerce. Europeans and North Americans alike were using spa treatments and visiting beauty salons in an attempt to appear younger for social events. As there was still something of a stigma to the wearing of makeup, women would enhance their lips with lightly shaded beeswax, and they used very fine liners and powders on their eyelids and lashes.

With the explosion of sales at the outset of the 1900s, cosmetics vendors saw a huge increase in laboratory research. Earlier, in 1862, Abraham Lincoln had established the Division of Chemistry (later the Food and Drug Administration) as part of the Department of

Agriculture. It went on to answer the gradual increase in calls for safety regulations for food, cosmetics, and pharmaceuticals.

In the nineteenth century, an interest in health and wellness was kindled across North American society. Middle-class health prophets such as Sylvester Graham, inventor of the graham cracker, foretold a new moral order resulting from dietary reform. By 1896, when Dr. John Harvey Kellogg, who believed that optimum health could be achieved only through bland food, sexual abstinence, and a daily yogurt enema, was awarded his patent for what we now know as corn flakes, the scientific investigation of nutrition had begun in earnest.

Question: When my kids had chicken pox, I put a few tablespoons of oatmeal into an old clean sock, knotted the end, and let it steep in the tub before I put the kids in the bath. It made the water nice and soft, but was there anything more than the placebo effect in making the kids feel better?

Answer: Oatmeal has the ability to soak up dirt and oils from the skin and exfoliate dead skin cells. It can help relieve the pain and itching of psoriasis, sunburn, and dermatitis. I think the sock just keeps the oatmeal from going down the drain and plugging up the pipes, which is an important consideration.

Seventh-day Adventists, like Dr. Kellogg, are vegetarians and very serious about their diets. Kellogg and his brother, Will, invented the flaked cereal during their studies on the use of whole grains such as rice, wheat, oats, and corn in the diet.

Dr. Kellogg is one example of how the habits of day-to-day life were being put under the microscope during this period. The popularity of breakfast cereals grew out of the vegetarian movement. Heavy meat-centered meals, especially breakfasts, were seen as contributing not only to gastric problems but also to society's moral degeneration.

In the last twenty years of the nineteenth century, the number of American manufacturers in the cosmetics industry would nearly quadruple to a whopping 262 firms. During World War I, the door-to-door salespeople of the California Perfume Company sold five million of their products (toiletries as well as perfumes). In 1920, the company's sales exceeded $1 million. The company still operates under a brand name, Avon, that is still calling on households across the world through face-to-face and digital interaction.

When the twentieth century detonated with Art Deco, health fads, spas, and flappers with their short skirts and wild dances such as the Charleston, research about all the chemicals used to adorn and pamper the body was still limited. After the global suffering and devastation of the First World War and the flu pandemic, people were ready to enjoy being happy and alive. They spent more and more of their money on what earlier generations might have considered "frivolous luxuries." Women refused to hide their use of makeup, and lipstick and eye-shadow colors became bolder and darker. As the industry's cash flow increased into the multimillions with the Roaring Twenties, the cosmetics companies hired a new wave of scientists. They became an army of laboratory staff hired to develop formulas.

Cosmetics companies that had begun in the early 1900s, such as Max Factor, L'Oréal, and Maybelline, exploded on the scene in the 1920s. Women, inspired by movie stars such as Theda Bara and Clara Bow were making use of dark eyeliner and deep red lipsticks. The therapeutic benefits of sun exposure had begun to be understood earlier in the century, and when Coco Chanel fell asleep in the sun and awoke with a tan, her followers loved the look. In 1936, L'Oréal invented the world's first ever sun cream. Throughout the rest of the century, as the cosmetics industry made new progress, Congress was regulating the industry regarding safety in matters such as quality of ingredients, factory-workers' rights, and use in therapeutic treatments.

While beauty concoctions and formulas became the concern of cosmetics companies, serious investigation of the skin remained largely a part of medicine and disease studies. The twentieth century proceeded with many breakthroughs in our understanding of the body, but new cosmetics knowledge was primarily confined to the discoveries around the importance of oils and other complements to our skin or integumentary system. For the most part, this separation remains in place today.

The Language of the Lab versus Discoveries from the Lab

This new scientific focus means that the users of cosmetics and skin-care products, men and women like you and me, have a lot of investigation and critical thinking to do.

The examination and cross surveying of the many trillions of bytes of data stored in current databases, as well as the actual physical investigation being done in laboratories today, is amazing. The amount of human knowledge, energy, and expertise being deployed on these issues is truly remarkable. At the same time, it is sorely hampered by the profit-driven mentality of corporations. That is the one fact everyone can see, and it wisely tempers our trust in the skin-care industry's claims. In spite of all the hoopla in magazines, on the Internet, on television, and on billboards, we all need to be aware that often "information" is being pulled out of the hats of advertising copywriters, not from scientific papers and research studies.

We all know that the skin is our largest organ and that it is absolutely essential to our lives. If things leak in or out of it in the wrong ways, we are goners. That scenario also makes the skin one of our most vulnerable organs. Look at what a fire, a car wreck, or even too much sun can do to the epidermis and the dermis beneath it.

Serious life-endangering conditions, though, are not the concern of the cosmetics industry, even if it does ultimately benefit from what we learn in dealing with skin catastrophes. In addition, because of the association between skin care and profit motives, deep, trustworthy, and profound research related to skin care is less well funded than many of the other platforms in the medical spectrum.

The dermis and epidermis are absolutely among the most critical parts of our anatomy; just like the lungs bringing oxygen into the body and the stomach extracting nutrients, our skin keeps us in our bodies and shields us from invaders. Still, approximately one-third of America's population is suffering from skin problems at any given time. Our largest organ is the most susceptible to injury and disease simply because it is out in the open. It has no protection and can be bombarded by toxins and abrasive agents at any moment.

Our skin resides in the never-never land between the inside and the outside of our bodies. We can see it, but we cannot see how it works. In addition, the act of caring for the skin is often seen as pure vanity. Because of this difficult physical position and misguided moral judgment, those who fund serious professional investigation often overlook the skin. The only labs that are loaded with research funding are those that are part of the beauty industry. In the United States, for example, only 2% of the National Institutes of Health (NIH) budget goes into funding lab work related to skin disorders.

There are groups such as the American Skin Association (ASA) that fund research and are not directly owned by the beauty corporations. The ASA funds over US$1 million a year for research using a team of scientists and physicians to select the groups that receive grants for advanced work related to the skin. They direct funds toward young people just starting their careers as well as to seasoned veterans, paying attention to the vexing effects of melanoma, psoriasis, and childhood skin problems, with investigations ranging from acne to stem-cell replacement.

These research studies are conducted all around the world and are varied, resourceful, and fascinating. They typically begin with medical issues; however, all of the medical discoveries spill out into the skin-care and beauty world through the various journals and conventions that bring researchers from the two worlds together. Following ten years of research at the Skin Research Centre (SRC) at the University of Leeds, the human skin model LabSkin™ was launched in 2012 by the UK dermatology company Evocutis. Continued refinement in the creation and growth of a human skin equivalent has meant that serious ongoing testing, observation, and other lab analyses can continue despite the restrictions on animal testing now in place. With this kind of work, researchers can observe how various afflictions behave on and inside the skin.

Naturally, this kind of work also has commercial applications. Recently, the Fraunhofer Institute in Germany designed a fully automated production system for the manufacture of human skin models that can create five thousand one-centimeter by one-centimeter tissue disks a month for less than €50 each. Since cosmetics companies in the European Union are no longer permitted to do their testing on animals, the primary consumer of these models is that industry. However, when they buy pieces of skin, are they paying for the research that went into discovering the process of skin modeling or the cost of the actual automated process?

The bottom line is that there are labs working seriously on making models of the skin—from the epidermis clear down through the dermis—for investigation. This means we can now conduct experiments on skin we have manufactured, rather than on animal subjects first and human volunteers later, taking the risk and cruelty out of testing. We can now watch how the skin reacts to substances, and how certain conditions develop in the short and the long term.

This is research that pioneers treatment for everyone from burn victims, to certain cancer patients, to acne sufferers, to those who want more effective antiwrinkle creams. The more of this type of research that receives funding, the more you will be able to tend to your skin and achieve greater success in healing.

The biggest concern is determining how much money the big beauty corporations will slip into the budget for research. And if these companies take a greater role in funding scientific skin research, will they seek a greater voice in determining what that research should focus on?

Research facilities such as the ASA and the SRC are interested purely in comprehensive real-world medical science. They build their financing systems so that they are not restricted or directed by the desires of corporations. However, the huge amounts of money spent on beauty products inspire corporations to be determined to find information that makes their products sound sensational. That means the language of the cosmetics corporations comes from the medical laboratory, and dictates how cosmetics are sold.

However, just because cosmetics industries are appropriating the language of the lab, it does not mean that they are using the discoveries to maximum benefit.

The cosmetics industry enjoyed strong growth throughout the twentieth century, but huge breakthroughs in medical science have come since our focus has been on understanding genetics. With the final mapping of the gene code, knowledge is expanding, and we have been looking at the real-world causes of our skin's aging processes. Some of those publically funded advances have found their way into our cosmetics. In many other cases, we are only *being told* that these advances have found their way into our cosmetics. It is important for us to be able to tell the difference.

In the next three chapters, we're going to examine how this understanding of genetics, coupled with our understanding of stem cells and growth factors, can truly form the scientific basis of modern skin care and where these breakthroughs are being touted only for marketing purposes.

C H A P T E R 3

Genetic Research and Your Skin

The appearance of your skin is permanently affected by your unique genetic code. This is the same code that gave your grandmother her musical talent, your father his wild left eyebrow, and you get heartburn whenever you eat tomatoes—a trait you share with your little brother.

The DNA that makes up your genes also instructs your cells to create specific proteins according to your unique code, which affects every structure and every process in your body. As human beings, we have between twenty thousand and twenty-five thousand different genes, which blend in a magnificent array of patterns to produce variety in our characteristics. Many of the unique factors governing our appearances, our diverse personalities, our overall health conditions, and the full spectrum of being human is encoded in this poetic operating system.

The influence of the code is so integrated with all parts of us that a great many discoveries about our similarities and our unique qualities are destined to be made over the next few decades. Scientists now believe genetics is responsible for a person's predisposition toward optimism or pessimism, and, of course, genetics controls physical factors such as skin color and type too.

During the first decade of the new millennium, scientists began to direct genetic discoveries toward every aspect of science and medicine. Decoding the human genome does not mean we understand it, but molecular genetics, the study of gene structure and function, is now the most prominent sub-field of molecular biology.

The Human Genome Project has enabled scientists to isolate genes that may contribute to specific diseases. It is also improving genetic testing to assess predisposition for disease and is allowing us to see the beginnings of customized therapy to target specific genetic profiles. However, it has also meant a reassessment of earlier assumptions. Genes, for example, are not necessarily self-contained units with defined roles. The reality is proving far more complex. In addition, we now know that genes are not the only determinates of heredity: Characteristics acquired during one's lifetime may indeed be heritable.

As the data build, the researchers' findings will come in to sweep away everything that has come before. New discoveries occur from moment to moment rather than decade to decade. Understanding is often very simple after the scientists in the lab have gathered the findings to examine.

Genetics is complicated by the fact that there is no one-to-one correlation between traits and genes. Many genes work together to create individual traits, and dozens of characteristics are affected and determined by a single gene. Everything related to skin care is complicated even further because genes significantly influence the production and use of proteins in the body.

The primary knowledge for real-world skin care is that both the dermis and the epidermis are composed of an array of proteins, including collagen, which increases the skin's strength and elasticity, as well as the pigment melanin, which is the prime determinant of skin color, and which protects us from the damaging UV rays from the sun.

Inheritance versus Mutation

Most people believe that skin color, texture, and type are inherited genetically from one's parents. This assumption is partly true, but environmental and lifestyle factors can significantly influence these traits. Exposure to toxins in the environment, high or low levels of sunlight, extreme temperatures, poor diet, lack of exercise, cigarette smoking, overindulgence in alcohol, prescription medications, and a host of other factors can prompt genes to mutate and change skin characteristics.

Some people also mistakenly believe that there are specific genes for each of the many possible disorders of the skin. However, genes themselves do not cause or control any disorders. If a gene's DNA sequence is altered or mutated, it causes the protein encoded by the gene to malfunction, resulting in irregularities.

Although some disorders are passed down from one generation to the next, it is also common for skin maladies to develop later in life. The wave of skin cancers that besieged us during the development of the hole in the ozone layer is the best-known example. This is but one known environmental trigger. Chlorofluorocarbons, or CFCs, the main cause of the depletion, were phased out of production by international agreement and the hole has now stabilized, but we have no real idea of what other environmental hazards are doing to our skin. Volatile organic compounds (VOCs), such as benzene and solvents, along with particulates such as the black carbon produced by automobiles, cover the earth and create a toxic soup over our skin, even while we are sleeping in our beds. The epidermis and dermis are composed of cells that are in no way immune to being damaged by environmental conditions, lifestyle factors, or exposure to harmful chemicals.

Inherited Skin Disorders

There are skin disorders that may be genetic, and you cannot do anything about your genetic makeup. The most common of the disorders that are at least partly hereditary are psoriasis and rosacea.

Rosacea is generally recognized by a splotchy redness on the face, whereas psoriasis leaves red and white scaly patches, due to the overproduction of skin cells, frequently on joints such as the elbows and knees, as well as on other parts of body. Another genetic skin condition, though not as common, is albinism. People who suffer from albinism have little or no melanin, or pigment, in their skin, eyes, and hair.

These disorders are not reversible and cannot be healed or cured, but their symptoms can be alleviated by certain treatments, and care must be taken to avoid as much discomfort as possible. The most important strategy is to avoid excessive sun exposure. Stay in the shade and cover up with a wide-brim hat when you know you are going to be in direct sunlight. Remember, you are still being exposed to the sun through the windshield when you are driving, so ensure you wear sunscreen even if you will be out of doors only for the time it takes to walk from the front door to your car. Also, avoid the use of harsh cleansers and skin products. Disordered skin is especially sensitive. Using the most gentle products and treatments can help to minimize damage.

Remember that a certified dermatologist should see any abnormal mark, condition, or discoloration of the skin. Skin cancer is deadly, and it is important to rule out the possibility of a serious skin disorder.

Aging and Your Genes

One of the biggest concerns for many people when it comes to skin care is looking old. How the skin ages is one factor that is strongly influenced by genetics. In a society where prejudice against senior citizens is rampant, and where youth is perceived to afford privilege and adoration, aging is feared. Ours is not a society that reveres those who have lived long, prosperous lives and gleaned ample wisdom to share as elders of the tribe. Instead, attention and reward often go to those exhibiting exuberant youth.

The antiaging sector is the fastest growing market in the skincare industry, and it has been for some time. Most of the research completed this century has provided scientists with information about the structural changes in the skin resulting from aging. However, modern-day researchers are only beginning to examine the causes responsible for the rate and effects of aging on the human body.

Intrinsic Aging, Extrinsic Aging, and Photoaging

There are two kinds of aging; intrinsic, which is largely genetic, and extrinsic, which is caused by external factors. Included in this later type is photoaging, or aging caused by exposure to the sun, which requires a section of its own.

INTRINSIC AGING

Intrinsic aging is what happens when skin ages naturally, and for most people the process begins in their mid-twenties. With all the other perks of growing into adulthood, collagen and elastin production slows down, and elastin, which is responsible for allowing skin to spring back into place once stretched, begins to lose its snap.

During this phase of life, not only do new skin cells begin to develop more slowly but the skin is also more reluctant to shed dead cells. Although the changes often arrive with the onset of adulthood, their results can take decades to show up in the form of fine wrinkles, visible veins, bags under the eyes, hollow cheeks, and dry or sagging skin. Intrinsic aging is also responsible for changes in the hair. Whether your hair is thinning, showing up in unwanted places, or just turning gray, intrinsic aging is to blame.

EXTRINSIC AGING

Extrinsic aging occurs with exposure to external factors such as pollution, tanning, gravity, or cigarette smoking. Even our facial expressions and sleeping positions play a part in premature, extrinsic aging. External factors are the biggest reason for the skin to age prematurely, and although we are unable to stop some of the changes, there are quite a few signs of extrinsic aging that we can prevent through healthy lifestyle choices, such as getting enough rest and exercise and eating a healthful diet.

Women who practice daily facial exercises in the hope of preserving the smooth, clear skin of their youth are actually inviting the very wrinkles that they are trying to prevent. The movement of facial muscles creates grooves in the dermis, the second layer of the skin. As we get older, the elasticity in the skin begins to wane, allowing the groves to become permanently etched on the face, as well as the hands and other parts of the body. Couple this problem with gravity and you have a conundrum. Gravity changes your face substantially, elongating the ears and nose and forming jowls, and the upper lip can disappear almost completely.

Even how you sleep is a factor in extrinsic aging. Sleeping the same way every night can cause sleep lines, otherwise known as wrinkles, to develop. You can avoid these by lying on your back to sleep at night.

Finland, Germany, the Netherlands, Belgium, France, and a number of Canadian provinces, among many other jurisdictions, have banned tanning salons from serving anyone under the age of eighteen. The Canadian government also requires the industry to display cancer risk warning stickers on the devices. In other words, tanning beds are now treated as controlled substances like alcohol and cigarettes. If minors have to be protected from tanning beds by the state, should the adults not take responsibility for protecting themselves from the devices?

There aren't many things you can do to prevent yourself from coming into contact with pollutants in the air and water, but you can try to give yourself a place to breathe fresh air at least some of the time. That might mean growing plants such as English ivy, bamboo palm, or Boston fern in your home; creating a green oasis with tall plants on your balcony; or organizing with other tenants in your building to plant a rooftop garden.

One pollutant that is easy to avoid is cigarettes. The chemicals in cigarettes are not only harmful to your respiratory tract but they damage your skin as well. The nicotine leaves a residue on the skin and teeth that turns them a deathly yellow hue. Deep wrinkles and brittle hair and nails result. Not only should you not smoke but you should also prevent others from smoking around you and your loved ones.

PHOTOAGING

By far the most-discussed form of extrinsic aging is "photoaging." This term is used by dermatologists to describe aging caused by exposure to the sun. The amount of pigment found in the skin, along with an overall history of sun exposure, will affect the severity of the sun damage. The truth is that spending too much time in the sun, especially in the tropics or at midday in the summer months in the northern hemisphere, without some kind of protection can cause fine wrinkles, freckles, age spots, dry patches of skin, and even types of skin cancer. It is important to get some sun on our skin since the skin synthesizes vitamin D from sun exposure, promoting the absorption of calcium to ensure strong bones and prevent rickets, among other benefits, such as resistance to cancer and cardiovascular disease. The best source of vitamin D from food is in fatty fish.

Signs of photoaging often lie dormant beneath the skin's surface for a long time, and then they seem to appear overnight. Repeated exposure to the ultraviolet light in the sun's rays damages existing collagen and hinders your body's ability to create new collagen.

Inflammation and Immune Responses

Regardless of whether we are talking about intrinsic or extrinsic aging, the genes that have some of the strongest effects on how we appear as we age are those associated with the immune system's inflammatory responses. These responses can seriously affect the epidermal barrier.

The epidermal barrier prevents penetration of harmful substances, irritants, and allergens. It also traps moisture and regulates hydration of the entire skin organ. These protective and hydrating functions work together to keep the skin supple and healthy. When the epidermal barrier is functioning properly, it minimizes the cellular damage that can cause premature aging and skin disorders.

When the body is exposed to allergens, toxins, or other irritants, inflammatory responses occur to fight infection. The same immune responses that help our bodies heal can cause damage to the skin's appearance, texture, and health. That is why any activity you undertake to support your immune system is ultimately good for your skin too. Eating healthful food, getting enough sleep, and minimizing stress will not only help you look younger but also help you enjoy every moment of the life you have.

Oxidative Stress

Genetic testing is being used to customize nutritional supplements and skin-care products. One of the most practical discoveries genetic research has brought to skin care surrounds the response to oxidative stress.

We all have different abilities to handle this kind of stress, depending on our genetic makeup. Oxidative stress occurs when bonds between the molecules in our bodies' cells are broken and create free radicals. Our immune systems create free radicals as part of their normal metabolism to spur healing during an infection or virus. Our bodies generally control the level of free radicals by releasing antioxidants. When exposure to cigarette smoke or chemicals in the air spur the free radicals to keep attacking other bonds, the chain reaction creates so many free radicals that there may not be enough antioxidants to bring them under control. The amount of antioxidants available depends on our genetically determined response. A shortage is called oxidative stress. Scientists can now specifically examine individuals' personal genetic profiles to determine their ability to handle oxidative stress. Oxidative stress, if left unchecked over time, leads to wrinkling and skin aging. Genetic testing can provide critical information to assist scientists in formulating skin-care products with just the right amount of each ingredient to counter antioxidant deficiencies in any individual.

Vitamins C and E are important antioxidants that fight free radical damage in the body. However, fried food, smoking, excessive alcohol intake, stress, air pollution, and the birth control pill can all deplete the body of these vitamins. Lifestyle changes, such as eating a healthful, well-balanced diet that includes fruit, vegetables, nuts, and seeds can help to maintain high levels of vitamins C and E.

Products and Technology Rule

We already know that when it comes to having beautiful, healthy skin, products and technology rule, not genetics. Science has come a long way in providing safe ways to soothe even the most difficult skin conditions. Many of nature's best healing remedies are still used in a wide variety of products designed to take care of the skin and to prevent toxic or genetic damage. As with all good things, top-notch skin care will take some time out of your daily schedule. Patience on your part is required, but great-looking skin is now attainable, regardless of most challenges you may be facing.

CHAPTER 4 Stem-Cell Research and Your Skin

Stem cells are in the news so much that the cosmetics industry touts them as a miracle-making ingredient in many of their products. Unfortunately, in the real world, there is no scientific basis behind including them in the cosmetics vendor's lines. Skin-care marketers are excellent at finding and using current buzzwords to promote their products, and, to them, stem cells are just another buzzword.

The science of stem cells, though, is remarkable. In mammals, a stem cell is a cell that divides, through *mitosis*, into different types of specialized, tissue-specific cells on exposure to signals described as *tissue-specific biochemical signals*. Stem cells are self-renewing, which means they can self-produce more stem cells.

Normally, human cells age as they divide repeatedly. Most cells stop dividing when they reach what is called the *Hayflick limit*. In 1965, Leonard Hayflick, a professor of anatomy and microbiology at schools such as the University of California, San Francisco, and Stanford University, observed that cells are programmed to divide about fifty times before dying out. However, stem cells defy this limit and go on regenerating for the entire lifespan of their host organism.

That means that stem cells you were born with are still dividing in your body and will continue to do so until the day you die.

Embryonic, Umbilical, and Adult Stem Cells

There are three types of stem cells that are of special interest to medical researchers. These are embryonic, umbilical (or cord blood), and adult stem cells.

EMBRYONIC STEM CELLS

As you may know, there is controversy surrounding stem-cell research, and that controversy is related to one of the three specific types of stem cells, our primordial cells, or embryonic stem cells, which are derived from embryos.

The administration of George W. Bush blocked all public funding of stem-cell research that made use of embryonic stem cells. Early in 2009, the FDA reversed this order and approved initial clinical trials that made use of stem cells derived from human embryonic sources. They approved the trials because of the promising properties of regeneration associated with embryonic stem cells. These stem cells, because they are not yet developed, can potentially take on the properties of any tissue found in the human body. The hope is that one day, we will be able to program stem cells to repair injured spinal cords and treat multiple sclerosis and any number of cancers.

The controversy arose in the first place because obtaining these stem cells used to mean the destruction of leftover human embryos that had been created for the purpose of in vitro fertilization (IVF) treatments. Often couples who have successfully undergone IVF treatment have more embryos frozen than they need to use. These frozen embryos would often be donated for stem-cell research, but harvesting the cells used to mean destroying the embryo, and that was unacceptable to those who believe life begins at conception, even when conception may occur by introducing two cells in a laboratory.

Recently, new methods of harvesting stem cells have been developed that preserve the viability of the embryo. When couples carry recessive genes for hereditary disorders, their embryos are tested for the disease in question before being implanted. This type of testing is called *preimplantation genetic diagnosis* (PGD). A single cell from the embryo is biopsied for the test. If the sample is left to divide overnight, there is enough material to conduct the test and to harvest stem cells from which a colony of cells can be grown for research.

UMBILICAL STEM CELLS

Another type of stem cell is found in the umbilical-cord blood. This stem-cell-rich blood is taken from the umbilical cord and placenta after a woman gives birth, and banked on the assumption that stem-cell therapy will become viable at some point in the future. Banking cord blood means that stem cells can be made available to the donor baby, and his or her siblings, at any point in the future should they have a health emergency or issue. However, this method of obtaining stem cells increases the risk of conditions such as anemia, respiratory distress syndrome, or an array of other potential complications during the harvesting and banking of the cord blood.

Banking cord blood is also big business, so there is the risk that profit-driven medicine during childbirth procedures will take precedence over the immediate postpartum care of the mother and her new baby. Although this sort of situation is directly related to the choice of medical caregiver and not a medical condition, there is always the added risk of profits controlling the operation, but that is a risk one has to assume with any medical procedure, regardless of the type.

ADULT STEM CELLS

The final type of stem cells are those taken from adults. Unlike embryonic and umbilical stem cells, which can replicate themselves without differentiating into specific cell types, adult stem cells are undifferentiated, but they are found in specific tissues or organs and are already "programmed" to maintain and repair the specific tissue in which they are located. For this reason, the potential for their use in other humans is limited to the original tissue from which the stem cells were derived.

Stem Cells and Your Skin

Human skin holds nondifferentiated stem cells that mimic embryonic stem cells and are found in the erector muscles of all of the body's hair follicles. These cells work constantly to renew your skin and are signaled by extracts called *growth factors*. An explanation of growth factors is presented in greater detail in the next chapter. The bottom line is that skin stem cells continuously regenerate new skin. This is how scar tissue forms over a cut finger or scraped knee, for example, and eventually heals. Our skin does not need more stem cells to regenerate; it just needs a substance or method for signaling the cells to produce tissue-specific cells.

Market-speak aside, there is no skin-care brand that uses entire human stem cells in the development of their products. As the fine print will explain, some of them are using extracts from human skin cells.

It is important to know that the FDA only requires skin-care manufacturers to prove that the ingredients in their products will not cause harm. They do not have to prove that their ingredients have the benefits their marketing material suggests they may have. However, it is comforting to know that cosmetics and pharmaceuticals are regulated in completely different ways. Whereas stem cells may be used in medical treatments, it is nearly impossible to utilize an entire human stem cell, or any other living cells, in any product labeled for skin-care use.

Furthermore, the extracts that skin-care manufacturers use come from cells in the skin, which do not harm anyone. Essentially, the extracts are skin growth factors, not stem cells that signal the skin to produce specific new cells. Thus, if the skin is getting orders from headquarters, the new cells it produces have the ability to revive and heal dry, cracked, or otherwise damaged skin. By stimulating your body's current cells, growth factors in skin-care products encourage your body to build collagen and elastin, which can even reverse parts of the skin's aging process.

What Are the Stem Cells the Cosmetics Companies Claim to Use?

If it is almost impossible to use whole human stem cells in cosmetics products, what are the stem cells they claim to use? Well, they are stem cells—from plants.

Most of the skin-care market is composed of people who are drawn to "natural" botanical products. However, combining the language of stem-cell research with nature's plants only makes sense in sales propaganda and has nothing to do with an understanding of true science.

The truth is that plants are driven by completely different DNA than our own, and stem cells do not have the ability to jump species. Apples and human beings are obviously completely different species. There may be some possible aid in hydration or similar requirements that your epidermis requires, but nothing like what the marketing copywriters claim on their very expensive bottles.

Green Marketing Is Not Always Honest Marketing

All of us want to be earth friendly, and the green market is one of the reasons why manufacturers of cosmetics and skin-care products are using plant stem cells to reverse the process of skin wear and tear. The scientific work is still in its infancy, but plants have been used to rejuvenate skin to a more youthful appearance and radiant glow for a long, long time. Unfortunately, plant stem cells in skin-care products do not work in a way that is similar to human embryonic stem cells in medical research, but it is possible to circulate cells from plants with antiaging properties into liquid cultures that can be used in products meant for application on human skin. That does not mean the properties that keep a plant looking youthful will keep you looking youthful.

One plant that provides botanical stem cells for use in antiaging skin-care products is the Swiss Alpine rose. This plant grows at altitudes of a mile or higher in conditions of extreme dryness, frigid winters, and summer afternoons with dangerously intense UV index levels. The plant is something of an abnormality. It not only defies the conditions of the atmosphere in its native home, but this plant also blooms with spectacular roses season after season.

Roses are some of the most classically beautiful flowers on earth, and I'm not sure I know of a woman alive who would turn down using beauty products that would promise to lend her the same exterior traits as the luster and softness of rose petals—but stem cells still cannot jump species.

Algae have also been touted as the next big thing in skin care. These single-celled organisms flourish in fermentation tanks, open ponds, and photobioreactors. None of these three methods of cultivation is in any way a threat to our farmlands, forests, or countrysides. Microalgae that come from the sea provide proteins, antioxidants, vitamins, and pigments necessary for good skin health. They also have natural abilities to help shield the skin from its environmental enemies, such as overexposure to ultraviolet rays and dryness. Algae are a beneficial ingredient in some types of skin-care products. However, microalgae are of benefit when taken by mouth as a food, drink, or supplement, but not when rubbed into the skin because the skin does not have the enzymes needed to put them to use. Microalgae hype, like Swiss Alpine rose stem cells, is simply another fancy marketing trick.

Plant stem cells do not currently—and will probably never—regenerate new cells in humans. There is some potential for plant stem cells to provide their unique benefits to humans, such as protecting existing skin stem cells and helping to prevent future harm from coming to them. However, the average person who is wading through the swamp of skin-care propaganda may have a very difficult time ascertaining any actual benefits from plant-based DNA. When in doubt, the best plan is to save your money.

CHAPTER 5

Growth Factors and Skin-Care Products

Human skin is amazing. If all of the cells in our bodies regenerated and regrew like the ones found in our skin, the average lifespan of humans would be much higher than it is today.

When the epidermis is injured, the skin signals the dermis, which is the next layer beneath the surface of our skin, to create enough new cells to heal the damage. These biological signaling mechanisms are called *growth factors* (GF), and they are beginning to appear in skin-care products everywhere we look. Unlike many ingredients, there is tremendous potential for all of us to use growth factors to turn back the clock and improve the appearance of wrinkles and a host of other skin problems.

You may be wondering, if the natural self-healing ability of growth factors is so perfect, why they even need to be added to skin-care products. As we age, our bodies slow down, and that slowing includes processes involved in the time it takes skin cells to divide into new cells and renew the skin. Aging causes skin to thin and sag. Working on its own, our skin cannot hope to do everything required for it to appear as it did in the days of our youth.

Growth factors perform two necessary tasks for our skin: They protect the cells we have from harm, and they stimulate growth of new cells while repairing damaged ones. Adding growth factors to skin-care products benefits skin of all types, regardless of pigment, age, or any other conditions. They flatten and fade acne scars. They erase wrinkles. They even out blotchy pigment. When used in conjunction with a healthful diet and other positive lifestyle choices, the advantages of caring for your skin with products that contain growth factors only multiply. Properly engineered growth factors really are a skin-care miracle.

The science of GF usage is still in its infancy. The most commonly known type of growth factor is the hormone, whether it is protein or steroid in nature. Individual growth-factor proteins occur in groups called *families*, and the growth factors that affect skin are called *epidermal growth factors*. Because epidermal refers to skin, many people believe that epidermal growth factors are found only in the epidermis, but platelets, plasma, urine, saliva, and even breast milk contain epidermal growth factors.

Until 1986, no one had ever heard of epidermal growth factors. American biochemist Stanley Cohen and Italian neurologist Rita Levi-Montalcini were working together at Washington University in St. Louis, Minnesota, in the 1950s. The research they started on cellular growth factors at that time not only led to the discovery of epidermal growth factors but also proved essential in the understanding of how cancer develops. This understanding helped scientists design more effective drug treatments to fight the disease, reducing fatalities from cancer every year.

Thanks to Cohen and Levi-Montalcini, we know which of the growth factors are protein in nature and which are essential to maintaining healthy skin. These growth factors create a kind of road map of stimulation that promotes repair and regeneration of damaged skin cells. The collagen and other factors that give your skin its elasticity are enhanced by growth factors, and without them, the dermis and epidermis would have a difficult time interacting with each other. Most importantly, when growth factors are exposed to the skin's surface, they penetrate the epidermal layer and are believed to act like a fertilizer for your skin cells.

True Cosmeceuticals

Growth factors add an interesting dynamic to skin-care products. Considering they were once used in a strictly therapeutic or medical capacity, products containing growth factors are now used for purely cosmetic reasons. Labeled as antiaging serums, the products are chock full of natural proteins that rejuvenate and rebuild the collagen and elastin that keeps skin looking vibrant and youthful. Unlike most skin-care ingredients, growth factors penetrate the topmost layer of skin. Using growth factors from the right source, in the right combination, and in the right dose really does increase the skin's ability to repair itself from the damage from both intrinsic and extrinsic aging.

Topical skin creams are usually only therapeutic or only cosmetic in nature. Due to the way growth factors change the nature of a skin-care product, the New Zealand Dermatological Society labels skin products that contain growth factors that were produced in the body with the term *cosmeceuticals*. In other words, these products display properties of cosmetic applications and therapeutic treatments. When they are mixed with other beneficial proteins, the presence of growth factors in skin-care products is invaluable for reversing the signs of intrinsic and extrinsic aging.

The growth-factor products are successful in helping the skin to build new collagen. This reduces the size of wrinkles and can completely eliminate fine lines. These innovative, genetically enhanced beauty products have even been known to even out the appearance of blotchy pigment and cancel age spots. They can even minimize rough, patchy areas and smooth the texture and elasticity of the skin.

For growth-factor products to be effective, you need high-quality growth factors in the right combination. This requires a highly knowledgeable and skilled staff, as well as a specially designed facility so the right growth factors are combined correctly. There are many different growth factors in the body, and all of them have unique functions, so you can immediately see that knowing the right grouping of growth factors in the products will give you the desired results and prevent unwanted side effects.

The Myths in the Magic of Growth Factors

Like any scientific discovery that makes its way into skin-care products, the use of growth factors is open to abuse and misuse.

Many of these new products have no real growth factors in them, or they contain growth factors made from either stem cells or recombinant *E. coli*. Even if they are made from platelets or other parts of the body, such as the umbilical cord or bone marrow, the fact is that none of them have scientific backing that is relevant to skin rejuvenation.

You must beware of the words *green* and *organic* in GF cosmetics marketing, such as the claim that a product contains plant stem cells; growth factors from other species will not work for humans. The receptors on human cells are specific to human growth factors and will never accept growth factors from different species. So when you see that the vendor is using growth factors that are made using rabbit cells, plant cells, or recombinant *E. coli*, it is time to look elsewhere.

Once again, the language of stem-cell research is being misused when it comes to growth factors. Stem cells do produce growth factors, but the stem cells are not the main GF producers in the body. Stem-cell growth factors mostly serve a developmental purpose; they are not typically involved in the renewal or repair of tissue. Stem-cell growth factors are not the growth factors that are relevant to our skin, and products from stem cells fall into this same group of misleading claims of genetic breakthroughs in skin products. All pseudoscientific blather about genetic boosts for your skin should be seen as a red flag that the product is probably no more effective than any other product that hydrates and lubricates the your skin. Glowing words about stem cells in conjunction with growth factors are a warning sign that the company is selling snake oil.

It should come as no surprise that not all companies that use growth factors are honest about how they use them. Doing your homework before putting something on your skin is just common sense. When making the choice to use a skin-care product that uses growth factors as one of the beneficial ingredients, the manufacturers' claims should be backed up by scientific and government certifications. Many of these seemingly miraculous cures for symptoms of aging are available over the counter, but consumers choose to purchase these products from a retailer with whom they have built some kind of relationship, such as the shop inside their local day spa or their dermatologist's office. Having a professional in your corner to manage your skin care is always an asset.

The following information provides basic skills and advanced tools that you can use as a checklist when you are shopping for products that say they include beneficial growth factors.

Basic Skills: Four Ways to Find the Fake Factors

There are many products that are now being sold with growth factors in them, but a witch's brew that contains some sort of growth factors gives us a sad message about the intent of skin-care product manufacturers. When growth factors are made from plant stem cells, recombinant *E. coli*, platelets, or cells from parts of the body such as the umbilical cord or bone marrow, there is absolutely no scientific backing that the growth factors are actually relevant to skin rejuvenation. Only a few kinds of growth factors will benefit your skin, whereas the others just use the scientific buzzwords to no end. Following is a basic checklist of four simple ways you can find the "fake factors" used in skin-care products.

1. **Check out the packaging**
   Growth factors used effectively in skin-care products are proteins, so they are sensitive to light. That means any product that comes in a clear bottle is of questionable merit.
2. **Look for the origins of the growth factors**
   It does not matter if the manufacturer is using growth factors from the rarest plants on earth, or if they are using rabbit DNA to produce them. If they come from a different species, they will not work with humans. It is just a cheap source of growth factors that lets the corporation put the words "contains growth factors" on the packaging, even though they do not do anything.

3. **Rule out "human origins" from stem cells or organs**
   Remember, growth factors have to be combined in the right quantities to work. Simply taking the stem cells or organ cells left over from laboratory testing and research does not work. The firm has to put in the hard work and expense to correctly combine the right growth factors with other effective ingredients, not just slap something together so they can use the buzzword.

4. **Check out the country of origin**
   Most of the research, development, and patents for GF technologies are based in the United States, where attention is still paid to authenticity. Products that originate from outside of the United States should be examined carefully.

The Advanced Class: The GF Top Ten

If you have the time and patience to get beyond the basic checklist, it is time to join the advanced class. Following is a list of some of the more common growth factors found in over-the-counter skin-care products on the market today. Not only do they contain growth factors but they are also combined with antioxidant ingredients to combat free radicals and ingredients that hydrate the skin to keep it feeling smooth and supple. Many product ingredients lists are included as long inserts inside the package rather than printed on the outside where you can read them before you buy. If you want to examine the ingredients before you make a purchase, you will have to visit the company's website for complete product documentation or ask the sales assistant at the counter to provide you with the binder they keep with details about the product.

It may take some time to research and investigate, but the following scientific names and symbols are synthesized and isolated growth factors. These are the active ingredients you should look for in products that contain growth factors and what they are intended to accomplish.

1. **GM-CSF (granulocyte-monocyte colony-stimulating factor)**

   This growth factor leaves the circulatory system and goes into your tissues, where it multiplies your existing white blood cell count to encourage healing. It is thought to reduce inflammation.

2. **bFGF (basic fibroblast growth factor)**

   This growth factor came to cosmetics after being used clinically for the treatment of burns. It initiates the formation of new blood vessels, prevents tissue death, and supports skin regrowth.

3. **HGF (hepatocyte growth factor)**

   This growth factor plays a role in organ regeneration and wound healing. It also initiates the formation of new blood vessels.

4. **IL-6, IL-7, IL-8 (interleukins)**

   These interleukins are said to support the development of cells to reduce inflammation and swelling.

5. **IGF-1 (insulin-like growth factor 1)**

   This growth factor behaves like insulin in the body and encourages cells to grow and multiply.

6. **KGF (keratinocyte growth factor)**

   KGF is a signaling molecule that triggers wound healing and initiates the formation of new blood vessels.

7. **PDGF (platelet-derived growth factor)**

   PDGF is also a protein that polices the growth and division of cells.

8. **TGF-ß (transforming growth factor beta)**

   TGF-ß is a signaling protein that triggers cellular growth and division. In particular, it plays a role in initiating collagen production.

9. **TGF-ß2 and TGF-ß3**

   These variations of the same protein secrete triggers that initiate collagen production.

10. **VEGF (vascular endothelial growth factor)**
    VEGF is a signaling protein that restores oxygen where blood supply has been limited and encourages the initiation of the formation of new blood vessels.

Therapeutic Use Is Short-Term Use

With all of the benefits of growth factors in skin-care products, it is easy to ask why people are not running out to buy skin-care products that list them as ingredients. The primary reason is that these products come at a high cost. Serums that use the most effective forms of growth factors typically cost between $240 and $280 per ounce.

Other potential users are wary of products containing growth factors because they are worried about using genetically engineered hormones, or about their skin bulging as epidermal growth factors moisturize the skin. Where skin cancer is a concern, potential users might worry about speeding up the rate at which the cancer grows when growth factors are introduced. Talk with your physician about the risk of unwanted side effects, including what could happen should you ever be diagnosed with certain types of cancer. Remember, any product should be used only when the advantages will clearly outweigh the potential for harmful side effects.

Much of what has been studied about growth factors to date involves short-term use for supporting wound healing after cosmetic surgery and for line erasing. Because it is still a relatively new way to treat the effects of aging, much is still to be learned about the use of growth factors in skin-care products. Well-controlled clinical studies have not yet been carried out to confirm or prove wrong any speculation on the matter.

While short-term use of skin-care products containing growth factors seems safe enough on the surface, repeated use of them over a long period of time may have unforeseen consequences. Therapeutic skin-care products are best seen as an alternative to minor plastic procedures. Their use should be short-term and discontinued once the healing process has been completed.

SECTION

TWO

Products and Procedures

Over the past two decades, many new skin-care products and procedures have been developed and offered on the marketplace at an incredible pace. In the chapters that make up this section of the book, you will examine exactly what those products and procedures do to your skin.

CHAPTER 6

Do Customers Really Demand Quality?

How We Got Where We Are

I do not have six-pack abdominal muscles (abs). I am a doctor who has worked with patients around the world treating serious disorders and diseases of the skin, and I work in the beauty industry. I have presented at conferences and worked on studies that have been quoted in the media around the world. I have even been on television.

It is acceptable for me to talk about my professional accomplishments, but I have to tell you about the physical "flaws" that cause me to feel insecure.

Think about it. Think about the social conditions that create the mindset of perfection and imperfection. When was the last time you heard a man describe himself as handsome? Alternatively, for that matter, when have you ever heard a grown woman describe herself as beautiful?

Most people, when asked to describe themselves to strangers, talk about their height, weight, shape, and coloring before they start to list what they perceive to be their faults rather than their attractive qualities. When we do meet someone who talks about how attractive they are, we tend to judge them as vain, stuck-up, and full of themselves.

There is no serious need for a man to have six-pack abdominal muscles (abs). In fact, striving for this unneeded condition can promote serious psychological aberrations in men and in women. We have all heard about people who suffer from hernias or back injuries from overtraining their abdominal muscles. The desire for six-pack abs can readily promote the purchase of all sorts of products, from speed drinks to clothing. The ubiquitous photographs of six-pack abs that we see in fitness magazines and other publications are just another trend. It is the one trend that promotes feelings of insecurity, but there are plenty of other fashions that attack everyone's confidence at some level.

The vast majority of the seven or so billion people on earth will never be model thin or have six-pack abs, nor do they need to push themselves to such extremes.

Advertisements are powerful. With great aplomb, they generate revenue for the corporations by zeroing in on our insecurities about being attractive, and they prompt billions of dollars in sales year after year because humans will never live up to the ridiculous values promoted in the endless barrage of advertising. It is impossible for us to begin to discuss how effective skin-care products and procedures are, or are not, until we confront what we want to believe about them and how we adopted those values.

The beauty industry, whether it is fashion, cosmetics, or plastic surgery, is worth about $200 billion a year. The industry incomes are at the mercy of human self-doubt, or insecurity about our alluring qualities, and this makes the industry especially vulnerable to unscrupulous practices. Vast sums of money are poured into the advertising agencies, and market hucksters rabidly promote ideals that they know as few as 1% of the world's population will ever achieve.

In addition, life, we all know, is usually not perfect, even for those who meet the current standard of perfection. The tiny group of people whose photos the ad agencies broadcast all over the media, the bone-thin girl-women models and the carbohydrate-free six-pack-abs boy-men, often very publically suffer from all sorts of psychoses, ranging from stimulant addiction to bulimia, not to mention the toll from all the stress, anxiety, and competition involved in achieving "the look."

When we combine all the tricks of modern marketing with the normal and abnormal psychology of beauty, as well as with the use and abuse of science, we have a cosmetics sales machine that really has brainwashed so many of us. Often, when we try a new cosmetics product or procedure, it is very hard to admit that the product has not been effective. Our reflexive action is to blame ourselves more than declaring that the product or procedure does not work. When a product fails, it is not because you did not use it often enough, or at the right time of day, or in the correct order or combination with other products, but the seeds of doubt will have been sown. A whole realm of guilt can now come into play and be in conflict with the self-satisfaction of being conscientious about self-care and good behavior. The simple fun of adorning oneself is lost in the maze of confusion. The marketing groups watch the research on this type of behavior with an eagle eye. They know that guilt can be an amazing tool. Circulate negativity and the consumer will come running to get past it.

Men's Increasing Concern over Skin Health

It is a mistake to associate the mental or physical health concerns surrounding skin-care products with only girls and women. An increasing number of men are becoming more aware of the importance of healthy skin. In fact, a research study at the University of the West of England showed that more than 80% of men are concerned with imperfections and flaws in their physique.[1]

Men also like to have smooth, touchable skin. Razors for shaving date back to the middle of the eighteenth century, when the blades had to be carefully removed and sharpened after every few shaves. Finally, in 1895, an English traveling salesman, King Camp Gillette, invented the disposable double-edged blade, and by 1903, he had found a manufacturer who could make them and he was soon selling

[1] University of the West of England press release, "Beer Belly Is Biggest Body Issue for Men" (January 6, 2012), http://info.uwe.ac.uk/news/uwenews/news.aspx?id=2178.

them in America as well—and making a fortune. That was the first and only revolution in men's skin care for almost the entire twentieth century. Now, in just the last fifteen years or so, men can get more than just basic shaving products. They can find products geared toward male skin types that contain sunblock, moisturizers, and ingredients that claim to help prevent wrinkles.

More men are going to the gym and doing things to make their bodies look better, so why not improve the quality of their skin too? Products once intended for women are now as unisex as Levi's jeans and a cold beer at the end of a long workday. Advertising for men's skin-care products is placed anywhere that might catch a man's attention. In 2005, Hendrick Motorsports driver Brian Vickers began driving lime-green racecars sponsored by Garnier Fructis, a brand of "green" hair and skin products for men and women.

In 2007, Datamonitor, described on its website as "a world-leading provider of premium global business information," reported that of all the sales of cosmetics products (including skin care) in the United States that year, nearly 20% were sales geared toward male consumers. Pharmacy shelves hold four times as many products for men now than they did just a few years ago.

How Do We Reverse the Brainwashing?

We know that archeologists have pieced together evidence of art and rituals dating back forty thousand years. We also have some sense of the beauty habits of ancient cultures such as the Aztecs, Egyptians, and Persians. With their henna, intense eye makeup, and elaborate jewelry, we can easily see the cosmetics industry advancing from ancient times to more complex societies and evolving into today's cosmetics industry.

We might imagine our ancient ancestors whipping up cosmetics from local clay and organic dyes with a group of friends and trying them out. If the sweetheart they had set their sights on was attracted by their come-hither looks, the new concoction was a winner. If there was no magnetic effect, the love potion was a loser. Marketing was simple and factual, and the results were obvious and trustworthy.

What remains sweet and simple is the urge to attract and hold the attention of those we've set our hearts on; however, today's constant sensory and intellectual bombardment of information from advertising in the media about what to buy to please our loved ones, makes what should be instinctual and natural a confusing and complex exercise.

Nothing requires us to give over that confusion to marketers in the beauty industry. We have it in us to reverse the brainwashing. It will not be easy, but the process can be spelled out in five simple steps.

Step one: Consider how deeply you have been affected by negativity in advertising

Our self-esteem has been deeply affected in many ways by advertising. For some of us, it means that we always have the nagging feeling that something about us could always be better and may never be good enough. Others sink into feelings of helplessness when looking at so-called beauty magazines. They feel alone and lost, as if they do not have a chance of finding love or being sexually fulfilled. This is a kind of mental breakdown, and it can lead to eating disorders such as anorexia and bulimia and physical-perception disorders such as body dysmorphic disorder (BDD). Whether mild or strong, advertising can pose a threat to our feelings of self-worth.

Following is an exercise to help you consider how pervasive negative marketing is in your own life:

On day one, consciously count the number of times in the day that you are confronted with images that promise "a better you." Keep a journal or a scrap piece of paper handy and make a tick mark every time you see a commercial for a weight-loss program during a television show, a placard for a tooth-whitening service on the bus or subway, a print advertisement for mascara or makeup, and even when you scroll past a link to an aesthetic services clinic or day spa on social networking sites.

The second day, take a fresh piece of paper and make a tick mark every time you are told something positive about who you are and how you look. Every time a friend pays you a compliment, every time you think it is a "good hair day" when you pass your reflection in a mirror or window, every time someone flirts with you or smiles at you in passing, make a tick.

On the third day, compare the number of "you could be better" messages from the first day with the "you are great right now" messages from the second day. Think of ways you can make the second number higher—for yourself and for others.

Step two: Separate the beauty trends from the timelessness of looking healthy

Conforming to the current beauty mold is random and capricious. Whatever trend is popular at the moment: big breasts, small breasts, a little weight in the face or around the hips, bone-thin, short hair, long hair, clean shaven, bearded, and so on. Fashion is simply a look found in the magazines. In the real world, where we really live, very few people look like the models, male or female. Throughout history, regardless of time or place, very few people have ever looked like the "ideal" their society has championed. Yet, without ever approaching that ideal, most of us manage to find love and have children, and when we do not, it probably has less to do with physical appearance than with personal choice.

Looking healthy, on the other hand, has little to do with the trends of beauty. Good health and confidence remain the most attractive features. The clear skin and bright eyes that result from drinking enough water, getting enough sleep, and from giving and receiving enough affection remain essential to being and looking healthy. Emotionally speaking, the more certain people are of themselves, the more guilt-free and self-assured they are and the more they radiate their innate beauty, regardless of their body type. Each of us has an inherent, unique beauty that we should learn to respect.

Step three: Focus on the good guys in the cosmetics industry

Marketing is a sophisticated machine. The psychology of marketing and its constant presence in our lives can make the entire beauty industry seem like one giant snake-oil sales machine. The news, though, is not all bad. People with integrity, inside and outside the industry, are advocating the need to get rid of this insidious invasion of the psyches of the general public.

Skin-care advances have never been better. The benefits of substances such as growth factors, all the great hydrating lotions, and information about protecting ourselves from UV radiation and environmental toxins are positive steps forward. However, separating the solid research from the hype is the problem. For now, it is best to use the Internet and watch for great companies that are sincere about using sound research and benign testing to make effective products that are not harmful to you or the environment in the short or the long term.

One of the "good guys" who comes to my mind in this respect is Horst Rechelbacher. As "going green," organic gardening, and all things natural began to shape up as an industry in the 1970s, he encountered ayurvedic medicine, the system of natural medicine founded in India, while visiting that enchanting country. Mr. Rechelbacher came into contact with the healing powers of holistic practices and herbal remedies, and the focus on textures, colors, and scents caught hold of his entrepreneurial spirit.

Once back in his native Minnesota, he formulated his clove shampoo, designed suave packaging, and was off and running with an organic line of cosmetics called Aveda, which he later sold to Estée Lauder for $300 million. Throughout the development of his business, Mr. Rechelbacher maintained strict guidelines for organic products, and one can still smell the wonderful, wild-herb quality when using the line. He was imminently successful without resorting to hype or other seedy behavior. In the end, Aveda was one of the first cosmetics firms to bring environmental principles into play, and it remains an excellent illustration of quality. Aveda products still have a strong and loyal following.

Step four: Demand quality from the industry

One of the reasons the beauty industry generates so much money is that consumers are seldom loyal to any one product or line. That said, loyalty is not something the industry has earned. How many times have you bought a product to treat pimples and ended up with a red, dry patch on your skin that looked worse than the pimple? How many times have you bought an antiwrinkle cream to stave off the signs of middle age, only to end up with pimples reminiscent of your teen years? If you were to look in your bathroom cabinet, how many unfinished bottles and jars of skin-care products that did not follow through on their marketing promises would you find? Chances are you would find several products that had not worked for you that were made by the same company. Consumers of skin-care products are often forgiving of past mistakes, when they should be demanding higher quality.

Quality inspires customer loyalty. In cosmetics, skin care, and all parts of this vital industry, paying attention to quality as well as design anchors firms with a strong toehold in the market.

Remember our discussion in chapter 2, where the women by the stream combined ash and clay to make the first eyeliner? If a cosmetics concoction had not worked, the wise woman who blended it would have had to face the wrath of her tribe. Why should modern cosmetics companies get off any easier? Products that are truly successful are talked about and gain a following by word of mouth. The fact remains that your friends and neighbors with great skin are better sources of information about great products and procedures than any spokesmodel or salesperson. In this same vein of enjoying true quality, the great brands of the beauty world that are blessed with rock-solid staying power are always based on integrity, results, and trust; all of which cause customers to come back, year after year, and tell their friends, which increases the bottom line exponentially.

Step five: Separate the emotional response from the rational response

Here is a sad fact: The assurances of solid testing and lab work, real science and environmentally friendly production, in other words, the science and sustainability of cosmetics products, are rarely investigated by the consumer. The fact that you are reading this book is a signal to the industry that you are not prepared to be tricked any longer.

We often become too emotional about the spin on the product. High-pressure or status-pushing salespeople can turn the heat up further still to close the deal. Everything from design to the choice of scent in products is meant to turn off the intellect and turn on the emotional response. Bottles and pumps remind us of the containers we took our earliest nutrition from, while scents takc us back to spring days or freshly cleaned laundry and creamy textures suggest mother's milk and infant formula.

By learning how to quiet your mind to these marketing pressures, and by learning the facts about the science of skin care, you will automatically develop a critical sense of what you are dealing with when you begin to search for vendors and technicians. When they are ethical, the vendors and technicians should insist on supplying their clientele with reliable, scientifically true, well-tested, and accountably produced information. They should also be consistent about giving you this information and ensuring that you understand it perfectly.

In the next chapters, I present this mind-saving and money-saving information about the most modern skin-care products and procedures.

CHAPTER 7

Potentially Toxic or Perfectly Safe?

What Do Skin-Care Products Actually Do?

It is only rational to ask what skin-care products actually do. Often the answer is that skin-care products do absolutely nothing. Sometimes the answer is that they protect, hydrate, and soften the skin.

As we will see later, some products do have real benefits, but skin-care specialists often cannot tell explicitly what those benefits are.

The one thing that no skin-care product or procedure can do is work miracles. Human beings are imperfect. Programs to enhance photographs like the ones on magazine covers are an easy enough way to obtain beautiful, glowing skin. Getting those perfect results in real life is an entirely different story.

Body-enhancement products range from organic-inspired creations that are safe to eat to synthetic substances with ingredients also found in products like antifreeze. Regardless of where or how a cosmetics product is derived, each has a common purpose: to enhance outer beauty.

That there is widespread confusion should come as no surprise. There are more types of skin-care products on the market today than there are skin types. It does not matter if you have naturally flawless, unblemished skin free from unsightly pimples or freckles, a mishmash of types that consists of an oily face but dry limbs, or any combination in between; somewhere in the retail cosmetics industry there is a product that promises to help you look and feel better. Because half of feeling good is looking good.

Are Skin-Care Products Safe?

Unfortunately, for the past seventy years or so, we have been offering ourselves up as human guinea pigs. Since the advent of commercial television, consumers everywhere have been flocking to their local pharmacies or salons to purchase things such as artificial skin-tanning products, roll-on deodorants, and toothpastes promising to fight cavities.

The one thing cosmetics and skin-care products are not supposed to do is cause harm. That is the fundamental principal of the FDA's regulation of these products. There is no testing to ensure the products deliver on their promises. They are only tested to ensure that they do not hurt the people who use them.

In spite of the best attempts of the federal government to keep Americans safe from the adverse effects of using over-the-counter cosmetic treatments, there are some ingredients still found in products that cost some of us the price of our well-being.

Although not everyone will fall victim to side effects from potentially toxic ingredients, it is safer to avoid putting anything on your skin that might contain these. It is a sad fact that many people miss the connection between their skin products and good health. They wrongly assume that whatever they put on their skin can just as easily be washed away. In truth, topical products that go on your skin penetrate the surface, and absorb into your body, where they reach the circulatory and nervous systems. Traveling through the skin is a more dangerous way for toxins to enter our bodies. When we eat or drink the toxins, our kidneys and liver can help our systems to filter them out. Toxins absorbed through our skin cannot be easily eliminated.

Prolonged use of certain chemicals, of which there are no less than eight major categories, have potentially toxic side effects. Sadly, by the time side effects begin to appear, it is often too late to repair the damage.

Eight Toxic Topical Ingredients to Avoid

Toxins are found in a variety of skin-care and cosmetics products, including hair products, moisturizers, shaving products, tanning creams, makeup, and dental aides. It is not just products for adults that are the culprits. Children's bubble bath, shampoo, toiletries, and laundry products also contain them. Carpet cleaners, household detergents, and fabric glue all use these same chemicals as well. Even manufacturers that market their products as being all-natural are not above reproach. Following are the top eight offenders:

1. Fragrance

Fragrance is commonly used in skin-care products of all kinds. One of the earliest and most common fragrances used in skin-care products is rosewater, a natural, plant-derived product. In addition to its pleasant scent, rosewater has a distinct taste, making it a popular ingredient in Iranian, Arabian, Malaysian, European, and even American cuisine. Essential oils are also used for their pleasant aromas as well as for the beneficial properties they are thought to have, such as soothing and moisturizing skin. However, just because these products are "natural" does not make them perfectly safe to use. Some of these fragrances cause allergic reactions, such as the condition known as *allergic eczema*, sometimes referred to as *atopic dermatitis*. The reactions can be similar to those caused by contact with the industrial-strength chemicals that are often used in commercial or household cleaning products. People with such sensitivities need to seek out fragrance-free products.

Some people cannot even tolerate being in the same room as someone who has used a scented soap, lotion, or hair gel. As a result, more facilities such as schools, offices, fitness clubs, and yoga studios have adopted scent-free policies.

2. **Imidazolidinyl urea and diazolidinyl urea**

   You may have noticed that none of the unused products in your bathroom cabinet have gone bad or suffered from age. This is because of the use of chemical preservatives that can prolong the shelf life of cosmetics and skin-care products almost indefinitely.

   Imidazolidinyl urea and diazolidinyl urea are just two of the inexpensive preservatives used in skin-care products and other cosmetics. These chemical compounds slowly emit the organic compound formaldehyde. In June 2011, the United States National Toxicology Program finally admitted that formaldehyde poses a cancer risk in humans.[1] Formaldehyde is used in making certain types of glue, fabric that resists creasing, automobiles, paints, and explosives. In addition, this is what millions of humans put into their bodies each day via topical applications of skin-care products.

3. **Mineral oil, baby oil, and petroleum jelly**

   Mineral oil is one of the least expensive forms of petroleum, which is why it is so popular for use in skin-care products. It costs more to dispose of mineral oil (it is a by-product created during oil refining) than it does to process it for use in skin-care products. That alone should be a big clue that it is probably something we should not be putting on our skin. And let's be realistic, if you handed someone a bottle of mineral oil from the hardware store, even if it was distilled and refined, and told them it was as safe to use it on their skin as it is to lubricate their lawn mower engine, most people would question the practice.

   Manufacturers of skin-care products disguise the use of mineral oil with its other names, which include baby oil, petroleum jelly, liquid soap, and petroleum lotion. All of those names sound safe enough, and some of the name brands are

---

[1] U.S. Department of Health and Human Services, Public Health Service, National Toxicology Program, "Report on Carcinogens: 12th Edition," (June 2011), http://ntp.niehs.nih.gov/ntp/roc/twelfth/roc12.pdf

trusted because they have been around for so long. However, since the advent of oil refineries, skin-care manufacturers have seen mineral oil as an inexpensive ingredient that has no expiration date. In fact, it clogs the pores, and that prevents them from releasing toxins that are then held in our bodies. These toxins are sent through the liver where they are broken down before being pushed through the intestinal track. Along the way, they pick up vital nutrients, which not only cause dietary insufficiencies but also depress the immune system, causing potentially deadly conditions such as pneumonia.

4. Parabens

Parabens are the most widely used chemical preservatives in the skin-care industry. Like imidazolidinyl urea and diazolidinyl urea, parabens are known carcinogens. What makes them a double threat is that when they are used over long periods, they mimic the female hormone estrogen. This can lead to breast cancer and, in the case of exposure in young girls, can cause puberty to occur early.

Ironically, the use of parabens as a preservative can undermine the active ingredients in antiaging creams. Because of the way parabens react with ultraviolet light, they speed photoaging and actually cause skin to appear older. Instead of preventing the skin traits associated with old age, such as wrinkles and age spots, parabens wreak havoc on human DNA. Those who suffer from paraben allergies are most at risk from using skin-care products that contain these chemicals. Parabens can potentially trigger rosacea, dermatitis, and other types of skin reactions.

One of the most common parabens found in skin-care products is listed as methylparaben among the ingredients, but many other chemical prefixes may appear in combination with the term *paraben*.

5. **Propylene glycol (PG)**

Propylene glycol is another petrochemical that is widely used in household products. This one is found in baby wipes and eye makeup removal products, among other toiletries and cosmetics products. Would you believe it is also found in antifreeze?

Like petroleum jelly or mineral oil, propylene glycol is also made from crude oil. The ingredients list on the label of your skin-care products may not contain propylene glycol, but it may appear as "PG" followed by a plant name. PG is even found in skin-care products that market themselves under "organic" labels. Although it has not yet been linked to cancer, when used in body sprays and other "mist"-type skin-care products, it can cause vision and respiratory damage if sprayed in the wrong direction.

6. **Sulfates**

Sulfates may also be listed as SLS (sodium lauryl sulfate), or as ALS (ammonium laurel sulfate) among skin-care product ingredients. Sulfates are also used in products we use to wash cars and degrease engines. Originally derived from the coconut, sulfates are used as foaming agents, and supposedly their origins in the coconut would make them a "natural" product. Does that make them safe? No! Like some of the other harmful chemicals listed here, they are inexpensive and therefore widely used by manufacturers of skin-care and other cosmetics products. Between skin cleansers, soap, shampoos, toothpaste, mouthwash, dish detergent, and other household cleaning products that may come into contact with your skin, you could be exposed to as many as eight or nine products containing sulfates each and every day.

Since it is a degreaser, SLS removes the protective healthy oils from your skin, which leaves you wide open to conditions such as dry skin, allergic reactions, and environmental contamination. SLS also mimics estrogen, a steroid hormone secreted chiefly by the ovaries that promotes the development and maintenance of female sexual characteristics. Agents that mimic estrogen have been linked to female problems such as pseudomenopause and cancers of the female organs. Men who are exposed to these chemicals can suffer from lower fertility rates.

7. **Synthetic colors**

Synthetic colors include nonhenna hair dyes and are usually labeled as D&C or FD&C followed by a number and a color on ingredients labels. On international products, dyes may be marked just by the letter C followed by the color and number. They are everywhere. In cosmetics, Yellow 6 and Red 4 are common, but many processed foods include ingredients such as FD&C Red 40 or FD&C Blue 2. The problem with synthetic colors is that they are derived from chemical compounds created during the process of distilling coal. They are found not only in skin-care products and food but also in pesticides.

Colors derived from coal tar have been found to cause cancer in mice and allergic reactions in humans. The worst part is that the process to create them leaves behind a type of dye sludge that has polluted rivers and streams all over the world. Since what we take into our bodies also affects the health of our skin, it is wise to avoid foods as well as skin- and hair-care products that contain synthetic colors.

8. **Triethanolamine**

Tricthanolamine is produced from the reaction created by combining the highly toxic substances ethylene oxide and ammonia. It is used in a broad range of personal-care items, including cosmetics, perfumes, hair products, shaving products, and sunscreen. However, the FDA has approved the ingredient only for brief, occasional use followed by complete rinsing. Meanwhile, in products intended for prolonged contact with the skin, the concentration of this ingredient cannot exceed 5%.

The reason for the strict limits is that it is potentially toxic to the skin as well as the immune and respiratory systems.

Studies indicate that triethanolamine mutates cells around the mouth, eyes, and lips of certain animals and causes cancer of the bladder and liver. It can also cause testicle deformities. Allergic reactions include itching, burning, vision loss, dry scalp, dry or scaly skin, hives, and blisters. The higher the concentration of triethanolamine, the more likely symptoms are to present themselves. If you have experienced any of these symptoms, consider them as indicators that you may actually be having a reaction to your skin-care or other beauty products.

How to Protect Yourself

The best thing you can do as a consumer is read the labels and look for potentially toxic ingredients. Consider any of the above ingredients you find listed to be a warning sign and look elsewhere for your skin-care and cosmetics products. There are reputable local and Internet retailers who provide organic, green, or otherwise eco- and skin-friendly products that you can use without causing damage to your body, even with long-term use. Two good places to look are local farmers' markets and e-commerce sites such as Etsy, where small businesses sell their wares to consumers all over the world.

HOLD A SKIN-CARE INVENTORY AUDIT

Go through the list of potentially toxic ingredients and decide which are the most important for you to avoid. If your grandmother swore by petroleum jelly, lived to be one hundred years old, and never looked a day over seventy-five, you might decide that it is a product you will keep as part of your skin-care regimen. If, on the other hand, you have a family history of breast cancer, ovarian cancer, or cancer of the organs, you may decide that no level of exposure to parabens or sulfates is acceptable.

Once you have defined your priorities, go through the ingredients lists of the three skin-care products you use most to see if they contain potentially toxic substances.

If you find they are present, you have to decide if you will (a) eliminate them completely and immediately, (b) use them less often, or (c) use them up and not replace them once they run out. Will you look for a replacement product that does not contain the toxic ingredients? How will you research the alternatives? Getting information is only half the issue in deciding how to care for your skin. Deciding what to do with that information is how you empower yourself.

What Goes In Your Body Should Determine What Goes On Your Skin

More people than ever are turning to organic diets that include raw foods or foods that avoid certain ingredients, such as soy, gluten, eggs, dairy, or other common food allergens. Since everything we put on our skin is absorbed into our bodies, this means we also have to watch what goes into our skin care.

As the body's largest organ, the skin can be a blessing or a curse to your health, depending on how you take care of it. Unbeknownst to most people, quite a few perfectly safe skin-care products are already in their homes. Most of these are so common that if you have any problems with allergies, you already know about them. If there is any food your immune system cannot tolerate when you eat it, you probably cannot tolerate it on your skin either. Most of the following safe products will not be found in the bathroom storage closet or medicine chest, but in the kitchen pantry or the refrigerator.

Seven Safe and Effective Skin-Care Helpers from the Kitchen

1. Strawberries

Take strawberries, for instance. Some people are allergic to them, but for most people they are a good source of vitamin C and dietary fiber. Cut in half and rubbed on the skin, strawberries open pores without causing them to appear dilated. This summertime fruit makes a tasty snack that also naturally whitens teeth; you can even try rubbing your teeth with a strawberry half. However, the acids in strawberries can lead to tooth erosion, so wait before brushing your teeth and only rinse your mouth with water so that the natural saliva in your mouth has a chance to neutralize the acids.

2. **Lemons**

   There is a reason so many household cleaners use lemon peel and juice. This citrus fruit is a natural disinfectant and kills even strong odors. When used in homemade cosmetics products, it acts as an astringent, lifting dirt from the skin without removing oils that help protect our bodies from unwanted environmental toxins.

3. **Sea salt**

   Fruit is not the only thing that is good for use on the skin. Sea salt, when rubbed over the skin while dry relieves dry, flaky skin. Added to bath water or used in a foot soak, it helps to soothe aching muscles and relieve stress.

4. **Coffee**

   Coffee is highly recommended for use in exfoliating the skin. Use coffee grounds as a mild scrub that can also reduce puffiness. Benefits come from the fact that coffee contains vitamin E and magnesium as well as antibacterial properties.

5. **Oatmeal**

   Oats are recommended to help relieve dry skin and relieve itching from conditions such as poison ivy and chicken pox. The natural chemical makeup of oatmeal moisturizes skin, and, when mixed with milk and brown sugar, you'll have not only a more healthful skin-care product but one that's edible as well—and less likely to harm children and pets, who might accidentally drink the mixture. Like coffee, brown sugar acts as a natural exfoliator that opens pores and cleanses the skin. You can make a face mask by mixing some oatmeal with coconut or olive oil and lemon juice, and it will leave your skin soft and glowing with freshness.

6. **Olive oil**

   Harkening back to the days of ancient Rome, olive oil is returning to the cosmetics industry. More people in the world than ever before now suffer from allergies, and olive oil is a wise choice as an ingredient. Not only is olive oil eco-friendly but it is also not likely to cause any kind of allergic reaction.

7. **Beeswax**

   Beeswax offers another option for green or allergen-free cosmetics that help to lubricate and moisturize the skin. Two companies famous for their beeswax-based cosmetics products are Aunt Bee and Burt's Bees. At sites such as Etsy, an online community marketplace where craftspeople buy and sell products that are handmade or vintage in nature, home-based businesses offer a wide range of cosmetics with natural ingredients, such as beeswax.

Where There Is Worry, Head for the Kitchen, Not the Cosmetics Counter

There is plenty of room to experiment with good skin care using items from the grocery store. Around the world, people have used the bounty of their gardens and farms to feed their skin, using the same plants they used to feed their bodies.

Although there is plenty of room for science and technology in modern skin care, the discoveries made have to be used responsibly and ethically by the cosmetics industry. You may have noticed when conducting your own skin-care inventory audit that there is not necessarily a relationship between the cost of a product and the quality of its ingredients. For example, an $80 face cream from a department store cosmetics counter is just as likely to contain PG as an $8 face cream from the cosmetics aisle at the discount store.

That does not mean that healthy skin care should be available only to the rich. If you cannot find a product in your price range that is free of the potentially toxic ingredients that worry you, then do not buy anything. Where there is doubt about safety, or worry about long-term health effects, the solution to good skin care can easily be found in the kitchen.

CHAPTER 8

Cosmeceuticals and Nutricosmetics

How Drugs and Cosmetics Are Catching Up with One Another

Cosmeceuticals and nutricosmetics are two ways that the cosmetics and pharmaceutical industries are becoming more entwined, at least some of the time. As with anything that has to do with the cosmetics industry, we have to separate the actual science from the use of scientific words in marketing campaigns.

Let us start with a few simple definitions. It is not hard to see that the term *cosmeceuticals* is the result of the conjoining of cosmetics and pharmaceutical. The main characteristic with this category of products is that, like cosmetics themselves, they are utilized topically, rubbed onto the skin. There is one strategic difference: Cosmeceuticals actually interact with the biology of the skin.

Nutricosmetics can be used alone or in conjunction with cosmeceuticals. Nutricosmetics are generally vitamin pills or liquids that are supposed to promote antiaging. They allegedly fight wrinkles with "natural" ingredients such as beta-carotene and tannic acid.

Remember the caveat that governs all decisions about skin-care products, because it applies to cosmeceuticals and nutricosmetics as well: Cosmeceuticals and nutricosmetics are tested to see if they are safe, but in the United States, there is no regulation to assure testing to make sure that they perform on the claims they make. No matter what the vendor claims about testing and lab work, there is nothing to back up their claims. There is no testing monitored by outside third parties who have nothing to gain from the sales of the products. There are no public-service labs designed to protect the public from false claims. The FDA does not review them at all. Nothing about cosmeceuticals or nutricosmetics is, or has been, scrutinized under the Federal Food, Drug, and Cosmetic Act (FD&C Act). The terms are not even in their lexicon.

Strengths and Vulnerabilities

Ironically, it is in this regulatory no-man's land where we find the source of greatest difficulty and the greatest hope of making true skin-care progress. Let us go through the list of strengths associated with cosmeceuticals and nutricosmetics and look at the vulnerabilities that exist. Remember, information that appears to be contradictory can often hold the source of the truth. The first item on our list, the use of green marketing—organic compounds and other botanicals—is one of those contradictions.

STRENGTH: GREEN MARKETING

We all love Mother Nature. Her botanicals have provided us with medicines and beauty treatments since the dawn of time.

Some botanical treatments do provide temporary softening, and others moisturize the skin. Top-notch researchers have analyzed a number of the skin treatments enhanced with botanical substances very closely, and the findings are pretty much unanimous: The wonderful-sounding extracts such as citronellol, primrose, and wild yam do lubricate the skin and offer some temporary protection in shielding it from the numerous toxic particulates and volatile organic compounds found in the air. Some of them also offer a limited shielding from the UV spectrum of light.

The deep understanding of the actual effects of the contents of Mother Nature's medicine cabinet is still in its infancy. Although we do know that some of her botanicals and minerals have been used as remedies for millennia, the depth of analysis available today with spectrographs and electron microscopes and so forth has not been fully engaged. As time unfolds, the dedicated laboratory professionals will engage in more in-depth science. There may yet be great discoveries ready to emerge from Mother Nature's storehouse.

VULNERABILITY: GREEN MARKETING

Botanical products can lubricate, moisturize, soften, and help to protect the skin, but this does not mean we can expect anything truly transformative.

The list of organic ingredients that are promoted in cosmeceuticals is extensive, and the expectations marketers try to build up in our minds are huge. The ingredients compilations are extensive, with the list including everything from well-established folk remedies such as aloe vera, baking soda, and apple cider vinegar to exotic concoctions such as frankincense and star anise. Add to that list *Juniperus oxycedrus*, Peru balsam, foraha (tamanu) oil, sweet basil, coconut oil, apricot kernel, beeswax, astragalus root, bay leaf, avocado oil, tea tree oil, and grape seed extract and any gardener can become a cosmetics chemist.

In chapter 7, I recommended using strawberries and beeswax as home skin-care remedies, but those are well-known and common ingredients. If you have an allergy or sensitivity to those ingredients, chances are it was discovered early in your life. We do not have the experience with foraha oil or astragalus root to know what our unique sensitivities might be. Most of us have some allergies to Mother Nature's bounty. We all know how poison ivy and poison oak affect the skin! Even milder astringents such as peppermint oil, which is in almost universal use, can have a harsh effect on the skin of certain individuals, whereas it can be soothing for others.

THE TAKE AWAY

Do not assume that products labeled with the terms *green*, *organic*, or *natural* are of any more benefit to your skin than other products. In some cases, as we have seen in earlier chapters, you might be better off using a mashed avocado from your fridge as a face mask than you would be with a prepared avocado-oil treatment that is laced with a potentially toxic paraben preservative.

STRENGTH: SCIENTIFIC DISCOVERY AND IMMEDIATE APPLICATION OF DISCOVERIES

For now, all the discoveries we have made about understanding our gene code and the behavior of cancer cells are most probably the direct route to discovering the methods of truly transformative skin care. Regarding the regeneration of skin, the work on growth factors is the most promising of all.

Many brilliant scientists, medical research doctors, chemists, geneticists, and others can and are putting products on the market quickly in true American fashion. These are people with expertise in new technologies who can deliver the desired results all of us have been dreaming of. These are the results that the multinationals' marketing teams can only hint at and make confusing in their marketing campaigns.

VULNERABILITY: SMALL VENDORS CANNOT TELL YOU WHAT REALLY WORKS

Talking about the virtues of ingredients used in cosmeceuticals is seriously limited. The extracts, compounds, and components of formulas cannot be discussed as to their therapeutic benefits. Vendors cannot broadcast statements to the effect that their offerings penetrate the skin to the body itself. They cannot state that their new products offer the effects to the buyer that are offered by drugs, or that they are a panacea. All the components of these special compounds are lumped together, whether they are active or inert.

If a doctor, research chemist, or geneticist invents a product based on his or her research that will transform your skin, he or she cannot make any claim to that effect or tell you how it works. The FDA will stop an honest firm and tell them not to make any claim unless it is a drug approved by the FDA. Registering a drug with the FDA is such a long and expensive process—the costs have been listed as being up to $850 million, and the process can take up to ten years—that the ordinary businessperson could never afford to launch a government-approved product. The big drug companies are so wealthy that it is a drop in the bucket to them, and they pay lobbyists a great deal of money each year to keep the cards stacked in their favor.

THE TAKE AWAY

If a product really works, it probably will not say so. The trend for the last ten years has been for cosmeceutical companies to avoid the FDA altogether. This is done with the verbiage used in labeling and advertising the product. The use of fuzzy terminology such as "may help" and sharp-sounding, trendy names that only hint at product function, without making a direct claim, are used. For example, the fuzzy term "long lash" does not make a direct claim that the product will absolutely grow long, thick lashes for the end user, but the warm and fuzzy feel of the term hints that it will.

Remember the great minds from scientific history? Curie, Edison, Ford, and Pasteur, who had great ideas that benefited us all, were not wrapped up and stifled by a corporate cocoon and, if they had been, may never have brought their amazing discoveries and the truth that accompanies them to market.

Society may miss out on skin care's next greatest innovation unless consumers like you find them and talk about those discoveries.

How to Find Products That Actually Work

There are products available that can and will improve the appearance of your skin, reduce redness, fill in wrinkles, and help spots disappear. Just because the developers of those products cannot tell you what their products will do does not mean you cannot find them. Here is how to find them:

1. **Work with a skin-care partner you trust**
   Your own dermatologist or primary healthcare provider should keep information about new advances available in the waiting room. When you are being examined, you should be able to

ask what he or she has learned about at conferences and from reading journals. If the practitioner does not bring up skin-care difficulties during your annual checkup, you should feel comfortable bringing it up yourself.

2. **Talk to your friends, relatives, and acquaintances whose skin has improved**

   "She has great skin" is a lovely thing to say about someone. It is not necessarily true that someone has always had great skin. We have all seen people who have had terrible acne and then see improvement. We have seen scars fade, rashes clear up, and redness calm in other people. If you have a similar problem, try to find a private moment to ask people whose own conditions have improved for their recommendations. Although the stigma of talking about cosmetic treatments has reduced in recent years, few people whose problems have been solved broadcast their successes. At the same time, no one wants to watch others suffer from a condition that can be controlled. If you think someone has triumphed over difficult skin conditions, ask them how they did it.

3. **Lament failures and broadcast successes**

   Skin care is something that consumers experiment with until they find products whose outcomes they are truly happy with. When your new antiwrinkle cream gives you pimples, tell your friends so they do not waste their money too. When you discover a treatment that reduces redness and makes you look younger, tell your friends so they can get some too. Although the mystique of having a "beauty secret" is tempting, without word-of-mouth support, small businesses fail, and everyone loses access to a product that really works.

   In recent years, beauty-industry magazines and bloggers have launched product reviews, but these have not proven to support new products from small vendors. Beauty and fashion magazines are dependent on advertising revenues from the big cosmetics companies, and bloggers are often dependent on fees for their reviews and/or "free product" provided for reader contests and other marketing techniques meant to promote their blogs.

4. **Look for expertise and evidence**
   When you are searching for skin-care products that address your specific skin issues, medical terms and symptoms should take you to real experts. When an individual has created a product, he or she should have the credentials to back up that creation. Degrees and affiliations with recognized universities and foundations are one clue that you are looking at the work of a truly qualified individual. Photographs and testimonials from users of the product should be available. In addition, there should be references or links to publications in medical and/or scientific journals authored or coauthored by the person behind the product.

5. **Track your own observations**
   Much of the research touted by the cosmetics industry is not scientific research, but market research. For example, when a new under-eye cream is launched, a number of women between the ages of thirty-five and fifty-five who use under-eye cream will be contacted and given the product. Six weeks later, after having used the product, they will answer survey questions about how they felt about using the product and their overall impressions of its effectiveness. Later, television and print ads may state that eighty-three women out of 113 said there was "noticeable improvement" after using the product. Where and how that improvement actually took shape is never reported.

   Market research may soon be up to a few challenges. With the advent of digital cameras, it has never been easier for consumers to "self-test" their skin-care products. Simply take a photograph of yourself the day you start using a new product and repeat the process in the same room, under the same lighting, every day. If there are visible improvements, you should be able to see them and describe them for yourself when you compare the day one with the day thirty photograph.

The Bottom Line

The bottom-line problem is that the general public has nowhere to turn for accurate information about skin-care products. Taking care of ourselves is a wonderful thing to do for a good quality of life, for financial reasons, and for personal fulfillment. Where we cannot rely on government bodies to protect us, cosmetics companies to tell us the truth, or the media to give us facts, we have to conduct our own investigations and share what we discover with others. Along the way, we will become informed consumers, and we will create caring communities as well.

CHAPTER 9

Aesthetics and Medicine

The New Procedures

As we have seen, one can never stop questioning the do-they-or-don't-they-work nature of skin-care products. Skin-care procedures, on the other hand, often leave no questions. When performed properly, by qualified experts, under managed expectations, there is no question that the host of new aesthetic procedures can make truly transformative changes to the skin.

The many procedures related to weight reduction and reversing signs of aging have become mainstream rather than hush-hush events that are only whispered about at cocktail parties in Westside Los Angeles. This new era of openness and honesty about cosmetic procedures has created a culture that finally allows us to deal with issues about our appearance that cause us discomfort.

Aesthetic medicine is more a healthcare service than it is a practice meant to restore our physical health. Men and women plagued by conditions such as unwanted hair, superficial spider veins in the legs, thin lips, crow's-feet, and other unsightly signs of aging often turn to a medical professional to take care of the problems. These professionals study a branch of medicine called aesthetics, which relies on both invasive and noninvasive measures to treat the needs of each patient, regardless of whether the procedure is laser tattoo removal or nonsurgical liposuction. The primary scenario with aesthetic medicine is that the majority of patients choose to come to the doctor's for a procedure that is not life-threatening. These patients have different degrees of the choice in the matter in contrast with those who have been disfigured by a calamity such as fire injury.

In 2006, the International Association for Physicians in Aesthetic Medicine (IAPAM) was founded. Its goal is to unite physicians who practice aesthetic medicine. Their medical advisory board is made up of skilled doctors, including dermatologists, whereas the administrative board is business-related and made up of industry experts. The main focus of the association is to provide clinical instruction for laser hair removal, Botox and other cosmetic injections, chemical peels and other treatments to rejuvenate skin, and medically ordered weight management through procedures such as liposuction. Whether a doctor is already practicing aesthetic medicine or plans to offer the services through their practice, it is a good idea to make sure the doctor you want to work with is a member of this association and receives the most current information about how to perform the procedures. Membership in the IAPAM also ensures the medical practitioners have a support system in place to take their questions and address their concerns.

Most patients who go to a doctor who practices aesthetic medicine are looking for a quick fix or prevention of signs of aging. People choose aesthetic medicine as a way to reduce or prevent the signs of aging because the treatments involve high-tech equipment such as lasers, Botox, and collagen fillers, and the treatments are easy to endure and affordable. Some people can have a quick fix during their lunch hour and never miss a minute of their workday. Whereas plastic surgeries are more invasive, more expensive, and sometimes take weeks of recovery time, aesthetic medicine is the answer for someone looking to reduce a few lines or treat a blemish.

Many American states require certain aesthetic procedures to be completed by a doctor or a physician's assistant who is under the direct supervision of a licensed medical doctor. It is important to remember that the American Academy of Aesthetic Medicine

(AAAM) will certify any doctor who completes their program. The board accepts physicians from podiatrists to proctologists as long as they are licensed to practice medicine.

This is certainly where some buyer-beware examination of the doctor you want to work with is required. Whether your doctor's education specialty is feet or family medicine, the payoff for doctors who perform aesthetic procedures is easy to see. Skin-care products might see fads that come and go rather quickly, but procedures used in medical aesthetics, on the other hand, are tried and true. These procedures tend to remain popular with patients because they use credible medical science, show valid results, and are performed rapidly during brief appointments.

There are other rewards too. Patients give higher feedback to doctors that offer aesthetic-related services, and those patients are more likely to pay their bills at the time of service, often in cash. The work is less demanding, and because of the way companies are constantly developing new products for doctors who deal in aesthetic medicine, aesthetic service providers have an opportunity to average less time in the office than other types of medical professionals.

Out of all of the branches of medicine, dermatologists are most likely to offer aesthetic services. This is because dermatologists already deal with issues of the skin, and it seems natural that, in addition to finding causes of rashes and testing blemishes for the presence of skin cancer, a dermatologist would be a patient's first choice for removing wrinkles, erasing blemishes, or using some other more invasive treatment. Many of the dermatologists who operate in aesthetic medicine perform cosmetic interventions that make skin look younger, clearer, and healthier in people who suffer from sun damage, rosacea, and other skin ailments.

THE PROCEDURES

Procedures used in aesthetic medicine include laser treatments and collagen injections that help to reverse the signs of aging and the aftereffects of years spent participating in unhealthful activities, such as tanning, smoking, or just not drinking enough water. Aesthetic medicine is something that can be taken care of during the lunch hour without the use of anesthetic. Most procedures subject the patient to little discomfort and require little or no recovery time.

Procedures fall into two categories, either surgical or nonsurgical. In 2009, physicians performed almost ten million of these procedures for cosmetic purposes alone. Of those procedures, nearly 85% were nonsurgical. That represented a 147% increase in the number of procedures since 1997, according to a 2009 report by the American Society for Aesthetic Plastic Surgery (ASAPS).[1] The top nonsurgical procedures in aesthetic medicine include the following:

Botox injections

First used on wrinkles in the late 1980s, Botox was initially studied in the United States and Canada. The chemicals used are linked to botulism, but the procedure was an instant hit with celebrities looking for ways to erase wrinkles and other types of age lines. It is also used in Europe to treat pain disorders involving the muscles.

Hyaluronic acid injections

These injections are used to treat osteoarthritis of the knees, but when injected into the lips, nasal folds, or around the eyes, they can also erase wrinkles and smooth scars from acne and other kinds of skin trauma. They can even erase superficial blemishes.

Chemical peels

This treatment is also known as *chemexfoliation*, or even more commonly as *derma peeling*. A chemical solution is applied to the skin that causes it to blister. When the blisters peel away, the new layer beneath is revealed and appears smoother, clearer, and younger than what was there before. After this procedure, the new skin is extra sensitive to sunlight and other forms of UV damage. It is highly recommended that people using the technique

---

[1] The American Society for Aesthetic Plastic Surgery (ASAPS), "Quick Facts: Highlights of the ASAPS 2009 Statistics on Cosmetic Surgery" (2009), www.surgery.org/sites/default/files/2009quickfacts.pdf.

take extra caution to avoid damaging the newly revealed layer of skin.

Laser hair removal

Lasers were first used to remove unwanted hair in the 1970s. Most people need a minimum of seven treatments that are spaced anywhere from three to eight weeks apart. This gives the shedding hair time to fall out on its own without any kind of extra manipulation. Laser hair removal is also used to treat ingrown hairs and certain types of cysts associated with them.

Venous treatment

Spider veins are the red and violet vessels that appear on human legs as they age. Unlike varicose veins, which are fat and cause pain, spider veins are superficial. Most treatment involves an injection that irritates the vessels. The vessels then scar and nearly disappear from view to the naked eye. The injection most commonly used is a concentrated form of saline solution. It is important to point out that this procedure does not remove the veins, but it does make them less noticeable.

Curl lifting

Hollywood calls this the "lunch-hour facelift" because of its quick results without surgery or anesthesia. During a thirty-minute appointment, doctors use sutures, which are very thin threads, under the skin to lift sagging areas without having to make any kind of incision. Patients walk out with a tighter brow, cheekbones, and jowls, and aftercare is as noninvasive as a cold compress and an oral antibiotic.

Liposuction, or lipoplasty

This procedure literally sucks the fat right out from beneath the skin. There can be negative aspects associated with removing too much fat at one time. These include sagging skin and dimpling. Avoiding these pitfalls will often take multiple appointments to achieve the desired effect slowly over time. Recovery time can be as short as a couple of days or as long as a few weeks. However, liposuction can cause bruising, swelling, or scarring, which, in turn, could cause the patient to seek out another type of aesthetic treatment to try to solve the problems created by this procedure.

The Benefits of Aesthetic Medicine

Aesthetic medicine is one of the most life-changing experiences that a person can go through. Whether it's vanity-related, such as removing a mole or a birthmark, or to boost a person's self-esteem, such as surgery to repair a cleft palate or cleft lip, the risks are the same. There is nothing wrong with a person wanting to take steps to alter their appearance, as long as they have an overall healthy outlook on life. Someone who is not pleased with who they are on the inside will not be pleased with the effects of aesthetic medicine, regardless of how much more physically appealing they appear to be. Some of the benefits include an improved sense of well-being. This may even act as motivation for taking on healthier lifestyle habits and making healthier choices. Other benefits of this branch of medicine are what we call *off-label*, meaning the procedures are used for something other than that for which they were originally intended. For instance, Botox is used to treat stroke victims, children with cerebral palsy, and those who suffer from migraines or a condition of excessive sweating known as *hyperhidrosis*.

The Disadvantages of Aesthetic Medicine

Unfortunately, aesthetic medicine has its share of disadvantages. Sometimes people who just wanted to feel better about how they look, instead of addressing who they are on the inside, end up suffering serious consequences. Some of the more common side effects and risks, especially with plastic surgery, include infection, internal bleeding, nerve damage, skin-cell damage and tissue death, fluid buildup, and painful bruising or swelling. One of the most serious medical side effects is blood clots, which, if left untreated, could cause death. Another side effect to look at is the financial side. People must be able to pay for these treatments as a luxury item without taking away from paying for their basic needs. Ignoring both psychological and financial well-being leads us to the problem of becoming addicted to pursuing an ideal "look," which can lead to extreme aesthetic procedures that eventually make the patient look disfigured or unreal.

The Future of Aesthetic Medicine

The field of aesthetic medicine is growing like a magic beanstalk. People are much more confident in themselves if they feel that their looks are appropriate for their lives. This is unlike the hard-edged vanity that occurs when a person lives only to maintain their looks. A balanced intent for feeling happy with one's appearance can cure some psychological ailments such as shyness or lack of confidence.

Technology is going wild with skin resurfacing, the freezing of fat, and a host of other cures. Before the turn of the twenty-first century, many of the mountains of new discoveries would have been unheard of to the ordinary person. Amazingly, the number of procedures is expanding well beyond our current offerings. The lightening of skin pigment in Asia and, of course, a plethora of treatments to combat signs of aging around the world are just two directions seeing rapid expansion and development. Laser and sonic-beam treatments are right on the edge, and more applications for these technologies will be discovered.

The most powerful breakthroughs are going to come out of discoveries we have made about the genetic structure of our bodies and the manipulation of stem cells. We are already enjoying a mammoth breakthrough with topical treatments that enlist growth factors to rejuvenate and repair the skin.

CHAPTER 10

The Limitations of Lasers and Light

Professionals and Their Equipment

There is a huge range of people involved in skin care. There are medical doctors who are skin specialists. We have been required to complete intense education and training into the composition and workings of the skin. Then there are the technicians who operate the tanning beds and other equipment in salons. The only things more diverse than the people involved in skin care are the devices that are used in the treatment of our skin.

Skin treatment machines come in many forms, shapes, and sizes. As a patient, the first thing that you notice is the vast array of devices once you leave the waiting area of a skin-care facility and are taken into the treatment area. These are the tools which the doctor, technicians, and other individuals use during your skin-care visit.

With the thinning ozone layer, exposure to heavy solar radiation is common, and the practitioners who are occupied with everything from skin cancers to the treatment of wrinkles are more and more in demand. With the rapid growth of the treatment practitioners and their facilities, the equipment they use is more and more in demand.

There are wide ranges of medical devices related to skin care: lasers, radio frequencies, lights, and so forth. As you have seen in previous chapters, the marketing never stops. The skin is so personal to us, making us vulnerable to psychological triggers, or the weak spots in our armor, which lowers our ability to protect ourselves against aggressive sales talk. The fact is that many devices promise to enhance the skin, but mostly they do nothing but make a temporary improvement, if they actually offer any enhancement to the unwitting client at all. The vast majority of the so-called beauty machines do more damage to the patient's skin than good.

The Truth about Lasers

As discussed in the previous chapter, most procedures in aesthetic medicine are noninvasive and show real results. When it comes to laser ablation or laser resurfacing of the skin, you must use extreme caution. Most of the lasers and related devices are among the biggest skin-care lies of the twenty-first century.

Like stem cells, *laser* is a catchy buzzword, but unlike stem cells, lasers have caused a great deal of pain and loss for patients during the first decade of this century. Dermatologists and plastic surgeons made more money in the first ten years of the twenty-first century than they did in the fifty years before it. There are plenty of reasons for this. Many people have experienced damage to their skin from environmental toxins and from UV rays from the hole in the ozone layer. In addition, there have been changes to the public's attitudes about altering one's looks for the sake of beauty alone.

There has been, financially speaking, a skin-care free-for-all at every level of the business. However, there are enough legitimate methods for dermatologists and other practitioners of aesthetic medicine to treat their patients without resorting to big machines that bring little in the way of results.

Lasers and other such devices are expensive pieces of equipment that look impressive to a person with little or no knowledge of the skin itself. They are great tools for enhancing the skin-care professional's cash flow, and it is not uncommon for the devices to cost more than a luxury car. However, just because there is a large price tag on mechanical equipment for skin care does not mean it was expensive to build. Like so many other electronic tools, they are manufactured in China, Southeast Asia, and Indonesia, where labor costs are low and safety standards are not often maintained.

The costs are driven up because the ordinary person's understanding of the truth about the actual effect of the procedures is so limited. These flash-in-the-pan mechanical wonders launch a sense of hope in the patient and prey on a subconscious belief that the doctor is going to bring them a new life, free of skin problems. Their awareness of what is true and what is not true is so sparse that the skin-care people can charge exorbitant prices for their services. Often patients are too worried about cancer and wrinkles to say no.

The equipment sales representatives usually live stateside and represent a Chinese manufacturer who is much more interested in revenues than healthy skin. The sales mantra is easy to repeat: The equipment pays for itself fast.

Most American doctors who treat skin conditions have a laser machine in their offices. They may be red or green lasers and suitable for many conditions, but all of them work the same way. All lasers assault the epidermis, while the skin-care team hopes that our natural healing systems will repair any damage done by the laser-induced trauma.

The problem is that while the operator of the laser device controls the level of trauma to the skin, we cannot control how the natural mechanisms that heal the skin will function. Dr. James Green is an American medical doctor (MD) who has been involved in laser treatments for more than a decade. He says "that because new collagen growth turns white when it is denatured, ablative lasers cause the face to first turn red and then a strange white color, which is noticeable even under makeup." He feels that better results can be achieved with other kinds of treatments, saying, "The problem with ablative lasers is they cause too much pigment change."[1] Dr. Green faced the problems head on and quit using lasers.

---

[1] James Green, "Skin Care, Laser Treatments, Chemical Peels, Microdermabrasion & Microneedling" (n.d.), http://jamesgreenmd.com/plastic-surgery-articles/skin-care-chemical-peel-microdermabrasion.php.

The trend of buying laser equipment and then randomly using it to shoot everything on the skin that bothers a patient arose from marketing rather than medical or laboratory research and investigation.

The Myth of Photorejuvenation

As we know, *photoaging* refers to the signs of aging and skin damage that result from UV exposure from the sun. *Photorejuvenation*, as the term suggests, is the idea that the damaged layers of skin can be removed using controlled light, thermal heat, or chemical-peel treatments to make someone look younger again, as well as treat some skin conditions.

There are many contradictions to the theory. First of all, photons are particles of light. In the process of photoaging, sunlight causes damage to the skin. How can we expect the use of controlled light waves by a laser to correct what has been damaged by light? The whole group of photorejuvenation treatments, whether they are meant to combat wrinkles, acne scars, and pigment spots from sun damage, or redness from rosacea, are designed to injure the skin and activate natural healing mechanisms. As we age, our skin loses the ability to heal itself, and after the body addresses the healing of the trauma, it does not keep producing new cells to prevent the damage from recurring.

It is important to remember that the doctors and technicians using the equipment are trained by the company that produced it, not by a medical school. This lack of real knowledge from a capable institute of learning such as Irvine or Harvard or the Mayo Clinic creates situations in which the doctors and their staff are freewheeling, using certain procedures and limited understanding on the go, rather than under the careful supervision of professors and senior doctors with many years of experience. If you are the person who ends up with a strange coloration of the skin after your body has created new cells to heal the wounds the machine inflicted, you are in a horrible situation.

Each tool differs in its power, wavelength, and duration. Therefore, each tool may be best suited to specific skin conditions. Light, heat, and chemicals are the basic forces on which machine-oriented photorejuvenation is built. Light treatment consists of the focalizing of extreme beams of light on the troublesome area of the skin. Commonly known as IPL, or *intense pulsed light*, the idea—as with lasers—is that the injury to the epidermis from the light will force the body to create new cells for healing the treated area.

The wavelengths of the light stream are controlled by filters according to the requirement for any particular skin condition, and the light bombardment is concentrated on the problem area of the person's skin. Rapid-fire photons then "injure" the specified area in short spurts. In the process, collagen production is enhanced, which can be beneficial, but the deep concern is that the skin is injured so that the body can create new cells.

In this respect, growth factors promise to be leagues above the use of all the machines. Growth-factor treatment is launched with the application of a soothing serum, and the same process of instructing the body to create new cells begins, but without the application of techniques that injure the skin. With the comfortable application of a serum to the problem areas, healing begins, without the chance of a quirky regeneration of cells by the body.

How to Protect Yourself

It is now normal to undergo procedures to improve the appearance of the skin and to talk about the results. In an ideal world, you would know someone who has undergone treatment and get to see the results for yourself before beginning treatment yourself. If you do not know anyone who has undergone treatment for your specific condition at an accessible, affordable clinic, the only way to protect yourself fully is to ask your local clinic to refer you to past clients of theirs and spend some time with them. If the clinic will not provide names, this should be your first warning that all is not as it appears.

When you do find a past client to meet with, look closely at the results of their treatment. Try to have a long leisurely meal together to give the former patient time to relax so you can have an in-depth conversation about their experiences. Do this with several of the clinic's clients to find out about their condition and the treatment that was used. Was it a treatment involving thermal heat, chemical rejuvenation, controlled light, or a new treatment such as the highly promising, truly noninvasive growth factors? What do they remember of the good and the bad aspects of their treatment and recovery? You will see the results for yourself, not just in photographs that are meant to look terrific. This will give you an idea of what the treatments are really about, and the likely outcome. Only with this candid information will you be able to make the most effective decisions about your own treatment.

In dealing with the clinic staff, you should be able to speak to the person who will be doing the treatment to learn what results you can expect. If it sounds too good to be true, it probably is. Furthermore, the staff should be completely forthcoming about the maximum number of treatments and the recovery time you will need, what kind of aftercare you may need, and what will happen in case of infection or other difficulties. Although it is fine to assume that you will experience the best-case scenario, you must know how to prepare yourself and how the clinic is prepared to deal with potential emergencies.

You should also be informed of the costs and additional expenses of partial and complete treatment. There can be a huge variation in how much these therapies cost, depending on where the treatment is conducted, under what conditions, and by whom. The cost of treatment should never come as a surprise, so make sure you know exactly what to expect.

Remember, there are many claims about cures, fantastic results, and so forth, but the photorejunevation machines are designed to damage tissue. Although the operators of these machines can control the level of injury, they cannot control how your skin will heal itself.

CHAPTER 11

To Lift It or Leave It: Thoughts on Plastic Surgery

Earlier in this book, I have tried to give you a sense of what the marketing gurus do to brainwash ordinary people into feeling they need the latest miracle cosmetic product or skin-care treatment to hold onto their youthful appearance or clear up a skin problem or imperfection. Some people can become addicted to the search for this "perfection," and often at great monetary, physical, and emotional expense to themselves.

Although I am concerned about skin care, and I make my living trying to help people reduce or delay the signs of aging, one fact is true and will always remain true: We age and our bodies change. It is a part of knowing ourselves that we can accept this and mellow into our later years.

The quest for beauty can bring risks with it, and maturity is required in deciding whether those risks are acceptable or not, especially when it comes to cosmetic plastic surgery, which has the potential for risk. The unfolding story of cosmetic surgery is not just a vainglorious tale, but as we age and surgeries become more common, we must reexamine the fact that just as how we look on the outside is of great importance to us, so is who we are and how we want to be on the inside.

The History of Plastic Surgery

The rudiments of cosmetic surgery have been with us for a very long time and have always been integral to medical practice. The growth of knowledge has included the discovery of many medical procedures, of which the facelift, or *rhytidectomy*, is the most well known. At its foundations, plastic surgery addresses medical needs that are as serious as any disease treatment. Many procedures on the cosmetic surgery list are also on the reconstructive surgery list. These include work on burns and other massive traumas. Plastic surgeons also work with various congenital situations, such as cleft lip, cleft palate, and septum deviations. The most requested cosmetic procedures are facelifts, liposuction, breast work, eyelid surgery, and stomach tucks.

The first recorded account of plastic surgery is found in ancient India around 600 BC, when noses and ears that were lost in battle or through punishment for crimes were reconstructed using skin from the cheek or forehead.

By the first century BC, the Romans were practicing plastic surgery to enhance appearance, such as breast reduction in an overweight man, as described by the encyclopaedist Aulus Cornelius Celsus, and the removal of battle scars.

With the fall of the Roman Empire, when many medical texts were lost, and then the Middle Ages, when surgery was akin to magic and deemed sinful, plastic surgery went into decline, only to rise again in the Renaissance.

The Italian Gasparo Tagliacozzi (1546–1599) wrote the first textbook on plastic surgery and did many experiments using skin, subcutaneous tissue, and vasculature from other parts of the body to cover wounds in another area.

The United States came into the picture in the early nineteenth century with John Peter Mettauer (1787–1875), a surgeon and gynecologist, who is said to have been the first to repair a cleft palate in

1827 using tools he designed himself. By the end of that century, what we recognize as a modern nose job had been captured in a scientific paper and the interest in cosmetic surgery, right alongside restorative work, was off and running.

The First World War, with its massive death count and severe trauma, proved to be a medical testing ground for many medical specialties. Horrid burns and disfigurations of soldiers and civilians were common. In Great Britain, Harold Delf Gillies (1882–1960) established the first hospital devoted to reconstructive plastic surgery, where he and his colleagues developed many techniques to repair damage to soldiers' faces as they came home from the war.

During the same period in the United States, Varaztad Kazanjian (1879–1974), Vilray Blair (1871–1955), and a number of others who were working for the US Army developed innovative medical treatments for some of the worst injuries to soldiers caused by trench warfare. When they returned to the United States, they set new standards and established the American Association of Plastic Surgeons, putting an end to unregulated plastic surgery and the association by many of plastic surgery with the term *quack*.

For centuries, the progress of plastic surgery, along with all of sciences, had inched along. It was carried out by people of amazing fortitude who possessed an endless desire to help others. The progress was at the mercy of religious beliefs, capricious changes in government priority, funding, and the moods of the time. However, progress sped up with the move into the twentieth century, when medicine made further groundbreaking advances, with painkillers and antiseptics readily available.

The history of plastic surgery is another story of human ingenuity. We not only figured out how to swim across the river, but we also worked out how to build a bridge, dam the river, and even change its course. As a species, we are driven to collect and sort data and use the information to make life more workable. No one wants to return to the early days, when having plastic surgery was considered a vanity to keep secret or an indulgence to be ashamed of.

By the first decade of the twenty-first century, people of almost all economic backgrounds could engage in surgical procedures for the sake of beauty. According to the International Society of Aesthetic Plastic Surgeons, about fifteen million procedures took place around the world in 2011.[2]

Do not Forget the Dark Side

The popularity of cosmetic surgery has increased dramatically with technological advances and changing attitudes toward the acceptance of such treatments to improve one's appearance. At the same time, tragedies do happen. The front covers of tabloids broadcast shocking mistakes made on celebrities. Then there are the heartbreaking stories of mothers who die because of complications after liposuction, leaving their children orphaned.

The unwanted events related to cosmetic surgery are not only physical but also mental, and though less obvious, they can be just as difficult to deal with.

Electing to go ahead with a procedure and then having postsurgical remorse is not an uncommon occurrence. Many people are devastated after plastic surgery and want their original bodies back. People sometimes feel as if they were disfigured by the procedure and it can affect their overall well-being, and when a procedure cannot be rectified, the mental despair can be overwhelming.

A matter of great concern is how the desire for cosmetic surgery can turn into a fixation. The obsessive desire to be beautiful at any cost can cause people to become addicted to surgeries and latch onto an unrealistic image of what attribute or look constitutes ideal beauty.

Now that the shame of being seen as vain and other stigmas associated with plastic surgery have disappeared, and the cost is no longer a barrier to many people, a whole new wave of obsessing over getting ever more procedures has come into play. *Body dysmorphic disorder* (BDD) is the condition whereby a person becomes preoccupied and excessively concerned with a perceived physical defect. The situation is similar to anorexia, only the solution to the problem is

---

[2] ISAPS, "International Survey on Aesthetic/Cosmetic Procedures Performed in 2011," (2011): 10, www.isaps.org/Media/Default/global-statistics/ISAPS-Results-Procedures-2011.pdf

seen not as having to lose weight, but as needing to have surgical treatments to correct the "defect." The reported rate of cosmetic-surgery patients in the United States who have BDD is from 7% to 8%.[3]

New Solutions to New Problems

Of course, we will find solutions to some of the problems with plastic surgery. At the same time, as the first few generations of people who have to deal with the signs of aging, we have to adapt our way of thinking about this time in our lives.

A hundred years ago, the global average life expectancy at birth was only about thirty years. In 2010, it had risen to more than twice that long. Aging is a sign of privilege, but looking young has become a sought-after luxury. Even modern men have abandoned their fathers' macho principles and now head for the clinics of teams who profess to be able to help them fight aging—the most extreme of whom are the surgeons.

Cosmetic surgery is readily available, but we must keep a very close eye on anything that cuts into our flesh, no matter what. The results are so final and can be bleak beyond our wildest imaginations. Besides, is there really a cure for aging? Probably not, but to protect yourself from syndromes such as BDD, the surest route is to learn to think clearly, accept yourself as you are, and use surgical techniques only if they will add to your enjoyment of life. Eating well, rubbing some healthful oil on your skin, and accepting the fact that we begin to age from the moment we come into the world are probably the best attitudes to protect yourself. The healthiest among us can accept that the process of aging is not only a privilege but also a profound part of being alive.

---

[3] Canice E. Crerand, William Menard, and Katharine A. Phillips, "Surgical and Minimally Invasive Cosmetic Procedures among Persons with Body Dysmorphic Disorder," Annals of Plastic Surgery 65, no. 1 (2010): 11–16.

SECTION THREE

Calamities and Concerns

There are a number of serious skin disorders and injuries that can happen to anyone at any time. In this section, we will discuss what your treatment options are if you ever have to deal with a serious skin-care problem.

CHAPTER 12

Skin Diseases and Disorders

What is Normal Anyway?

A disease is an abnormal condition that impairs the structure or normal functioning of the body. When it comes to our skin, before we can address abnormal conditions we have to ask ourselves what is normal. However, the real question is, what is normal for you? I have noticed that there are three types of "normal," each of which has different signs and requires a different level of care. In addition to asking which type you fall under, if you are responsible for children, your spouse, or elderly parents, you may want to consider what their needs might be as well and watch out for danger signs.

1. THE NEUTRAL-NORMAL TYPES

As a medical professional, I would tell you that if your skin feels comfortable, that is, there is no itchiness or other irritation, no noticeable dryness or no abrasions, and you do not feel greasy, then your skin is normal.

The vast majority of people fall into this category. Many never even think about their skin at all. If they get a thorn or a splinter stuck in their skin, or have a small cut or some other minor injury, they may not notice it until long after it happened. Not until an infection sets in and there is pain do they become aware of the intrusion or injury, at which point they address the problem themselves or seek help from a doctor if necessary.

Our skin is normally tough and resilient, and if you have a splinter, your body will create just the right amount of fluid to force the little spear of wood to the surface, where it will be easy to remove.

The neutral-normal people rarely have to see a doctor for skin problems, and they tend to take care of their skin anyway, for example, by protecting it from intense sun.

2. THE TOUGH-GUY (AND GAL) TYPES

Those in this second group generally live in harsh climates and have tough lifestyles. They develop calluses and weathered skin from hard outdoor work and generally pay no notice to their skin, as the way they look is as everyone in their culture and society looks. These people include farmers, cowboys and cowgirls, construction laborers, serious surfers, desert dwellers, and lifelong sailors.

Many of these people consider the severe weathering of their skin to be a symbol of a full life marked by accomplishment and adventure. Weathered skin in these people is a sign that they are at home in the natural elements.

Question: Is yogurt beneficial to the skin?

Answer: Yogurt is rich in protein, calcium, and several B vitamins, as well as probiotics (the "good" bacteria that aid digestion) and benefits the skin when applied topically. The bacterial cultures *Lactobacillus bulgaricus* (*L. bulgaricus*) and *Streptococcus thermophilus* (*S. thermophilus*) and enzymes in yogurt can help to heal the skin as well as our digestion. Yogurt also contains lactic acid, which can help to moisturize the skin and remove excess oil and dead skin, helping to reduce the signs of aging. After a sunburn, yogurt can rehydrate, cool, and soften the skin. Yogurt is often applied as a mask to moisturize and clear the skin, helping to heal blemishes and acne and restore healthy pH balance. Yogurt can also be used as an ingredient in a natural mask to smooth and rejuvenate the skin.

3. THE CAUTIOUS TYPES

The third type of normal is composed of people who are aware of the harm that can come from the sun's UV rays and the pollutants in the atmosphere and how they can influence our overall health and our skin health. This type wants their skin, and the skin of those they love, to remain supple and healthy throughout their lives. They do what they can to avoid weakening the skin through exposure to the sun and pollutants.

This group will often enlist a dermatologist to examine their skin for concerns such as melanoma. They may also rely on skin-care specialists and spas for advice, diagnostics, and treatment. The very fact that you are reading this book suggests that you belong to this group of "normals."

When Things Become Abnormal

It does not matter what group of "normal" you belong to, when something happens to the skin, there is no way to pretend it is business as usual. When disease flares up and affects the skin, we are immediately aware of how important and amazing our body's largest organ truly is. Taking it for granted is no longer an option.

Many people do not know when a skin flare-up is a situation that calls for a dermatologist, a spa visit, or an over-the-counter medication. Following are five steps you can take to help you decide what action to take when a problem with your skin pops up:

Step one: Be honest about the differences between normal and abnormal

A simple breakout, bump, or blackhead will often just appear; you notice it and go on with your life, and often the blemish will disappear. Neutral-normal types will wait for the blemish to go away even when it is not normal. If you are used to not thinking about your skin, it can be hard to teach yourself to be honest and think about it.

Besides first noticing an irregularity on the skin, the first sign that you need to pay attention to is discomfort. Soreness, sometimes sharp and concentrated, sometimes dull, achy, and spread out, as well as itching and dryness should be investigated.

Step two: Look for triggers

Skin afflictions, such as rashes and itchiness, can result from an allergic reaction to a food, especially if you have eaten something you have never had before, which could be a clue to the trigger. Another culprit could be a new skin-care product; discontinue it if you suspect this is the cause. The side effect to a new medication could also show up on the skin, and you should consult your doctor. If unpleasant skin conditions interfere with your day-to-day routine, you should see your doctor or a dermatologist. If it is just a mild nuisance, you can ask your pharmacist for advice on a topical product that might help; the pharmacist may also advise you to see your doctor or a dermatologist.

Skin conditions do not flare up without a reason. No matter how mild or unimportant you consider a condition to be, try to discover the possible trigger. In addition to reactions to food or medications, skin flare-ups can result from daily stress aggravated by lack of sleep and relaxation time and contact with chemicals in the atmosphere, indoors and outdoors.

Step three: Do not be macho about your symptoms

This step is clearly aimed at the tough guys and gals. The threat of disease should never be underestimated and that applies as much to conditions of the skin as to any other. Any time you have the slightest worry about your health, do not be the macho and ignore your suspicions. If you think there might be a problem, you are probably right.

Naturally, you need not be hypersensitive about every little flaw that pops up on the skin. A bump, red spot, bruise, or discoloration may indicate that something has distressed the skin, but it does not necessarily point to anything serious, though you should watch the area to make sure it is not spreading and soon disappears.

Step four: Remain calm and act with a level head

If a simple bump, rash, bruise, or other affliction does appear on your skin and it does not go away, it is best to remain calm so you can act with a level head. If a simple bump shows up, goes away, then recurs, or if it spreads, it is time to visit the dermatologist or doctor without hesitation.

Step five: Have a trusted physician in place

This is a step the cautious types will certainly have taken care of in advance. The time to find a doctor is before you are forced to deal with an emergency. It is important to have a physician who knows you and your family's medical history and any predisposition you might have for any particular disease. In chapter 19, you will learn what to look for when choosing a dermatologist. Hopefully, you will never have an emergency, but if you have a medical doctor and a dermatologist you can turn to, an emergency will be much easier to deal with.

Skin Diseases in Daily Life

The far-reaching effects of skin disease are not to be dismissed by the assumption that worrying about skin care is a sign of vanity. One of the most basic arguments against labeling skin care as unimportant is that healthy skin is a sign of overall good health and a strong immune system, which are vital to the body's ability to prevent and battle melanoma. The pride one takes in their appearance is also a sign of a positive outlook, which itself can help us to ward off disease.

Our emotions also affect the immune system, and our outward appearance can affect our emotions. When we have blemishes, and especially when we have more serious skin afflictions, such as severe burns, we may feel embarrassed and want to go into hiding. This negative emotional state can depress the immune system.

Our daily routines are the playground and the battleground of skin diseases. When we are in harmony with our environment, we can enjoy the normal function and appearance of our skin. Being informed can make a huge difference to our emotional response when a problem arises.

What Causes Skin Diseases and Disorders?

Everyone should know certain basic information about the most common disorders of the skin in case they, or someone they love, are ever affected.

First, you need to know about the skin disorders and diseases that originate from outside our bodies. Organisms such as bacteria, viruses, protozoa, fungi, and worms can cause disease on our skin. Some are transmitted from person to person, by animals, or from the environment, such as public washrooms and swimming pools. Skin disorders that originate from outside the body also include manmade and natural products that the skin is exposed to, such as chemicals, gases, and particulates, as well as traumas to the skin, such as burns and cuts.

Second, you need to know about the skin disorders and diseases that originate from within. These include genetic skin disorders that are passed down through families, which can include a susceptibility to skin cancer, as well as certain food sensitivities. Some are caused by disturbances to the embryo while it is developing. Allergic reactions to foods and medications also originate from within, and conditions such as acne can result from disturbances of the endocrine system. Circulation problems can also trigger skin diseases and disorders because healthy skin depends on a good supply of oxygen-rich blood.

The most serious skin disorders are caused by the overproduction of cells, which can lead to cancer, and is exactly what happens when exposure to UV rays triggers melanoma.

As you can see, there are numerous triggers for skin diseases, and the issues we have in dealing with these triggers are compounded as we age. The emotional stresses of day-to-day life, coupled with poor nutrition and the toxins that invade our space are powerful contributors to skin disease. Although common skin diseases and disorders may occur, developing the habit of lavishing your skin with the best of care can go a long way toward prevention.

The Common Skin Diseases and Disorders

ACNE

Acne is the most common skin disease, especially in teenagers and young adults. An estimated 80% of people between the ages of eleven and thirty have acne at some point.[1] We all know what acne looks like and can identify it quickly, but only those who suffer from it know what a social catastrophe it is when their face is swollen and covered with moist sores. The sufferers can feel isolated and experience emotional pain. This is such an important condition to understand, and I discuss it in detail in chapter 13.

DERMATITIS

Dermatitis is a family of diseases that together are the second-most common skin condition. Eczema and dermatitis are often classified together, although dermatitis is usually acute and eczema is usually chronic. Your dermatologist can diagnose which condition a person might have.

There are several forms of dermatitis, but they are all caused by an allergic reaction to substances such as chemicals, bacteria, plants, or fungi, and they are not contagious. Dermatitis can manifest as rashes, redness, swelling, itching, and sometimes blisters that result in scarring. The prime symptom is itchy inflammation.

People afflicted with dermatitis need a competent dermatologist to treat the condition and help alleviate associated problems such as dry skin. Following are a few of the more common forms of dermatitis:

Atopic dermatitis (also called atopic eczema) tends to be cyclical and often occurs in people who have asthma or seasonal allergies such as hay fever. This type of dermatitis usually runs in

---

[1] National Institutes of Health (NIH), "Facts about Acne: Who Gets Acne?" (November 2010), www.niams.nih.gov/Health_Info/Acne/acne_ff.asp.

families and is often associated with stress as well as allergies and asthma. It is most common in children and usually disappears after adolescence, although it can persist into adulthood. In infants, an itchy rash with lesions can appear on the face, scalp, hands, and feet, whereas in older children and adults the rash is often seen inside the knees and elbows. Atopic dermatitis can be made worse by contact with pollen, mold, environmental toxins, and perfumes and dyes, as well as by certain foods and stress.

The main treatments for this condition are avoidance of the triggering substances and medications prescribed by a doctor.

Contact dermatitis is a condition whereby the skin becomes red, sore, or inflamed after direct contact with a substance. There are two types of contact dermatitis: allergic and irritant. Irritant dermatitis is the most common and is caused by contact with substances such as soaps, detergents, pesticides, and other chemicals, and the effect can be severe, usually looking like a burn. Allergic dermatitis occurs when a person is in contact with substances to which they are sensitive or allergic and can include fragrances, cosmetics, certain fabrics and metals, latex, and certain plants. Treatment for this type of dermatitis demands removing the allergic agents from the home and avoiding contact. A person might not be allergic to certain substances at first, but with repeated use, a sensitivity can arise.

Nummular dermatitis is caused by dryness of the skin, often caused by a dry environment and taking frequent hot showers. It manifests as red plaques on the legs, hands, arms, and torso. This condition can be combatted with the use of lotions and oils that keep the skin moist, and by avoiding substances such as caffeine, which dry the skin. A dermatologist can prescribe corticosteroids to help heal the condition.

Seborrheic dermatitis is called *cradle cap* when it appears in babies and leads to dandruff. In adults, it manifests on the scalp as dandruff and as oily scaling on the face, typically near the eyebrows and sides of the nose. It can be aggravated by stress.

IMPETIGO

Impetigo is a highly contagious bacterial skin infection caused by *Staphylococcus* or *Streptococcus*. It occurs most often in children from two to six years old, when bacteria enter an open wound and take up residence in the skin. It produces small, red, pus-filled sores on the skin that can break open and form a thick crust. Treatments may include prescription topical and oral antibiotics.

MOLES

Many people worldwide have moles. They have even be known as "beauty marks" when found on certain spots of a woman's face. Moles are pigmented growths, or lesions, that are generally benign and can form under or on the skin. However, not all moles are harmless; some have the potential to develop into melanoma. Any new moles, or changes to existing moles, should be noted and checked by a medical doctor or a dermatologist, and *only* a dermatologist, not any other so-called skin specialist.

PSORIASIS

Psoriasis may look like certain other kinds of dermatitis, but this chronic skin condition is a distinct disease that is believed to be caused by an overactive immune system, whereby normal skin cells are mistaken for a pathogen, causing an overproduction of new skin cells. Psoriasis is a nontransmittable condition that can run in families. A mild case of this condition can manifest as a small rash, but in more severe cases, the skin is inflamed and itchy, with loose, silvery scales that can join together and cover large areas of skin.

Although there is no cure for psoriasis, it can be managed through a holistic approach with diet, stress management, and lifestyle changes, as well as with the care of your medical doctor and a dermatologist.

ROSACEA

Rosacea is one of the most frustrating skin diseases because it often seems like a simple rash, but it is a chronic condition that can manifest as frequent flushing of the face, similar to blushing; redness on the face that looks like sunburn; small cysts on the face that come and go, look like acne, and produce pus; and dry eyes and sore eyelids, among other symptoms. Like psoriasis, there is no cure for rosacea; however, a medical doctor or dermatologist can help in the management of the condition.

SKIN CANCER AND MELANOMA

It would be irresponsible not to include a more in-depth look at skin cancer in this chapter. Skin-cancer rates have been climbing and are largely due to changes on our planet. The thinning of the earth's atmosphere has been one of the most serious results of pollution. The hole in the ozone layer has grown to the point where just walking out into the sun can be risky. It is important that we protect ourselves from the UV rays from the sun.

Skin cancer is the most common form of cancer in the United States. More than 3.5 million Americans are diagnosed each year with the less serious forms of skin cancer, basal cell and squamous cell skin carcinomas, and melanoma, the most serious type of skin cancer was diagnosed in 76,600 Americans in 2013.[2]

Melanoma develops in the cells of the skin that produce melanin, the pigment that gives skin its color. Melanoma can develop anywhere, but most often in areas exposed to the sun. Warning signs of malignancy include the appearance of a new mole; a painful, itching, red, or bleeding mole; and changes in the size, shape, color, and elevation of a mole.

The good news, if you can call it that, is that skin-cancer growth can be stopped if caught in the early stages. As with all skin cancers, avoiding getting sunburn from excessive UV exposure is the best way to prevent skin cancer from developing.

Again, I cannot reiterate often enough the value of having a trusted dermatologist. This is not only to maintain beautiful skin as you mature, but it is also a matter of life or death when it comes to skin cancer. I personally know of a case in which an MD told a patient that a suspicious, nonhealing sore was a wart and not to worry about it. After a consultation with a dermatologist, the patient was sent to a surgeon. The surgeon scheduled an operation immediately and

---

[2] American Cancer Society, "Skin Cancer Facts" (March 25, 2013), www.cancer.org/cancer/cancercauses/sunanduvexposure/skin-cancer-facts.

explained that he would have to excise a much larger area of epidermis than would have been necessary if the patient had come to the surgeon earlier.

Once you find a skin specialist, schedule ongoing checkups and always follow through on your appointments. Remember that even if you are fortunate enough to have found a malignant skin cancer before it can lead to death, the longer you wait, the bigger the scar will be from the removal of the cancer cells.

WARTS

Warts are common around the world, and they are among the most annoying infections caused by a virus. The many varieties of warts are contagious, entering the body through broken skin, and most are harmless. Warts can be found anywhere on the body, but mostly on the hands and feet, and they tend to appear as small, grainy bumps of thickened skin. They may be itchy, but are typically painless, though ugly. Warts are caused by the human papilloma virus, or HPV. Warts should be checked to rule out a more serious condition. Your doctor can remove them safely and prescribe medications to help prevent them from spreading.

Question: A Ugandan friend of mine says that children's warts can be cured if you rub them with a raw potato and then hide the potato in a dark place. Obviously, the dark place is a superstition, but is there any chemistry of merit in the raw potato?

Answer: If rubbing a potato on a wart does work to remove it, the possible explanation might be that the naturally occurring acids, enzymes, sugars, and starches combined with the high vitamin C in the potato could help to dissolve the wart and slough away the dead skin cells. The placebo effect could also come into play with the positive thinking of the person who believes the potato will be effective.

CHAPTER 13

The Hows and Whys of Acne

Acne, the most common skin disorder in the United States, affects forty to fifty million Americans, and nearly 85% will have this condition at some point in their lives.[1] It is worse in boys than girls during puberty; after puberty, girls have more trouble with acne than boys.

As we all know, acne is an affliction that shows up as bumps and general inflammation of the epidermis, primarily of the face, neck, shoulders, chest, and back. Three factors are involved in the cause of acne: (1) enlarged oil glands that overproduce oil on the skin, (2) blockage of the hair follicles with oil and dead skin cells, and (3) bacteria that grow in the clogged pores.

The scientific name for common acne, *Acne vulgaris*, sounds like something out of a horror movie. In addition, for those affected, it is as horrid as it sounds. It can affect preteens and young adults up to the age of twenty-five, but it mainly affects adolescents, who already tend to be socially insecure and can be teased or ridiculed by their peers, intensifying their insecurity and possibly resulting in serious psychological and social problems.

[1] American Academy of Dermatology, "Stats and Facts: Acne," (2013), www.aad.org/media-resources/stats-and-facts/conditions/acne.

Acne on the face cannot be easily hidden. It manifests as blackheads, whiteheads, and pimples. When it is severe, the face and other parts of the upper body can be covered in pimples, which can also become infected, red, and inflamed, especially when the sores are picked or break open.

How Acne Happens

Our bodies produce an oil called *sebum*, which naturally keeps our skin moist and healthy. The glands that produce sebum are called *sebaceous glands*, and they are found just below the surface of the epidermis and are connected to the hair follicles. As young people begin to produce adult hormones, they may produce too much sebum. They also slough off skin at a higher rate, and the combination of excess oil and these skin cells clog up the follicles, creating a blockage so that dead skin cannot slough off normally. As this condition continues, blackheads and whiteheads form in the pores, and the blocked follicles attract bacteria that are normally found on the surface of the skin. If the sebaceous material is pressed, it can leak out onto the skin, and because it contains bacteria, the skin cells around the pores become infected, creating what we know as a pimple, or an *inflammatory papule*. Pus forms when the immune system produces white blood cells to fight off the infection and the white blood cells pile up, creating a *pustule*. When the sebaceous material spreads to the skin surrounding the pore, the infection spreads and can cause scarring, nodules, and cysts.

Experts do not know exactly what causes acne, but hormones are believed to play a part, especially androgen levels at puberty, mostly in boys, and hormonal changes at the onset of menses in girls. There may be a genetic link to a person's susceptibility to get acne; some medications can cause acne; some cosmetics, especially greasy ones, can cause acne in susceptible people; there may be a dietary link; and environmental toxins and stress may also be factors.

The Bad News: Bacterial Mutations and Antibiotic Resistance

There have been numerous treatments for acne over the years. Antibiotics are one form of treatment; however, the bad news is that although they may be successful a first time, if you are treated again, even years later and with a different antibiotic, chances are the drug will not work. The bacteria that cause acne have been with us for a long time; however, they are clever critters that we now know can mutate and become resistant to antibiotics.

For years antibiotics were a breakthrough in the treatment of acne, and even though they are not as effective as they once were, they are still prescribed by doctors and dermatologists. An example of the serious consequences of antibiotic resistance is the case of MRSA (methicillin-resistant *Staphylococcus aureus*), whereby this "Staph" infection becomes resistant to antibiotics, including penicillins such as methicillin. Recently, hospital, prison, and nursing-home deaths have been traced back to MRSA infections.

The bacteria that cause acne, *Propionibacterium acnes*, are also learning to resist the antibiotics such as tetracycline that are used to treat acne. This makes people who are given this drug more vulnerable should they need antibiotic treatment for another infection. With the emergence of these antibiotic-resistant strains of bacteria, dermatologists and medical doctors are more aware that they must limit the use of antibiotics.

Recent research has shown that by combining benzoyl peroxide, which has antibacterial and anti-inflammatory properties, with an antibiotic, the benzoyl peroxide can help to suppress the emergence of resistant strains of *Propionibacterium acnes*.[2]

Following is a list of other possible treatments that your dermatologist may prescribe or discuss with you:

Antiseptics such as benzoyl peroxide can be used topically to combat bacteria.

---

[2] Maha Dutil, "Benzoyl Peroxide: Enhancing Antiobiotic Efficacy in Acne Management," Skin Therapy Letter 15, no. 10 (2010): 5–7.

Blue and red light phototherapy uses combined blue and red light wavelengths to kill the bacteria as well as shrink the sebaceous glands, which decreases the production of oil. Multiple treatments are usually needed, and they can cause temporary redness, crusting, and peeling, and some people may feel the results are not worth the cost.

Cortisone or other steroid injections placed directly into a painful or swollen cystic pimple can be used for a temporary or occasional fix, such as before a prom or job interview. It takes a few days after treatment for the pimple to disappear.

Dermabrasion is a technique using a rotating wire brush that removes the upper layers of the skin. Dermabrasion is a very painful procedure that requires anesthetics and a good deal of time for the skin to repair itself.

Laser therapy, like blue and red phototherapy, also uses light. And also like blue and red phototherapy, laser therapy can destroy the sebaceous glands and result in long-term skin damage.

Retinoids are compounds that are related to vitamin A, an essential nutrient for the skin. They are used topically to speed up the shedding and regeneration of skin cells, which at the same time helps to unplug clogged pores and reduce the frequency and severity of outbreaks. Retinoids can also be taken orally.

Surgery may be recommended for the removal of severe cysts.

Vitamin A, when taken orally in the right dose, appears to normalize levels of oil on the skin.

Vitamin B3, like vitamin A, when taken orally in the right dose, has an anti-inflammatory effect and may reduce swelling.

A Quick Note about Natural Remedies

Nature has been the source of humankind's pharmacopeia for millions of years. Some enthusiasts believe that the natural approach is a panacea, arguing that the people living before the development of modern medicines were healthy, had no tooth decay, and certainly never had acne. However, this idea has not been proven by archaeological evidence; for example, it seems that the ancient Egyptians had acne, and they used sulfur to treat it.[3]

Like any other over-the-counter chemical remedy, treatments marketed as "natural" or "organic" acne remedies should be treated with caution. You cannot take claims made by purveyors of so-called natural products any more seriously than you can take the claims of the large multinational cosmetics companies. Remember, the ingredients have been tested to make sure they do not cause harm, but no investigation has been conducted into whether or not those substances deliver on their promises. That does not mean you should not try time-tested home remedies. Minor ailments may need only minor treatments, but beware of those who overstate the role of the natural approach.

Aloe vera is one plant that does soothe pain. If you break open a leaf from your own plant and apply the juices to a minor burn, you are likely to get immediate relief; however, serious burns with blistering skin require immediate attention from a doctor.

Aloe vera has also been used to heal abrasions and to treat skin conditions such as acne and psoriasis; however, although it can reduce the inflammation of acne, its use as a cure on its own is doubtful.

Question: A traditional American treatment for teenage acne is to beat a raw egg, apply it to the face, and leave it until it dries before rinsing it with cool water. Does this work to improve acne? And if so, why?

Answer: Eggs are loaded with two very important substances: albumin and vitamin A. Albumin is a filmy substance that, when combined with the salts in the skin, acts as a drying agent. It can dry out acne and tighten

[3] Jonette Kerri and Michael Shiman, "An Update on the Management of Acne vulgaris," Journal of Clinical, Cosmetic and Investigational Dermatology 2 (2009): 105–110.

the pores. Vitamin A is a major ingredient in modern acne medications, and it is naturally present in egg yolks, but not the egg whites. Egg yolks, however, should probably not be used as a skin mask if you have acne. They contain a pigment called xanthene, which can interact with hydrogen peroxide and make your skin more sensitive to sunlight, and a small amount of hydrogen peroxide is released by the bacteria *Propionibacterium acnes*—and by acne treatments that contain benzoyl peroxide.

What You Can Do to Treat Your Acne

Just because Mother Nature cannot give us a "cure" for acne does not mean we are powerless against it. Anything you do to support the functioning of your immune system will help your body recover from acne. You may not see dramatic changes, but every little bit helps. While I have written this section with teens and preteens in mind, it serves as a good reminder for everyone to focus on the following healthful habits:

1. Get physical exercise, meditate, and take time to relax every day to reduce stress.
2. Maintain close relationships with family members, especially with the teens and preteens in your family. Healthy family relationships support overall mental and physical health.
3. Eat a well-balanced, healthful diet. It is common knowledge that our modern diets laden with heavily processed fats, flour, sugar, and sweeteners are causing many maladies, such as diabetes. There is no question that a healthful diet supports a strong immune system, which can only help to prevent and improve acne. Include lots of greens and other vegetables, fruit, unrefined grains, sufficient protein, and healthful fats in your diet. Teens and preteens who eat some of their meals away from home should challenge themselves to eat a raw or steamed vegetable with lunch and dinner and a piece of fruit for snack.

4. Wash your face twice a day with a mild soap suggested by your dermatologist. If you can, make sure your soap does not contain any of the potentially toxic ingredients listed in chapter 7 under "Eight Toxic Topical Ingredients to Avoid."
5. Refrain from squeezing and pinching pimples and blocked pores; this will only make it worse and can cause scarring.

The Good News: Genetic Research and Growth Factors

The tools that have come out of genetic research are available just in time. Genetic research means that we can now signal the cells to get busy and cure acne with the use of growth factors. Growth factors are now the most promising tool in the new dermatological arsenal. The bacteria themselves do not react to the application of growth factors. Instead, growth factors prompt the body to create new tissue that replaces the malfunctioning follicle structure and wipes out the infection.

As researchers continue to explore the gene code and everything related to it, we will see more waves of scientific discoveries that will allow us to find new ways to deal with bacteria and viruses. For now, the growth-factor breakthroughs remain the most amazing step forward in skin care.

CHAPTER 14

Skin Pigmentation and Its Purposes

In the vast realm of skin treatment, the healing of acne and removal of its scarring are the main reasons why people enter dermatologists' offices. Dermatitis is the second-most common reason, and the third-most common reason is for issues around skin pigmentation. This includes people seeking to lighten or whiten their skin, as well as those wanting to darken their skin, such as by tanning.

Trying to change our skin color, as we will see, is a huge threat to our overall health. It is important to learn to love the skin you are in; the way it works and what it does for you are so amazing that there is a lot to love.

Our skin and hair color are adaptive traits related to climate and geography, as well as diet, and they connect us to our history. Darker skin protects people who live in tropical areas from the UV rays from the sun. In northern climates, such as the Arctic, where there is not much sun but the people consume a lot of seafood, they can have darker skin because their diet is rich in vitamin D, which is otherwise obtained through the sun on the skin.

There is so much to learn about our bodies in order to care for them properly. In the case of skin pigment, or color, it is important to be informed and loving.

All about Melanin

Melanin is the natural pigment that colors our skin; it is produced when we are exposed to sunlight, causing the skin to tan. Genetically, people have different skin colors depending on their geography, as mentioned above. We can all trace our origins to Africa. Some of our prehistoric ancestors migrated to northern climes, where the need for melanin decreased and skin coloration became paler and paler. Later, some of those lighter-skinned people headed toward equatorial zones, where they tanned and grew darker. Melanin is more abundant where there is more sunshine and it functions to protect us from ailments such as skin cancer and other effects of solar radiation. People with less melanin are better able to produce vitamin D when they live in areas of weak sunlight and dark winters.

Although melanin acts as a sunscreen and can protect us from cancer, it may also reduce the amount of vitamin D that is produced in the skin from the action of sunlight. People with naturally darker skin living further away from the equator may need to be diligent about eating foods such as fatty fish or taking supplemental vitamin D, which is needed for healthy bones and teeth. Melanin also determines hair color and the color of the iris of the eye, and is found in the brain. Melanin in the skin is produced by *melanocytes*, which are found in the lower level of the epidermis. There are many types of melanin, including *eumelanin*, *pheomelanin*, and *neuromelanin*.

There are two types of eumelanin: black and brown. When it is deficient, it can cause albinism. In the absence of other pigments, a small amount of black eumelanin causes gray hair, and a small amount of brown eumelanin in the absence of other pigments causes blond hair.

Pheomelanin imparts a pink to reddish-brown color and is found in large quantities in red hair. It is responsible for freckles and is concentrated in the lips, nipples, penis, and vagina. This pigment may also be responsible for damaging DNA, leading to melanoma without exposure to UV rays.[1]

Neuromelanin is a bluish to brown-black pigment that is produced in the brain and easily identified during autopsies. Its function is not completely understood, but it has been shown to bind with certain metals such as iron and other heavy metals, indicating that neuromelanin plays a protective role in the brain. Scientists have now found a link between decreased neuromelanin and increased iron in the brain and Parkinson's disease.[2]

When we are born, we do not have all the melanin that we are destined to have; it will build up as we mature and even change over our lifetimes. As the melanin increases, the irises of nonwhite babies can begin as blue and change to green, hazel, or brown by the time they are two years old. Babies' skin is lighter when they are born, and it darkens as they age and are exposed to the sun over time. Hair color can also change from black, brown, blond, or red to gray as we age.

As we learn more about the biology of our skin and the effects of environmental changes on it, practices in skin care change and develop.

Skin Pigment Affects Treatment Results

Understanding that melanin protects the skin from UV rays, we can apply this knowledge to improve the skin's condition by intentionally injuring the skin to promote healing in a cosmetic treatment. For example, the same properties that protect dark skin from the sun's rays also protect it against medical lasers. Whereas lasers are very effective in removing a class of birthmark known as a *port-wine stain* from white skin, lasers are less successful in removing them from the skin of people of Asian or African descent. The higher concentrations of melanin in darker-skinned individuals simply scatter the beams from

---

[1] Devarati Mitra et al., "An Ultraviolet-Radiation-Independent Pathway to Melanoma Carcinogenesis in the Red Hair/Fair Skin Background," Nature 491, no. 7424 (2012): 449–453.

[2] Florian Tribl et al., "Identification of L-Ferritin in Neuromelanin Granules of the Human Substantia Nigra: A Targeted Proteomics Approach," Molecular & Cellular Proteomics 8, no. 8 (2009): 1832–1838.

the laser and soak them up. This renders the treatments weak. Freckles and moles generate the same pattern under the laser because they are the result of a healthy supply of localized melanin on otherwise typically light skin.

This same diminishing effect spills over to other skin treatments as well, such as dermabrasion. There are health advantages and disadvantages to being any color. It is the interfering with nature and nature's gifts that causes problems.

Hyperpigmentation and Hypopigmentation

Few people are aware of conditions such as hyper- and hypopigmentation, which are serious disruptions in pigment production. In hyperpigmentation, patches of skin become darker due to an increase in melanin. Hypopigmentation results from a reduction in melanin production, causing white patches. These dark or white patches can appear on the face, backs of hands, neck, and back.

Hyperpigmentation is more prevalent among people with darker skin, and it typically occurs on areas of the skin that are usually exposed to the sun as it can result from the production of melanin, called *melanogenesis*, in response to UV damage to the DNA. The mechanism is actually the body's attempt to protect against skin cancer. Hyperpigmentation can also be caused by various drugs and injury to the skin.

Hypopigmentation, or loss of skin color, can occur in people with light or dark skin and can be caused by genetic abnormalities, disease, fungal infection, injury, and burns or other trauma.

People of all races can be vulnerable to hyper- and hypopigmentation. There are several acquired and genetic disorders that we cannot easily control, such as Addison's disease, vitiligo, celiac disease, and porphyria, which can lead to either of these conditions. There are, however, two causes of hyper- and hypopigmentation that we can control. These are excess sun exposure and cigarette smoking:

1. **Excess sun exposure**

   Sunlight stimulates melanocyte cells to produce more melanin. Because our bodies' ability to regulate melanin is compromised as we grow older, if you have a spot that has been injured through sunburn or the use of chemicals, then its increased sensitivity can cause hyperpigmentation to occur. By being careful about the time of day and length of time you spend in the sun and wearing sunscreen and protective clothing, you can protect your skin as you age.

2. **Cigarette smoking**

   Smoking cigarettes can lead to a condition called *smoker's melanosis*, which is characterized by hyperpigmented lesions on the gums and inner lining of the mouth and sometimes the lips and surrounding area of the mouth. When the sufferer quits smoking, the lesions usually heal in one to three years. Quitting benefits the skin in other ways too, as the free radical damage from smoking causes the skin to age prematurely.

The Horror of Products and Procedures for Changing the Pigment of the Skin

Hyperpigmentation can also be caused by lowering the skin's resistance through the use of skin-lightening lotions. In the "bad old days," some skin-lightening treatments were known to contain mercury and mercury derivatives. Some home-based purveyors of "traditional" whiteners still offered for sale in India and Pakistan still contain this poison. Of greater concern is hydroquinone, a bleaching agent that is a known carcinogen. Applying this ingredient to the skin before it is exposed to the sun can intensify its effects and lead to both hyper- and hypopigmentation.

Hyperpigmentation can also occur after an outbreak of acne that has healed, and hypopigmentation can occur following laser dermabrasion for the treatment of acne scars.

If you have white spots on your skin due to a fungus or another condition, a visit to the tanning salon will not help to even out your skin tone. In fact, if you take a medication as benign as the birth control pill or an acne medicine, tanning beds can interfere with the skin's normal melanin production and make it even more sensitive to the tanning bed's lights. The process can intensify white spots you may not even have noticed before visiting a tanning salon.

It is important to love the skin you are in. The processes by which melanin is produced are only beginning to be understood, but what we have learned is truly amazing. Do not mess with these remarkable processes by trying to change your skin tone, which has evolved naturally over many generations of migration, intermarriage, and exposure to different climates. Our skin is part of a human story that we are only beginning to understand.

CHAPTER 15

Hair Loss and Regeneration

Naturally, as with all other parts of the skin, the hair follicles are wrapped up in a lot of snake oil and fluff from the corporate world of marketing. Hair loss, like everything else the marketing machine makes us feel insecure about, has its roots in history and its present in misrepresented science and questionable surgeries.

The worries are deeply etched within many of us. When we see a bad hairpiece, we feel apprehensive about the condition of our own hair as we age. We feel empathy for the person wearing the goofy disguise and an aversion to the distressing subject.

The uneasiness about hair loss throws us off balance because that longing for a healthy head of hair never goes away. Naturally, what constitutes feeling good varies for everyone, but no matter what the latest style happens to be, everyone wants to feel at ease under their own hair.

Male Pattern Baldness

Baldness happens. It is a fact of life, but most men with a scalp that is as smooth as a baby's bottom would prefer a head of gray hair. Adding insult to injury is the fact that baldness does not happen overnight.

Most of it starts with a type of pattern baldness, such as a receding hairline and thinning hair on the top of the scalp.

A single strand of hair can last just over four years. After it falls out, it takes about six months for a new one to grow in its place. The average scalp holds approximately one hundred thousand hairs and about one hundred fall out every day.

Standard hair-care practices such as shampooing, brushing, blow-drying, and curling with a curling iron can all contribute to hair loss. Anyone over thirty years of age could lose more hair than younger people. In addition, if you are male with a male parent who went bald, chances are you could be headed down the same genetic path.

In almost all cases of baldness in men (and less commonly in women), because of their genetic makeup, men produce more of a male hormone called *dihydrotestosterone* (DHT), which is converted from testosterone. DHT prevents the absorption of nutrients needed by the hair follicles, and these gradually shrink and *male pattern baldness* results. Male pattern baldness begins with a receding hairline that advances to the top of the head.

We have known that there is a relationship between balding and testosterone since the 1950s, but even the ancients noticed a correlation between hormones and hair loss. Around 400 BC, Hippocrates observed that eunuchs (men castrated before puberty) did not go bald, a fact that counters the idea that baldness indicates a man's lack of virility.

Rest assured that men do not need to be castrated to keep their hair. Although not much can be done to counter one's genetic heritage, the thinning of hair in men and women can also be caused by nutritional deficiencies, stress, and sleep deprivation, as well as thyroid disorders, blood pressure problems, diabetes, and other conditions. Certain medications, especially those that can affect the body's hormones, such as birth control pills and steroids, can also cause hair loss.

A Look Back

Concern about hair loss is as old as recorded history. Ancient Middle Eastern cultures considered baldness to be shameful as it was a sign of loss of virility. Throughout history and to the present day, people have strived and continue to strive to find a "cure," from swallowing a combination of iron oxide, red lead, onions, alabaster, honey, and fat from a variety of animals in ancient Egypt to herbs, nutritional supplements, lotions, and laser treatments today.

Wigs and various hairpieces have also been employed for thousands of years to signify power as well as to camouflage thinning hair.

Wigging Out, from King Louis XIII to the American Presidents

By the seventeenth century, King Louis XIII was a regular bigwig around France, and not just because of his seat on the throne. He began wearing a wig to cover his premature baldness, and soon other members of the court began to wear wigs. They became the fashion, spreading to the courts of England and later to the upper-class American colonists, and by the eighteenth century, many wealthy Americans wore hairpieces to signify their elevated class.

Wigs became so popular in America that the first few presidents of the United States wore them. However, when the upper classes fell out of favor during the American War of Independence and the French Revolution, wigs were no longer worn, and by the twentieth century, Dwight D. Eisenhower was proudly displaying his uncovered bald head, even when appearing on the newly adopted magic of television. However, he was the last; since then, nearly half of the American presidents have had no visible signs of hair loss.

Plugging Away at the Cure for Baldness

Science and technology have given new hope to those with shiny pates. Once considered impractical, hair transplants have transitioned from something resembling a doll's head to something nearly indiscernible from real hair. The first hair transplants took place in Japan during the 1930s, when micro grafts of follicular units were used to replace damaged eyebrows and lashes, but not treat baldness. The advances made by the Japanese doctors remained unknown to the rest of the world because of the outbreak of the Second World War.

In the late 1950s, an American dermatologist, Norman Orentreich, made patients with hair loss the focus of his clinical research. He theorized that hair extracted from the back of one's scalp, where there is good hair growth, could be transplanted into the balding top of the head, where it would take root and grow permanently. He coined the term *donor dominance*, which means that donor hair would maintain the same characteristics at the "recipient" site as it had at the site where it originated.

Today, stereo microscopes allow doctors to see in three dimensions so they can avoid damaging the follicular cells that will be used for grafting to the bald area. This microscope has led to the successful procedure called *follicular unit transplantation*, which allows as few as one to four follicular units of hair to be moved at a time. This is important because the follicular unit contains oil glands and nerves necessary for hair to look and feel natural. Thousands of follicles might be grafted in a single transplant, improving both the cosmetic appearance and emotional well-being of the patient.

Hair Regeneration Procedures Are a Global Phenomenon

Since Dr. Orentreich's intrepid dive into hair transplantation in the 1950s, attitudes have shifted with regards to cosmetic surgery. In the past, it was often interpreted as an ego trip on the part of the person seeking a new head of hair. However, this is no longer the case; attitudes have changed, and the treatment of patients for hair loss has expanded.

According to a survey of members of the International Society of Hair Restoration Surgery, there were over 900,000 hair restoration patients worldwide in 2010. About one-third were for surgical procedures and two-thirds were for other techniques.[1] Taking into account the number of procedures conducted by nonmembers of the society

---

[1] International Society of Hair Restoration Surgery, "2011 Practice Census Results," (2011): 4, www.ishrs.org/sites/default/files/users/user3/FinalPracticeCensusReport7_11_11.pdf.

would increase this statistic substantially. Treatment for hair loss is an area of the skin-care industry with a great potential for business. Male pattern baldness is common around the world. In the United States alone, it affects about fifty million men, and thirty million women now experience hereditary hair loss.[2]

Medications

In addition to surgery, there are two FDA-approved medications for hair loss: Rogaine (minoxidil) and Propecia (finasteride). Rogaine is an over-the-counter topical medication that is rubbed into the scalp and works by reactivating the hair's growth cycle. Within a few months of using the product, hair loss slows down and regrowth takes place. Some people experience an itchy scalp when using this product. Propecia is a prescription medication that is taken orally as a pill. It promotes hair growth for some men with male pattern baldness; however, the potential side effects include low libido and erectile dysfunction that can last long after the drug is discontinued.

Growth Factors Are Changing the Hair-Loss Scenario

The most promising treatments for hair loss are related to the discovery and use of growth factors. The beauty in growth factors is that they work in a logical and straightforward way. Growth factors are the team players in the body that send out signals that prompt the production of new cells. In the case of hair growth, lab teams isolate the chemicals in growth factors that send the signals to the scalp, and the body kicks in and brings hair back for troubled patients.

To be effective, the growth factors used in products to treat hair loss must be the specific growth factors that are related directly to human hair development. The growth factors also have to be supplied from human sources. Plants and other living things have completely

---

[2] American Academy of Dermatology, "Hair Loss in Women," (2013), www.aad.org/media-resources/stats-and-facts/conditions/hair-loss

different gene codes from humans, and the chemicals cannot cross species. Following are all the growth factors related to human hair growth that any worthwhile product must contain:

1. Hepatocyte and insulin growth factors
2. Fibroblast growth factor
3. Macrophage-stimulating protein
4. Keratinocyte growth factor
5. Endothelial growth factor
6. Platelet-derived growth factor
7. Human parathyroid antagonist peptide
8. Epidermal growth factor (for scalp improvement)

To ensure that your product contains all of the growth factors, contact the director of research and development for the product. He or she should be able to give you a breakdown of the ingredients and their source.

Growth-factors treatment for hair loss involves simply applying the product to the balding areas, and assuming the product has all the above ingredients from human sources, the growth factors will signal the scalp to produce new cellular material for hair growth; the chemicals send the signals, and the body does the work. Remember, too, that we are not concerned just with hair on the head; growth factors can also support eyebrows and thick, luxurious eyelashes.

SECTION

FOUR

Healthy Hope

In this section, we will look at how you can take control of your skin care in a proactive, positive, and practical way. This is where you can apply all the knowledge you have gained in the preceding three sections to make a lifetime plan for your skin and find the professionals who will guide and support you.

CHAPTER 16

Getting Back to Basics

Creating Your Personal Skin-Care Regimen

The neutral normals, the tough guys (and gals), and the cautious types are the three typical attitudes toward skin care that we defined in chapter 12. Notice the use of the term *typical.* All three of these attitudes represent the range of normal responses to thinking about the skin and skin care. What we have to define here is the danger of being fanatical about skin care to the point where it interferes with your enjoyment of life.

Does seeking to protect your skin from the harm of the sun's rays mean you will never walk along the beach and feel the warmth of our nearest star again? Does the worry about chlorine exposure mean you will stop diving into swimming pools and stretching into your elegant strokes through the water? Does fear of laugh lines or crow's-feet mean that you prevent laughter and tears of joy from being part of your experience of life? Of course not! The important point here is to avoid any sort of fanatical behavior or extreme indifference. You need to assume a calm, simple, and intelligent attitude about caring for your skin. This is skin care for the real world, and you need to get back to basics to create a skin-care regimen you can live with.

First, we are going to do a simple test to discover what type of skin you have. Second, we are going to talk about what your results mean. Third, we are going to talk about the most important components of any skin-care regimen. Finally, we will do a little troubleshooting on common issues that might arise from time to time.

To guide you, let us look at some real-world truths. These may sound shocking after years of exposure to cosmetics advertising and makeup marketing, but the truth is often shocking:

- Skin care should not cause you stress or worry. If you are on vacation and all the skin care you do one day is to drench your face under the water of a cool stream, your skin will be fine.
- Taking care of your skin is like taking care of your financial assets. You want to see long-term returns, not short-term successes in booms and busts. Doing a little bit all the time is better than doing something dramatic that will have short-term results and unknown side effects in the future.
- What happens on your skin is often a sign of what is going on inside. Learning about how to care for the outside is a small part of the equation. Taking care of your insides is just as important for your skin health as taking care of the outside.
- When you have a problem with your skin, see a dermatologist. Beauty magazines do not cure cancer. Makeover segments on talk shows do not prevent fungal or bacterial infections, and stylists do not offer protection against environmental damage.

Discover Your Skin Type: A Home Test

Before you can develop an effective skin-care regimen, you need to know what type of skin you have. The three base types are ordinary (or normal) skin, oily, and dry. Many people's skin combines more than one of these classifications, and they have what is called *combination skin*, meaning that it is oily in some places and dry in others.

If you are already working with a dermatologist with whom you have developed a good relationship, he or she will have already evaluated your skin's natural level of oil production and will probably have told you what type of skin you have. However, if you do not know, it is easy to find out with a simple home test. To do the home test, you need the following materials:

1. A trusted soap or cleansing agent. This should be a product that you are certain removes everything from the surface of your skin and dissolves without leaving residue or parching your skin dry.
2. Five tissues.
3. A make-up mirror in a well-lit room.

Step one: Cleanse and relax

First, cleanse your face well and wait for an hour while you do something calm such as answering emails or reading. Stay inside and don't engage in activities such as exercise or gardening that may stimulate your body to release fluids through your pores. Do not apply any treatments of any kind after the cleansing.

Step two: The oil-absorption test

Take the make-up mirror and turn on the lights. Avoid hot lamps, which will cause you to secrete fluids through your pores. Lay comfortably on you back and take your time so you can carry out each action carefully. Press one of the five tissues flat against your chin. Take another and press it against one cheek. Use the third on the other cheek, and then use the fourth for the fatty part and the bridge of your nose. Next, press the last tissue flat against your forehead using the whole span of your thumb and forefinger to cover the entire area.

Step three: Determine your type

Hold each of the tissues up to the light one by one. You can feel relatively certain that you have ordinary skin if none of the tissues are oily when examined in the light. If the tissues are damp with oil residue, you probably have oily skin. If there are scales of skin on your face or on the tissues, your skin is probably dry. If the tissues you used on your chin, forehead, or nose are oily, whereas your cheeks are dry or normal, then you probably have combination skin.

What Skin Types Mean in the Real World of Skin Care

This is a very simple test meant to give you a baseline for making decisions about skin care based on your skin type and your individual needs. Over time, products can trigger an excess of oil production, and they can even cause dry skin. If you have any suspicions about what you are already using on your skin, stop using it for a few days and do the tissue test again. Do not rely on the cosmetics industry for advice. Following are the key facts you need to know about your particular skin type:

ORDINARY OR NORMAL SKIN

Congratulations! This is the type of skin that has been praised in dramas, poetry, and songs. Naturally, you do not have to spend a fortune visiting your dermatologist for reassurance that your skin is not going to dry up and crumble off your bones. It also means that you do not have to spend a lot of money on skin-care products to maintain your skin or prevent future damage.

When you have normal skin, your body is secreting the right amount of oil on your skin. You can also tell at a glance that your skin is in good condition, which is quite a litmus test to pass. Your skin is robust if it has managed to mend itself throughout your life; it is obvious that the basal cells are fully active in their endless pursuit of renewal.

It is important to remember that when you are blessed with normal skin, your first point of reference when a problem occurs should be the dermatologist, not the cosmetics counter. Use cleansing agents or soaps that are mild and free of harmful chemicals. We have already discussed the potentially toxic ingredients in chapter 7. If you have read about them and are still confused, remember, you are trying to work out a lifetime regimen, and it must apply specifically to your own skin.

The need for great advice is one of the main reasons for establishing a relationship with a doctor who understands the skin and has seen how various chemicals react with it. After you learn how to determine what products can be trusted, the process itself is simple for normal skin. You will use a trusted product to cleanse your face thoroughly at least once every two days. When you exercise or engage in other activities that might coat the skin with oils and particulate, remember, just cleanse again.

CHOOSING THE RIGHT SOAP

Soap is such an innocuous household item that we almost never think about it. Perhaps it is time that attitude ended. It could very well be that every member of the family needs their own soap based on skin type, age, and hormonal and health status.

Even if you have used the same soap for years, it is probably a good idea to look at its more recent ingredients list. You can never trust marketing hype. Companies that claim their products to be "honest," "pure," or "real" use the same ingredients as products that claim to work miracles and those who do not make any claims at all.

Remember the list of potentially toxic ingredients from chapter 7? Look to see if they are in your soap. You want to be sure that it does not contain the chemicals or substances that you are worried about. It is also safer for pregnant and nursing women, people undergoing cancer treatment or other intense drug therapies, and children to avoid the entire list of potentially toxic ingredients.

Look for the source of all fragrances and colors in the soap. Does the wonderful scent come from natural lavender or spruce, or is it from chemicals? Natural colors are always suggested, but even white soap that might look cleaner is not naturally white. Traditional homemade soaps made from lanolin after the sheep are sheared each summer, or from the final pressing of olive oil, are not white, but a yellowish light brown.

DRY SKIN

The idea behind the care of dry skin is to encourage it to look and feel like normal skin. We want to support the moist feel of supple skin that is naturally balanced with sebum. The application of good-quality moisturizers after cleansing with soaps that are infused with fats is the approach you need to pursue.

Your dermatologist will have seen what oils work well for skin similar to your own, and this is a very important reason to find the right doctor to work with while developing your regimen. Washing the skin is something you will do each day, and it can have a harsh effect on your whole body. Remember to look at the list of potentially toxic ingredients and rule out their presence before you buy any new soap or moisturizer. Remember also that if you have any food or plant sensitivities that will trigger a reaction on your skin, you need to avoid them as well.

The main thing is to wash your skin daily and avoid harsh soaps. Use products that moisten the skin with ingredients that your doctor recommends, not those you read about in a beauty magazine. Soothe your dry skin with moisturizer daily and before bedtime when it is especially dry. Your skin may not be as well protected from the sun as normal skin, and, therefore, a good-quality sunscreen is necessary. Again, if you cannot rule out all the items on the list of potentially toxic ingredients, consult your doctor about finding an effective sunscreen that is free of harmful ingredients.

If you suffer from severely dry skin of any kind, it is imperative that you seek professional help and follow your doctor's suggestions. Though dry skin sounds less critical than oily skin, the ailments related to dry skin can lead to sores, rashes, lesions, and other severe symptoms.

OILY SKIN

As you know, the most common skin malady on the planet is acne. It is extremely frustrating and must be dealt with aggressively. Your treatments must be directed by a doctor if it is severe, or it can become more complicated and you may never be completely free of the sores and the residual scarring.

Everything from a simple breakout to severe acne is related to oily skin. The culprit is *Propionibacterium acnes*, a bacterium microbe that grows on the human flesh all the time. Sebum, the wonderful material that keeps our skin moist, is food for the bacteria. Acne comes into play when people have an overabundance of the bacteria in their pores. White blood cells then come pouring in to combat the excess bacteria by producing an enzyme that damages the pore walls. This allows the mess to leak into the dermis and cause the bumps.

All of the ordinary treatments such as regular cleansing and not picking at the sores make sense and can be effective, especially in mild cases, where the oiliness can be cleaned off, putting a halt to acne here and there. Simply keep the oils washed off morning and evening with a cleanser that you and your doctor have discussed. Keep your hair, the rest of your body, and your clothing clean and avoid greasy cream rinses and other lotions.

COMBINATION SKIN

Usually combination skin is a little oily on the T-zone, which consists of your forehead, nose, and chin, while the cheeks remain normal. If you overcleanse the cheeks when caring for the T-zone, your cheeks can become dry, so focus on the oily T-zone and try not to expose the cheeks to the cleanser as much. If your cheeks become dry, see a dermatologist for help. He or she will recommend a mild moisturizer you can apply only to the dry area.

See a doctor if acne appears on the oily areas of your face since the normal or dry areas can become aggravated by acne treatment, and it is important to have trusted products that can help to protect these areas of the skin too.

The Three Components of Any Skin-Care Regimen

Though it may appear that there are a great many things to consider when planning a real-world skin-care regimen, the secret is to relax. Get over any anxiety you might have about your skin, any vanity you might have regarding your appearance, and do not compare your skin with anyone else's.

You should be concerned only with taking care of your own skin—and note that concern is not stress or worry. Concern is an act of paying attention and taking action when required. There are three essential components to master regarding skin care: cleansing, moisturizing, and protecting.

1. **Cleansing**

   Cleansing your skin almost every day is imperative to having beautiful, supple skin. However, this can become a fanatical pursuit, which is not the correct approach. Stress is very hard on the system, and relaxation is healing, so always find balance as you keep up your cleansing regimen.

2. **Moisturizing**

   Moisturizing should also be an ongoing way of life. It feels great to have moist and soft skin, and once the habit is in place, it will feel awful when it is dry and tight. When your skin is uncomfortably dry, you will naturally go out of your way to learn about the best lotions to have on hand for a quick fix.

3. **Protecting**

   Protecting your skin is clear-cut, but some of the dangers may be more obscure. Obviously, if you were going to learn welding, you would make sure to protect yourself with the appropriate gloves, masks, and aprons. However, the particulates and toxins in the air around you are not quite as obvious! Protecting yourself from perceptible environmental substances, such as smoke from trucks and buses, could even involve changing locations. You also need to read up on ways to make your home nontoxic.

   This can be simpler than it sounds. Watch out for toxins in your home that you can eliminate, including chemical air fresheners, old appliances that leak chemicals, or furniture that gives off chemical vapors. Apply the skin-care inventory audit lessons you learned in chapter 7 to other products you use, such as shampoos, laundry detergents, and bathroom and kitchen cleaning products.

As well as protecting yourself from indoor and outdoor toxins, you also must protect your skin from the sun. We need to enjoy the outdoors and the sunshine, but it is important to protect ourselves from the sun's UV rays. Staying in the shade, wearing protective clothing, using sunscreen, and wearing sunhats can all reduce our exposure to these harmful UV rays. When choosing a sunscreen, look for ones that are suitable for your skin type and approved by your dermatologist.

Trouble-Shooting Common Issues

FUNGAL INFECTIONS

Fungi are everywhere, and they are always looking for a host. What allows a fungus to start growing out of control is a warm, dark, moist breeding ground. In this regard, you have to be most concerned about the skin on your feet. Heavy socks and unventilated shoes can create the perfect conditions for a fungal infection to survive and grow, affecting the toenails as well as the skin. If your feet perspire a lot, change your socks a few times a day and wear breathable materials such as cotton or wool rather than synthetics. You could also have more than one change of shoes and alternate between them. Fungus can also grow in moist areas of your body, such as under the arms. To prevent a fungal skin infection, wear breathable fabrics, especially in hot weather. Dry yourself well with a clean towel, and when swimming in a public pool, be sure to shower (wearing waterproof sandals) and dry yourself afterwards, as fungal infections are contagious. If you are ever suspicious that you might have a fungal infection, see your dermatologist immediately.

NUTRITIONAL DEFICIENCIES

When it comes to skin care, nutrition is as important as protecting yourself from UV rays, getting fresh air, avoiding toxins, and using good-quality skin-care products. Eating poorly deprives your body of the nutrients it needs to support healthy skin that will not be easily damaged.

A well-balanced diet with lots of fresh greens and easy-to-digest protein is naturally low in sugar and high in essential vitamins and minerals, which allows your body to create new cells wherever they are required, efficiently and ceaselessly. If the skin appears dull and pale, look to improve your nutrition.

I go into more detail about the important topic of nutrition in the next chapter.

CHALLENGES TO THE IMMUNE SYSTEM

Challenges to the immune system also weaken the skin. Ongoing, lifelong exercise, as well as rest, relaxation, and a healthful diet keep the immune system powerful. You do not have to become a gym rat, you just have to get out and move your body until it sweats. Find activities that you enjoy, and your skin will glow with health.

A LIFE OUT OF BALANCE

The importance of finding a healthy balance in our lives is one of the most important aspects of skin care. If we are too rigid in our routines, we become dreary and stagnant in mood and bearing. This can actually be reflected in the pallor of the skin, which lacks luster and becomes sallow. At the same time, if a person lives too far out on the wild side and goes out drinking and partying all the time, the skin becomes dried out and ruddy until the capillaries under the skin burst.

Between the person who has not had any fun for a long time and looks washed out and the perpetual partier with a puffy, red face is a healthy person with glowing skin. Find a balance between work and fun to ensure overall good health, including skin health.

CHAPTER 17 Nutrition and Your Skin

You can impact your skin's health positively through good nutrition. The largest organ in your body is made of millions of cells and is nourished from the inside by a vast network of blood vessels and nerve fibers. As with every cell in your body, your skin cells are built by the materials and nutrients you take in through your diet and from supplements. Since the skin is a permeable organ, nutrients can be absorbed topically when you rub them directly into the skin's surface.

In addition to providing the building blocks for healthy skin cells, the nutrients we consume also support several other skin-nurturing functions such as hydration, protection from damage and mutation, and long-term improvements in appearance and overall health of the skin.

To maintain nature's delicate balance, you must consider the quality and quantity of the nutrients you consume. Many internal health problems are reflected on the skin. Though aging affects us all, most skin conditions are caused by poor nutrition and exposure to toxins. Poor food sources, beauty products that contain low-quality ingredients or those that are not suited to your skin, and other materials applied topically can all make these conditions worse. Due to the body's constant renewal of skin cells, problems can be turned around quickly with simple changes to your diet and the use of growth factors.

In this chapter, I outline the most important building blocks for providing optimal nutritional support for your skin. Remember, though, that what is good for the skin is good for the rest of your body and your emotional health as well.

Quality Proteins

All of the cells in your body are made of a variety of proteins, and dietary protein is necessary for the growth, maintenance, and repair of all tissues, including the skin. There are over twenty amino acids, which are the building blocks of protein. These are called *essential* amino acids because they are not synthesized by the body and must be obtained from food. Proteins from animal foods, such as meat, poultry, fish, eggs, and dairy products, contain all of the essential amino acids, and are often called *complete proteins*. Vegetarians need to combine foods such as whole grains and legumes to get these complete proteins, though not necessarily at the same meal.

Water

Water hydrates the skin and prevents dryness, making it more resilient. Water also helps with digestion, it helps the liver and kidneys flush out wastes, and it regulates body temperature through sweating, all of which contributes to clear, healthy skin. It also helps dissolve minerals and other nutrients so they can be used to nourish the body, including the skin. We cannot survive without water.

Pure water is better than caffeinated beverages and alcohol, which are dehydrating, and juice, which can contain too much sugar. The recommendation to drink at least eight glasses of water a day is a good rule of thumb, but keep in mind that this includes fruits and vegetables, broths and soups, and herbal teas, and it depends on your level of physical activity.

Omega-3s

Whereas protein provides the building blocks for new skin cells, it is just as important to eat a good balance of healthful fats. Every cell in our bodies and in our skin is surrounded by a membrane composed of fats, or *lipids*, that provide a protective barrier against disease. They are necessary to produce hormones and to absorb the fat-soluble vitamins A, E, D, and K, among other functions.

There are different classes of fat; some will harm us and others are essential to our health. The harmful fats include manufactured hydrogenated and partially hydrogenated oils that contain trans-fatty acids. Among the healthful fats that benefit the skin are the omega-3 essential fatty acids, called *essential* because they cannot be manufactured in the body, but must be obtained from the diet. The best sources of omega-3s are fatty cold-water fish such as salmon, mackerel, and tuna and raw flaxseeds and walnuts, as well as free-range meat and dark green leafy vegetables.

One of the primary functions of omega-3s in the skin is to help keep water and nutrients in the cells and allow wastes to pass out. Without omega-3s, the skin begins to sag and wrinkle.

HONEY-SWEET FACE MASSAGE AND MASK

Honey has a long history of use as a beauty aid. This all-natural substance is readily available and minimally processed. Honey really is one of nature's best humectants; that is, it can draw in moisture and retain it in the skin's cells, and combined with ingredients such as oatmeal, it works well as an exfoliant. Honey also has antibacterial, antifungal, antiviral, and anti-inflammatory properties. Raw honey is best because pasteurization can destroy its beneficial enzymes.

To use honey as a facial massage and mask, first cleanse your face, leaving it slightly damp, and then apply about a tablespoon of raw honey, a little at a time on your forehead and cheeks, and massage it into your skin, being careful not to massage around your eyes. After a few minutes of massaging, leave the mask on for at least fifteen minutes before washing it off—thirty to forty-five minutes is ideal.

Antioxidants

Antioxidants are especially important to our skin because they neutralize free radicals—which cause oxidative damage—by inhibiting oxidation. Free radicals are molecules within a cell that have unpaired electrons in their outer orbit, making them unstable and highly reactive. The unpaired electrons need to pick up another electron from another molecule, causing that molecule to become a free radical, and a cascade begins that eventually damages or destroys the cell itself. These reactions will alter cells in ways that accelerate aging and can lead to cancer and other diseases. Antioxidants protect the body by contributing electrons to stabilize the unstable molecules.

It is important to understand that we do not want to wipe out free radicals entirely. The liver uses free radicals to detoxify chemicals, and our white blood cells use them to kill bacteria and viruses. Free radicals also result during normal metabolic processes in the body. However, in our modern environment, free radical damage to cells often result from toxins such as air pollution, radiation, tobacco smoke, and herbicides. It is the excessive production of free radicals, compounded by the under consumption of antioxidant-rich food, that create extensive damage to the cells, and the damage accumulates with age.

Certain nutrients act as antioxidants, including vitamins A, C, and E and the mineral selenium, as well as enzymes or special proteins that are produced in the body. Antioxidants can be consumed in the diet or applied topically directly onto the skin. Sources of antioxidants include the following vitamins and minerals:

Vitamin A protects the skin from the damaging effects of the sun, and it repairs damaged cells and encourages new tissue growth. It is helpful in fighting fine lines and wrinkles, but it also combats acne and dry skin. Active vitamin A is found only in animal sources, including butter, eggs, dairy products, liver, and fish. Beta-carotene, which can be converted to vitamin A in the body, is found in highly pigmented fruits and vegetables, such as carrots, sweet potatoes, and dark green leafy vegetables.

Vitamin C is necessary for the formation of collagen, and it prevents inner-cellular DNA sun damage and can reverse some of the early signs of aging. Good sources of vitamin C are broccoli, sweet peppers, tomatoes, and strawberries. Citrus fruits such as oranges and grapefruit are not high in vitamin C, but their skin, and especially the white pulp inside the skin, is high in bioflavonoids, which increase the amount of vitamin C that is absorbed.

Vitamin E is a powerful antioxidant that can slow down the aging process and prevent premature aging. Vitamin E is able to prevent the oxidation of polyunsaturated fats, which form free radicals when they react with carcinogens, and it reduces the symptoms and damage attributed to sunburn. Good sources of vitamin E are avocados, nuts (especially almonds), olive oil, whole grains and legumes, and dark green leafy vegetables.

Selenium is a mineral whose most important biological function is its role as an antioxidant. It also helps the body use vitamin E effectively. By protecting cell membranes from free radical damage, selenium supports the skin and connective tissue in the body, and one of the symptoms of a deficiency in selenium is hair loss. Selenium content in food depends on the selenium content in the soil; however, it is found in whole grains such as brown rice, almonds, Brazil nuts, and pineapple, as well as seafood, organ meats, and meats.

ANTIOXIDANTS USED IN SKIN-CARE PRODUCTS

Antioxidants are used in topical treatments to provide anti-inflammatory and firming effects, and they help to reduce wrinkles and treat scars.

Alpha-lipoic acid (ALA) is a fatty acid with antioxidant effects that is found naturally in every cell in the body. ALA is often added to skin-care products to soothe minor inflammation.

Coenzyme Q10 (CoQ10) is added to moisturizers and eye creams to tone the skin and reduce wrinkles, especially around the eyes (crow's-feet).

Vitamins C and E are often added to products for use around the eyes and other wrinkle-prone areas. Vitamin C helps to plump up skin cells by increasing collagen formation, and vitamin E helps to regulate moisture, giving the skin a more youthful appearance.

Aloe vera contains antioxidants and other components that help heal wounds and break down scar tissue. It also protects against UV damage from the sun, moisturizes the skin, and has anti-inflammatory and antiseptic properties.

Other Skin-Friendly Nutrients

In addition to antioxidants, the skin also requires several other important nutrients to be healthy. The **B-complex vitamins** help build and repair cells; they are most plentiful in whole grains and liver, as well as in dark green leafy vegetables, meats, poultry, fish, eggs, nuts, and legumes. **Sulfur**, found in garlic, onions, egg yolks, asparagus, meat, poultry, fish, and legumes, enhances skin structure and helps to keep the skin smooth and youthful. **Zinc** is a mineral that is important for skin elasticity—low levels make the skin sag and droop—and it helps sunburned skin repair. Stretch marks, especially when red, indicate a zinc deficiency. Alcohol depletes the body of zinc. This mineral is found in almost all foods, but especially in oysters, fish, meats, liver, dark poultry meat, egg yolks, legumes such as peanuts, and whole grains.

What Foods to Feed Your Skin

To optimize skin health, your diet should be as natural as possible. Avoid processed and junk food, caffeine, sugar, and foods containing trans-fatty acids, such as margarine and hydrogenated and partially hydrogenated vegetable oils. The following foods are considered to be the optimal skin enhancers. Try to eat at least two servings each day and all of them over the course of a week.

Almonds are one of the richest sources of vitamin E, which combats aging and helps keep the skin moist and soft. Almonds are easier to digest if they are soaked overnight and eaten raw or lightly toasted. The brown skin can irritate the stomach and should be removed, which is easy to do once the almonds have been soaked.

Avocados contain healthful monounsaturated fats, omega-3 fatty acids, protein, beta-carotene, vitamins C and E, and selenium, all of which support healthy skin.

Blueberries, especially picked wild, may be the highest source of antioxidants among fruits and vegetables, including beta-carotene, which is converted to vitamin A in the body, and vitamin C, which protects the skin from premature aging.

Carrots are high in the antioxidants beta-carotene and vitamin C. They help to repair skin tissue and protect against UV rays from the sun.

Citrus fruits contain some vitamin C, along with bioflavonoids, which enhance the absorption of vitamin C. Vitamin C supports collagen production, helping to keep the skin smooth and taut.

Cottage cheese contains selenium, a powerful antioxidant mineral that enhances the absorption of vitamin E. Selenium protects against skin cancer and fights dandruff.

Flaxseed oil is one of the best sources of omega-3 fatty acids. This delicious oil reduces inflammation and can help in the treatment of acne, eczema, psoriasis, sunburn, and rosacea.

Green tea is high in catechins, antioxidant compounds that prevent the breakdown of collagen. Among these catechins is a polyphenol antioxidant called *epigallocatechin gallate* (EGCG), which is thought to reactivate dying skin cells.

Mangoes supply 100% of the recommended daily amount (RDA) of vitamin C in just one cup, and they are rich in beta-carotene. This delicious tropical fruit can help reduce inflammation from sun exposure.

Mushrooms are rich in the antioxidant mineral selenium and have anti-inflammatory properties that can help improve acne.

Salmon is the most popular fatty cold-water fish, which contain high levels of omega-3 fatty acids that help strengthen skin cells, protect against sun damage, and reduce inflammation and dryness, keeping the skin smooth and glowing.

Sweet potatoes are considered by the Center for Science in the Public Interest to be one of the most nutritious vegetables.[1] High in vitamin C and beta-carotene, they combat the free radicals that cause skin to age prematurely.

A HEALTHY-SKIN MENU

If you are planning on cooking a special dinner for friends, here is the basic framework for a feast for your skin:

Starter: Mushroom, red onion, and spinach salad served with a dressing of orange juice (or other citrus) and flax-seed oil. Top each portion with a tablespoon of crushed almonds.

Main course: Grilled salmon served with a baked potato topped with avocado guacamole and steamed carrots and broccoli on the side.

Dessert: A fruit salad of mango and blueberries drizzled with honey and topped with a little ice cream (just because fun is also good for the skin).

[1] Center for Science in the Public Interest, "10 Worst and Best Foods," Nutrition Action Health Letter (2009), www.cspinet.org.

Supplements

A well-balanced diet of natural foods is the best source for nutrients; however, in our fast-paced world, with busy schedules and often little time to prepare well-balanced meals every day, you may not be getting all the nutrients you need to support healthy skin. You may also have a particular skin problem that needs extra support. This is where nutritional supplements can be helpful, preferably under the direction of a healthcare professional.

When you purchase supplements, read the labels carefully to ensure that you are getting the ingredients and dosages that you need, and always choose the best quality, least processed products that you can afford. You can have some fun exploring the world of supplements online, but beware of marketing hype.

CHAPTER 18

Caring for Skin Injuries

Injuries are a part of life, and our outer protective layer, our skin, is the most susceptible. Whether you stumble and fall, bump into something, or get stung by a bee, your skin is always affected. An injury can be serious enough to require stitches or just a minor scratch. Fortunately, most of us do not give the possibility of an injury much thought, which is a good thing because constant worry is not healthy and it can spoil our enjoyment of life.

We all get minor flesh wounds, hangnails, scratches, and small burns throughout our lives, and we have all observed the miracle of healing as the skin repairs itself.

Simple injuries are generally limited to the surface tissue, where the body usually heals itself quickly with no complications. However, all skin injuries should be taken seriously and treated with care to allow the body to heal the injury.

Three common types of skin injuries are wounds, bites, and frostbite. Following is a discussion of each of these in terms that a dermatologist or other medical specialist might use when discussing the condition, diagnosis, and expectations with you or a loved one who has such an affliction.

Wounds

Wounds are the most typical of all skin injuries, and they can be open or closed. Open wounds are injuries such as abrasions, punctures, lacerations, or a gunshot wound. Closed wounds manifest as bruises, bumps, swelling, or other injuries that do not break the skin. When you present a wound to a medical professional, the first thing he or she will assess is whether the wound was the result of an internal or an external event or condition.

An external event would be a fall or a bee sting that injures the skin. Internal wounds can be caused by conditions such as poor circulation, or illnesses such as neuropathy as a result of diabetes, whereby the peripheral nerves are damaged so that the sufferers lose feeling in their extremities, leading to injuries that can become infected.

Chemical wounds can result in wounds on the skin as well as internal wounds. Contact with a caustic chemical can result in burns and blistering skin, whereas chemicals that are inhaled, for example, can damage the linings of the lungs.

Once the medical professional has assessed the source of the wound, he or she will base their treatment on whether it is an open a closed wound and whether it is clean or contaminated. A clean wound is free of foreign material. A contaminated wound will have foreign material embedded in it, such as glass, dust, or gravel. In addition, the practitioner will note if the wound is acute or chronic. An acute wound heals in well-defined, orderly, and predictable stages without complications, whereas a chronic wound does not heal in an orderly way, infections can set in, and healing can take years, or never happen at all.

Bites

There are many creatures, indoors and outdoors, that can bite us. Bites are a common source of skin injury and can be inflicted on us by creatures such as stinging bees, wasps, and mosquitoes; biting spiders, horseflies, and other insects; children trying out their young teeth on our flesh; horses taking sugar cubes out of our hands; a pesky dog feeling overly protective; and cats who get annoyed by a poorly placed stroke.

Some spiders, snakes, scorpions, and other critters leave behind powerful poisons when they bite; fortunately, they are not as common or as life threatening as fantasies would have us believe. This is not to suggest that we should be careless about venom, but no one should live in fear of it. Deaths attributed to bites from these animals are more frequently caused by complications than they are by the actual injection of venom. However, if you are ever suspicious about a bite, do not hesitate to get to an emergency facility for expert treatment. Even snake and spider bites that release no venom, also known as *dry bites*, can be dangerous, so all such bites should be taken seriously.

Question: For generations, Canadian kids at summer camp have taught each other to make X's with their fingernails into the bump of a mosquito bite and then rub it with toothpaste to cure the itch. Are the kids onto something with their word-of-mouth pharmacy?

Answer: Yes! Toothpaste is used to stop the itching. It needs to be left to dry on the skin and not washed away. There is no chemical mechanism to explain how it works, but it is probably because the toothpaste keeps the air out, and thus relieves the itching.

Frostbite

Frostbite results when skin is exposed to frigid temperatures for too long. It can happen when we are a long way from help, such as out in the backcountry cross-country skiing. Frostbite occurs when the temperature is at or below freezing and the body, in its wisdom, reroutes its blood supply to warm the heart, brain, and other organs essential to life. This cuts off the blood supply to the extremities, such as the fingertips and toes. At first the skin becomes numb and develops white, red, and yellow patches; if this does not develop further, the frostbite will heal on its own. If freezing continues, blisters can appear, sensation disappears, and eventually the frostbite deepens and affects muscles, tendons, vessels, and nerves and the blisters turn black. If you plan to go on an expedition or trek in cold weather, you should educate yourself on how to handle frostbite. For one thing, you should never rub the frostbitten area because it may cause more serious damage. Instead, wrap the area in blankets or clothing or move to a place that is at room temperature to allow your body to heat itself.

The Language of Healing

No matter what kind of skin injury you experience, the healing process will always be amazing. *Cicatrization*, or scarring, is the formation of scar tissue in wound healing, which takes place in four phases.

The first phase is called *hemostasis*, in which our bodies seal off any damaged blood vessels by forming a blood clot to stop the bleeding. In the second phase, *inflammation* takes place, whereby plasma and neutrophils that fight infection are released from the blood vessels and envelope the bacteria and debris in the wound so they can be removed. An example of this is the common splinter, when, in an amazing engineering feat, the skin around the splinter fills with fluids, which cause pressure that can push the foreign material out of the body. In the third phase, which consists of *proliferation* and *granulation*, new tissue is formed through the secretion of collagen on which new skin cells can form, and in deeper wounds, *contraction* takes place to form a protective layer over the wound. The fourth phase is the *remodeling*, or *maturation*, phase, in which the new dermal tissue is remodeled to increase its strength, making your body safe and sound again. Each phase can vary in length, depending on the seriousness of the wound and the patient's overall health.

It is important that the dermatologists and other specialists pay attention to the underlying causes and closely watch this four-phase process because, if a chronic wound is disturbed, the healing can be exacerbated by conditions such as diabetes.

What You Should Do If You Have a Skin Injury

MINOR CUTS AND SCRAPES

If you get a minor cut or scrape, then clean it with tap water, being careful to wash out all the debris, and then clean it a second time with hydrogen peroxide. Finally, apply an antibacterial agent to the wound. A small cut will heal more quickly when it is exposed to the air, but if it continues to bleed and needs to be under pressure and protected more carefully, then put a bandage or dressing on it.

Be certain to change the dressing frequently and note how well the cut is healing. Swelling and redness are signs of infection, and you should have it checked by a professional before any complications set in. Your dermatologist may also be able to treat a mild or serious wound to prevent scarring or other damage to your skin.

If a wound seems to be quite large or deep and there is some bleeding, do not hesitate to go to a clinic or a doctor. This will set your mind at rest and could save you years of grief and aggravation if the wound were to become more serious. Even the cleaning of the wound may require a second go-round with professional equipment and the application of professional dressings.

SERIOUS WOUNDS AND INJURIES

When you encounter a trauma wound, you understand immediately that you are involved in something much more serious that the minor wounds described above. These kinds of injuries can result from events such as automobile accidents, falls, and natural disasters. There can be severe abrasions, cuts, and bleeding, as well as trauma wounds that do not break the skin but leave a bruise or swelling. You may also suffer from shock.

Never take chances with serious abrasions caused by events such as slipping on concrete or gravel, having a part of your body compressed, puncturing yourself with a tool or household item, or having your skin penetrated by things such as glass shards or bullets. All of these conditions are serious not only because of blood loss but also for the potential damage to organs, muscles, and tendons. Such wounds and injuries are also critical launching pads for serious infections.

A number of symptoms can accompany this sort of wounding: loss of color to the skin, swelling, loss of consciousness, dizziness, trouble breathing, and retching. You or someone else must call 911 immediately or get you to an emergency facility or a doctor as quickly as possible. Apply lifesaving pressure to the wound to stop or slow blood loss and cover the patient with a blanket or coat to keep them as warm as possible.

Other Important Knowledge

Typically, we take injury in stride, but we need to be aware of what happens when injuries occur. Abrasions do not go deeper than the epidermis, and we have all suffered from them as kids when we were riding our bikes, skateboarding, or just playing hard. These injuries can leave scars that can last a long time, and we are often happy to have a little reminder of childhood's big adventures.

Deep lacerations often require stitches and leave prominent scars. Rescue units are skilled in using the latest healing techniques such as a surgical glue called *octyl-cyanoacrylate* that can mend a cut right on the spot and prevent this kind of scarring.

It is also important to consult your dermatologist as soon as possible after you are injured. Skin begins to mend within a couple weeks, so do not delay the visit. Skin mends more quickly in children, who have robust skin, and more slowly in older people, whose skin can be 50% percent thinner than a child's. In either case, early intervention can prevent later problems.

In Australia, children are taught early to protect themselves from the damaging UV rays from the sun. Most schools require them to wear wide-brim hats to shade their heads, faces, and shoulders. If they show up at school without the proper protection, they have to play under cover at recess. Pump bottles of sunscreen are also commonly provided in classrooms. These measures, as well as continual advertising on television, keep parents aware and encourage them to think about their children's overall skin health and its protection.

A Realistic Outlook Means Being Prepared

We are all vulnerable to skin injuries all the time, and children are probably the most vulnerable of all. Of course, we should all watch out for ourselves and others, but it probably is not realistic to expect to go through life without getting a mark on your skin. What is realistic, and desirable, is to teach yourself to deal with injuries immediately and properly. This support will allow your skin to carry out its remarkable process of healing.

CHAPTER 19

Choosing a Dermatologist and Other Specialists

Ideally, you should have a dermatologist who can help you design a lifelong regimen for your skin care. Most people see their dentists twice a year for a checkup, and then when a problem pops up, they have a regular dentist to consult. Yet, when it comes to caring for our largest organ, we usually do not have a specialist in place.

The skin is amazingly resilient. It is also excellent at sending out signals when it needs care. Acne, redness, swelling, blisters, bumps, pain, and itching all tell us something is going on. The skin's alarm system is hot-wired and will always be there to warn us when there is a problem. Even when symptoms are absent, we may feel irregularities, such as when we wash ourselves and our fingers feel something on our bodies that is not normal. If we learn to credit this self-knowledge fully, we will always know when it is time to visit our dermatologists. This is where nurture takes over from nature, because the time to get to know a dermatologist is not when we find a skin problem; it is before!

Quite often, hairdressers have discovered funny-looking moles on their clients' necks that have turned out to be cancerous. As well, many mysterious rashes have been allowed to progress after being covered up with makeup instead of having them examined by a professional. In cases like these, the lack of a dermatologist at the ready is a barrier to quick treatment. That barrier can put your life at risk.

Other barriers include the availability, or lack of, qualified dermatologists. In many communities, there are not enough dermatologists for people to have a choice of treatment providers. In other areas, there is so much choice that practices compete for new patients and neglect patients already on their lists. Insurance providers often have recommended, or preferred, providers with whom they pressure their subscribers to work with. Some dermatologists practice only cosmetic or aesthetic medicine, whereas others manage only serious skin conditions or diseases.

In an ideal world, you would be able to work with the same dermatologist all of your life. He or she would be familiar with your medical and family history and work with you to follow a regimen that would change as your skin's needs change. Unfortunately, dermatologists retire, patients and practices move, treatment areas of interest change, some personality combinations just do not work effectively, and some practitioners just do not do their jobs as well as others. However, none of those reasons should be a barrier to your getting treatment for your skin from a qualified and competent dermatologist.

The romantic partner of your dreams will think you are the most beautiful person on earth. The dermatologist of your dreams will help you achieve the most beautiful skin on earth.

Finding a Dermatologist Using the TREATMENT System

You might be searching for a dermatologist for the first time, or you might be wondering if you need a new one. To help you through the process, I have organized the topics you should consider under a system called TREATMENT.

T IS FOR TRUST

The first quality you should look for, even if it is on an intuitive level, is an easy and relaxed trust between you and your potential dermatologist.

R IS FOR REFERENCES

Every practice should be able to provide you with an up-to-date list of patients you can consult who have undergone procedures similar to the ones you are considering, whether their results were positive or negative.

E IS FOR EXPERIENCE

The magic number for years of experience is ten. This length of time is enough for a practitioner to establish a reputation and build a reliable practice team.

A IS FOR AFFILIATION

Your potential doctor should be affiliated with a local hospital or medical center.

T IS FOR TRAINING

All dermatologists have medical degrees followed by specialist training in treating the skin. In addition, the field of dermatology is changing so rapidly that ongoing training is not just desirable, it is necessary.

M IS FOR MEMBERSHIP IN MEDICAL SOCIETIES

Be sure to get a list of the medical societies and organizations your potential doctor belongs to. You can make a follow-up call about their current standing.

E IS FOR EQUALITY

Never think that you have to be subservient to a doctor. If your instincts tell you there is something not right about a diagnosis or treatment plan, you must seek out a second opinion, and perhaps even a third.

N IS FOR NATURAL EASE

Dermatologists love to talk about the skin, and they should have no difficulty in sharing information and knowledge with their patients.

T IS FOR TRACK RECORD

The best indicator of how someone will treat you in the future is how they have treated you in the past. If you have had bad experiences with a dermatologist, it is probably time to find another one.

When you apply the TREATMENT system to your search for a dermatologist, it is very important to avoid being combative or aggressive or to take on the role of a know-it-all. After reading about so many treatments and products that do not work, it is easy to be suspicious about skin care. At the same time, dermatologists are the "good guys" in the quest for safe and effective skin care, and once you find a suitable one, you will be able to achieve the best results for you.

Simply use the TREATMENT system, define your priorities, remain clear and interested, and be determined to have the best overall results. Remember, the goal is to meet someone with whom you feel comfortable and want to establish a long-term relationship.

Trust

Being able to look your dermatologist in the eye and having the doctor able to do the same with you is the beginning of the path to excellent skin care. In Western cultures, eye contact is a sign of trust. If you look closely at your life, you will notice that the relationships you have with friends, relatives, and associates that run smoothly are those with people you trust.

Your potential dermatologist should also show his or her trustworthiness in other ways. If you express an interest in laser dermabrasion, for example, he or she should tell you about the limitations of the procedures, not just its perceived merits. You should be told in a matter-of-fact way about the cost of procedures, availability of payment plans, and other financial matters without any degree of embarrassment or assumption.

The role of trust when choosing medical professionals has weight that is not present when choosing many other service providers because your life is involved in the case of the former. If you have risk factors for skin cancer, then you need a dermatologist you trust to ensure you do not use products or have procedures that could increase that risk. Ultimately, you are weighing the merits of different dermatologists regarding getting advice about how to keep your skin healthy for the rest of your life. You have to be able to trust that advice and the person who gives it to you.

References

Finding a suitable dermatologist can be seen as a game of discovery. There are things that must be investigated, such as an up-to-date list of references. All medical practices provide reference lists, and you should be able to ask for the contact information for patients who have undergone similar treatments to your own. A reluctance to offer a list of a dozen or so patients is a sure sign that something is not quite right with the practice. Most doctors use photographs and videos to document treatments they have done, and seeing them is a top-notch way to get an idea of a doctor's skill.

You can also talk with the patients sitting in the waiting room to learn how efficient and reliable the practice, the doctor, the staff, and the outside services are.

Never underestimate the importance of referrals and references from trusted friends and acquaintances. They are always one of the best paths toward finding new doctors and specialists. Friends and acquaintances who have enjoyed a great experience with a doctor are always some of the best resources you have. After that, the Internet provides ready access to a good deal of information, including from the Federation of State Medical Boards and other national regulatory bodies. There are also the numerous sites online that offer lists of doctors with recommendations. When you visit these sites, you must remember that they are most likely run as for-profit businesses, such as "content-mill" companies that simply collect comments and testimonials from questionable sources. You will still have to check the doctors out in person after you check them out online.

Experience

One reason to choose a doctor who has been in practice for at least a decade is that they will have a local network of well-qualified professionals in other fields so that if you ever need a specialist such as an oncologist, a bacteriologist, or a geneticist, your dermatologist can give you a reliable referral. More years of experience also means the dermatologist will most likely have dealt with a broad range of conditions and will have treated a number of others with problems similar to your own.

Affiliation

Your doctor should have standing at your local hospital or medical center. This means that they visit their patients who are in hospital while on rounds, and they have relationships with specialists and other members of the hospital team. It also means they have access to facilities such as surgical rooms, MRI machines, specialized equipment, and emergency services if and when they need them. It also means that your dermatologist plays a role in protecting the health of your community when emergencies occur. For dermatologists, this ensures that there is someone available on-call when a fire sends people to the burn unit or trauma center, as well as in cases of other urgent skin injuries.

Training

Your dermatologist will be a doctor of medicine; that is, a physician with a full degree from a school of medicine. He or she must be well trained in technique and up to date on all new knowledge in this very complex branch of medicine, as well as in the relationship between the skin and other parts of the body. These requisites equip the practitioner to diagnose and engage in ongoing, long-term treatments for skin disorders.

Remember, ongoing education about the latest treatments are demanding tasks for any doctor. A prospective practitioner who is enthusiastic about keeping up with advances in the field is a sign that you will have a great ally in maintaining your skin-care regimen.

Membership

Some doctors may use their memberships in organizations simply for marketing and not take advantage of the many educational platforms that these organizations offer their members. The websites of various medical organizations often list upcoming and recent events in the area. Discuss these with your potential doctor to find out if he or she attends these events or at least reads the follow-up reports. This will give you a sense of how important gaining ongoing knowledge is to the practitioner. You will easily recognize natural enthusiasm about skin medicine and skin care when it is there.

Equality

Earlier generations often put doctors on pedestals and placed their words in the "without question" category. That is a disservice to yourself and to your doctor as well. Do not get upset over matters that are of no importance, but if you have serious questions, do not wait to ask. Proceed and pursue them immediately. You should never be embarrassed to question a doctor, and the doctor should never show any reluctance to answer your questions.

Natural Ease

Consider the first meetings as getting-to-know-you sessions. You should both be able to relax and listen to each other. During the conversation, you can observe the doctor's reactions first hand. Enjoy yourself and engage in conversation about their education and time in practice just to feel out their self-assuredness and truthfulness. Remember that certificates on the wall themselves are not bona fide guidelines for finding a good practitioner, but a willingness to listen and respond are.

Be sure to check out what the office feels like. Is the staff harried, or are they happy and efficient? What is the wait time like? Is the equipment modern and well cared for?

In addition, you have to make sure the practice is easy for you to deal with. Can the doctor or a member of the staff speak your native language? Do you feel comfortable with the doctor's age? The distance from your home and office are also factors that you must consider. Do not be shy about your concerns, even if they are as simple as the availability of parking. The key is to eliminate anything that might make you reluctant to make an appointment. Feeling at ease with your choice prevents worry and stress in obtaining skin care.

Track Record

There may come a point during your lifetime when your ongoing skin-care regimen needs changing and that may mean seeing another dermatologist. You may need to see a condition-specific specialist, or just move on to a dermatologist with another area of expertise or outlook. People change, medicine changes, and all things change through the years. If you ever go see your doctor and have doubts about the diagnosis, always trust yourself.

Patient Intuition Is Always Right

I was recently told about an experience that illustrates the effectiveness of the TREATMENT system in finding any kind of healthcare provider. It is easy to see how all of the elements from trust to track record are covered in this single experience.

A good friend of mine once went to an MD for a large bump. My friend had been walking barefoot around a deck that was being built at a friend's home. The carpenters had left a two-by-four in the yard with a sixteen-penny nail through it and my friend stepped on it.

Being a rugged outdoorsman, or one of the "tough guys," he simply ripped the nail out of his foot. There was little bleeding, so he simply put iodine on the wound and thought no more about it. The injury seemed minor, and he expected it to heal on its own. Instead, a knot began to grow in the arch of his foot. It grew and grew until it was the size of half a golf ball, and putting on shoes became a serious difficulty.

The first thing he did was to go to a general practitioner, who identified the bump as a wart. My friend had experienced a few warts in the past, and he knew this diagnosis was not accurate, so he sought a second opinion from yet another MD, who also diagnosed the bump as a wart. My friend asked about the procedure for removal, and the doctor explained that he would burn it off just like any wart. My friend thought the diagnosis was so ridiculous that he walked right out of the doctor's office.

With two professional conclusions that did not feel right, he decided to go to a podiatrist. This specialist was a veteran and immediately told my friend that the bump was an epidermoid cyst. The podiatrist was immediately certain of his diagnosis, whereas the two MDs had been a bit indecisive before making their diagnoses. In another show of expertise, the podiatrist immediately sketched a section of epidermis with the nail penetrating it and explained how the blunt piece of steel had forced a bit of epidermal tissue down into the dermis. With the bit of epidermis lodged in the dermis, the body had instructed growth factors to start growing new skin at the wound. As the tissue grew in size, it forced a cyst to rise on the epidermis, and the bump got bigger and bigger.

The podiatrist also sketched out his plan of action without a moment's hesitation. He would perform surgery, going down into the area of the cyst, and attempt to remove the entire growth of epidermal tissue. He also explained to my friend that although he was experienced, he could not guarantee that he would be able to take out all of the cystic tissue with the first surgery.

The podiatrist's surety inspired my friend's trust immediately; the fact that he had been honest about the possibility of his not being successful meant that he was skilled enough not to be overly sure of himself. My friend decided to have the surgery immediately, and it was completely successful.

It Is Worth the Time and Care

It takes work to find a dermatologist you feel comfortable with in the long term. You may one day change your mind and have to find another one, but it is always worth the time and care it takes to find the right person. Remember, with the many services you require during your lifetime, the closer the bond with the person who takes care of you, the more effective the achievements of the service provider will be. This is true no matter if the service is shoe repair or brain surgery.

You must be fully aware that an appointment with your dermatologist is not like going to the cosmetics counter and chatting with sales reps about which product to buy and how to use the latest applicator. The ability to keep the skin safe, protecting it from the sun; keeping it hydrated to aid it with its own lubrication; and keeping it healthy, vibrant and beautiful are hugely important reasons for finding just the right skin doctor.

CHAPTER 20

Caring for Your Skin in the Real World

You are in control of your skin care. You are the one who gets to decide what substances you will use to keep it clean, moisturized, and protected. You decide which lines, freckles, or blotches on display tell the story of your life and your personality and which should be removed according to the method of your choosing.

What I hope this book has done is give you the tools you need to find dermatological support you can trust and to find products and choose procedures that will be truly beneficial to your skin. I also hope you have learned how to avoid dangerous chemicals and to save your money when salespeople try to sell you snake oil dressed as science.

Following are some key conclusions I want you to remember as you apply these lessons to caring for your skin in the real world.

The Nature of Your Skin

Although your genes may influence the kind of skin cells you were born with, avoiding habits that can damage your DNA and spur mutations will determine what kind of skin cells you will live with. Beware of those who tell you the destiny of your skin is determined by what your parents and grandparents experienced. Your habits are different, and if those habits become harmful, they can be changed. Avoid cigarettes and exposure to harmful chemicals when you can, and protect yourself from the harmful rays of the sun.

Most importantly, learn to love the skin you are in. Do not try to change your skin color with lightening products or tanning procedures. Your skin color is a complex reflection of your ancestors' gifts, your adaptation to the world you were born into, and your unique part in the story of humanity. All skin tones are beautiful and deserve respect. You may not be able to do anything about the prejudices of others, but you can build up your own self-esteem and self-acceptance.

The Nurture of Your Skin

Remember to eat properly; drink enough fresh, clean water; and engage in activities that bring you joy and support your immune system. All of these things are reflected in the appearance of your skin and make it a blessing to care for.

Wash the surface of your skin with your hands to discover any lumps, bumps, or irregularities. Deal with signs of irritation, rashes, or outbreaks immediately before they become bigger problems. Do not be macho or tough about injuries of any kind; this only allows infections to take root and reversible damage to become a permanent scar.

Trust your intuition. If something does not feel right about a diagnosis or treatment plan, there is probably something wrong. Get a second or even a third opinion until you are certain your skin problem can and will be solved.

Choose products that you have investigated for potentially toxic ingredients, and, when there is nothing "safe enough" available, remember that your kitchen is your best bet for safe supplies. You may not be able to trust parabens and sulfites, but you can trust berries, bananas, and honey.

The Science of Your Skin

Learn about new discoveries in depth; do not just latch onto the words and catchphrases that describe them. Remember that stem cells and growth factors cannot jump species. Plant growth factors cannot signal human cells to step up the pace of healing, only human growth factors can do that. If companies cannot or will not tell you the source of their ingredients, they probably have something to hide.

Try to stay rational when you are shown a product that promises miracles. Marketing that attacks your self-esteem has to use that method because it is low on real expertise. Remember that the functions of the skin are already miraculous. Products and procedures should solve, control, or prevent problems, not promise miracles they cannot deliver. Remember that products and treatments are tested to ensure they do not cause harm, not to ensure they deliver on their statements. The only line of defense between your skin and cosmetics marketers is your intellect.

Research and plan on using skin-care procedures that solve a single problem in the most successful way possible. Do not allow yourself to be sold a new procedure simply because your provider has new equipment. Set goals and make plans according to research and reported outcomes, not a sales job.

Genetic, stem-cell, and growth-factor research are all sources of fascinating discoveries in skin care that are available to you right now. They are not too difficult to understand, and it has never been more important that you resist marketing efforts designed to confuse you.

Most importantly, use the TREATMENT system to find a dermatologist you can trust or to replace one with whom you do not have an easy rapport. Whenever the options for skin care seem overwhelming, your skin specialist is your best ally in creating a skin-care regimen you can live with in the real world.

About the Author

Dr. Al-Qahtani is an emerging figure in antiaging and skin care, who focuses his research on growth factors and their contributions to skin rejuvenation. He is the president and founder of AQ Skin Solutions, which he founded in 2008. The company is known for its Growth Factor (GF) technology—an advanced collection and production of the purest form of human growth factors that are utilized in topical skin care products, hair, and other therapeutic applications. Dr. Al-Qahtani has developed GFIT—Growth Factor Induced Therapy, which is now used worldwide for the treatment of a multitude of skin conditions.

Prior to the launch of the company, Dr. Al-Qahtani began his career researching mechanisms underlying antibodies maturation and response in B-lymphocytes, and later the medical applications of growth factors for healing wounded tissue and burns. As a researcher in Immunology, he developed a process for producing the highest quality of growth factors utilizing a specialized cell line that was recognized and authenticated by the American Type Culture Collection (ATCC). Dr. Al-Qahtani holds US and international patents on Growth Factor technology.

An accomplished speaker, he has spoken at numerous international conferences on the role of growth factors in skin care. These include:

- 2013 Dubai Derma, the Dubai World Dermatology & Laser Conference & Exhibition
- 2013 Kuwait Derma Update and Laser Conference
- 2012 and 2013 FACE Conference, United Kingdom
- American Academy of Anti-Aging Medicine (A4M)

- International Master Course on Aging Skin (IMCAS)

Dr. Al-Qahtani received a PhD at the Institute for Immunology at the University of California, Irvine. He also holds Masters Degrees in Medical Microbiology and Biotechnology from the Royal Melbourne Institute of Technology in Australia. His undergraduate study began at the Royal College of Surgeons in Ireland and the University of San Francisco.

Currently Dr. Al-Qahtani is assistant professor with the College of Medicine and Health Science at United Arab Emirates University in Al-Ain.

Index

B

E

H

L

M

Q

R

S

U

V

W

Within These Walls

Holly Hill Mangin

This book is a work of fiction. Names, characters, businesses, organizations, places, events and incidents either are the product of the author's imagination or are used fictitiously. Any resemblance to actual persons, living or dead, events, or locales is entirely coincidental.

Book design by We Got You Covered Book Design
www.wegotyoucoveredbookdesign.com

Editing by Nadara "Nay" Merrill
www.naysnotations.com

ISBN—Paperback: 978-2-9576979-2-2

ISBN—E-book : 978-2-9576979-3-9

First Edition: August 2023

With love to my family and friends:
those who were, those who are, and those
who've yet to be.

Prologue

The Mysterious Hillfield Manor

June 10, 2013

According to legend and based on more than one historical fact, Hillfield Manor, built in 1642 by Lord Jonathon George Cena, has been host to paranormal activity for more than 300 years. The first reports of ghostly activity occurred in the late 1700s after the manor house changed hands and came under the ownership of the Eason family in October 1788. Throughout the family's history at the manor, servants have complained of seeing transparent "silkies" walking the halls, hearing strange noises, and being touched. Chambermaids have refused to enter rooms alone, and a stable boy was reportedly pushed by unseen hands into a horse that subsequently kicked him. He died from his injuries.

As recently as 1993, disturbing and skin-tingling events have inspired storytellers and paranormal investigators alike who have come from far and wide to experience the multiple sightings within the walls and upon the grounds of Hillfield Manor. One of the more illustrious guests, a well-known television paranormal investigator who recently walked away from retelling haunting accounts of ghosts and the unusual, even commented that it was the

> most disturbing thing I've ever experienced. To walk the halls and be in the presence of more than one apparition just on my way to dinner was enough to make me turn around and run back to my room. I had promised to stay the night, but I couldn't. I was gone within an hour, and for most of that hour, I was out front waiting for someone to pick me up! I won't be back.

But ghosts are only part of the mystery. Disappearances also abound. With no less than eight disappearances between 1785 and 1993, possibly the most famous story of intrigue stemming from Hillfield Manor is that of Bartholomew James Eason, who lived at the estate between 1878 and 1880. A cousin to Lord Eugene Hamilton Eason, Bartholomew moved to the manor to help oversee the estate's operations due to the lord of the manor's poor health.

Accounts state that in early March or April 1878, Mr. Eason reportedly encountered a "most enchanting" gray lady who walked the Long Gallery on the second floor of the manor. Despite attempts to dissuade him, which are documented in family journals and dated between April and July 1878, Mr. Eason was determined to attempt some form of discourse with her. After months of occasional glimpses and failed attempts at communication, a breakthrough occurred, and he was later often seen in the presence of the gray lady.

Dated August 22, 1878, Lady Georgianna Maurgettie Eason, wife of Lord Eason and the lady of the manor, wrote:

> It has become such a common occurrence that I dare say neither the family nor the servants, save a few of the newer maids, bat an eyelash upon her sudden arrival or her just as sudden departure. Bart is so happy in Marie's presence (he assures us that is her name) and although she never speaks to us and is often merely just a shadow to our eyes, she has softened him and has made him a better man. I sincerely regret that time separates the two, for despite her translucency, they make a most handsome pair.

Just who this elusive "gray lady" was remains the subject of considerable speculation. Records suggest she could be Marie Louisa Cena, sister to Lord Jonathan George Cena, the original owner of Hillfield. Regardless, her presence came to a sudden halt on October 13, 1880, when both she and Bartholomew were seen walking in the main hall of the manor. They were never seen again.

There are several theories about the disappearance. One suggests the lovestruck man committed suicide to be with Marie by jumping into the 32-foot-wide moat that once surrounded the manor. Another proposes that Bartholomew, heartbroken over the fact that he could never be with his true love, left Hillfield so he would never have to lay eyes on her again. Conclusive evidence as to the actual whereabouts of Mr. Bartholomew James Eason has never been provided.

With a history of ghosts and disappearances, why not throw in a bit of eccentricity as well? Legend has it that, because of the disappearance of his cousin, Lord Eason lost touch with reality. He began to require members of the household to wear period clothing "to dress and speak in a manner best befitting the gentry of the 1800s" in the hopes Marie would return and tell him what became of his cousin. After his death in 1885, the family continued the tradition in his memory, and by the early 1910s, Hillfield Manor was widely recognized for its quaint style in dress, speech, and understated elegance, which continued until a little over thirty years ago.

Sadly, misfortune saw fit to continue its visitations upon the walls of Hillfield Manor. In 1976, the current Eason's eldest son, Christopher Bartholomew Eason, mysteriously disappeared without a trace at the mere age of nineteen. Most recently, under the shroud of yet another unexplained, yet unconfirmed, disappearance—this time of the Easons's remaining child and sole heir—the manor which had been used as a museum and tourist attraction since the 1920s was closed in September 1993.

But the lights are back on at Hillfield Manor. On April 8, 2014, James and Marie Gale, the proprietors of Homecomings, a highly recommended refurbishing company, installed themselves within Hillfield's walls. In a statement, James Gale confirmed that members of the Eason family would return in the coming months.

Until then, we can only wonder if the traditions of ghosts, disappearances, and period costumes will continue.

Chapter 1

***Last night, I dreamed of** Evelyn again. Evie. I know the conversations I have with her in my mind aren't real. How could they be? She died six months ago.*

No, these are conversations born of memories and desires, words said and left unsaid, scripted by my mind in such a way as to keep me hoping that maybe, just maybe, she's trying to tell me something, something she wants me to know.

They're not real. They can't be.

But they seem real. And it's because they do that I'll keep searching for answers. Because as much as I want our conversations to go on indefinitely, there's something I want more: peace.

"The owners are interested in hiring someone discreet, efficient, and trustworthy. And they asked for you specifically." Mr. Johnson taps his index finger on the top of the desk. "Honestly, even if they hadn't, I can think of no one more suitable." Pleased, I redden a bit under the quiet praise.

"Thank you, sir. I've learned so much from you and working here." I hesitate, unsure how to continue without sounding ungrateful, but I need to think of practical issues as well. "Could you tell me more about the position?"

"Of course. It's over at Hillfield Manor and—"

"Hillfield!" I can't help interrupting, but I try to tamp down my enthusiasm.

Mr. Johnson's eyes light with suppressed humor as he continues. "Well, if you like that piece of information, this might interest you as well. It pays a bit less than what you're currently getting, but the owners have suggested you live at the manor for the duration of the job."

"Could you tell me how long that would be?"

"Oh, Emma." Mr. Johnson stretches his arms behind his head and leans back in the oversized leather chair in which he sits, his substantial paunch more noticeable even with the desk obscuring the lower half of his body. "I've not set foot in that place in years, not since it was closed up in 1993, before that even." He narrows his eyes in thought. "If memory serves, the collection is extensive, and the personal volumes take up a good percentage of it. No one knows how long they've been keeping records of everything. You'll be one of the few alive—maybe the only one—who knows what's so important they felt the need to write it all down!" He brings his hands together with a clap as his eyes widen, and we share a laugh before he continues.

"All the Eason family journals are to be copy typed and filed. I believe the owner would like to be able to find information by date or by subject, so indexing will be required as well. I've heard it's a bit disorganized at the moment, so everything will have to be put to sorts before you even attempt to get started. I would think at least half a year."

At this point, I'm almost dancing in my shoes, and I think Mr. Johnson can see it. I can't help myself. "Mr. Johnson, you are the best human being ever! Thank you so much." I wonder what he would do if I decided to throw my arms around him for the biggest hug imaginable but decide against it and instead, I step forward, grasp his hand warmly between my own, and shake it enthusiastically.

Mr. Johnson laughs. "I had nothing to do with it. You did."

"You said the owners asked for me by name. How

do they know of me?"

Mr. Johnson shakes his head, a look of bewilderment flashing through his eyes. "Your guess is as good as mine, Emma. I was given a directive by one of the lawyers for the estate. He gave me your name and was even able to give me a physical description. He asked me to tell you about the position and to get back to him with your answer."

I've worked for Mr. Johnson long enough to know he wouldn't encourage me to accept an offer of employment he doesn't believe is legitimate, and although it's strange that I was asked for by name, it's not enough to have him doubt the sincerity of the offer.

Hillfield. The manor is a grand, imposing structure with a Gothic facade. Its windows are heavily barred and its doors are shuttered, giving it a forbidding air. It's perfectly maintained on the outside. Every year, a company comes and fixes anything damaged or rusted. As far as the yard, it's kept meticulously manicured. Even the walks are cleared of snow in the winter. The house gives every appearance of someone living there, save for the fact that no one ever enters or exits its doors. Walking by the high gates that surround the manor, a sense of eeriness hangs in the air, as if something unknown lurks within the walls. Ever since I can remember, there have been rumors that the place is haunted.

I've always been interested in the paranormal. I read every book, article, and documentary on the supernatural I can get my hands on. I eagerly seek out haunted locations, and I'm always wanting to hear accounts of paranormal experiences. I'm drawn to the mystery and the unknown, and I often find myself trying to explain what can't be explained.

My sister's death fueled my need to know about the other side even more, especially since she's been coming to me in my dreams, reminding me with aching awareness that she is no longer here in my waking life. I went to my fair share of psychics and paranormal investigators. Most were obviously fake—and I needed that. I wanted them to be frauds because then I could get my brain to acknowledge the fact that there is no way to bring Eve back. Once you're dead, you're dead. That's it. Life goes on, so to speak.

All the psychics would assure me my loved one was in a better place. But I'm not interested in heaven and hell. I believe those places exist—my upbringing has instilled that faith—but I'm talking about the spirits who never made it to those places. Ghosts. Do they live on too, wondering what happened or not even realizing what happened? The thought of Eve being stranded here, "living" life on a loop, torments me. I question if she had any unfinished business. After all, I have the distinct impression she's been trying to tell me something in my dreams . . .

"So, Emma, what do you say? Emma?"

Lost in my thoughts, it takes me a moment to

realize I haven't even given a final answer. "Yes! Yes, I accept," I say, nodding emphatically. "When do I start?"

"Well, your job here ends at the end of the month." Mr. Johnson recently suffered a heart attack and decided to cut back on the hours he spends at work, making my job unnecessary. "They'd like you to start soon after." He gives me a date. "Will that give you enough time to get everything in order?"

"Yes, that's fine." My degree in Library and Information Science is a gateway to a lot of opportunities, but I have to get my foot in the door, and Hillfield will be the perfect first step.

"Then, Emma, the job's yours. I'll let them know, and I'm sure the solicitor of the estate will get in touch with you shortly."

After a few more pleasantries, I leave his office to go back to my desk with a bounce in my step. I'm going to Hillfield Manor, entering a place I've always longed to enter, and walk down the halls that centuries' worth of others walked, possibly even encountering one of their spirits. What family secrets will I learn? I can't wait to find out.

Chapter 2

***"So, Hillfield Manor is opening** up." Eve's face fills the screen of my laptop, and her eyes widen as she hears my news. "I sent you the article."*

"That old, boarded-up place by Grandma's?"

"Yeah! I saw the article about it in the newspaper. Once it opens, we have to go!"

"Will it be open to the public?"

"The article doesn't say, but we'll find a way around it, even if we have to pose as Girl Scouts selling cookies!" Eve laughs. "I think we're a little too old for that now . . . I wonder if it really is haunted."

"That's what we have to find out!"

"Emma—" The screen freezes, and Eve's words warp into a weird robotic vibration. When the line is secure once more, Eve looks different, more like she did the last time I saw her in the hospital, her skin sallow, her body too still. "You'll have to go without me. Find what it is you're looking for."

"But I need you to come with me." My tone has taken on a desperate pitch.

"Nope, sorry, I've got a retirement party to go to that day. They rented a yacht! How can I pass that up?"

"You can't go on the yacht! Eve, promise me you'll come with me and stay away from the yacht."

"Emma, what are you going on about? Everyone has been planning this for the last three months!"

"You're going to drown!"

Eve laughs. "I'm a pretty good swimmer. After all, that's why I'm a licensed lifeguard and swimming instruct—"

"No, Eve. Please!" Tears course down my face. "Please, listen to me. Don't go!"

Eve regards me through the camera on her phone. She looks happy, her face once more radiant with life. She doesn't acknowledge my tears. Instead, it's as though she looks through me, to some faraway place. "Find what you're looking for, Emma. At Hillfield Manor. Find it."

I wake up drenched in sweat, my heart beating double time. Despite the chilly January morning, I kick off the blanket and blink a few times, letting reality settle upon me. The conversation I had with Eve comes back to me. The real one. The one where I told her about Hillfield and we strategized on how we'd get in. The other conversation comes back to me as well. The one where I tried to talk her out of going to the retirement party. That conversation hadn't ended the same way either. I had asked her to come for a visit, having forgotten about the party planned for her boss, and when she turned me down, my attempts to get her to change her mind were halfhearted. I knew she wanted to be there. It was important to her.

But that was the last yacht she'd ever step foot upon, the last party she'd ever go to. Had I known that, my attempts would have been more forceful. I would have tackled her to the ground, boarded up the exits to her apartment from the outside, or held her at gunpoint if necessary.

What's that thing they say about hindsight?

The loud chimes of my alarm go off, reminding me that I'm about to start my first day at Hillfield Manor. At least I'd slept through the night. Sometimes I'm not so lucky.

Shutting off the alarm, I sit up and dangle my feet over the side of the bed. My outfit for the day is already waiting for me in the bathroom, and my luggage is already set by the front door downstairs. I'm not taking too much. I don't need to. A twenty-minute train ride would bring me right back should I need anything. Besides, I'm planning on coming back in a week for my day off anyway.

Although I grew up in upstate New York, my father is English, making me a dual citizen. Every summer, we'd come here to visit his mother, my grandma. She died several years back, leaving the house to my father, her only child, and my parents have kept it. It brings my dad peace to think of Grandma as still alive, roaming the halls where all his most cherished childhood memories took place.

Since the house was empty save during the times they visited, they graciously allowed me to move in when I decided on a change of scenery. It's a win-win situation. My parents know the neighborhood and the house where I'm staying, so they don't worry about me as much—although they seem to worry incessantly since Eve's death, not that I blame them—and I pay for utilities and any minor maintenance issues, saving on rent while having a nice place to stay.

As I drink some tea and eat a blueberry muffin, my foot taps impatiently against the floorboards. I have plenty of time, but I still hurry to get ready. I'm going to Hillfield Manor! I've always wanted a peek inside and hope the Gales, the owners of the company refurbishing the manor, are keeping everything as original as possible so I can see what the house looked like in its former glory. They've been there for roughly seven months already, a lot of time to do major work.

The taxi pulls up to the high wrought-iron fence a little after nine thirty. I could have walked from the train station, but with my luggage and the steady drizzle, a taxi seemed the better option. Butterflies flit away in my stomach, and an excited anticipation wells within my chest. After assuring the driver this is where I want to be dropped off, he helps me with my bags—one suitcase and a smaller computer bag—and eyes the mansion with curiosity as I take out money to pay. "This place open, then? It's Hillfield, init?"

I crane my neck toward a blue plaque on the fence above my left shoulder, Hillfield Manor clearly written in white letters. "Yeah," I say, turning back to the man. "But it's not open yet. Keep the change."

"Cheers." Sticking the money into his pocket, the driver shuts the trunk and gets in behind the wheel. Shutting the door, he waves before pulling out and merging into traffic. I may have visited every summer since I was born, and I've been in England for close to six months, but it still amazes me to watch people drive from what, to me, is the passenger seat.

Taking a deep breath, I hoist my computer bag higher onto my shoulder and face what is essentially my new home for the foreseeable future. An older couple, both in rain ponchos, stand just outside the fence door and wave, and I smile in return, rolling my luggage up to them. The woman has graying blonde hair cut in a stylish neck-length bob. With a petite frame and pixie features, she reminds me of a real-life Tinkerbell without wings. The man, only slightly taller than me, holds himself erect. He's bald-pated but sports a neatly trimmed gray mustache and beard. I was told I would be met by James and Marie Gale, the owners of Homecomings, who are also staying at Hillfield, and I assume this is them.

"You must be Emma," the woman says.

"Yes, Emma Beckett. Mr. and Mrs. Gale?"

"Call me Marie." The woman smiles. "Mrs. Gale makes me sound so old. And this is James."

"You may call me Mr. Gale," the man said gruffly before breaking into a wide grin. "No, Marie is correct. It does make us sound old. Call me James." He winks at his wife and pulls her closer into a one-armed hug, then holds out his hand. "Was your trip satisfactory? You didn't run into any trouble on the train?"

Shaking his hand and then Marie's, I shrug. "No, I had no trouble at all. And I lucked out at having the seat next to me empty."

"Oh, that's always nice," Marie says. She moves to close the gate and lock it, nodding to a few people under umbrellas who have slowed to stare. "Here, let's get you inside before you get soaked and we gather a crowd. I don't want people to start asking if they can come in. We already had that happen yesterday."

James grabs hold of my suitcase, lifting it easily and foregoing the wheels. I'm about to tell him when Marie touches my arm and gives a slight shake of her head. "It's no use saying anything. He won't use them. We saw you wheel the suitcase up. I swear, the man doesn't believe in modern convenience!" She laughs.

"I'm merely trying to prove to you how young and strapping I am, my dear," he says with a twinkle in his eye. "Now, move along before my strength fails me and I'm positively humiliated in front of you and our young guest." With a slight tip of his head, he motions Marie and me forward and follows a few steps behind.

"I can't believe I'm here." My voice comes out breathy, excitement welling in my chest with each step closer we get to the front doors of Hillfield.

The manor is an old estate that was boarded up when I was still a child and living thousands of miles away in the States. At the time, my grandmother was still alive, and when we made our yearly visit, my parents would sometimes take Eve and me to the small park across from the manor. I would sit and stare at the house, wondering what happened to the people who lived there to make them close such a beautiful place.

Eve, who was a couple of years older than me, would scare me by telling me she saw a curtain in one of the windows on the upper floors move or heard the rattle of one of the doors, even if we were too far away for that to be possible, but she was just as captivated by the house as I was. Ghost stories about the place were rampant, so much so that even my parents would look over at the house, their eyes filled with fascination and wonder.

Then, when I was in my teens, I was watching an old TV series on ghost investigations, and Hillfield Manor was the topic of the episode. I learned more about the supposed gray lady of the manor and the disappearances that had taken place on the Hillfield property. I watched as the lead investigator, shaken and pale, talked to the camera about seeing multiple ghosts, and I felt a chill run down my spine even though there was no documented proof of what he'd seen. Eve told me it was all fake, that he was only acting that way for ratings, but a few episodes later, there was another lead investigator, the first supposedly having left because of his experience at Hillfield.

And now, here I am, not only about to step over the threshold but also about to live and work at the manor and possibly discover more about them than anyone alive knows.

As we step under the portico, I pause, taking a deep breath. "I can't believe I get to do this."

"That's how I felt when I first got here." Marie's eyes twinkle. "I don't think the feeling ever really goes away. At least, it hasn't for me."

I smile weakly, feeling the importance I place on entering Hillfield Manor as more than just the awe I have for it. In some ways, I feel obligated to take it in as if I were two people: Eve and me. And I force myself to visualize things as I believe she would see them, just as I attempt to take in everything myself. In this way, I can at least pretend we are doing this together, the way we agreed, instead of moving forward alone.

Of course, stepping over the threshold throws me back into reality. Eve isn't here. Her spiritual presence doesn't magically present itself, suggesting that in some way she is still a part of my life and knows what is happening. I don't feel her at all. Disappointment courses through me, and I blink rapidly, willing myself to keep the tears that threaten to fall in check.

I inhale deeply and step forward into a large, mostly empty foyer, except for a large, prominent double door in the center of the opposite wall, a door large enough for a horse to walk through. High above, a mass of clear crystal fashioned into a giant swirling chandelier hangs from a vaulted ceiling. Although off, light dances off the facets, thanks to a few lit table lamps below, creating a myriad of rainbows, sparkling and glittering. The walls are bare and slightly dingy, waiting for a fresh coat of paint, and there is a marble floor, inlaid with veins of black and gray, its rough nature rubbed down to a sheen. Even without its decor, it's obvious the foyer was designed to impress. James sets my bag on the floor, looking no worse for carrying it. "I'll take that up to your room once I've had a chance to catch my breath," he says with a wink.

"Oh, you!" Marie admonishes, nudging him in the ribs and laughing. "If you keep that up, people are going to start to wonder if we can handle projects like this, and I have no desire to lay down my hammer and paint samples just yet."

Marie turns to me. "Let's go into the parlor and sit for a moment. I've prepared tea, and I'd love to learn a little more about you and what you're going to be doing here."

She leads me across the foyer to a room somewhat dated and musty.

"We haven't done in here yet," she says as she watches me. "We're working from the back of the house to the front. To tell the truth, I'm not sure what I want to do in here. I want to be true to the original design and decor, but it definitely needs to be updated. Save for a few additional pieces, I think this room looks about the same as it did when I worked here."

My eyes widen. "You used to work here?" I ask as Marie points me to a couch and sets about preparing the tea.

"Yes." She smiles. "That's how I met James."

James takes a seat on the couch next to Marie. "The only difference is that I used to live here."

"Really?" I study James with renewed interest. "That must have been amazing."

James's expression sobers. "It was. But it was also a lot of work. An estate this size . . . Only many hands coming together could make it work."

"Cream or sugar?" Marie asks. When I decline, she hands me a cup filled with what smells like Earl Grey tea and places a saucer on the coffee table in front of me.

"And now you're both back again," I say after taking a sip. "That must be strange."

James barks out a laugh. "I expect it's more so than you think. Sometimes I wander into a room expecting to see the faces of those I encountered back then. Who knows, perhaps I will."

He gives me an opening to a conversation I probably shouldn't bring up within the first few minutes of arriving, but as I open my mouth to speak, a glance at Marie and the sparkle in her eyes tells me she has already gathered what I'm about to ask.

"So, is it true? What people say about this place being haunted?"

James sets his cup of tea down and leans forward as if to impart a great secret. "Yes."

"I knew it!"

James tsks and wags a finger. "That is the simple answer. I think there's more to it than that. In my experience, the manifestations represent so much more. Don't you agree, darling?" He picks up his tea again and turns to Marie.

Marie nods and the corners of her mouth turn up. "I do."

"You've seen them too?"

"Emma, I think it best for you to know that if you *can* see them—and there are many who can't—then there will most likely not be a day that goes by where you won't see one or two."

Disbelief must clearly show on my face because Marie just smiles. "Just wait," she says, but then she frowns. "You aren't the type to throw hysterics and go tearing through the place scaring our workers, are you?"

I glance at James, trying to determine whether he's in on a joke Marie is playing, a sort of Hillfield Manor initiation, but his expression holds nothing but curiosity and perhaps a little apprehension.

"You're serious?" I ask when neither of them cracks a smile or even hints at being anything other than sincere. "You really see ghosts every day?"

They nod.

"I don't think I'll be hysterical," I say hesitantly, focusing on Marie once more. "I've always been fascinated by ghosts, but I've never run into one before, so I can't say I know how I'll act."

"It can be disconcerting, to say the least, but please understand that none of them will hurt you. And it's not as if any of them are out to scare you as it seems they are in all these movies. As a matter of fact, some may be more scared of you than you are of them."

"I'll try to keep that in mind . . . but, and I'm sorry to be so morbid, but if I'm going to run into them every day, I want to be prepared. Do they show signs of their deaths?" At this point, images from *The Sixth Sense*, where ghosts exhibit grotesque gunshot wounds and other horrible indicators of their demises, are taking control of my brain.

James chuckles. "That's the fear, isn't it? I can honestly tell you I have never seen a ghost that looks like anything other than a man or woman going about their daily routine. Am I right, Marie?"

"I completely agree." She takes a small pastry from a dish piled high with them at the center of the coffee table. "Now, tell us what you're going to be doing here, Emma."

I give them a rundown on what I'll be doing at the estate, adding, "I've always been fascinated with history . . . okay, and gossip too, and here I am, basically walking into these people's lives and reading their private thoughts, and if people continue to do that, their words are going to live forever. *They* will essentially live forever. I think that's pretty cool, don't you?"

"Well, when you put it that way! But why now? Those journals have been around for quite some time, and no one has seemed particularly interested in them."

"I'm not sure exactly. I spoke with a representative. From what I understand, due to the age of many of the volumes, the quality of the ink is degenerating, not to mention the fact that the library itself, I was told, isn't necessarily the best location for the books. Apparently, with the house closed up, there's a touch of mildew."

James nods. "Yes, that's one of the things we need to fix. That room seems to get a lot of moisture and was never properly insulated. We went in to open it up and it's true. We noticed the smell as well. It's on our list of things to do, but we were told not to touch anything in there until you could get in for organization and storage. Is there anything we can do to assist you?"

"To tell the truth, I won't know until I can get in there and see everything for myself. That's part of the reason I came early. I'd like to get my bearings and get a sense of where I'll be working." I smiled. "And yes, I'm crazy curious about this place too."

"That sounds like the perfect introduction to a tour!" Marie smiles. "But first, would you like some more tea?"

"No, thank you," I say as I set my cup down on its saucer. "That was great."

James stands up, and despite his spry form, I can hear a few quiet snaps and cracks as he stretches and looks at his watch. "I'll leave you to the tour, dear, if you don't mind. I'll take Emma's bag up to her room, but then I have to get out and make sure everyone's doing what they're supposed to be doing."

Marie and I rise too, and I thank James before he heads out.

"I'm sure you want to see where you'll be spending the majority of your time, so why don't I show you to the library first?" Marie walks me to the foyer where we entered. "We'll start from here so you can remember, although I'm sure you're going to be doing a lot of exploring and will know your way around in no time. So, from here, it's really easy."

Marie leads me to the far side of the foyer and walks through the double doorway into a large hall. I don't have much time to look around because she's already hustling us across the room to the far side and walking through another set of double doors. "This is the garden entrance." In front of her are two sets of double doors that lead to a large terrace and the grounds beyond, and this is what she motions to when she says, "It may not seem like much now, but gardeners will come in and really tidy everything up. It's true, general maintenance has been done on the lawns, but when this place is put back to its former glory, it's going to be incredible." Marie smiles and extends her left arm. "And if you'll just walk through this door . . ."

Holding my breath, I cross the threshold and release said breath in a rush. The room is smaller than I expected but nevertheless impressive. It's the size of a large classroom, one with every single wall covered from top to bottom with heavy wooden bookcases filled with books save where heavy French doors overlook the garden on the right-hand side of the room and a fireplace in the center of the left-hand wall.

I'm about to turn to Marie and tell her my thoughts when I hear a phone buzz.

"Oh!" Marie says as she digs the phone out of her pocket and looks at the screen. "I have to take this. Feel free to look around." Pivoting, she exits, and I'm left to gape at everything around me.

The room feels rich and luxurious. I picture men of old, in their finest suits, drinking port and discussing finances and the government while they puff away at heavily scented cigars. Looking over at the fireplace, I imagine the faint appearance of a man with his elbow resting on the mantel, staring out at the garden across the way. Curious, I turn to find out what draws his gaze, and when I glance back, the man is gone. I frown, wondering if I indeed conjured him from my imagination or if he was one of the ghosts Marie and James told me about. If so, are they all so faint and subtle? "A bit anticlimactic," I say softly in the direction of the hearth.

"How are you getting on, then?" Marie asks as she comes back into the room. At my silence, she steps closer to me. "Emma? Are you all right? It's a lot of work, but it hasn't scared you off, has it?"

The statement snaps me out of my stupor, and I laugh. "No," I say, realizing I haven't even taken in the enormity of the job, too busy I was with ghosts, real or imagined. I assess each shelf, noting that one wall, the back, has shelves reaching up to the twelve-foot ceiling and that one of those little ladders had been attached at some point to allow for easier access to those shelves and their contents at the top. Overall, a little over half of the shelves in the room look like they contain journals of some sort. The rest are overfilled with books—some with very old-looking spines—as well as magazines and small to medium-sized knickknacks.

I smile at Marie. "I love organizing too. This is going to be fun."

Marie takes me around the rest of the house fairly quickly. It allows me to get my bearings while still granting me ample opportunity to explore on my own. We arrive back at the foyer, and Marie turns to me.

"This is where I will leave you." She looks at her watch. "Lunch is in an hour and a half or so. We don't do anything formal. A lot of the workers leave. There are quite a few restaurants around here they go to, or they go home. Some of them stick around too. During lunch is when you'll see a lot of our people wandering around, poking their heads into the different rooms. I don't know if they're looking for ghosts or just curious about the place." Marie touches my hand. "You're more than welcome to join James and me. We're planning on making sandwiches and hanging out here."

I nod and tell her I'd like that. My eyes wander toward the location of the library, willing me to see past the mortar and stones holding the place together to the reason I'm here—all those journals. "I have a lot to do here." I sigh. "And this place is so beautiful that I'm sure I'll never get bored. I'll be too busy looking through all the rooms and seeing the progress you're making."

"It seems pretty isolating, what you're doing," Marie says after a moment, her expression thoughtful. "But I guess it's necessary. You make sure to come see us if you're ever feeling lonely, though. Everyone here seems to be friendly, but you let me know if they're not."

"Thank you. I have tons to occupy myself with, but you'll be staying over as well, right? The idea of ghosts roaming the halls scares me a bit even though I want to see them at the same time."

"Yes, we'll be here. And like I said, there's nothing here that will hurt you. You might not be able to see them, and if you can, well, if anything, of those who see you as well, more than half of them will be just as scared or more so about it." She laughs. "I can't tell you how many times I've seen a ghost run from the room when I've entered it." She breaks off and waves her hands in the air in mock horror. "It's definitely a sight to behold!"

I join Marie in laughing, thankful that she is so nonchalant about the possible encounters I might have. Her ease puts me at ease, and if the gentleman I spied in the library really was a ghost and not a figment of my imagination, I have every confidence that I'll get along just fine.

I walk into my room, what Marie had called the Rose Suite, and the name suits—pale-pink wallpaper hangs from the high walls and darker shades are graced within the carpets scattered throughout the large room. A cherry-chocolate colored three-seater leather sofa with a deep-buttoned scroll pattern along the arms and back beckons from beneath a large window that faces the back of the estate. *You and I have a date,* I promise silently as I grab my tablet that contains several e-books I have yet to read and place it on the low coffee table in front of the sofa.

Moving away from the seating area, I focus on the queen-sized bed, its head against the same wall as the door. Sitting on the edge, I bounce up and down a few times, testing the resistance of the mattress, then lie back. Yes, comfortable. Nineteenth-century style was retained, but everything must have been upgraded in the 1990s before the house was closed. Because the room is in decent shape, it won't be refurbished at this time. Marie apologized for not giving me options, most of the other rooms undergoing transformations, but I think I would have chosen this room regardless.

Squinting, I search my room, hoping, yet dreading, to make out faint shadows or outlines of people who no longer exist. If they are real, why aren't they at rest?

And whereas I always thought they were real—or said I did—there was always a shadow of doubt. Television shows want ratings, after all, some people just want attention, and everyone wants to believe there's something more. I know I do, especially after losing Eve.

I've never seen a ghost before, so it's something I highly anticipate. And after being told that they really do exist, I wonder what that means for Eve. She underwent a traumatic event that caused her death. She must have been scared. So now, is she out there wandering, wondering what happened? I hope not. I hope there is a heaven, a beautiful, wondrous place where people who've passed are only ever happy. A place where she can still check in on me occasionally, even if I can't do the same.

Sighing, I open two remaining doors, one the en suite bathroom, which is small but well appointed, and the other a small walk-in closet. In the far corner, five cotton garment bags hang from wooden hangers, and I wonder what they contain. Since no one currently lives at the manor and the closet is empty save those bags, my curiosity is piqued.

Instead of snooping, though—there will be plenty of time for that—I go back to the door of the room and grab my luggage, which James placed just inside. It doesn't take long to unpack, and there is still plenty of room left on the shelves and available hanging space after I've finished.

Placing the now empty luggage on the floor near the garment bags, I grab my toiletry bag off a shelf, exit and close the closet, and enter the bathroom where I take a look at myself in the mirror.

I look tired. I *am* tired. But the thrill of being at Hillfield is enough to have me set down the toiletry bag, rinse my face with cool water, and pinch my cheeks. Using one of the hand towels, I pat my face and dry my hands.

It's time to look around.

Chapter 3

Reaching a landing, I have to cross a small corridor before I come to the final set of steps to the second floor. From there, I enter the first door on my right.

I stop upon entering the room and draw a breath. This is the Long Gallery, and it very much lives up to its name. Not only is the room the entire length of the house, but the ceiling is also twice the height as it is in any other part of the manor. My eyes are drawn to the wall of floor-to-ceiling windows along one length of the room and all the way up to the eighteen-foot plaster ceiling complete with architectural moldings. With my eyes drawn upward, I slowly enter the room until I stand at the center in front of the massive fireplace made of white and black marble. Slowly, I turn in a circle. I see on the walls in between each window portraits of what must be dour-looking men and women gazing out unseeingly into the room. Opposite the windows and on the same wall as the fireplace, large and medium size portraits and scenery paintings compete for the attention of the room's occupants.

This is the room pictured in the article on Hillfield Manor I shared with Eve. I hug myself, thinking of what she would have thought had she gotten the chance to see it with her own eyes. I'm sure she'd be just as impressed as I am.

It doesn't take me long to start thinking of all the other rooms I have yet to explore, though, and when I consider the length of time I'll be working here, I decide to cut my exploration of the gallery short and go look at another room.

On the other side of the Long Gallery, and taking up roughly half of its length and width, there are three good-sized rooms, one with a smaller room off to the side that may have been used for an accompanying maid. In addition, taking up the remaining floor space, there is an apartment of rooms.

Into each room I move, touching the walls and looking out windows, trying to capture the essence of what it must have been like to stay here in a different time. Some of the rooms are furnished, but many are not, and in each empty room, I try to imagine furniture placement as well as the lives of the former occupants. Had someone died in this room from smallpox or during childbirth? Had there been a clandestine affair? How many secrets and pieces of gossip had the walls heard over time? If only walls could talk!

The bright light coming in through the windows helps illuminate the larger rooms such as the Great Hall, which, save for the furniture, is stripped of all decorations. According to Marie, these things are either being cleaned or will be purchased later.

Looking around once more, I'm about to move into yet another room when my heart seizes in my chest. Not more than five feet away from me stands a woman, and she's looking straight at me. Confused, I glance around, wondering how she came upon me without my hearing her.

Processing several pieces of information at once, what is most striking, of course, is the fact that I can literally see through her to the wall on the other side. Not completely transparent, though, she looks to be in her midtwenties, and had she been standing next to me, would probably come up to my chin. I can't clearly discern the type of clothing she wears, for although her face is relatively clear, everything past the shoulders is blurred, like a chalk drawing after rain, but it looks like a servant's uniform.

My heart beating furiously, I back up, my eyes never leaving the vision before me. I'm not so much scared as I am shocked. Until, that is, she reaches out to me, advancing slowly. It's one thing to see her, another thing entirely to have her approach me. My breath comes to me in short gasps, and my mind runs through my options: run, scream, stand here frozen to the ground. She doesn't look like she wants to harm me, but I've watched enough scary movies to know the benign-looking ones are always the ones to watch out for, their faces slowly morphing into grotesque skulls. I shake my head, denying what I am clearly seeing, and put my trembling hands up in front of me to ward off her advance.

Observing me observe her, the woman gives me a small but sad smile and nods in acknowledgment. She hesitates briefly and glances toward a side door that leads to one of the auxiliary rooms whose use I can't fathom. I can tell she's letting me in on her intention, but it doesn't ease my mind. My body remains rigid as she looks back at me again. Turning, she moves toward the door, losing what definition she had until she fades from view completely.

It takes a minute for my heart to reestablish a more regular rhythm and for my limbs to completely lose control. I find myself on the floor, my hands shaking as I push my hair out of my face, staring at the door with equal amounts of excitement and fear.

That was just the biggest adrenaline rush of my life, and I'm not quite sure what to think of it.

Looking around, I vainly search for someone, anyone, who can corroborate what I just saw. There's no one. I debate yelling for help or running to find someone, but what would they be able to do? I don't really know James or Marie, and after our conversation this morning, I'm not sure I want to let them see my reaction. Taking a deep breath, I try to rationalize. It isn't as if I need help. The woman hadn't attacked me; she smiled.

I need validation, though. I want another person to tell me that my eyes are indeed not playing tricks on me. All these thoughts pass through my head within seconds as I again search for another witness. Finding none, I slowly rise from the floor. My legs still feel weak, and I'm still shaking, but instead of running away from the incredible sight, what any person in their right mind would do, I cautiously move toward it. My curiosity outweighs my fear. A few steps before the room into which she walked, I slow my steps even more. Taking a deep breath, I peek around the doorframe, ready to bolt back into the Great Hall, through it, and down the hallway if needed.

Hesitantly, I find myself walking into the room. First, I only stand fully in the doorway, my eyes the only parts of my body moving as they dart back and forth around the room in pursuit of the woman. The ghost is gone, but a sense of unease and the shaking of my limbs remain with me. Leaving the room through another door, I see the hallway is empty, and suddenly, I feel very alone. My pace increases. I run down the stairs and through the manor, each room I pass devoid of familiarity or warmth.

Where are James and Marie? I search the kitchen, the library, and the sitting room. Then I move through a conservatory, another sitting room, the dining room, a ballroom. The offices are next, and despite the fact that they are crammed with miscellaneous objects and furniture covered with dust cloths that unsurprisingly remind me of the woman I had encountered moments ago, they don't have the human contact I so desperately crave at this moment. All of a sudden, the rooms seem smaller, the air thinner. It's too much to digest. My breath comes faster, and I sob.

When I look up, James and Marie are standing in front of me, concern and sympathy written on their faces.

"I was looking for you. I couldn't find anyone. I couldn't . . ." My words trail off as I remember the feeling of being trapped.

"We were just in the room next door," James supplies. "What happened? See a spider?" James's attempt at levity falls short, but I muster a smile anyway.

"I saw a ghost. It's the first time I've ever seen a ghost."

Marie nods sagely. "They won't hurt you, dear."

"I've always wanted to see one." My eyes wander the corridor, and I sink into a crouch, fearing I might faint.

"I wanted them to exist, and I . . . I wanted . . . But I wasn't prepared. They're real! And then I felt so alone, and I didn't know where you were . . ." I shake my head, feeling foolish. "I'm sorry. I never thought I was, but I guess I *am* the hysterical type."

"Yeah, they can do that. I remember my first ghost. But really, I promise you that I've never known any of the spirits here to be malevolent. Okay?" Marie kneels beside me, her face filled with concern. "Would you like me to get you some tea?"

"No, no. I'm fine. I feel better, I think." Lifting myself from the floor, I smile at James and Marie. "I'm sorry. Really. I'll try not to do that again. It was just so . . . unexpected."

James smiles and pats my arm before looking at his watch. "Well, look at that. It's lunchtime anyway. You'll join us, won't you, Emma?"

With my body still trembling with the aftershocks of an adrenaline rush, hunger isn't exactly what I'm feeling, but I'm not in the mood to be alone either. I nod and walk with them, pausing for a moment at the window. Gray clouds overhead threaten more rain, and from my vantage point, the grounds appear more barren than they had before. A few of the trees have lost leaves in the storm, and their skeletal branches wave frantically in the greenish glow before yet another storm.

"So, tell us a little more about yourself, Emma. You're American. I can hear that right away." James holds up a hand and shakes his head when I open my mouth to speak. "I'm not saying I'm offended by your accent. After all, I hear it all the time when Marie opens her mouth. I'm just stating a fact."

"Okay. And just so we're clear, there's two of us and only one of you, so no bashing on the Americans," I tease.

"I wouldn't dream of it. Once upon a time, I would have, and to be frank, when it comes to whose culture is better—well, Marie can be dreadfully stubborn and opinionated. But so can I!" he says, an attempt at a backpedal upon seeing Marie's lifted brow.

I laugh at Marie, whose brow is still raised, a mock mask of anger upon her face. "Yes, I grew up in the States, upstate New York, to be more precise, but I have dual nationality." I explain how my dad was born in England and moved to the States and spoke about my grandmother and how my family came to visit her every summer.

"It sounds like you were granted a pretty nice childhood, living in two worlds almost."

"It did seem that way on occasion, but when it comes right down to it, people are people wherever you go."

Marie nods. "I agree with you there. Do you have any brothers or sisters?"

My heart skips a beat at the question. I should have expected it. It's a natural one to ask. And I guess I *did* expect it. What I didn't expect was the way my chest tightens and my eyes tear up. "I h-had a sister, Eve."

Marie grabs my hand, and her eyes glisten with unshed tears of her own. "I'm so sorry, Emma. I can see I stuck my foot in my mouth. Was it recent? I'm sorry, we don't have to talk about this."

I squeeze Marie's hand with my free one. "No, it's okay." I pull in a breath and then another before continuing. "Eve died by saving someone's life. She was a fantastic swimmer. A boy went overboard at a retirement party she was at, and she went in after him. He made it back, but there were boulders under the water and . . . That was six months ago."

"She sounds like an extraordinary young lady," James says gruffly.

"Yeah." I smile sadly. "She was. She's part of the reason I'm here. My parents wanted me to come home after, but there are too many memories there. At the funeral, I could feel it. She was everywhere. I could hardly stand it, expecting to see her around every corner, the hope that maybe around *this* corner it would be different." I pause for a moment before continuing. "Anyway, we spent a lot of time together here, but it's not as fresh somehow. The last time we were here together was over five years ago. Other things took precedence, especially after our grandmother died."

"It sounds like you two were close."

I harrumph. "We were, and we weren't," I say with a smile. "We had our sibling rivalries. Eve could get on my nerves like no one else, trust me, but she was my biggest cheerleader besides my parents, and she was always there when I needed her." I feel hot tears on my cheeks and wipe them away hastily. "And I thought we had a hell of a lot more time together."

James coughs roughly and hands me a napkin from the pile on the table so I can wipe my eyes.

Silence settles upon us for a few minutes while I collect as much of my sadness as I can and put it back on a shelf. Marie and James continue to eat in a subdued manner, and I feel bad for bringing them down.

After taking a drink of water, I open my mouth to ask a question, anything to try to revive the convivial tone from before. Marie touches my arm, though, and says gently, "Emma, put your water down."

Startled by the wariness in her tone, I freeze for a moment before slowly doing as she asked. "What is it? Is there a ghost?" Fear and excitement mix within me as I follow her and James's gazes to the corner of the room. I gasp.

There, seemingly unaware of her captivated audience, is a woman dressed in what looks like simple nineteenth-century clothing. Although I can clearly see the wall behind her, I can also make out most of the details of her person and her dress, save for the colors. She stands with something in her hands I can't see, and she paces back and forth as she regards it.

"Can she hear us?"

"Sometimes they can and sometimes they can't," James says. "I guess we'll have our answer in just a moment." He projects his voice a bit more. "Excuse us, miss. Hello?"

The vision continues to pace—four steps forward, pivot, four steps back—oblivious to the three of us sitting at the table not more than ten steps farther as she peruses whatever it is in her hands before she begins to fade and then disappears altogether.

"Wow!" I suck in a huge breath and exhale loudly. "That was incredible!"

"I must admit that's the first occasion in a long while where I've found myself paying attention to one."

"How can you not?" I ask, my heart beating maddeningly now that the ghost is no longer present. "I don't think I'll ever get used to it."

"But you weren't afraid?" Marie asks anxiously, her brows furrowed.

"No, just . . ." I shake my head. "I don't know how to describe it—awe, excitement, disbelief . . . okay, a little bit of fear."

Marie grins.

"Why aren't they at rest? Do they realize, do you think?" I wonder aloud. *And what does that mean for Eve? Is she out there too?*

"Know what? That they're dead? I don't think they are. Not in the way you mean it. I think they live in different times, and whereas they may be dead in our time, time for them is moving at its usual pace. They're living their lives, their real lives, just as we are. It's something at Hillfield that enables us to see them. I would not be surprised if they're wondering the same about us."

"Well, I'm really glad you two were with me this time, and if it's always like that, I don't think I'll have any problems. The other one seemed like she wanted to talk, and that was a bit unnerving."

"Well, sometimes they come up upon you, or you come up upon them, when you least expect it. When we first opened the house for renovations, that's what took me a while to get used to again," Marie says.

"Are any of them ones you remember from your stay here?" So excited about seeing another ghost, I forgot that James used to live here and that some of these ghosts might be family members of his.

"James, I'm so sorry. That was completely tactless of me—"

"Miss Becket," he says, shaking his head. "Please don't be alarmed. I assure you I only lived here for a short time, and since I've been here, I've seen no one with whom I was acquainted."

"Really?" Marie chimes in. "Not one?"

James eyes Marie intently, a silent conversation playing between the two of them, then James says, "I'd like to amend my answer. I've seen no one with whom I was acquainted, save one, and that is not a story for today."

Standing, he gathers his plate, cup, and paper napkin. "It's one thirty, my love," he says. "We should go out front and wait for the truck. Lord help us if they drive by. It's not as if they could miss the place."

Marie gathers her stuff and stands as well. "They won't miss us. If anything, they're already waiting out there, hoping to get a peek inside."

I watch the two of them as they speak to one another and feel a smidge of envy. I want to find the same type of love these two share, that my parents share as well, but now that Eve's gone, I don't know if it's worth it.

Familial love is tight, and losing Eve was the hardest thing I've ever had to go through, but I can't imagine losing a romantic love, one with whom I'd share everything.

"Well, I hope you have a good afternoon," I say when there's a break in their conversation. I know they're anxious to get back to their work, and I've already taken up the better half of Marie's day.

"Thank you. You as well, Miss Emma," James says with a slight bow. "One of these days, if you're up for it, I'll tell you about one of the ghosts I saw. The whole encounter was quite extraordinary."

"Really?" I ask, my eyes widening with interest. "I love ghost stories! I'm looking forward to hearing all about it."

"I'm not sure if I will be able to put the experience into the right words, but I will endeavor to do so."

"Great, because you're not getting out of it. You brought it up. You can't leave me hanging!"

James stares at me for a moment and then turns to Marie, but not before I see a glimmer of mischief in his eyes. "Leave you hanging? As if I would ever . . . Marie, you're not going to use such barbarous turns of phrase, are you, darling? I've only just learned your strange vocabulary without having to learn a whole new generation's worth."

"Don't sweat it," Marie says as they walk toward the door. "You've gotta get used to the lingo, daddy-o."

"Good Heavens! Not that blather again." James raises a hand over his head in farewell. "We'll tell you all about it at some point, Miss Emma. For now, go to your exploring! But please, remember what we said: If you get lonely, don't be shy."

They disappear around the door frame, and I can hear them make their way toward the kitchen to drop off their dishes. I smile softly at their teasing and briefly wonder once more if I'll ever want to trust having that type of relationship in the future.

Taking a quick glance around the hall to make sure everything is clean, and also to see if I'm alone—I am—I walk in the direction of the kitchen myself. From there, I plan to explore as much of the house as I can before calling it a day. After all, I might as well get used to it. It'll be my home for the next half year at least.

Chapter 4

My alarm goes off at 8:00 a.m. Frankly, I'm startled by it since I normally wake before it rings. Although my eyes feel a bit raw from my crying fit yesterday, the rest of me is in top form. If I had any dreams of Eve, I don't remember them, and not having them, or not remembering them if I did, makes me feel a little more *me*. I feel energized and ready to take on the work I've signed up for.

Stretching, I rise and eye my surroundings, looking for any transparent visitors that may have walked through the walls while I slept. Seeing none, I grab the outfit I set aside last night in haste and make my way to the bathroom, praying no ghosts of peeping toms or tinas are in there either.

I think I set the record for the quickest shower I've ever taken. There's a lock on the door, sure, but it won't keep out any of the other "people" who want entrance. What if they want a shower too? I almost laugh as I imagine dragging the shower curtain to one side, only to see Casper scratching his back with a bath brush.

Actually, that would probably freak me out more.

Once I'm dry and have clothes on, I feel better about slowing down. Making a fool of myself by tearing down the halls naked is not on my list of things to accomplish on my first full day here—or any day, for that matter.

Taking a deep breath, I steady myself before opening the bathroom door and doing a quick scan. Nothing. So, I open a window and then the door to the hall to get a nice cross breeze, then make up the bed and store yesterday's clothes, which I left haphazardly on the floor last night, in a laundry bag I left in the closet.

The cotton garment bags I noticed yesterday draw my attention once again. There's no harm in a peek. I take them out, lay them on the bed, and unzip the topmost bag.

It's a dress, a beautiful, dusty-rose skirt with layers of white petticoats underneath and an attached bodice of a lighter rose. According to the photos I see on my phone, it's a replica of late-nineteenth-century fashion and must be what guides wore when giving tours. Holding the dress up to me, I twirl, imagining how it would look.

I'm rifling through the other two bags when there's a knock on the opened door.

"Good morning, Emma. I wanted to check on you and see how you're getting on."

"Hi, Marie. I'm fine. Thank you. No ghosts in the room or bathroom, so all good there." I chuckle to hide my unease.

Marie shakes her head and her brows furrow in concentration. "You know, I've never heard anyone mention seeing one of them in any of the bedrooms or bathrooms. We're just two doors down, and I promise, we haven't seen anyone. If we do, I'll introduce you," she says with a wink. "What have you got there?"

I wave my hands over the garment bags and exposed dresses and accessories, which are held in smaller cotton bags attached to the hangers. "You caught me snooping," I say. "It's not my best trait, but I like to think my honesty makes up for it." I smile and bat my lashes a few times, earning me a laugh.

"You're not the first to snoop around here, and you won't be the last." Taking up a position next to me, Marie scans the dresses and assorted accessories. "Oh! You've found our costumes." A smile lights up her face as she touches the fabric of one of the gowns. "You've heard that those who used to work at the manor were required to dress up in nineteenth-century clothing?"

"Yes, I read about it in several articles I've come across."

Marie nods as she caresses the soft blush material. "I always enjoyed dressing up. I never got to wear something like this, though. Since I cleaned the house, I had to wear dresses fitting the status of a housemaid. The women who led the tours are the ones who wore day dresses like this."

"They're beautiful," I say as I, too, touch the fabric. "That must have been fun, but it must have been a pain to wear the dresses a servant had to wear to clean the house."

Marie chuckles and then groans. "Oh, I could tell you stories! It was the hardest in summer. As you know, we're not known for excessive heat here, but when you add roughly five pounds of layers and had to bustle about cleaning things the way they had to be cleaned in the nineteenth century, it wasn't exactly fun."

"Wait a minute, you had to act like you were in the nineteenth century? So, you couldn't use vacuums or anything?"

"Not in the rooms for the tours, no. At least, not while tours or any other business matters were being conducted. Then, after the last tour group would go through for the day, we were able to take the dresses off, get into some comfortable clothes, and yes, use a vacuum.

Ugh, I can't imagine having to do what they did—lifting those rugs and beating them. Do you know how heavy they are?" She shakes her head. "No, thank you, especially with all the foot traffic. We would have had to beat the rugs every day!"

"Wow, so in a way, you've experienced what it was like to be a servant in the eighteen hundreds."

Marie nods. "They must have had hard lives, and I'm quite satisfied with the one I have in this century." Marie takes the dress out of the bag and holds it up next to me. "You should try it on. It would complement your skin tone beautifully. If the dresses are in these bags, they're clean, even though they've been here for a while."

I take the dress from Marie and walk to the full-length mirror, holding the dress before me. It looks even better out of the bag. The petticoats poof the skirt out nicely, and in full sunlight, the colors are enhanced.

"Obviously, these dresses were made fairly recently, with comfort and ease of putting them on in mind. There's a hidden zipper under the arm here," Marie says, moving to my left and lifting the sleeve of the dress, "and the petticoats have been sewn in as well, but I think they look remarkably similar to what I've seen in portraits."

I glance at Marie's reflection in the mirror before setting my gaze once again on the dress. It is so different from my normal style of leggings and T-shirts or sweaters, but I really want to try it on and walk around the manor, pretending to be a lady of the house or even a guest. “You don’t think it would be weird? What would the workers say?”

“Who cares! I’m sure you could easily avoid the workers, and other than them, there’s just James and myself. I’d love to see you in the dress, and I’m sure James, if he sees you, would be reminded of his time here as well.”

Marie pats my arm. “You think about it.” She looks around the room before moving to the door. “I have to be getting back, but you’re sure there’s nothing you need? Any questions?”

“I’m fine, Marie. Thank you. Don’t worry about me, though. You’ve got enough to do around here getting this place ready, and if I have any questions, I promise I’ll let you or James know.”

I walk her to the door, my thoughts still on the dress and whether I’ll try it on, when I hear her greet someone in the hall. She’s just made her way past a filmy man in period clothing who nods, does a double take, and then sidles up to the wall to gain as much distance from her as possible. He inches his way along the wall in my direction when he looks up and sees me as well. His eyes widen even more in fear. Glancing between me and back at Marie, who has reached the staircase, he spins around and rushes past her and down the hall, his form completely disappearing as he runs.

Marie, chuckling, sees me standing at the door and winks. “See? That’s what you’ll get the majority of the time. Others might try to talk to you or wave at least. Have fun with it. I always do.” She waves and continues down the stairs.

The hallway is clear, with no sign of the man or anyone else. I take a deep breath and let it out slowly. My heart rate is a bit elevated, but I don’t feel nearly as frightened as I did yesterday when encountering the woman in the Great Hall. I don’t know if seeing ghosts will ever become something I get used to, but I think I can handle it.

Excited to get to work, I make my way to the library. The brooding clouds blanketing the sky once again bombard the roof and grounds with relentless rain. It’s the perfect weather to start organizing. Thankfully, the electricity is still working, so being able to see won’t be an issue. Walking slowly through the buttery and the narrow passage joining it to the Great Hall, I can’t help but scan the rooms, anticipating another encounter. There are none, and I begin to think two encounters are the limit of what I’ll experience in a day when I come upon the library without incident.

Looking at one wall, I'm happy to see the journals are more or less in chronological order, although interspersed with a random novel here and there. The other two walls are more of a nightmare. It seems journals and volumes alike were haphazardly strewn upon the shelves, only to be crowded out by arbitrary items of interest. A journal from 1859 sits next to a fashion magazine from 1951, which lays atop a rare 1922 first edition of *The Velveteen Rabbit*. The first order of business will be to sort all the clutter and determine which of the novels, magazines, newspapers, and other miscellaneous items the owner wants to keep.

I settle on starting on the shelves along the top of one wall, using the rolling library ladder some thoughtful and progressive individual installed. The shelves are massive. At the top of the ladder, I spread my arms wide and notice its span isn't even half the length. Mr. Johnson had definitely been correct about the size of this place, but he underestimated the amount of time it would take to go through everything. Six months? I hazard a guess it will take more than that and make up my mind to email my former boss and tell him. I can imagine him laughing as he reads it and wonder what kind of response I'll get in return.

I put on the cloth gloves I was asked to wear when handling the books and begin taking them off the shelves, wondering when they last left their niche. It takes about four trips up and down the ladder before I get smart and take a large plastic container found in a corner of the room up with me. Balancing it on one of the rungs, I'm easily able to get twice as many items into the box as I was able to carry previously. I still work carefully, however. I don't want to be responsible for destroying precious heirlooms or pieces of literature worth more than I could make in several years.

When half the upper shelf has been cleared, I grab my laptop from the table where I set it down upon entering and bend down next to the items to begin an inventory. Many of the texts are extremely fragile, their pages on the verge of crumbling. Not being a collector or historian, though, I can't estimate their cultural or monetary worth. All I can do is be extremely careful not to ruin them through mishandling. Opening up the laptop, I create a new spreadsheet and begin listing titles, authors, and dates. Later, I'll copy and paste the inventory into the database where everything can be categorized alphabetically by title, author, or date.

When I've gotten through the majority of the books I've taken down, I look at one that appears to have been handled much more than the others. It's a journal. The cover is starting to deteriorate around the edges, and when opening the cover, pages come away from the binding. I search the inside cover for a date, noting the faint etching of a name I can't quite make out. Due to its condition, it has to be one of the very first journal entries. In the back of my head, I knew I would come across it, but actually holding the journal written so long ago in my hands makes me feel all giddy inside.

I scan the remaining shelves I have yet to tackle. I'm not about to start typing all the entries yet, as there is still way too much to do, but there is no reason I can't take a peek at what was written, especially since I'll eventually see it again anyway.

Expecting to find the first entry in January—new journal, new year—I'm surprised at an October date. Squinting, trying to make out the handwriting, I hold the journal closer to my face to decipher some of the words. Given what I experienced not more than just a few hours before, I read with growing amazement what transpired so many years ago.

October 15, 1788—Hillfield Manor is ours. The final papers have been signed, and all matters have accordingly been settled. It's a fine house, fine land. I believe we will be happy here . . .

October 18, 1788—I can't make sense of it, and I wonder whether I should commit the words to paper. There have been a few strange occurrences. Thomas, the footman, reported seeing a woman walking through one of the downstairs corridors. When he went to confront her, he claims she disappeared in front of his eyes. Then, one of our kitchen maids caused quite a commotion downstairs. She refused to say what she encountered, but she promptly quit us. Even Lawson, our butler, who's as tight-mouthed and loathe to gossip as can be, reported an incident in the entrance hall, claiming to see no less than ten "phantoms dressed in the most extraordinary outfits."

I carefully turn several pages before reading once more.

October 22, 1788—Strange encounters continue every day, and I can now admit to being privy to more than one confrontation. It pains me to say that Hillfield Manor, our beloved home, is cursed with apparitions of the most unusual sort. This, however, is tempered by the fact that the hauntings do not come with horrid shrieks and moans or the hair-raising sounds of heavy chains. In fact, no one has been more than unsettled or frightened. We've asked the household to keep these events quiet, but although we're blessed with a most loyal staff, it's certain word will get out eventually...

November 7, 1788—An interesting development in the whole ghostly saga of our home. I had assumed that those who hadn't seen one of our ghosts hadn't been in a location that merited an encounter. Perhaps that may be true to some extent, but today, I learned that not everyone can see them. I walked with Sir Philip Collins, a friend from my university days, and his wife, Eleonore. It was Eleonore who, upon seeing a woman materialize in front of our eyes, turned pale and lifted a finger to point to the offender. I hastened to tell her that all would be well when Philip turned first to his wife and then to me to ask what the devil we were on about. We pointed out the location of the ghost, mere feet before us, and verbally observed different aspects of the ghost's appearance. Philip could not see. Nor does it seem that the ghost could see us, for she carried on with whatever business she was about before fading from our eyes.

A chill passes through me as I carefully close the journal, set it down, and look around the room. It corroborates what Marie said and also makes me wonder about those ghosts who want to communicate. *What exactly do they want to discuss?*

While I resume taking books off the upper shelf, I try recalling the five theories of ghosts I learned when reading *Hamlet* back in high school. First, supposedly, people back in the 1600s and 1700s believed that ghosts could be the spirits of dead people who, for some reason, hadn't crossed over into the afterlife. They continued living life as if they were alive, seeing and hearing the things they wanted to see and hear, because they didn't want to—or couldn't—face the reality of their death.

The second theory was that spirits had divine permission to give loved ones a message and would return to heaven after having delivered it. This theory doesn't seem to fit the ghosts at Hillfield Manor, though, and I quickly dismiss it.

Another theory was that ghosts could be demons trying to trick us. From my understanding of the ghost stories I heard surrounding Hillfield Manor—and that's primarily based on rumors, a television ghost show, and newspaper articles I've read—the ghosts hardly interacted with people except for the story about the guy who disappeared, so the only tricking the demons would be doing is having people believe they were ghosts. I dismiss this theory too.

The fourth theory was that ghosts were residual and were recordings of past events. This one certainly could hold some truth except for the fact that the ghost I saw yesterday looked right at me and was about to speak. No, if anything, she was an intelligent ghost, which leads me back to the first theory that she was just a dead person. Maybe she doesn't even realize she's dead and is busy living in her own little world.

The last theory was that ghosts were only figments of the imagination, which, of course, is possible, except for the fact that other people see them at the same time. Mass hysteria? Doubtful.

As I continue with the mostly tedious work, I picture the woman. She looked friendly enough as she stepped toward me, and now I wish I hadn't freaked out. I've always wanted to believe in the paranormal, and now I have my proof. But I'm not convinced that ghostly phenomena can be explained by sixteenth-century theories or even science as we know it. It seems to me that there is something more to it. Perhaps James's theory is correct.

Every couple of hours, I take a break from the library and explore and admire the manor, its many wings, turrets, and hidden corners. Although I don't run into Marie or James, workers are bustling around, taking up tasks, and chatting with each other, their voices punctuated by laughter and the occasional cries of surprise. A small smile of sympathy crosses my lips each time.

At lunchtime, I hear a low murmur of voices echoing in the middle of the manor and, making my way toward it, find a few people sitting at one of the tables in the Great Hall, their body language relaxed and inviting.

A woman glances up and calls out for me to come and join them, and I'm happy to do so. Sitting down with a microwaveable meal I bought late yesterday afternoon, I smile and introduce myself, and the others do the same.

"So, the question of the manor is, have you seen 'em?" a guy named Steve, who's sitting across from me, asks.

All attention turns to me, and I nod as I chew and swallow. There's no point in pretending I don't know what he's talking about. "Yeah, a couple of them. You?"

"Nah, I'm not one of the fortunate ones. Louis, down at the end, can't see 'em either."

Louis waves over to me. "It's a load of shite," he complains. "It's the main reason I took this job."

"Seriously? They scare me half to death," Brenna, the woman who called me over, says. "I can't be alone here. What about you?"

I shrug. "The first one was a shock, but I think they're cool."

Brenna tells me that most of the people here work on contract, so once they're finished, they move on to other jobs. "It works out well. We're not stuck, waiting around to get something done, and now that my time's almost up, I'm chuffed. The money's great, but I can't handle seeing dead people."

A few of the others make comments about their experiences before we move on to other topics, mainly about what they need to get done. When it's time to get back to work, I'm more refreshed and ready to go.

I continue to sort through the books, taking them off the shelf and, once having a nice pile, adding their titles and authors to my inventory list before starting again. After a while, I notice it has grown darker outside. I've been here for hours, and the sky is now turning a dusky color. Realizing I should call it quits soon, I look at the shelf I've been working on. Only four books remain. Taking them down and inputting the title and author information, I stretch as I finish, save the data, and log out of my computer. Tomorrow is another day.

Mr. Louis Wade arrives promptly at 10:30 a.m. I receive a curt phone call informing me he is down by the driveway entrance, so I hustle to a small room off the kitchen to automatically open the gate for him. Then, hastily passing through the rooms, I scurry to the front of the house, where I walk more sedately to welcome Mr. Wade. By the time I make it to the front entrance, he's turning off the engine and gathering items from the back seat of the car.

He's slightly younger than I imagined him to be. First, there is his occupation, which will always remind me of the now semiretired Mr. Johnson, and then there is the clipped baritone voice I heard on the phone minutes earlier. Instead of a man in his early to late sixties, the man in front of me couldn't be more than late forties, early fifties at most. He's handsome, with a strong jaw, high cheekbones, and a straight nose. He's wearing a well-tailored gray suit with a dark red tie and is close to six feet tall, with graying sandy-brown hair that's cropped short.

"This is the place all right!" he says as he stares up at the house.

"Mr. Wade. Good morning, I'm Emma Beckett. Pleased to meet you."

"I haven't been in this house in over twenty-five years." Mr. Wade looks around with an air of disbelief and wonder. The clear bright blue sky belies the chill in the air, but it's a nice day and I silently vow to get out of the house later and walk around the grounds.

After introductions, we climb up the steps to the front porch. Mr. Wade stands there and looks at the house, his face a combination of a smile and a frown. "I always loved it here," he notes.

"I got here the day before yesterday. It was my first opportunity inside," I reply with a grin. "I can't tell you how many times I stood outside the gate and would just gaze at this place. The inside is just as magnificent."

"I could give you a tour if you'd like. It's been a while, but I'm sure I remember the place as if I'd walked through the doors yesterday."

"You said you were last here twenty-five years ago?"

"Yes, the last time I was inside. I spent most of my childhood within these walls. Friend of the family, you know."

"Oh really? That must have been cool. I wandered all around yesterday and was overwhelmed by all the rooms. Despite the workers being here, it was a bit lonely. I can just imagine what it would be like to have people here all the time."

"Yes, well, the family wasn't very large, and tragedy struck more than once . . . Lots of sadness." He shakes his head at what he must be remembering. "But"—his smile grows—"we boys got into mischief as boys will." He gazes off into the distance, blind to everything save the memories playing in his mind.

I lead him through the entrance and into the sitting room Marie and James brought me to upon my arrival. Mr. Wade is still quiet, and after a few moments more of his internal contemplation, I cough, jolting him out of his reverie.

"So, since you grew up here, do you by any chance know Marie and James from Homecomings? Marie said she worked here when she was younger. And James used to live here."

Mr. Wade squints as though trying to bring into focus an earlier time, and his eyes light up. "Marie! Short little woman, who could play Tinkerbell in *Peter Pan*?"

I chuckle as I nod.

"I do remember her. She was one the ghosts seemed to take a liking to. You'd always see her talking to one or another, even if they didn't care to respond. It always made them seem more . . . normal, if you will."

"I've seen a few myself here. Marie and James acted as if it was a usual occurrence."

"Here, it is. Maybe it's the reason the owners want this place opened up again. Interest in ghosts keeps on increasing. Maybe they're planning on showing the place off."

"You disagree?"

Mr. Wade bites the inside of his mouth as he chooses his words. "I was friends with the owners' son. He died. At least, that's the only possible conclusion. No one knows what happened to him." He pauses. "That's the reason the place is closed. Seems they never really got over it, especially since the same thing happened to their first son. Until they know what happened to him—to either of them—they don't want to undertake anything more. At least that's what I thought until all this started happening," he says, waving his hand to indicate the house and the work going on.

I nod but remain silent. I think of my parents. After losing Eve, they didn't know what to do. Sometimes, I believe the only reason they keep moving forward is for me. Perhaps the owners needed to find a reason to keep moving forward too.

"The so-called paranormal activity brought them a pretty penny a year," Mr. Wade continues. "But after they lost their second son, they probably felt the place was cursed. The ghosts have something to do with it. I'm certain."

"But Marie and James said they're not evil."

"They don't have to be evil to have something to do with it, and I'm convinced they do." He nods as he looks around, and when he turns once more to me, he nods again. "The best thing would be to keep this place locked up and throw away the key. Even better, tear the whole place down. Maybe then the poor souls would be free." Mr. Wade's brows furrow and he tsks. "I apologize. Most of my memories of this place are fond ones, and Hillfield certainly is extraordinary, but I can't help the way I feel."

"I understand."

He shrugs as if it doesn't matter one way or the other and sits on the couch in front of the fireplace. "I guess we should speak about your job here. As you know, you'll be copy typing all the journals. Of course, the originals will be kept, but the owners seem to believe someone will someday want to read the memories of someone long dead, and the journals themselves are timeworn, the ink is fading with antiquity . . ."

Lunch is quite pleasant. We sit inside the Great Hall on either side of one of the long tables, sandwiches, chips, and soda in front of us with chocolate brownies patiently waiting in the center between us. Marie, on top of her regular work, had found time to fix a delicious lunch for all of us, and she and James sit with us, Marie next to me and James sitting next to Mr. Wade.

Keeping the conversation to small and polite topics, such as the town itself and the weather, it's surprising when Mr. Wade finally says, "So, tell me everything," before sticking a chip in his mouth.

I smirk. "I think it would take about as long as it will to get through those books in the library to tell you everything. Can you be a bit more specific?"

Mr. Wade laughs. "We're going to be working together for a little while. I like to know things about the people I work with. Take Marie, for example."

Marie looks across the table, swallows what is in her mouth, and asks, "What about me?"

"You used to work here back when I was a boy."

"You were hardly a boy, Louis. You're only ten years younger than I am."

Mr. Wade flicks his fingers as if shooing away a fly. "I was telling Emma here how you used to talk to the ghosts, regardless of whether they answered you."

"And why not? They are people, aren't they? Imagine going about your day, never knowing if you're going to run into someone you never would have known existed."

"I don't have to imagine. Living under this roof, it's exactly what one comes to expect."

"That's my point. We're used to it. We understand that that's what we'll encounter. From the looks on some of their faces, I don't think they do. A little common courtesy is in all our best interests."

Mr. Wade looks like he is holding in a roll of his eyes. "As I was trying to say, it's clear Marie is a kind woman from the way she treats everyone she meets. But you—what makes you tick? Are you the type who's only out for number one? 'It's a dog-eat-dog world,' as they say?"

"It's interesting you should say that," I pipe in. "But how do you know when you've taken it too far and are just being selfish?"

"There's a difference between sticking up for number one and being an arse. I like to think you can do the former without becoming the latter."

"True, true." I nod, stirring the straw in my soda. "In my experience, however, there are plenty who have been unable to make a distinction."

Mr. Wade laughs again, his eyes bright and carefree. I like his laugh. It's a rich baritone at first that fades into a whole body shake, as if every part of his being is sharing the joke. "I heard you've worked with lawyers in the past. Could that be part of the problem?"

I chuckle at the stereotype. "Aren't you a lawyer?"

"Touché," he replies, a sparkle in his eyes. "But not everyone is out to rake everyone else over the coals. If that were the case, what's the point of it all?"

We sit in silence for a few moments before I clear my throat. "So, we've established that you know Marie, but you never said if you met James."

Mr. Wade wipes his mouth with his napkin and turns to James. "No, I never did say. I don't believe we've had the pleasure before today. And if I'm mistaken, I do apologize."

James smiles softly. "You're quite right. We've never had the pleasure."

"That's kind of cool," I interject. "Here you both were staying in the same house, talking with the same people"—I nod at Marie—"and yet you never ran into one another."

"It's a big house," James supplies.

"It certainly is," Mr. Wade concedes.

"Yeah, it is, but it's kind of like history. You guys were walking where the other had walked and you had no idea of each other's existence. And unless it's a famous person or the person's history is written down, no one is ever the wiser. Anyway, that's why I'm doing what I'm doing. The personal aspect of it. We all have these hopes and dreams, and unless they're written down, poof. No one will ever know. I think it's neat when bits and pieces come together, when we learn about someone long gone. It kind of brings them back for a moment." I trail off, thinking of Eve.

"This sounds more like the type of conversation I would have had in my philosophy class back in college or one of the conversations I would have with one of my roommates over whiskey," Mr. Wade says as he pushes back his chair.

"Ahh, a nicely aged whiskey can make any conversation intriguing!" James quips, pushing back his own chair. "Unfortunately, it's not conducive to handling heavy machinery, and I have to return to work."

"Another time perhaps?" Mr. Wade asks. "I remember there being a billiard room, if I'm not mistaken," he says, motioning to the hallway.

"Another time. Certainly." James smiles. "But it'll have to be an imaginary game. The table is being recovered." He goes to pick up the plates, but Marie brushes him aside.

"I'll get those and meet you after I finish in here." James smiles and pats her arm, then looks at me. "Have a good afternoon, Miss Emma." Mr. Wade follows James to the door, where they shake hands. Then James disappears into the hallway, and Mr. Wade returns to the table.

He helps Marie and me bring plates and glasses into the kitchen, then turns to me. "I'll meet you in the library," he says, giving Marie a hug. "It has been wonderful to see you again, Marie. I expect it to be more often, at least until Emma is through here."

Marie pats his arm and smiles. "You haven't changed, Louis. Not one bit."

Excusing himself, he leaves through a side door, clearly remembering the lefts and rights he'll have to take to get back to the room I still have trouble finding.

Earlier, we set up a preliminary database for all the journals, which will definitely make things easier, but I still have questions that need to be answered before I can get underway with the work, and it's those questions my mind turns to as I absently wipe off the counter.

Marie bustles around the kitchen, wrapping the brownies and placing them on a table with a little sign that says Help Yourself, a note for any of the workers who might come through here later in the day.

Smiling, I tell Marie that I'll finish up in the kitchen, and she throws me an appreciative glance before hurrying out to meet James on whatever project they're working on. Sighing, I lean against the counter, my hands carrying out the mission of washing while my eyes roam over the garden outside the window. I still can't believe I'm here.

Placing the last glass on the drying rack and drying my hands on a bar towel, I walk back through the rooms to the Great Hall where we ate, making sure the table is wiped clean. I lean against it, the wood cool against my skin, and wonder again about the other people who used to live here, the ghosts I've encountered, especially the one who tried talking to me, and what more I will learn from the piles of journals and books I need to go over in the library.

I enter the library a few minutes later, and Mr. Wade is gazing out the window that looks out over the garden. I watch him thoughtfully for a moment, wondering what he's thinking, if losing his friend weighs heavily on his mind now that he's back in the very rooms in which they used to play.

Taking a few steps forward, I put a hand on his arm, but he doesn't look at me.

"It's beautiful out there," I tell him, my voice soft, and he doesn't move. "There's something about the gardens I find . . . peaceful."

He glances at me before turning to the view outside once more. "I feel like I've been transported back in time," he says, confirming my thoughts. He motions to the gardens. "It's almost like a dream." He laughs, a sound filled with both happiness and sadness. "And that I'm able to be near the place again, after all this time . . ."

I give him a small smile, and the smile he gives me in return is filled with longing, with a yearning for what was and would never be again, and at that moment, I think I understand. It makes me ache for Eve and what I will never share with her.

And so we stand, two people from two different lives sharing a similar pain. It's a connection I didn't expect but that I welcome just the same.

"Shall we get back to work?" Mr. Wade asks.

I nod, taking a step away from him, feeling a little awkward. It's one thing to get lost in my own feelings, but I feel as though I've intruded upon his, and I'm eager to get back to the task of separating and cataloging. Glancing at Mr. Wade, I can tell he feels the same.

After Mr. Wade leaves, and throughout the rest of the afternoon, the woman is never far from my thoughts. What keeps playing on a loop in my mind is the moment she opened her mouth to speak. What had she been about to say? Was she going to ask a question? Or was it simply that she was going to say hello? On more than one occasion, I'm tempted to stop what I'm doing and go back to look for her. Then I wonder if Marie or James have ever seen her. From what Mr. Wade said, Marie was friendly with everyone she encountered, ghost or not, and I saw it for myself yesterday morning when she greeted the man who ran away afterward.

I look around the room, curious whether I am alone. At some points, I don't believe I am. It's just a feeling, but I never see any sign of the woman or any other apparition.

It's late when I decide to stop. At one point, I hurriedly grabbed something to eat and ate it while catching up with Marie, but I wanted to get back to what I was doing. Now, hours later, all I have to show for it are three additional empty shelves. One by one, the noises around the place lessen. While they were happening, I never really listened to determine what they were, but now that they have stopped, the silence is loud. The movements from one room to the next, which I could only guess would have been James or Marie, cease. Before too long, they pass by to say good night, and Marie hands me a cup of tea before they head up to their room, the footsteps heading away from the library growing faint. Now I'm alone.

It's a strange thing to be alone in a big house at night. If you sit and let the quiet seep through you, you can imagine you are the only one in the world. You can imagine you are anyone from anywhere. At least, that's what I imagine.

Sitting on the sofa with a book in my hand and a cup of tea on the table, I feel strangely comforted by the fact that although I am by myself, so many people have been here before me. It feels like I am a part of something bigger than I had ever imagined before and that my part is just as important as anyone else's. We're all linked.

All of a sudden, I've turned into a philosopher, but as I look around at all the books, I get the feeling that my thoughts are more along the lines of truth than they ever have been before.

And that's when I know I'm tired and need to go to bed. It has been a long day, but looking at the empty shelves, I'm happy with what I've accomplished. Plus, I want to make sure I have a good night's sleep so I can do as much or more tomorrow.

Turning off a small lamp on the desk and then the larger ceiling light, I walk out of the library and through the silent rooms of the manor, flicking switches and plunging the house deeper and deeper into darkness as I go.

As I walk the halls in solitude, I touch the walls, the window casings, and places I think someone else might have touched when passing through. Even though I can hear the sounds of the house settling, and even though all of outside seems to be looking in at each window I pass, I feel a sense of belonging, a feeling I'm right where I need to be.

I don't even bother looking for ghosts as I make my way to my room. I won't see them tonight with it so dark. I'll just have to wait for another day.

I enter my dark bedroom, climb up onto my bed, and drop off to sleep. There is nothing for me to see, feel, or experience. And that is exactly how I want it.

Chapter 5

It has been a week since I began working on the books, and I'm pretty happy with where I'm at. I've cataloged all the books on the shelves of one wall. When I say it, it doesn't sound like much, but when I look at the result, it's definitely impressive.

I currently have twenty-six large boxes lined up in front of the fireplace, most of them filled, at least partially. Books will be alphabetized by author first, then title. Books that are extremely old or are first editions are in boxes near one corner of the room. I'll look at those more thoroughly later, determining which will be stored in a better environment.

Then there are the magazines and journals. Magazines are currently in stacks on and under a collapsible table James found and brought in for me. I need to ask what is to be done with these. And the journals, especially the old ones, have been carefully placed in special boxes used to preserve books. I keep sneaking peeks at some of the entries. I know I'll see them when I'm copying them, but it helps with keeping things interesting.

With the progress I've made, I have no problem taking a break. I'm heading back to my grandmother's house tomorrow. There's laundry to do, and I'm meeting up with some friends for dinner and drinks. But right now, the dresses in my room's closet are calling to me.

The ghosts of the house don't scare me as much as they did that first day, but I still make my way tentatively through the rooms and up the stairs. Right now, I equate them to being afraid of dogs, like I've been invited into a house where there are some, and I've been told they're friendly, but I'm still a bit afraid they'll bite if I move too quickly.

Marie and James were right, though. I do see several ghosts each day, and most of them retreat or flee as soon as they see me. There are a few who nod or wave, so I do the same, but it's disconcerting to act casually with someone I'm able to see through.

I haven't seen the woman who scared me so much on the first day, but I kind of hope to run into her again. I'd like to think I'll have the courage to listen to what she has to say. I make it to my room without incident, though, and close the door behind me, take the pink dress from the closet, and lay it on the bed.

Stripping off my clothes, I take the dress off the hanger, unzip the zipper on the side, and shimmy into it. One of the petticoats rides up the side, and I pull and twist until it flows freely around my legs. Once done, I zip up the side and move to the mirror.

The fabric caresses my skin like a gentle embrace. It is cool to the touch and luxurious to wear. I am comforted by the weight of history draped upon me, as if I have stepped straight out of the pages of a storybook, and the swish of the skirt as I walk is like a soft whisper, gliding through time and space in a never-ending dance. It's as if I've been transported.

I pull my hair back into a messy bun and put my tennis shoes back on—it's not like anyone is going to see my feet under all these layers—and leave my room to once again explore.

There are still parts of the house I have left to look at, and I debate which rooms to start with when I get an overwhelming urge to go to the chapel to be alone with my thoughts.

I'm not a particularly religious person, but given my thoughts on life and death lately, I guess it's only natural for my mind to go there.

The room is out of the way at the back of the house on the first floor. With three pews on each side and a small raised pulpit upon which a lectern stands, the focus of the room is the giant wooden cross behind the pulpit. It isn't decorative or adorned but just stands as a testament to the validity of the space and for all who seek its peace and sanctuary.

Just outside the door, my phone rings. It's the first time it's rung since I've been at the manor, and I jump at the sudden intrusion of noise and whisper a hello, backing away from the room and walking into the smaller room beside it to take the call. "Hi, Mom," I say as I walk over to the window to peek outside. It's raining once again, only this time, it's more of a sedate rain that promises days of lingering. The sky is a dusty gray, and everything appears somber and subdued.

"Hi, honey, I miss you! How do you like your new job?"

"It's good. Great!" I say as my eyes prick with unshed tears. I spoke to her a little more than a week ago, but each time I do seems more precious than it used to be. "There are so many things I have to tell you about this place. You won't believe it."

"I'm not bothering you, am I? I just had to call you up and hear your voice, hear you speak back to me." I can hear the sadness in her voice, and a tear slides down my cheek.

"You're not bothering me. I'm right here. But, Mom, this place!" I go back to talking about the house because I can feel my grip on my sorrow loosening its hold more and more. I'm so sick of being sad. "There's something about it. It's incredible. You and Dad are going to have to come inside the next time you're here."

"Just tell me this: have you talked to any ghosts?"

"What?"

"Ghosts. Have you talked to any?"

"But you always used to say the rumors were nonsense."

"You were young. I didn't want to scare you, but oh, the stories your grandma used to tell about working there." She chuckles softly.

"Wait, what? How come this is the first time I'm hearing about this?"

"Grandma worked there until she became pregnant with your dad. She'd tell us about all sorts of encounters she had. When you were little, she didn't want you to hear. She was afraid you'd get scared. Later, well, she started to forget. You know how she was."

"I can't believe you've been holding out on me."

Mom laughs on the other end of the line, and I smile. It has been a while since I've heard it.

"I've seen a few, but I haven't had the guts to talk to one yet."

"You're not all by yourself, are you?" Her words are accusatory, as if she's certain I'll lie, and I wonder why she thinks that.

"No, I'm fine. James and Marie Gale, the owners of the refurbishing company, stay here every night, and during the day, about five to ten additional people are working in one room or another. It's pretty cool because I know they're here, but the house is so big!" I decide to switch tactics. "How's everything going over there? Anything new?"

There's a pause before she responds. "How do we go back to normal, you know? But we're trying. We're okay. We miss you."

"Well, I'm fine. I promise. And I miss you guys too."

"You can always come home. Having you here sure sounds good to me." I inwardly sigh. Of all the things I could do, that's the last one on the list.

"Are you sure you're okay? Do you want me to come home?" It's something we've talked about before. My parents know how I feel about it, but if they really want me to, I'll go.

I hear her exhale. "I'd love for you to be here, but you need to make your own way. We understand that. And having you come home would just be to make us feel better, not you. Just bear with us if we call a little too much or ask to FaceTime."

"I love you, Mom."

"We love you, honey. So, so much. Dad says hi."

I hear "Email me!" shouted from him in the background, and I smile. Dad loves to get mail as long as it's not bad news or bills.

"You heard your father," Mom says. "Love you." Then there's the click as she ends the call.

I smile at my phone as I walk toward the door. Putting my phone in a small hidden pocket, I run through what feels like a bunch of spider webs. Disoriented by the sticky cling of what feels like thousands of tiny threads, I brush myself off even before I hurriedly turn around to make sure I didn't indeed just run through a huge spider web. Already I'm debating on whether to start tearing off my clothes to get what I'm sure are enormous spiders and all their babies off me.

I'm glad I don't. As I turn around, brushing myself off, I find myself looking at a man doing the exact same thing. His eyes widen, as I'm sure mine do, and when he sees me, he jumps back about a foot. The first thing I notice is his pants, which aren't pants at all but breeches. He wears them with a pair of stockings and shoes with buckles on them. On top, his broad shoulders and trim waist are only accented by the embroidered waistcoat and complimentary embroidered coat with large cuffs and pleats. It is only then that I can look at his face.

Stunning is the only word that comes to mind. His eyes draw me in, piercing me with their intensity. Hooded, they aren't quite brown, but I don't think they're hazel either. I wish I can see them more clearly, but it's almost as if I'm looking at him through a filter of some sort. His face is square shaped, with a hint of stubble along his cheeks, chin, and full upper lip. His hair, longer on top than on the sides, is a dark chestnut, and the length is enough to show a slight curl around his ears. I'm totally staring, and I have to stop. After probably way too much time, I find my voice.

"I'm sorry. You scared me! I didn't see you or hear you come in." I reflect on the entry that talked about how ghosts don't seem to realize they're dead and either see us as spirits too or think of us as just as "real" as they are. I know I'm looking at a ghost, and strangely, I'm not scared. I just wonder how he sees me.

"Please, I beg your pardon," he says in a soft, deep voice as he bows before me. "I'm terribly sorry for frightening you." Although I can hear his voice and see him much more clearly than I could the woman who approached me, the hazy quality of this man is still observable. He isn't substantial; if I were to put my hand out to touch him, I'm certain I would encounter that sticky spider web feeling again.

"It's quite all right, I assure you," I return, trying to remember words from historical romances I've read, but I don't know what else to say. We stand awkwardly for a moment before he continues.

"Allow me to introduce myself. My name is Alexander Jonathan Thomas Eason," he states formally, bowing slightly again. "I am at a loss, though, for although I know my own name, I find myself incomplete without yours."

"Oh, that is nicely said." I blush. "I am Amelia Beckett, but my friends and family call me Emma."

"I hope, one day, to be included in that exclusive list," he replies softly. "Please, what brings you to Hillfield Manor?"

I freeze. What can I say? I can't say I work here or else he'll think me one of the servants, and the clothes I wear would have been considered too fine for me to be relegated to their ranks. I could be a companion, but I'm sure if I say that, he'll ask me for whom. I try to stick as close to the truth as possible.

"The Easons have graciously extended an invitation for me to stay at the manor while I, uh, while I convalesce," I inform.

Alexander looks thoughtful for a moment before he comments. "The manor and the grounds are scenic, peaceful, and will, I believe, most assuredly help you recover, but if I may be so bold, you look the picture of health, Miss Beckett."

"Thank you," I say. "The Easons, er, your family, have seen to my every need."

"May I walk with you? I believe you were on your way to—" Alexander breaks off, unable to continue. He raises his eyebrow, a sign that I should help him by filling in the blank, but I'm so overwhelmed by his appearance and my ability to communicate with a real, live—ahem—ghost that it takes a moment for my thoughts to process.

"I was on my way to the chapel. It's just next door. I can find my way," I'm finally able to utter as I begin to walk toward the door. Then, realizing I may not have another chance to speak with him, I turn abruptly, "Do you believe in ghosts, Mr. Eason?"

His head jerks back as he looks me in the eye. Cautiously, he nods. "I do believe in ghosts, Miss Beckett. Why do you ask?"

Unable to tell him I believe myself to be talking to one, I think of the other apparition I've seen. "There is this woman," I start. "I've seen her once. I've been anxious to talk to someone about her, but I wasn't sure in whom I could confide. I understand I've just met you, Mr. Eason, but I feel it easier to talk to you about this versus someone else in the house. After all, I've only just met you whereas—"

"Whereas you have already established a relationship with others in the household. I understand, Miss Beckett." He walks around the room, his hands clasped behind his back and a slight frown on his face, always keeping me within peripheral vision. Then, eyeing me speculatively, one eyebrow raised, he asks, "How do you know this woman is a ghost?"

I stifle a snort, wanting to shoot my hand through his abdomen to prove my point. "Are you trying to placate me, Mr. Eason, or do you truly believe? I understand the idea is more than a little unusual, but I assure you I am neither mad nor hallucinating." I seriously wonder about that, though. Did Eve's death drive me over the edge? Am I really just locked up in some asylum somewhere with all of this as my biggest hallucination yet? Despite my sudden uncertainty, I try to maintain my act of confidence. "If you wish not to discuss this with me, please say so, and I will be on my way. I think I can tell when a person standing before me is corporeal or transparent."

His hands fly from behind his back, and he waves them in front of himself, his eyes wide. "No! No, no. I'm sorry, Miss Beckett. I didn't mean to offend you."

He runs a hand through his hair while he looks around the room as though searching for his next words.

"I . . . I guess what I should have said was that I wished for more details of your encounter. Did you hear any strange noises accompanying her appearance? Did she disappear before your eyes? Did you feel a shift in the temperature? Did . . . did she see you?"

I let out a breath and smile apologetically. *Way too many historical romances, Emma!* "Excuse me for being too quick to judge your intent, Mr. Eason. These are exactly the types of questions I'd like to discuss with someone who believes, with someone who has, perhaps, seen a ghost as well," I say, looking at him through a lowered gaze.

"I *do* believe, Miss Beckett, and my judgment lies in the fact that I, too, have been in the presence of an apparition." He runs his right hand through his hair again, a few tendrils dipping onto his forehead. "I know it isn't proper for me to ask. After all, we haven't been formally introduced, but seeing as we've already had a lively discussion—" he smiles "—and we do appear to have something in common, would it be possible for me to see you again? Maybe tomorrow? We could meet somewhere more public if you'd like, perhaps the hall or the Long Gallery? We could discuss this further."

"I'd like that," I return. The Long Gallery would most likely be unoccupied, and that is all the better, as far as I'm concerned. Would the others be able to see Alexander?

Would they be able to communicate with him? Just now, I'm not quite sure I want James and Marie or any of the workers to know about my ghost. It's a strange but welcome feeling to talk to one without fear, and for right now, I want to keep that to myself. I want to keep Alexander for myself. *Purely academic reasons, of course*.

"I do enjoy the gallery. Shall we say after lunch? Around two?" I wonder if it is that easy. Are ghosts able to follow a set schedule? I suppose I'll find out.

He bows again and extends his hand toward the door, allowing me to go first. Just in front of the chapel, he turns toward me. "I look forward to seeing you in the Long Gallery tomorrow, at two, Miss Beckett." A small smile plays at the corners of those lusciously full lips. "Until then," he says, and with yet another bow, he turns away and walks around the corner.

I wait a few moments before sneaking up to where I last saw him. I hesitate but finally peek around the edge. The long corridor with closed doors on either side is completely empty. Mr. Alexander Jonathan Thomas Eason is nowhere to be seen.

Once I get to my room, I open the door and peek inside, wondering if I will find myself disturbing someone whose room this used to be. Running into Mr. Eason—Alexander—is a solid reminder that I can run into a ghost at any time, and although I find myself open to an experience, so far, I've never seen one in my room, and for this I am grateful. I would feel violated on some level and then I wonder if that's how they feel coming upon *me* when doing whatever it is ghosts do.

Flopping down on the bed, I stare at the ceiling. Alexander's hazel eyes are what I picture. I think about how clear he was to me, very different from what I had seen of the woman. Maybe it was his proximity, or perhaps he was a stronger ghost? If the web-like sensation I felt when we literally walked through one another was any indication, he was pretty strong.

I wonder what will happen in the Long Gallery tomorrow, if he'll show up, if I'll be able to see him if he does. I also wonder about our ghost conversation. He said he believed in ghosts, but what does that mean? The manor has a history of ghostly sightings, so maybe as an Eason living in the house, he saw them before he became a ghost. Or maybe it's as James said, and he is alive in his own time, believing *I* am the ghost instead. It would explain why he jumped away from me. I want to ask him if I am a bit transparent like he is. At the same time, I don't want to say anything and chance breaking the spell or whatever it is that is allowing me to talk to him in the first place.

It's a conundrum, but having the same questions rattling in my head isn't going to get me any closer to answering them. Then I think about the journals. I've already read entries pertaining to ghosts. Most likely, there will be more. Although I'm not even close to being finished organizing all the books, I decide to take a break and begin copying some of the journals. If I don't find any entries about ghosts, then at least they might take my mind off Alexander and the lady for a little while.

After changing, I make my way to the library and stand staring at the room and the monstrous task ahead of me. There is a feeling of ownership, strange as that may sound. The responsibility of this room and its contents fall on my shoulders. Every decision I make will affect how this room will ultimately look in the end and, therefore, how people will see it. Again, I feel somehow like I'm a part of something. A part of the past and the future.

I push the thought away, and sighing heavily, I put on my white gloves as I walk over to a shelf on the opposite side of the room from where I've been working. Grabbing a journal at random, I begin to skim the passages as I amble over to the table that holds my computer, open book easel, and weighted bookmark.

December 3, 1988—Ok, here we go again. It's been about a month since the last time I wrote here, but Mum keeps saying it's for posterity, so whatever. If someone 100 years from now is reading this, you seriously need to get a life. And, Mum, if it's you, you shipped me off to the States for five years. <u>Now</u> you're interested?

Anyway, I saw her again today. I'm pretty sure she saw me too. She was sitting, reading a book, and she looked up and right at me. Then she looked back down really quickly, like she didn't want me to know that she saw me. In other news, prelaw sucks.

December 8, 1988—Ok, so I talked to her today. She was in the same spot. It was like she was waiting for me to walk by. Maybe she was. Sweet. Her name is ______ and she's seventeen years old. It's a little young for me, but she seemed mature enough. At least she seemed to have more in her head than New Kids on the Block or Bros. I didn't speak to her for very long, but maybe I'll see her again tomorrow. She seems pretty wicked.

February 8, 1989—And that's that. Delete everything I've said. I'm glad I never wrote her name (Mum, I know you read these when you're home). Her name wasn't worth mentioning anyway. She's with some Wellesley guy now. Her parents are all for the match, and really, she was starting to annoy me with her requests to see Hillfield. I understand that the history and mystery of my home intrigue people, but it would be nice to know someone is interested in me, not my family or where I live.

After the third passage, I realize the author isn't talking about a ghost, so I put the journal back where I found it and grab another one on a higher shelf.

*February 19, 1878—Ghosts, specters, demons. There are always abundant rumors concerning them, and seeing as it appears to be en vogue to witness one, I'm not surprised to hear the idle gossip surrounding them. At least, that's what I presumed. It's unlikely I would have ever considered the notion even remotely plausible had I not witnessed it for myself from the first day I stepped into Hillfield. Eugene and Georgie smiled—*smiled*—at what I'm sure was a dumbfounded expression on my face and assured me the occurrence was fairly common and that, with time, I, too, would regard them as ordinary rather than extraordinary should I happen to continue my stay at the estate. What may be regarded as commonplace in the future cannot be seen as so now, so I feel it incumbent upon me to record my thoughts and any interactions I may have with the paranormal for posterity's sake.*

As I turn the front cover of the journal, I see a beautiful engraving of the name Bartholomew James Eason. The letters are ornate and carefully crafted, with swirls and intricate line work. My mouth curves into a wide grin, and my arms and legs twitch with anticipation. I can't help but laugh out loud as I discover the journal's owner. *The* Bartholomew! He's the man who disappeared after meeting the gray lady, and his disappearance is the one most talked about whenever someone mentions Hillfield Manor.

Eagerly, I open to the first page and begin typing as I read. Bartholomew's journal reads like a novel. Every page is filled with vivid descriptions of his experiences, from the moment he arrived at Hillfield Manor to each and every encounter with the mysterious gray lady. He recounts in detail how he felt around her, as if she was an old friend he had known for years.

He also talks about the atmosphere of Hillfield Manor, and how it could be both sinister and beautiful all at once. *The feeling of mystery in the air was palpable*, he says, *as if time itself had stopped in this place and nothing ever changed or would change.*

Carefully, I place a small piece of paper between the pages to act as a placeholder, and with a gentle sigh, I close Bartholomew's journal and tuck it away. There is so much to absorb in these pages, and I want to make sure it lasts. I want to savor every word. I have become so entranced by my reading that I can't help but feel a little bit of sadness at having to close the book.

I've encountered two Easons today, Alexander and Bartholomew, and both men, long dead, have proved to captivate me more than many of the living!

Chapter 6

I'm in the library working on yet another shelf when Mr. Wade stops by to check on my progress and give me an update on what is to be done with the books. He has a clipboard in his hands and is consulting the paper on top when he looks up.

"Well, it already looks a bit bare with just that part of the wall empty now," he says, pointing to the empty space.

I step off the ladder I'm on and walk over to stand next to him, only to chuckle. From here, with the fireplace in the way, it hardly seems like I've made any progress, but it's half a wall nonetheless, even if I still have another two and a half walls left to do.

"I guess it's a start," I say and smile. Thank goodness the fireplace and French doors take up about half a wall each, cutting down on yet another wall I'd have to deal with.

"I have some news that might help it all go a little bit faster." He looks around the room again and reconsiders. "Perhaps not, but at least I can tell you where half of the books will be going, and then it won't look so crowded in here."

Mr. Wade straightens his posture and tilts his head until I hear a crack. Taking on a more serious expression, he reads the paper on the clipboard once more and then begins. "Go ahead and get rid of any magazines that you see unless you want one yourself. If there are any special editions, keep them in a separate pile. I wouldn't think there would be too many. As far as books, keep all the classics. If there happens to be two or more of a title, please keep the oldest edition in the best condition." He looks at me quizzically. "Does that make sense?"

"Totally," I say with a nod.

"Once you are done copying the journals . . ." Here he pauses and motions me to follow him. There are two entrances to the library, or so I thought. One is through a door to the left of the garden entrance, the door Marie led me through the first time I walked into the room. The other one leads to the garden itself and is always kept locked.

Mr. Wade leads me to a third door, hidden behind a bookshelf. It's cleverly concealed, and I never would have known of its existence had Mr. Wade not shown me what to look for.

"A secret passage! Oh, this is so cool!" I exclaim as I watch him press on a small dark lever very close to the frame of the shelf.

"I think so too." He winks.

After hearing a click, Mr. Wade pushes on the door and we are in another room. I was in this room only once before when Marie was showing me around the house. It had seemed an ordinary room, paneled, dark, and I never would have guessed it was connected to the library in such a way.

Mr. Wade smiles. "Once you are done copying the journals, they will go in here. Mrs. Eason has authorized this room to be converted, if you will, to a Journal and Rare Book Conservation Room. Storage furniture and special book jackets have been ordered to help with the preservation of the journals. They should be arriving in a couple of days. In addition, climate control measures will be taken in this room. I'm told the refurbishers have been informed of all of this, but I will make sure to tell them as well."

"Wow," I breathe, truly impressed. "That is wonderful news. Will any of the books be sold or loaned out to different institutions?"

"At this point, nothing will be leaving the premises as far as books are concerned, save the exceptions I've already mentioned. As a matter of fact, that door"—he points to the only "real" door in the room—"will be reinforced and a lock installed. It's about time. Some of these, I understand, are quite rare. Regardless, once Mrs. Eason arrives, it will be completely up to her what is to be done with them."

"Wow," I repeat, looking around the room. It's a perfect place. Upon entering, I noticed a slight drop in temperature. There is only one small window toward the corner of the room, so because the sun doesn't reach into the room, the books will be safe from sun damage as well as its accompanying warmth. With the addition of climate controls, furniture, and book covers, the journals will last for a long time to come.

"There are a couple more things I'd like to go over with you."

"Sure, no problem." Following him through the secret passage once again, I marvel at the fact that I had no idea it was there. If this passage exists, I wonder how many more do as well. I now know what I will be doing with my free time.

"First, before I forget. Here is a key to the library door." Mr. Wade hands me a heavy golden key, which I place on my keyring with the keys to my grandma's house.

Like my phone, I carry them everywhere. "If you'd please lock up anytime you are not present, it would be appreciated. Also, the door leading outside should remain closed and locked. It's on a security alarm." He looks at my computer lying open on the desk. "Have you just been organizing or have you been copying as well?"

"Funny you should mention that. I just started copying a little yesterday. I found one of Bartholomew Eason's journals! I had to start working on it when I saw who it belonged to."

"Remember, confidentiality. Don't tell me anything. But did you have any difficulty?"

"No, I had no trouble going through it. I managed to get half of it done, but I'm going to save the rest for another time. Draw it out." I chuckle as Mr. Wade gives me a baffled glance.

"Suit yourself," he says, clapping his hands together. "I spoke to James before seeing you, and he has assured me the room next door should be finished within a week, so if you wouldn't mind starting with the older journals—besides Bartholomew's, that is—you'll be able to place them in there once you're finished with them. The new shelving and archival storage boxes should be here by the end of next week, so that gives you a bit more time for sorting and organizing as well. All books that are not journals, rare, or old, will remain in here and can be organized by author and whether it's fiction or nonfiction."

Mr. Wade takes a pen from his pocket and ticks off items with a check. "Yes, yes, that's done, told her about this," he says softly as he goes through the list. Once he's through, he looks up. "Are we done with the business portion? Do you have any questions?" he asks, his eyebrows raised.

"Not that I can think of, no."

As Mr. Wade is leaving, James walks in, and the two men shake hands.

"You'll give me a call if there are any problems with the room? By the end of the week, you say?"

"There's not much to do to get it up to snuff. It'll be ready," James says, nodding.

Mr. Wade shakes James's hand again and moves toward the door.

"Emma," he says, at the threshold. "If you need anything, give me a call. You have my number. Otherwise, I'll stop by in a week or so and check on your progress."

"Thanks, Mr. Wade."

There's a small commotion just outside the doorway, and James and I walk over as Mr. Wade is saying goodbye to Marie and a young man standing next to her.

James turns to me. "I wonder if Marie and I can impose upon your good nature, Miss Emma."

"It's just Emma!" I admonish yet again. I've been telling him since I got here, but he refuses and either calls me Miss Emma or Miss Beckett. "What do you need?"

"Well, Just Emma," James says, his eyes twinkling, "Marie and I have to leave the manor for a couple of hours. Someone believes a permit is required, but said permit was acquired months ago, and we need to—"

"James, how can I help?"

He points to the young man who is now looking at the two of us. "This is Lucas. Lucas, please be so kind as to say hello to this charming young lady who is working in the library. Miss Emma Beckett."

Lucas steps forward. He's probably in his late twenties, slightly taller than James, and has Marie's smile. Ash-blond hair falls over his forehead as he takes my hand. "It's a pleasure," he says as he tips his head.

"Lucas has stopped by to take a look at the house. He is quite an accomplished carpenter and has offered to give us a quote for some of the work needed here. Would you be so kind as to show him around the place? I don't know why he can't wait until we're done, but apparently," he says, raising an eyebrow, "being seen in the presence of one's family, regardless of the absence of an audience, is unheard of in this day and age."

Although he sounds like he's joking, from the look on his face, I can tell James believes it. Behind him, Lucas narrows his eyes and huffs. I look down to hide my smile. "I would be happy to show Lucas around."

"Marie and I do appreciate it," he says, patting my shoulder. He leans in conspiratorially. "And if you could, try to keep him around until we return. We haven't seen our boy in a year. It would be nice to see him in person and not over a blasted contrivance."

I smile. "I will do my best."

Making our way into the library, I glance at my watch and am not surprised to see it is already close to noon. Lucas had spent considerable time in each room, walking the perimeters, commenting on the windows or the portraits in the Long Gallery and on the floorboards and ceilings in other rooms. All the while, I couldn't help looking for my visitor from yesterday. While in the gallery, I sought out his likeness in the portraits; while strolling through the multiple rooms on the ground floor, I hoped for his appearance—if only to confirm my sanity, especially if Lucas saw him too. It wasn't meant to be.

Lucas almost chokes as he follows me into the room. "*This* is the library? My parents told me there were a lot of books, but . . . I think this goes a bit beyond that." He looks around in awe, walking over to run his hand along the bindings of the books before thinking better of it and pulling his hand back. “You’re by yourself on this? You don’t have any help?”

“No, it isn’t needed,” I say, a bit disappointed at his responding look of doubt. “Right now, I like working by myself. I have a system.”

“Do you have a life?” Lucas laughs.

“What? This is my job. It’s not like I’m stuck here. I can walk out the front door any time, just like you.”

“Yeah, but doesn’t it put you to sleep?”

“Excuse me?”

He runs his hand over his face slowly. “It gets boring, right? I mean, the tour was great. I love old houses. I guess that’s something I’ve inherited. And this place is incredible, but what you have to do, why would you want to?” He lifts a finger and points at the journals on the shelves and in boxes. “Let’s look at some memories. Why? What are they going to do? Can you change them? No!”

I shake my head in confusion. “It’s not that much different from what your parents are doing. They restore old houses and give new life to history. I’m doing the same thing. I’m helping people today know what life was like back then, at least through the writers’ perspectives. I think it’s interesting.”

“I get what my parents do. They do this for the love of the houses, and most of the time, I do too, but the money that can be made with a place like this is a huge draw.”

He runs his finger over the spines of a few journals before picking one up and flipping through the pages. "What you're doing, it's nothing like that. How many people are going to be that interested?" He pauses, then looks me in the eye. "Unless there's something specific you're looking for that's of interest. That's it, isn't it?"

My eyes widen. "You just admitted being drawn to what you do, so why can't the same hold true for me? There is a lot of history here, and if I'm interested, there have to be other—"

"And you're losing me again," Lucas interrupts, his exaggerated glassy eyes clearing with a firm shake of his head.

He's acting like a child, and I hold back on my desire to roll my eyes and stoop to his level. "You know where the door is." I hold up my hand, indicating the way. "Feel free to use it, and since you have no interest in what happens in here, don't bother coming back."

It's obvious he's not used to being told off. Lucas looks as if he's been struck. His eyes are wide in disbelief, his mouth is slightly open, and his whole posture is like a marionette with its strings cut.

I turn away from him, waiting for him to storm off or say something to break the uncomfortable tension. But there is only the oppressive silence of the room. If he's waiting for an apology, he might as well settle in because that isn't happening.

"Easy there. Woah, okay? You're obviously dedicated to your work. I'm sorry if I crossed a line. I thought you could take a joke." He smiles as if his backhanded compliment will smooth things over. For the sake of James and Marie, I'm keeping a tight rein on what I want to say, but this guy's going to give me a run for my money.

Lucas exhales and relaxes his shoulders. "So, *is* there anything interesting in the journals?"

"Well, you know journals." I shrug. "For the most part, they're supposed to be personal."

"Yes, that's true. There's just so much here. It makes me wonder if the Easons were hiding some sort of secret, you know?"

I shift uncomfortably. "Regardless of whether I find one, I signed a nondisclosure agreement. I can't say anything."

Lucas snaps his fingers and points at me with a wide smile. "*You* are no fun, but yeah, sure. *Everybody* has secrets." Condescension drips off his words, and I struggle to maintain my composure as my dislike for this man continues to grow.

"And your name isn't on the list of people I can communicate with about it," I say, my ensuing smile as fake as the one he gives me. "So don't try to worm any information out of me. I take my job seriously."

"Yes, you certainly do." Lucas looks down and traces his finger along the edge of the desk on which he's leaning. "Em . . . ah," he starts, looking at me and then quickly looking down at his tracing finger. "Let's go get some lunch."

My eyebrows raise, and it's all I can do not to gape. What? Then it dawns on me, and I smirk. "So, asking straight out didn't work, so you figure you'll try to get close to me? How many lunches do you think it'll take before I'm divulging family secrets?" I cross my arms over my chest and glare.

Lucas blows out a puff of air and smirks. "Cover blown. Fine. You're officially off the hook. And I won't keep you out too long if you're worried about staying away from your precious work. It's eleven fifty now. The restaurant is just a quick five-minute walk. I can have you there and back before one. Come on, have lunch with me, so I don't look like the loser no one wants to sit with."

I'm supposed to meet Alexander at two, so I'll have plenty of time, but I still find myself searching for some reason to call off the lunch. He stands there, his stance wide, his arms crossed, and a devious gleam in his eyes. What does he want? I can also tell he's waiting for me to back down and prove I have no life. Nope. Not going to happen. And the thing is, I *want* to go. I know I need to get away from here for a while, even if I am going to be in the company of a jerk. Plus, I can honestly tell Marie and James I had tried getting to know Lucas a little better.

I notice Lucas is still looking at me and realize I've been quiet for a little too long. "You'll still be a loser," I say, my smile sickeningly sweet. "But I could use something to eat."

He ignores my first remark, turning to head for the door. "Well, then, let's get going. I'm starving!" He looks back at me. "Ready?"

I take a deep breath. I feel as if I'm about to test the limits of something, but I have no clue what that could be. I exhale and brush past him. "As ready as I'll ever be."

Chapter 7

Although as we're leaving Hillfield, Lucas assures me he'll be on his best behavior, it's not far into our walk when, once again, his claws are out.

"Tell me, Emma, why did you want to work at Hillfield?"

"Oh, I've always been fascinated with the house, with the stories about what happens in the house. Ghosts! And they're real! Come to think about it, I'm surprised we didn't see any on our tour."

Lucas's steps falter for a moment, and he rolls his eyes.

"You don't believe?" I ask. "You've heard the stories too, right?"

"Yeah, I've heard them. Have you forgotten who my aunt and uncle are?"

"What? I thought they were your parents?"

"You know what assuming makes."

Glaring at him, I move to turn around and head back to Hillfield, but Lucas grabs my arm. I shake it off and look him in the eye. Lucas inhales and then blows out the air forcefully. "Marie's my aunt, but they adopted me when I was younger after my parents died, so, yeah, whatever."

It's obvious Lucas doesn't want to talk about this, and although I'm curious, I let it go. The man obviously has some anger issues, and perhaps it has something to do with his parents' deaths. Mentally steeling myself against his abrasiveness, I smile sheepishly. "Well, why aren't you, you know, more excited about the ghosts? It's a big deal. I saw—"

Lucas stops and looks at me with narrowed eyes. "Don't."

I take a step back. "What? I saw some, and I even spoke—"

Lucas squeezes his eyes shut and pinches his nose. When he looks at me again, his eyes are filled with anger. "I don't want to hear it," he says slowly, punctuating each word.

I look away from him and back toward Hillfield. Marie and James have been great, but their nephew is the complete opposite. I debate—again—walking away now or going to the restaurant to see if I can get something to go. My hunger wins, and I push past Lucas. I'm almost at an intersection when his steps fall in line beside mine.

"There's something more to it, to the whole house," he says, his voice hard. "And if there's one thing I'm going to do, I'm going to figure it out."

He sounds like one of the bad guys from those old *Scooby Doo* cartoons, and I'm tempted to say, *Zoinks!* Instead, I ask, "What do you mean?"

He stops walking and turns to me. "Come on, Emma, don't be so naive. The same family has been in the house for generations upon generations, there are about a million journals in that library, the house is so well-known for ghosts that they actually used to give tours to showcase them, and there've been disappearances throughout the years. Disappearances that no one has been able to solve. You don't find all that strange?"

My hackles rise at being called naive, and yes, I find it all incredibly strange, but eccentricity is bound to thrive in a house where ghosts are rampant and servants and members of the family are asked to dress up in costumes and write in journals—which didn't nearly add up to a million, by the way.

"What are you suggesting? That the family, who is perfectly within their rights to keep a house for generations—it's not like they're the only ones—are only keeping it for nefarious reasons, and ghosts are in on the couple-hundred-year-old conspiracy? You don't think that sounds even more far-fetched?"

"You had to sign a nondisclosure agreement, didn't you?"

"Yeah, so?"

"So, they're hiding something!" Lucas huffs as he begins walking again.

I hurry to catch up to him. "Let's just say they *are* hiding something," I say. "What's it matter to you?"

He folds his lips between his teeth, and it reminds me of a little kid pretending to zip his lips and throw away the key.

"Lucas?" I rest my hand on his shoulder and stop walking once more. "Seriously, what's it matter?"

"I deserve to know. That's all."

"But why? If my family was as high profile as the Easons, I wouldn't want private stuff getting out either, so what's it to you?"

Lucas gazes into my eyes, his own troubled and angry, and then he smirks. "Don't worry your pretty little head about it." His eyes narrow. "And there's no need to go running to tell my aunt anything either. Understand?"

"You're an ass," I say, folding my arms in front of me. "You were, like, the class bully back in school, weren't you?"

Lucas sighs and runs his hand through his hair roughly. "I'm sorry, okay? I just—for reasons I don't want to go into right now—I feel I have a right to know more about the house. That's all." He sighs again and forces a smile. "Please tell me you'll still have lunch with me. The restaurant is just there," he says, pointing to a small pub across the street from where we stand.

The urge to just grab my food to go is strong. I don't need his drama and mood changes. The man is nearing thirty, yet he's acting like a moody, hormonal teenager, and it's getting old. Fast. At the same time, I find Lucas almost as interesting as the house. *What the hell is he looking for, and why?*

"Emma?"

I give him a glare of my own. "You're an ass, and I don't like you. Still want to eat with me?"

He smiles, his shoulders shaking a bit with withheld laughter. It's a look that's good on him if he'd use it more. "Yes, please," he says.

Seriously? Closing my eyes, I sigh before opening them once again. "Fine," I growl as I stride past him. "Let's go eat. You're buying."

The pub is quaint and dark inside, and there aren't many people. We pretty much have our choice of seating. As we're settling ourselves at a table near an oversized fireplace, a waitress comes up to tell us of the day's specials.

Not even asking if I'm ready to order and cutting the waitress off to boot, Lucas launches into what he wants and then turns to me expectantly, his brow raised. *How is this beast evenly remotely related to two such wonderful people as James and Marie?* I shake my head in wonder and ask for the quiche Lorraine, one of the specials the poor woman managed to get out.

We make small talk while we wait, and I feel like I'm tiptoeing on eggshells, wondering what'll set off Lucas again. We use the typical conversation starters, which seems odd after our conversations thus far. They're the *nice weather we're having* variety with a little *tell me something interesting about yourself* discussions. I'm more than ever aware that time is ticking away and surreptitiously glance at my watch or my phone throughout lunch, only slightly dismayed when Lucas catches me.

"I know I made a bad impression on you, but you could at least give me a second chance."

"That was the walk over," I say while guiltily putting my phone in my pocket.

Lucas smiles. "I guess I deserved that. I basically called you a prig, said your life was boring, and was derisive about your job. Then I berated you on the walk here. I apologize. Thank you for agreeing to lunch with me."

"I was hungry," I say as I polish off another fry.

"That's the only reason you agreed?"

"You basically called me a prig, said my life was boring, and were derisive about my job. Then you berated me on the way here," I parrot. "What do you think?"

Lucas grins again. "Touché."

"So, you've seen the house, and you know who your bosses will be. Are you going to take the job?"

Lucas looks at me thoughtfully. "It's something to consider, especially if there's the possibility of running into *you* occasionally. Maybe I can truly convince you how sorry I am."

I point at him with a french fry. "You are a flirt. Why?"

"Oh, come on. You like it."

I roll my eyes, stuff the fry into my mouth, and stand. "I'm heading back," I say, more than ready to be done with this prick. "You coming?"

We make it back to Hillfield at quarter to one. Thankfully, James and Marie are back, and they commandeer Lucas, allowing me to get an hour of work in before hurrying up to my room to change into the period clothing. Shortly after two, I slow my step just shy of the Long Gallery, take a deep breath, and enter. Finding myself alone, I meander through the room, gazing at the portraits once again. This time, not only am I searching for the visage of the female apparition, I'm searching for Alexander as well. Looking at the number of pictures on the wall, though, there is no guarantee I will find either one of them.

As I search, my gaze wanders to the door now and then, and I wonder, once again, how all this works. He said he would be here, yet yesterday, he faded into nothing moments after he walked out the door. I don't think he just disappeared. It was more like the door through which I could see him was shut. Is he able to control when he makes an appearance? If so, what gives him and the other ghosts here the ability to do so?

"Miss Beckett."

The voice is soft, almost a whisper, but when I turn around, Alexander's presence is quite strong. He's almost fully corporeal, to the point that I have to look twice to discern any translucency. His attire is similar to yesterday except for the color of his shirt, now a pale pink.

"Mr. Eason, it's nice to see you again."

"Please, call me Alex. Mr. Eason is much too formal."

"I will only agree if you call me Emma. We're confiding in each other about ghosts, after all. It seems only right we forgo the surnames."

"I'd like that . . . Emma." Alex's eyes hold me hostage, and my breath catches. It's as if my whole being is caught in that one sultry gaze. In one moment, I want to hide or run away, but I also want to throw my arms around him and never let go. I've never experienced such conflicting emotions before, and instead of confronting them as I know I should, I push them away. *He is dead. He is dead. He is dead,* I keep reminding myself.

I turn in a circle and nod, indicating all the portraits. "This is your family. Are you given lessons as a youngster as to who did what and who was married to whom? Did your school masters quiz you on your family history?"

Alex laughs. "No. I can tell you the history of some of the more prominent members of the family, but I don't believe I would be able to tell you about them all."

I look at the portrait of a particularly sad-looking young woman. "This was cousin Mary Josephine Louisa Eason," I say in mock seriousness. "She is looking particularly upset because she lost her favorite knitting needles."

Alex, too, studies the portrait. "I would say she looks particularly upset because she *swallowed* her knitting needles," he corrects, pointing to her extremely long neck. We both laugh. "Actually," he says, his eyebrows furrowed in concentration as he focuses again on the portrait, "I believe *Aunt* Letitia Annabelle Eason was an extreme recluse. From what I understand, she was almost afraid of her own shadow and very much disliked being in the company of others except her immediate family. It must have been torturous for her to sit for this picture."

"Oh, the poor woman! I can't imagine living life that way. So, she died a spinster?"

"Well, no. She ended up marrying and having seven children. She died at the ripe old age of sixty-seven."

"What?" I look at Alex, confused. I must not have heard correctly.

"It's true. Apparently, marriage cured her. Her parents hated having her around the house, moping and making everyone miserable with her delicate health and odd ways. They did love her, though, and wanted her to be happy, so they told her she could have her choice of husbands—from those who came calling, at least. She ended up marrying the artist who created this portrait. He was wealthy in his own right and was able to provide for Aunt Letitia in a very comfortable manner."

"No!"

"True story. Once she moved out of the house, she was a completely different person. Regard." Alexander points to another portrait several portraits away from the one we stand in front of. Walking over, I see a woman, beaming with pride and happiness, sitting with four children at her feet. I move closer for further inspection. It is indeed the same woman, years older, with what looks like a complete change of character.

"Amazing!"

"Isn't it? I guess that's what love does."

"I guess so."

I look down at my feet. Talking about love with a guy who's easily the most attractive man I've ever met suddenly makes me shy, and I search for words to change the topic. Alex beats me to it.

"Have you seen a portrait of the apparition you've seen in the house?"

Lifting my head, I meet Alex's kind eyes. "No. I've only seen her once. She looked as if she was about to speak to me, but, well, I admit she must have seen my terror, thought better of it, and continued doing whatever it was she was doing. She ended up just fading away."

"She tried communicating with you? Interesting. The ones I've seen are open to communication as well."

"Do you think they know they're dead?" I ask, really curious as to what his response will be.

"I don't think they *do* know. Your apparition tried communicating with you, and I, too, have experienced that.

Based on that fact alone, I would hypothesize that the apparitions do not have any notion that they are dead."

"Well, they aren't residual, so we're talking about intelligent hauntings."

"Yes. Yes, I guess we are. Strange. They are going through their daily routines, or what they think are their daily routines, when in reality, they are no longer alive. Think about it. You feel alive, right? You can feel your own pulse, feel the heat of your skin, think about all the memories you have stored away. Are you alive? Are you a ghost? It's something to ponder."

In addition to being genuinely curious, I wonder if Alex is asking me these questions partially because he doesn't know if I'm a ghost. Then again, maybe he seriously thinks I'm alive and am in what was his time. I have no idea what goes on inside the mind of a ghost. Instead of answering, I turn the tables. "What do you think time is like for them? Do you think they experience a day like we do, or do you think that certain moments are highlighted? And if that's the case, why?"

"You have given this more thought than I have, I must admit. For my family, ghosts have always been the standard. I grew up in this house and couldn't even tell you how old I was when I saw my first. Perhaps as an observer coming in, you are able to witness and think about things that we just take for granted now. A new and fresh pair of eyes, that's what you are, Emma, besides being exceptionally lovely."

Blushing, I bend my head. "Thank you. Those are pleasing words to hear, especially coming from a gentleman as dashing as yourself." I wonder if I'm being too forward. I'll have to do a search. Come to think of it, I have to look up Mr. Alexander Eason as well. He mentioned growing up here, which most likely means there is a journal with his name on it. And Hillfield Manor and the Easons are so well-known, there has to be something online. I'm almost tempted to ask him to come down to the library with me so I can look right away.

Alex smiles shyly before announcing he has to leave. "If it is all right with you, I would very much like to see you again. I noticed you weren't at dinner last night. Perhaps I'll see you there tonight?"

I think of some excuse off the top of my head. "Often at night, I find myself somewhat tired. I have taken to eating in my room."

He looks at me curiously. "That's right. You said you were here to convalesce." He pauses. "Is there anything I can do to make your stay more comfortable, Emma?"

"Alexander, you have entertained me with details of your family"—I indicate the portrait of Aunt Letitia—"you have given me food for thought, and you have been most pleasant company. I don't think you could do more."

"Shall we meet tomorrow? Perhaps we can have lunch together. We could meet at noon?"

I try to think through the ramifications of this. At best, James or Marie, or any of the others who stay to eat, would see Alexander, and although I don't need it, my encounters would be validated. At worst, well, I couldn't think of anything at the moment. "Noon tomorrow. The Great Hall?"

"Yes, that works splendidly. Until then, Emma." Alexander bows and swiftly walks out the door.

I let out a breath and rush to the door frame and peek around it. The faint *thunk*, *thunk*, *thunk* of a hammer can be heard in the distance along with a radio, but otherwise, it's quiet. There's no sound of receding footsteps; there's not even a trace of Alex. He's gone.

My heart pounds a little faster than normal thinking about him. *He's nice! And those eyes.* Curious, I pull out my phone, kept in a hidden pocket of the heavy skirt, and search for Alexander. I include Hillfield Manor and nineteenth century in the search, so I'm not bombarded with entries of other men with the same name. Nothing. I'm disappointed, but I also figure that if he didn't do anything major for his time, it's understandable he wouldn't be there. Plus, I still have a library of journals to search.

If Eve were here, she'd ask me—I freeze. Eve. How is it possible for her to have been out of my thoughts for so long? I inhale sharply and slowly let my breath out. This is a good thing. I know it is. I know my thoughts shouldn't be with her constantly. It's not healthy, but how come I feel so guilty when I find I haven't been thinking of her?

I try to steer my thoughts away from Eve and back to Alex, to the house and my work here. It doesn't work, not for long anyway, and since my phone is already out, I pull up some photos of us together and stare at her smiling face. I don't cry, and I try to see that as progress too, but there's a huge lump in my throat, so I shove the phone in my pocket, determined to push past the pain I feel.

I leisurely make my way down to my room, and my mind moves to Lucas. I hold on to the mental image I have of him when a spark of annoyance flares. This is good. I can work with irritation. And speaking of it, no one gets as angry as he got when I mentioned ghosts for no reason. There's definitely some animosity toward his aunt and uncle too. What's with that? They seem so sweet, so I find it hard to believe he feels he's owed an explanation—and an explanation for what? Why doesn't he just ask them? He wasn't afraid to express his opinions about anything. At the same time, there was something that he was hiding, and that's what intrigues me the most.

After I get out of the costume and put on my clothes from earlier, I walk out of my room, shaking my head in exasperation. I didn't come here to be bullied by a jackass or enthralled by a ghost. A ghost! I've never been the clichéd romantic type—not that I thought—but here I am, thinking about every detail I can remember, and ugh! I have to stop. The fact remains, he's dead. He's dead, and I'm alive. That's all there is to it.

Whenever I walk through the manor, I always go past the Great Hall in search of the woman. She hasn't been there each time I've looked, so I almost miss her this time when I glance over the room. Something in the corner is a bit distorted, and when I do a double take, her image becomes clearer to me.

Taking a deep breath, I move past the threshold and will her to turn around. She's just as transparent as she was the last time, but whereas I couldn't make out her clothing before, this time, I can tell she's wearing a dress, definitely twentieth century. My heart is pounding and my hands grip the sides of the long sweater I'm wearing as I wait, but she doesn't look my way. I move farther into the room.

"Hello," I say as I move into her peripheral vision.

She starts, her eyes wide as she turns, but when she sees me, her face lights up in a smile. Almost instantly, her smile fades, and she lifts her hands in a soothing gesture.

I grin. "I apologize. I wasn't expecting to see anyone here the last time, even though I've heard this place has a history of ghosts."

"Well, I warrant that's true," the woman responds, "seeing as I'm talking to one now."

I narrow my eyes as I take a step closer to her. "You see me as a ghost?"

"I don't see why that's so hard to believe since you see me as one too."

"I never said that."

The woman laughs. "You didn't have to. It was written clearly in the lines of fright on your face."

I feel my face turn red, but I chuckle as well. "You were the first ghost I've ever seen."

"I take it that's no longer the case."

"No. Where do you think I got the confidence to talk to you?"

The woman smiles again. "My name is Annie."

"It's nice to meet you, Annie. I'm Emma."

"So, Emma, why do you find it hard to believe that I see you as being just as transparent as you probably see me?"

"Because I'm not dead," I blurt, then slap my hand over my mouth.

Annie nods. "I'm not either. At least, not in the way you mean it. I've been at Hillfield for a few years now, and I've seen quite a few ghosts, so I've been able to think about this quite a bit. I believe the ghosts we see live in different times from us, and whereas they may be dead in our time, time for them is moving at its usual pace. They're living their lives, their real lives, just as we are."

I nod. It's what James suggested too. "There's no way you're a residual haunting or we wouldn't be having this conversation, but for the sake of your argument, what's the year for you?"

Annie smiles and says something, but I can't hear it. And as she talks, her face becomes even more transparent, so I can't make out her mouth clearly enough to read her lips. "You couldn't hear me, could you?" she says, her face coming into focus once again.

I frown and shake my head. "No, and I couldn't see you as well either."

"This isn't the first conversation like this I've had, and every time, it's the same. The face becomes blurred, and the voice loses volume. Perhaps we're not supposed to know. It adds to the mystery, don't you agree?"

"I—"

"I think we're out of time, Emma," Annie says, cutting me off. She's right. Even as she says my name, she's so transparent I have to squint to see her.

"Bye!" I say hastily, but I don't know if she hears me. She's gone.

"Emma? What's the matter?" Marie says, wiping her hands on a dingy cloth as she comes into the room. Her brows are lowered in concern. "I heard you call out."

"No, nothing. Sorry. I just talked to a ghost!"

"Well, now. It wasn't so bad, then, was it?"

"She was actually the ghost I was afraid of when you and James found me, but it was so cool! We were just standing there having a regular conversation about ghosts."

"You talked about ghosts?"

"Yeah." I go on to tell Marie about Annie and what we discussed.

"Interesting. For me, a few, but not many, have the wherewithal to even go that deep into a conversation, but as far as finding out *when* they're from, that has been my experience as well. Sometimes you get little clues based on what people are wearing, but that doesn't happen regularly. Anyway, I'm proud of you."

"Thank you!"

"Have you worn the clothes? You have to wear that dress you showed me. It's gorgeous and would look fantastic on you."

I grin, tempted to tell her about my experiences with Alex. For now, though, I want to keep him to myself.

Instead, I only tell her that I've worn the dress and will try to find her the next time I try it on, and I finish by saying, "I love it. If they decide to open this place up to tours again, I might ask to be one of the guides."

Although it has been two weeks, I haven't seen Annie again. Alexander, on the other hand, showed up the next day in the Long Gallery—three hours *after* the lunch we were supposed to have. From that day, there hasn't been a day that has gone by where we don't talk. It's more than a touch disconcerting how drawn I am to him. He understands my sarcasm, listens to my words, speaks intelligently about every subject we touch upon, and of course, there is the way he looks, both physically and *physically*. I can't get over the fact that he appears so much more solid than Annie. Sometimes, I feel like it would be nothing to place my hand on his arm, but whenever we get close, there is that strange tingling sensation, and one of us pulls away.

"What do you think it is, Emma, that causes this sensation that overcomes me whenever I'm close to you? Do you feel it as well?" he asked one day.

I didn't know what to say. "It is strange, isn't it?" I moved my hand closer to his without touching him. I could feel the electricity, and I was half tempted to just go for it, touch him, and see if the spider web feeling would happen. I stopped myself, though. I don't think a woman from the nineteenth century would have done such a thing without being considered too forward.

If he noticed, he made no indication.

Alexander acts very much like a nineteenth-century gentleman I've imagined from novels by Jane Austen and others, the way he speaks, his manner, his little courtesies, but I always come back to wondering whether he sees me as a living person or as someone truly dead. In addition to conversing with me without a chaperone and calling me by my first name, he'll do something or say something totally out of keeping with nineteenth-century behavior.

But just yesterday, he gave me an indication of his thoughts on my existence. We were talking about our childhoods.

"I find myself wanting to know all about you. What were you like as a little girl?" he asked. We were, once again, in the Long Gallery among all the portraits and landscapes on the walls. Light filtered through the long windows, making his somewhat solid appearance even more hazy.

"I'm sure I was similar to other little girls," I said, keeping my answer light.

"Do you have any siblings?"

"Yes, a sister. Evelyn. My family calls her Eve. She died earlier this year."

Alex hesitated, then said, "Yes, well, losing a family member, especially one so close, is difficult, but we all must put one step in front of the other." His words were not said without compassion, but the brusqueness struck me as odd, especially when he followed with, "Your parents, are they living still?"

"Yes."

He nodded absently and clasped his hands behind his back.

"Alex?" I asked, confused by his demeanor. "Is there something wrong?"

"Hmm?" His focus sharpened on me, and he shook his head. "Oh, no, Emma. Not at all. I only worry about you."

"About me? You worry about me?"

He nodded. "Yes, your enjoyment here at Hillfield. I just want it to be as carefree and content as possible as you convalesce. I cannot stand the thought of you not enjoying your time since you were invited to stay with . . . us."

I quickly ran through our conversation up to that point. We had been talking about Eve's death, and I had already mentioned I was here to convalesce. I wondered if he possibly thought that I, too, was dying. "I'm sorry," I said, mortified. "I didn't mean to make you uncomfortable."

"Uncomfortable?" He laughed, a gentle and welcoming sound that nearly provoked me to relax and smile. But I didn't. There was something in his eyes that suggested he wanted to say more. I tipped my head, willing him to continue. "No. I'm sorry for my behavior. It's just . . ." He paused, staring at me intently, his gaze lingering on my lips for a moment before meeting my eyes once more. "There are so many things I wish I could say."

He regarded me for a moment more before a look of alarm came over his face. "Oh, we've run out of time," Alexander said. "I mean, I'm sorry, but I, uh, I have an appointment." He was already backing up, and it was only then I noticed he was beginning to fade.

"Tomorrow?" he asked, but he didn't stay for an answer. He had already disappeared.

It was at that moment I knew. *He* knew. He had to know. The way the look of alarm came over his face, he must have seen, sooner than I did with him, that I was fading. I gave him the impression that I'm here because I'm sick or recovering from a sickness—after all, how many people would come right out and say they were dying to a new acquaintance? He said he was worried about me and my happiness.

Once I got to my room, I dropped onto my bed and covered my mouth with my hand, attempting to hide the giddy smile on my face. If I was a betting woman, I would say that Mr. Alexander Eason cared about me, at least a little. Even if he thought *I* was the one who was the ghost.

Chapter 8

All the shelves are empty of books. Finally. It has been weeks of sorting and indexing, but now, papers and books are stacked in piles on the tables, with notes and markers scattered around them. The walls have shelves that are now empty and clean, and, even if it's my own thinking, there is a satisfying feeling of accomplishment in the air.

Most of the journals have been placed in the adjacent room where they will be permanently placed once they are done being copied, but some of them line a library cart that sits next to me. Alex's. Once I found them, it seemed to take all my strength not to read them right there, but instead, I dangled them in front of me like a carrot, my motivation to finish indexing and sorting. A celebratory treat.

In some ways, I feel like I'm invading his privacy, like I should ask him for his permission to read his private thoughts. At the same time, no matter how much he's alive while I talk to him, he's been dead for hundreds of years, and there's nothing I can do to change that.

It's a sobering thought. Alex has been a highlight in my days here at Hillfield. But he's also been my buffer against others. I sometimes eat lunch with the workers while they're here, and more often than not, I've had dinner with Marie and James, but it's like I've erected this wall to keep them at a distance. Our conversations have always been pleasant, but it's like I'm trying to hold back from feeling too much, from getting too close. That's not the case with Alex. It's completely messed up, but I keep telling myself that since he's already dead, there's nothing to lose. I tell myself that talking to him is more like talking to a figment of my imagination. And as far as anyone outside of Hillfield is concerned, that's all he'll ever be. And perhaps because he's dead, I'm more at ease. I know nothing can happen to him. He's here, two hundred years later, and he'll be here after I'm gone too.

I pick up a journal off the cart and open it, savoring the moment as the words on the yellowed pages come alive before my eyes. The words may be old and faded, but his feelings are crisp and fresh. He writes about his life, his friends, and his dreams with a passion I can't help but admire. As I read through his writings, I find myself drawn into his world—even if it's only for a few moments—and I feel connected to him in a way I can't explain. I smile to myself, not in happiness, but in understanding. I understand what it's like to be lonely, to desire companionship, and to feel lost in a world full of people.

But then an entry makes me stop short.

Women are the silliest creatures known to man. Thank God they have pleasing forms and pretty faces, or mankind would be doomed, for men would surely have nothing to do with them. Take, for example, the woman I met today. She was most enchanting—save for when she opened her mouth. She regaled me with absolute rubbish about something or another. I, being the gentleman that I am, nodded sympathetically—I even graciously agreed with the twit—but when I endeavored to ask questions with the sole intention of allowing her to see the absurdity of her words, she got most upset.

Frowning, I look up from the journal. This entry sounds nothing like the Alex I know at all, and I skim through the next couple of pages, willing to give him the benefit of the doubt when another entry catches my eye.

Thank God my brother will become the next Lord Eason, Viscount of Hillfield, as I have no desire to take on the tedious burdens of the estate; however, as the second son, I am fastidiously encouraged to consort with the exquisite ladies of the peerage, to which I have no qualms. There are many things a "lady" will do when her eye is on one's name and wallet, and who am I to get in the way of her pursuit? No, I simply need not be compromised, for there's too much fun to be had.

I close the journal with more force than I should but less than I want to. Shucking the white gloves, I stand and stalk around the room, trying to reconcile the man I've encountered and spoken with to the one who wrote the entries. How could he be so thoroughly deceptive? Should I confront him about it? But then he'd know I read his journal.

Huffing, I stand next to the window and look out into the garden. Alex always seems interested in what I have to say, but then, maybe him believing me to be a ghost has something to do with it. He doesn't have to worry about his family's money or being compromised, but that comment about women being silly creatures with nothing in our heads . . . That just wasn't Alex.

Turning back to the room, I jump when I see the hazy outline of a figure. There have been more than a few times when this has happened here, and it always takes me a second or two to acclimate myself to the Hillfield

Manor way of life. My hand goes up to my chest as if its pressure can slow down the racing of my heart.

"Annie?"

The figure turns, and sure enough, Annie's smile greets me before her words. "Emma! I was wondering if you would be in here. I was just finished cleaning and on my way out. Have you been here the whole time?"

"I've been in here for a while, yes. It's so weird that we can both be in the same room without even knowing it until, all of a sudden, there you are."

She nods, smiling. "How have you been? What does it look like in here to you?"

"I'm good, thanks. All the books are off the shelves now," I say, my eyes scanning the room. "There are piles on the floor, piles on a few tables we've brought in—"

"Who are you talking to?" Lucas interrupts. He leans against the doorframe, a scowl on his face.

I glance at Annie and silently apologize for Lucas's rudeness.

"Annie, this is Lucas. He's been working here for the past week. Lucas, this is Annie. She works, worked, will work—I don't know—here too." Annie chuckles, but when I look at Lucas, his scowl is even darker. "She asked what the room looks like now. I imagine all the shelves are still fully loaded in your time," I say, taking my eyes off Lucas and focusing once more on Annie.

"Filled with all sorts of books and trinkets and journals. It's starting to become an eyesore, but short of a light dusting, staff have been told not to touch anything on the shelves."

I nod. With the journals and rare novels, it's understandable the Easons wouldn't want many people perusing the books. I'm about to respond when Lucas bangs on the door.

"Oh, cut the shit," he growls, his face mottled red. "What, did Marie put you up to this? It's not enough to have to watch her pretend she can see people who aren't there, but now she's got you doing it too?"

My eyes widen in surprise at his outburst and then narrow. "You really can't see her?" Annie stands next to me, focused on Lucas. She raises her hands in front of her and moves them up and down to get his attention, but if Lucas is aware of her actions, he hides it well.

Lucas grips the bridge of his nose with his fingers and lets out a long sigh. "Look, if you're trying to charm me with this"—he points a finger at me, which moves up and down to include my whole frame—"performance of yours, save it for the tours, and if you really think you're seeing ghosts, I'm going to tell you the same thing I told Marie: Get your head examined. There's no such thing, here or anywhere else."

He gives me one final look of disgust, then turns on his heels and stomps out of the room.

"He's an unpleasant fellow."

"You can say that again." I nod in the direction he took. "I'm sorry about that."

"There's absolutely no reason for *you* to apologize. He, on the other hand, could take some lessons." She snorts. "There are many who can't see what you and I can, but there's no need to be rude." Annie grimaces and then wipes her hands as if they, too, were tainted by Lucas's attitude.

I smile. "Well, I guess my break is over," I say as she starts to fade. "I hope to see you again."

"I believe we shall, sooner or later, Emma."

I reach for the white gloves once more when she has faded completely, slipping them on and reaching for Alex's journal. Sighing, I carefully pull back the cover, this time propping it open with a weighted book marker so I can begin copying. And as I type, I can't help thinking about Alex and wondering what it means that he is so different from the man emerging from his written account. I keep telling myself I shouldn't feel anything. What's the point? But it doesn't stop the dull thud of my heart or the disappointment coursing through me.

Chapter 9

*. . . **Take, for example, the woman** I met today. She was most enchanting—save for when she opened her mouth. She regaled me with absolute rubbish about something or another. I, being the gentleman that I am, nodded sympathetically—I even graciously agreed with the twit—but when I endeavored to ask questions with the sole intention of allowing her to see the absurdity of her words, she got most upset.*

Alexander Eason—1797
Eason Family Estate Library

I look up from Alexander's journal with a huff. A second reading has done nothing to improve upon the ugly words, and then I realize the entry just so happens to be the date, save the year, I met him in the room next to the chapel.

Is this really how he feels? Was I so drawn by the appeal of ghosts—not to mention the way he looked—that I let his condescension and misogyny go over my head? He had asked me why I thought I had seen a ghost. Had that been his "attempt" at illustrating the "absurdity" of my words? I push back from the desk, tempted to chuck the journal across the room. It would serve him right if I found him and "attempted" to punch him in the nose. He'd see the "absurdity" of my claims then when my fist went—literally—right through his face!

The alarm on my phone jangles loudly from the desk, and I swipe my finger on the screen to silence its shrill sound. I'm supposed to meet him in the conservatory and set my alarm to give me enough time to get ready, but I'm having second thoughts now. All this time, he has been playing me for a fool, and I don't know if I can look at him, knowing what he actually thinks of me. On one hand, despite my anger and hurt, there's a niggling guilt too. After all, I've been honest about *who* I am, but I haven't been honest about *when.* On the other hand, in a way, I'm almost glad. We're both lying, and the way I see it, my little deception isn't nearly as bad as the lies he's been consciously uttering.

Standing, I put everything away in a hurry, lock the library, and make my way up to my room to change into one of the period dresses.

My mind is running with the possibilities ahead of me, of what I might find out when I meet him in the conservatory and confront him. I take a deep breath, steeling myself for whatever may come. My fingers are clumsy as I fumble with the zipper on the side. Part of my lie. The prospect of what I have to face weighs heavily on me, but I have to find out the truth so I can stop thinking about him so much. Maybe he has a good explanation, and as I rush out of my room after checking my reflection in the mirror, I find that I hope he does, even if I can't imagine what it could be.

"I was looking in the library for a good book to read and came across several journals," I say. It has taken me ten minutes to work up the nerve to say anything after meeting with Alex, but I don't think I'll be able to sleep tonight if we don't get this out in the open.

"Yes, we Easons love our journals," Alex says wryly, his jaw clenching.

"Oh? You keep a journal too?" I ask innocently enough. "Tell me, what sort of things do you write about?"

"Well, most of my journals are filled with everyday occurrences that I think are important for me to remember. But there are also some more personal things in it—stories about my family, old tales from when I was young, things that only happened once . . . They're not written down anywhere else." His voice trails off as he remembers the entries in his worn-out journal full of secrets he's kept hidden away for so long.

I interrupt his reverie. "Tell me more about you. What sort of things do you write?"

Breathing deeply, Alex begins to recount the contents of his journal. He tells me about how alone he had felt growing up and how everyone seemed to be caught up in their own drama, leaving him feeling abandoned and neglected. He speaks about how his journal provides a space for him to feel seen and heard, like someone is finally listening without judgment or interruption.

He sounds so . . . sincere.

Doubt surges through me, and I can feel my blood racing with indecision. His words are so contrary to what's in the journal that I can only stare at him, my mouth agape. How can he stand there, knowing what he's telling me is completely false? Yet his tone and facial expression, soft with what seems to be real memories, tell me that everything he says, this elaborate construction of lies he has built before my very eyes, is actually true.

I can't contain myself as I confront him. "How can you do that?" My voice is filled with disappointment. "I read your journal. I'm sorry. It was a breach of trust on my part, but how can you stand there and tell me things that are so completely different from what you wrote?"

Alex remains silent, his face pale and his brow furrowed. He stares ahead for a few seconds, his eyes darting back and forth as if searching for the truth himself before finally turning to me, his face solemn and filled with regret.

"Emma," he begins softly, "I'm sorry for lying to you about what was in the journal." He bows his head slightly and hesitates. "But I thought it would be easier if I just—"

"Told me what I wanted to hear?" I can't contain the fury that has been bubbling up inside me any longer. "What's wrong with you?" I spit out, flames practically leaping from my eyes.

Alex seems surprised by my outburst, but I don't have time for his confusion; I'm too filled with my own. I liked Alex. I genuinely liked him; I still do, despite the two different sides he seems to have, and I don't know how that fits into the whole dead/alive paradox that just seems to be the icing on the cake.

I take a couple of steps back, willing myself to turn away from him, making this the last time I see him if I can help it.

"I'm sorry," he says, his voice almost a whisper. He looks at me pleadingly; his eyes full of regret and sadness as he searches for understanding in mine.

Despite how frustrated and angry I feel, my heart softens at this heartfelt admission, and instead of continuing our heated exchange, I shake my head and let out the breath I've been holding. Who is Mr. Alexander Eason? There has to be another way to find answers.

He hesitates, a thousand words swimming in his eyes that he refuses to say, before asking, "Do you want to talk about it?"

There are still too many unknowns, and until I have more answers, it's probably best if I just leave. "I don't think so."

"You can talk to me." He looks at me with sadness in his eyes.

"I know."

"You don't have to be so guarded. I'm your friend, remember?"

I watch him for a moment as he thinks about what he is going to say next. "It's easier for you than it is for me."

"What do you mean?" I ask, indignation and curiosity warring in my head.

He lets out a frustrated sigh. “I can’t explain it.” He shakes his head. “No, I’m not willing to explain it. Not to you.”

“Because I’m a woman?” I ask hesitantly, wondering whether I should use the words “twit” or “silly creature” instead.

He huffs. “Because you’re a woman, you might understand it better.”

“What’s that supposed to mean?”

“I mean no offense, Emma.”

Chapter 10

While I may not have faith in my ability to determine what's true and what's fiction regarding Alex, there is, however, the family Bible. I remember taking a look at it because it held a place of prominence on one of the shelves. It alone was placed on a small pedestal, and the area around it was relatively clean, meaning books weren't actually crammed right up next to it, although they came close.

Right now, it sits on a small table in the room next to the library yet separated by a secret entry, and that's exactly where I head.

The Bible dates back to when the original Easons owned the manor. In varying handwriting styles and degrees of neatness, the names and dates of the births and deaths of each Eason are recorded, as are the dates of marriages, from the first marriage in 1788 to the last entry made in 1950. It seems the latter Easons didn't stand so much on ceremony. That, or it could be because there's no room left. The first entry started on the front endpaper. Once names and dates had filled that, the entries continued onto the back paper. There was maybe a quarter inch of space remaining.

The years 1738 through 1767 yield no results for any Alexander. Then, there it is: *Alexander Jonathan Thomas Eason: March 23, 1768–May 21, 1798. Apoplexy.* I almost drop the Bible. He died when he was only thirty. Alex looks like he is nearing thirty now. And if he is, and he's not a ghost in the traditional sense but is actually living his life concurrently to mine, that means his death is coming up soon. May 21 isn't even a week away. I think about the man who, with me at least, seems—*seems*—to be filled with such vitality and warmth, albeit somewhat shy. To be cut down in his prime! I've not known him long, but upon finding out, I suddenly feel like I want to cry.

So many people want to know about the major events in their lives, and I wonder if Alex is one of them. Here I am, able to tell him about his own death, but since he's already dead, there's nothing he can do to save himself. It almost hurts my head to think about it because, when it comes right down to it, it doesn't seem to make sense.

Setting the Bible down, I move over to the desk where I have a dictionary and look up "apoplexy." I've heard the word before in terms of being angry but don't understand how someone can die from it. It sounds like some kind of fit, but if Alexander died from it, I want to know what it was, if he suffered.

The first listing states "cerebral hemorrhage or stroke" as the definition. It doesn't give me much to go on at all. What causes it? Is it something external like getting kicked by a horse, or is it something that just happens?

I sit back and rub my forehead. I can feel a headache coming on. I shouldn't have looked up the information. It's not as if I can do anything about it anyway. I'm thinking about a ghost . . . and, what is to me, the anniversary of said ghost's death. All I can do is shake my head, mourn a man who died too young, and wonder what will happen next week on May 21.

Between our last conversation and tonight, the eve of Alex's death, I'm ashamed to say I avoided him. It's a mix of reasons and excuses I've made to myself. I was still upset with him, wondering which Alex I should trust, the man who made me laugh and engaged me in interesting conversations or the one whose words were cruel and crude. There were several times that I told myself to confront him once more, tell him the truth about my situation—when I was from—as if that would somehow make everything better. If anything, though, it would only make me feel better about my actions. He would still be the same man who showed one face to me and another to the world in which he lived.

I thought about Eve too. Had I known she was going to die, knowing I could do nothing to stop it, I would have spent every moment with her. I would never have another chance afterward. But with Alex, it's like if I can avoid seeing him, then it'll be just another day. He's dead; he's a ghost, and he'll still be here. I don't know how I feel about that. There's jealousy, envy, but I'm also relieved. I'll still have him.

A couple of days after I confronted Alex about the journal, Marie finds me sitting on a window seat in one of the freshly made-up parlors, staring out at nothing in particular.

"Emma."

I turn, startled. I didn't hear her come in. "Oh, hi, Marie."

She comes over and sits beside me, extending her legs in front of her. "I love my job; I do, but I think James and I are going to have to start taking on smaller projects." A joint pops as she leans over to stretch. She sighs. "And how have you been doing? Have any big plans for this weekend? You're going home, aren't you?"

I smile. "Yeah, a few of us are going to hang out and watch movies."

"Aren't you supposed to be going out clubbing? I remember going out every weekend. Oh, to be young again." She sighs again as she straightens.

Shaking my head, I look down. "No, I don't really feel like dressing up to go out, and my friend Sarah just broke up with her boyfriend of six months, so we're going to get a bunch of junk food and bash men while we watch rom-coms." I look up, a sheepish grin on my face.

"Are you having any problems yourself? You've seemed a little down the last few times I've seen you. James and I have both missed you at dinner the last few nights."

As if she's just given me permission to unload, I tell her everything. I tell her about meeting Alex and how great he's been, and although I don't mention what he said in his journal, I tell her about the huge difference I see between his words and his actions. I also tell her about finding out about his death and my thoughts of Eve, and by the end, I feel worn out and like a huge burden has been lifted.

We sit in silence for a few minutes. Then Marie stands. "I think maybe all isn't what it seems," she says at last. "I think you have to trust what you see and how you feel." She crosses her arms and looks down at me. "Which one do you believe him to be?"

I shake my head. "I really don't know how he can be the man who wrote such awful things."

"Then he's not."

"But I saw the words with my own eyes!"

Marie nods and shrugs. "We see lots of things here with our own eyes that other people would swear don't exist." She shrugs again. "Just keep that in mind."

She pats my shoulder. "That comment I made about being young again? I take that back," she says with a smile, "but I could probably do with a good massage every once in a while."

Marie walks to the door and turns to face me. "It'll all work out, Emma. I have a feeling." Then she waves her fingers at me and leaves.

And so here we are on the eve of his death. Alex and I are sitting together on a window seat in one of the rooms on the ground floor. It's one of the smaller rooms just off the Great Hall.

"Is it too forward of me to say I've missed you?" he asks as he smiles at me shyly.

I've missed him too! I shake my head. "I'm sorry, again, about reading your journal," I say. "I guess I've been avoiding you, partly because of what I've read and partly because . . . well, it doesn't matter."

He frowns. "I've wanted to talk to you about that. Emma, I went into the library after we talked and looked for my journals. I was afraid someone had found them, but they're not there. In fact, I've made a point *not* to keep my journals in the library. My mother has, on more than one occasion, tried to pry into my private affairs, so I learned early on that the best course of action was to leave nothing where she could—innocently, of course—find them."

Now it's my turn to frown. How could that be? His name was clearly on the cover of three of the journals. "Really? I could have sworn I saw your name."

He opens his mouth to say something but thinks better of it and closes it once again as he rubs his face tiredly with his hand.

That's when I truly look at him. He appears exhausted, his hair is mussed, and his coat is disheveled. My heart shutters and I wonder what I should do. Should I tell him about his impending death? How does one stop apoplexy? "Are you feeling okay?"

"Yes, I'm just tired is all, and I have an awful headache. I should probably try to take something for it."

A gasp escapes my lips. Is that how it starts? After I looked up apoplexy and found little to go on, I researched some more. The amount of information I found was minimal at best. According to one source, it was "bleeding within internal organs." Another said it was a "brain hemorrhage." Without knowing what to look for or what it is I should tell Alexander to look for, all I have is my word that it would happen, and that isn't nearly enough to go on.

I couldn't find anything about precautions to take or treatments to give. And now, for the second time in my life, I wish I was a doctor. "Do you have any other symptoms?"

Alex's brow furrows. "Symptoms? Are you a physician now?" He smiles and closes his eyes as he puts his head back, appearing to rest it on a cushion I can't see. It's another sign of how unwell he is. He's never once before given any hint that his surroundings weren't exactly the same as my own. "Why, yes m'lady. I've noticed a bit of nausea as well. Tell me, am I going to die?" Alex snorts and then winces in pain.

I swallow the sob in my throat and quickly look away so he won't see the truth in my eyes. I need to tell him. Steeling myself, I mumble, "You die on May twenty-first. Tomorrow." Silence ensues and I turn, expecting to meet his shocked stare, but Alex is gone.

Did he hear me? And if so, would it make a difference?

Chapter 11

The sun may be shining, but when I wake up this morning, it's with a feeling of dread. Even before being fully aware that I am awake, I know in my gut I don't want to leave the sanctity of comfort in which I lie. Today is the day. I knew it was coming, but now that it's here, I don't know how I'll face it.

Last night, after Alex disappeared, I gave the whole thing a little more thought. If ghosts are just dead people, then I'll see Alex again because he's dead—obviously. But if, as a ghost, he's actually just living his life in his time, then, when he dies in his life, would he still be a ghost that I could see or would he move on?

I fold myself into the fetal position and huddle under the covers for a warmth that seems to evade me.

My eyes closed, I struggle to regulate my breathing and pull myself together. I try to think about work, what I have planned for the day. I'm not too worried about getting behind, and at the moment, I don't care.

Scrunching up into an even tighter ball, I tell myself that perhaps my meeting with him had altered the course of history. It's foolish. If meeting me had altered his timeline, then there would be no record of his death . . . unless I was the one who had somehow brought on the course of his death. I shake my head, trying to rid myself of such thoughts. I can't physically interact with him, so there is no way that I could interfere one way or the other. But if he heard what I said before he disappeared . . .

Sighing heavily, I stretch out, becoming straight as a board before again curling. I probably look like one of those potato bugs. Fumbling for my phone, I check the hour. I should be able to get in a few hours of work, if I can concentrate, before—my heart skips—meeting Alex for lunch.

I wait anxiously for his arrival. We said we would meet at noon and have lunch together on one of the window seats on the landing of the main staircase. Homecomings has done superior work here. When I arrived, the oak appeared dull and lifeless, an almost grayish-silver tinge cast over any part that had been exposed to the sun through the glass windows at the staircase landing. Steve and Brenna, who have both since gone on to other jobs, liberally applied some sort of gel to every wooden surface and then painstakingly scrubbed every inch to get it to its original natural hue. Afterward, a wood preservative was used and then later, the wood was polished so it gleamed.

The seven-foot wide, five-foot high window next to which I sit took some time as well. Inlaid with stained glass and iron, each piece, sometimes as small as an inch, had to be carefully wiped and cleaned until each section sparkled once again. Now finished, it's a dazzling sight to behold. The center panel depicts the Eason family coat of arms. On either side, beautiful geometric designs utilizing clear and colored glass are used. I stare at them, wondering about the men who shaped each piece, wondering about whether they ever really thought about the legacy they left behind.

Looking at my watch yet again, I'm not surprised to see a half hour has passed. The staircase and window are beautiful and awe-inspiring, but they're not enough to keep my mind from wandering to thoughts of Alex. I wonder what the days will be like without his presence, and my stomach clenches with unhappiness. So many rooms now contain a memory of him for me. My throat tightens, so, to stop myself from getting too emotional, I think about facts. I mentally go through a list of all I know about him. I know his name and age. I know he is a member of the Eason family. I know he likes the outdoors, and he enjoys sunsets. I know he had an older brother, and I know I liked talking to him. I liked how he seemed to hang on to every word I said. I knew he raked his hand through his hair whenever he was flustered or upset. I liked how he made me feel . . . and then I realize my "knows" and "likes" have become past tense "knew" and "liked," and I find myself crying.

He's dead now, a man I couldn't possibly hope to have in my time, yet I mourn for him, the man that I never even had the chance to properly meet.

Once again, I look at the time on my watch. It's after one. I pace, feeling numb, like I did in the hours after Eve's death. Maybe this is just one of those times when he doesn't appear. Maybe if I just go about my business, he'll appear again. It's the same illogical thoughts I had with Eve. *If I just go home, she'll be there; if I just go to sleep, I'll wake up and realize it was just a nightmare.*

It may be illogical, but in this case, it's a possibility too, isn't it? It's the only hope I have, and it's the only thing that keeps me from breaking down completely.

Chapter 12

***What if time is a** concept we've been thinking about all wrong? Her name is Marie. We've now had more than one conversation, and each time, I take extreme caution to not mention the date. I have an unnerving feeling that if I were to declare the year, she would realize the impossibility and fade from my eyes, forever lost to me from this day forward. All the same, I've made subtle inquiries as to her existence. The way she walks about the rooms freely suggests she was a frequent guest or perhaps a relative of the former owners. And as far as time, is it possible, from her interactions with me, that she is not dead at all, but living a full life in another time? Sometimes, the expressions she utters are unfamiliar yet make complete sense. And the way she comports herself is strange for a* *lady of breeding, yet it's obvious from our discussions that she's had education. I don't know what to think.*

—Bartholomew Eason, 1878
Eason Family Estate Library

I've launched myself into my work, trying to do anything that will stop me from thinking about Alex. Marie told me to trust my feelings about him, and now I have this massive regret that I didn't tell him I believed him about his journal. I don't know what's going on there, but there has to be an explanation, and if I could just talk to him again, maybe there would be a way to figure it all out.

It has been three days since the date of his death, and I haven't seen him. I've even resorted to wearing period dresses all day and roaming the rooms and halls whenever I take a break, on the chance I'll see him. I've become the new gray lady of Hillfield Manor, only this time in the flesh. I've had more than one odd stare from others working on the house, but I don't care. I'm losing hope I'll ever see him again, and it hurts.

"So, not only are you hiding away from the world, but now you're dressing like you've been dead and buried for a couple hundred years too," Lucas says as he sails into the room. I hastily wipe a tear from my cheek and continue typing.

"What do you want, Lucas? Do you ever think that maybe I stay in here because it's less likely I'll run into you?"

"Ouch," he says, but he's smiling. "I'm going to let that one go, though, because I've missed you."

I haven't seen Lucas since our first meeting, but I know from Marie and James that he's been around. I figured the feeling between the two of us was mutual, so his appearance now makes me suspicious. "What do you want?" I ask.

"Nothing. I haven't seen you, thought maybe you'd left because the boredom got to you." He saunters over and picks up a journal, thumbing through it. Closing the one I'm working on, I stand and take the journal from him. "I guess I was mistaken," he says.

"Yup." I'm not up to trading insults with Lucas at the moment, so I pick up a couple of the journals near him and turn away, placing them on a library cart out of his reach.

"So, have you found anything interesting?"

I look at him, confused. "What?"

"In the journals. You were so adamant about how fascinating it was to read the words of people who have long been dead. I'm just wondering if you've found anything interesting." He moves over to the desk and picks up the one I've been working on, causing the place marker to fall. "Take this one, for example." He opens the cover.

"Mr. Bartholomew James Eason," he says, squinting at the faded cursive writing. "What does he have to say?"

I march over to him and hold out my hand. "I told you before, I signed—"

"A confidentiality agreement. Yeah, yeah, I know." He hands over the journal. "But don't you want to talk to someone about it? I know I would. I'd want—" His eyes narrow and he moves closer to me. "Have you been crying?"

I jerk my head back and turn away from him, kneeling in front of the library cart in a show of straightening the journals on it. "No."

He lets out a soft laugh. "Don't tell me you're getting sentimental over something some centuries-old dead guy wrote?"

Some centuries-old dead guy. I know he's speaking of Bartholomew, but an image of Alex comes to my mind and a fresh wave of tears threatens to fall. Alex wasn't just some centuries-old dead guy to me.

I hastily swipe my eyes. "Damn it, Lucas!" I fume as I stand to face him. "Will you just tell me what you want and then get the hell out of here?" I take a deep breath, trying to control my emotions. My anger at Lucas isn't justified, I know, but I can't help lashing out at him, his words too close to the truth.

"Hey." Lucas grips my shoulder with one hand, and he uses the other to tilt my chin up, turning my head from side to side. "Emma, I was just joking." There's concern in his eyes, and he pulls me over to the chair at the desk and pushes me down onto it. "Do you want to talk about it? Despite what you might think, I'm a good listener, I promise," he says, crossing his heart and giving me a small smile.

I close my eyes, embarrassed to be seen crying by Lucas, of all people, then I shake my head and open my eyes once again. "I'm fine, just tired," I lie. I don't trust Lucas as far as I can throw him, and the fact that he doesn't even believe in the ghosts so clearly walking within the walls of Hillfield Manor makes starting a conversation about it pointless.

Lucas shifts a few of the journals on the desk, clearing a spot, and perches on the edge, looking down at me. "Are you sure that's all it is?"

Leaning forward, I put my head in my hands and sigh. "Look, Lucas, I appreciate the concern. Really. I didn't expect it from you." I sit back once more and look up at him. "But I don't want to talk about it, okay?"

He pulls his bottom lip between his teeth and nods slowly. Standing, he clears his throat. "Okay. I guess I'll get going then," he says. "Unless you want to go grab some lunch?"

That makes me laugh. "No."

Smiling, he walks backward toward the door, but he pauses in the middle of turning away. "So, we can go back to having animosity between us? This . . . moment isn't going to ruin what we've got going?"

"Just leave," I say with a wry grin.

"Because you had me worried there for a second. I thought I was going to have to—"

"Leave!" I shout, but there's no heat.

"Tootles," Lucas says before giving me another grin and walking out the door.

Although I enjoy the job, I'm starting to wonder if leaving Hillfield Manor would be best. If I stay here, I'll continue to wonder about Alex, wonder if he'll ever come back, and that would be worse than coming to terms with Eve. I can't live that way. I have maybe six months more of work if I really apply myself and possibly work overtime.

No.

I'll finish the job and then leave. If they offer me the estate manager and tour guide job I applied for, I'll turn it down. After all, I highly doubt the owner will welcome me in with open arms to make googly eyes at long-dead ancestors. *In the future*, I admonish myself, *don't fall for a dead guy. Lesson learned.* I have to put the past in the past. I almost laugh at the irony.

Looking up, I blink and then blink again. I can't breathe, and I swear my heart stops for a second before hammering in my chest. Alex. His familiar form, close to, but not quite solid, is across from me.

It takes a moment for him to see me, and when he does, I launch myself at him, realizing too late that he won't be able to catch me.

Practically flying through the air, I feel myself pass through him, the sticky spider web sensation stronger than ever. I close my eyes against my inevitable fall and grimace before any pain comes as I catch myself with my arm instead of falling face first into the, thankfully, cold hearth.

Hobbling toward me, his face filled with concern but more with amusement, he bends down so we are more or less eye to eye.

"Are you okay?" He reaches out as if to help but swiftly pulls back his hand and lays it on his thigh.

I take in the image of the man I was beginning to believe I would never see again, my eyes raking over him, relishing in the knowledge that he is still here, that I can still see him. I didn't realize how much he had come to mean to me until he was gone, a fact I should have learned from Eve, and now it's as if I've been given a new chance.

Still disoriented by the change of events, all I can do is stare. And that's when I see what I failed to notice at first.

"Emma? Emma? Are you all right? Talk to me."

"Yes, yes. I'm fine. But I have a better question." I regard the man I thought I would never see again with curiosity.

"What's that?"

"What are you wearing?"

Chapter 13

Truly looking at him, it's so blatantly obvious that I'm surprised I didn't catch it before throwing myself at him. His hazy form is clad in a white T-shirt, layered with an oversized blue and green flannel shirt and jeans. The jeans are ripped at the thigh and knee on the left side and completely torn off at the knee on his right leg to accommodate a massive cast that goes from the middle of his foot to halfway up his calf. Alex is *not* from the nineteenth century.

Alex looks down at himself and swears under his breath. "Uh, yes. About that. Um, Emma, I have something to tell you that you might not understand." Other than the night I thought he died, Alex always sat on furniture that has been in both our times—one of the heavy wooden benches in the Great Hall or on a window seat in one of the other rooms—but now, he straightens slowly and makes his way to what must be a couch or chair. To me, it looks like he's hovering in the air, and other than his hazy appearance, it's the most ghost-like thing I've ever seen him do.

"Alex? What is it?" I ask with exaggerated alarm, deciding to have some fun. "What's on your leg? And why are you wearing those . . . those rags?"

"I . . . Emma, I need to tell you something." He stands up and walks over to the mantel, taps the magnificent oak ledge lightly several times, and then rakes his fingers through his hair. Finally, he looks at me. "What year do you think it is?"

"Year?" Until now, I *thought* Alex had died in 1798, so I decide to use that. "Alex, you're scaring me. It's 1798. Did you hit your head?"

"No, no. I didn't hit my . . ." His voice fades as his eyes dart around the room, searching for someone or something to help him with his explanation. Exasperated, he shakes his head. He glances around the room again, and this time, I can almost see his mind working, probably thinking along the same lines I thought when I wondered if I should tell him about his death.

"Alex," I say, ready to put him out of his misery, "*when* are you from?"

His head jerks up and he eyes me with wonder. "1993," he says without hesitation.

And now it's my turn to be fascinated. I can do nothing but stare. Not only do I hear him say the year, something Annie said was impossible, but it's my timeline. I was a baby in Michigan at the same time Alex was—is?—having this conversation with the twenty-two-year-old me. Too many questions are going through my head all at once. Here, I had thought he was a ghost, and he still looks like a ghost, so does it mean he still dies, only later? Or is James and Annie's theory correct and his life will run its course, only in different years from mine?

"I know it's about two hundred years for you, Emma, and I can't explain it, but I'm living in the future. Please don't be afraid, though. I'm not going to hurt you." He rakes his hand through his hair. "Jesus, I can't even touch you," he mumbles before looking away, running his tongue over his lips and then biting them in mild frustration.

I smile softly. All this time, he's most likely been thinking of me as I have of him, and I'm touched he's so concerned about frightening me.

"Alex, I'm not two hundred years away. It's more like twenty-something."

"What?" Alex's brow crumples in confusion.

And now it is my turn to be honest. "I'm not living in the past. I'm living in *your* future. Alex, I'm in 2014."

"2014? Okay, wow. Why do you..." He breaks off and scratches his nose, trying to come to terms with the truth. "What about your clothes?"

I laugh. "I could say the same thing!"

He smiles and nods his head once in agreement.

"I'm sorry I was dishonest with you," I continue. "I saw you dressed in period clothing, and because of your name and the history of this place, I just assumed you were from the late 1700s. I didn't even think that you could be in costume too. I was—am—dressed like this because, well, I love the clothes!"

I laugh and feel my face grow red. I sound like an idiot.

"I don't dress like this all the time. I'm here typing all the journals up into a media format, and there is a refurbishing company here as well. We're the only people allowed in the manor for a while, and well . . ."

I look away, my face flaming. I'm rambling, but I can't figure out a way to stop.

"I know people who used to work here were asked to dress the part. We found period clothing in one of the closets, and, well, I wanted to see what it would be like to dress the way people dressed and walk around this place, kind of like living in history, you know?"

I search his eyes for any recriminations.

"So, like I said, I met you and you were nice, and I didn't want to scare you, and . . ." I look down, keeping my eyes on the floor. My embarrassment is complete, yet I keep on talking. I hope I'm just as hazy as he is, that it's working in my favor by masking the heat in my cheeks. "I like talking to you."

Glancing up to see his reaction, I see a brilliant smile come to his face. "You like me."

I should have kept my mouth shut. "I like talking to you."

"No, it's more than that. The way you launched yourself at me when I came in here." Alex starts toward me, nodding, a panther cornering his prey, until he's only a foot away. He looks down at me, so close and yet way too far away. I wish I could pull him toward me, run my fingers through his hair.

"You like me," he says again softly, his hazel eyes penetrating mine. It's not a question. He already knows. "Admit it."

The heat in my cheeks intensifies. He's too close. Too beautiful. This is getting ridiculous. "Yes, I like you," I whisper. "Okay?" I smirk at the look of triumph in his eyes.

Alex stares at me for a few seconds and leans toward me. It's as if he contains the strength of the moon, and my very soul, a tide pool of longing, can do nothing else but be drawn toward him. I'm afraid to meet his eyes, afraid of what it means going forward, but I'm helpless to the pull of his gaze that dares me to fully look at him before he huskily says, "I like you too."

My heart flutters. This is crazy. We stare at each other for moments, minutes. My breath hitches as he lifts a hand mere inches from my skin and traces it across my jaw. Perhaps I imagine the tingle of electricity and the way he seems to be breathing faster, his pupils dilated as he regards me. He leans in again, his mouth opening to say something. Instead, he closes it, takes a shaky breath, and turns away.

We stand together but apart, separated by inches and years. It all seems so right, but the timing is wrong and unfair.

Neither of us speaks for a while, both lost in our thoughts. Then Alex clears his throat.

"So, now that we've established that, there was more to it when I came in here. You looked so relieved to see me. What's going on?"

I shake my head to clear it. "Well, I looked up your name in the family Bible—did you know it hasn't been updated since the '50s, by the way?—and I saw your name and . . . Did you know that a guy with the exact same name as you died in 1798 from apoplexy? I didn't know what that was, so I googled it. I had no idea whether I should tell you because, if you had been him, well, what could you have done with the information?"

"Apoplexy? What the hell is that?" Suddenly, he's nodding, his mouth parting in understanding. "Ahh, that's why you were asking me about symptoms. I wondered. Women weren't known to be doctors back then." Just as quickly, his expression changes to amusement and he laughs. "That's why you looked so stricken when I asked if I was going to die! Oh, Emma, I'm so sorry." He laughs again. "Actually, I was nursing a pretty bad hangover that day. A friend of mine got married the night before." A small smile plays around his mouth. "No, the Alexander you must be referring to was one of my however many great-uncles. It's a tradition in our family to name the second son after him because he was so beloved. But as far as I know, his ghost has never been seen."

"*Beloved?* Have you read his journal? He was a misogynist!"

Alex grins as he nods his head. "The journal! *That's* why you were so upset. You thought you read mine, but you read his. I wondered what that was all about."

My eyes widen in horror. I totally forgot. "Oh, Alex. I'm so sorry! You must have thought I was insane."

He shakes his head. "I didn't know what to think, but it makes sense now."

Again, I find myself staring at him. Something has changed between us. There had been a tension before, like we had both been walking on eggshells. That's gone now, obvious in the way we now freely speak to one another. The boundaries and conventions of politesse we had erected to protect one another from the truth of when we existed are gone.

"So, why did you disappear for a few days? And what happened to your leg? When you didn't show up . . .well . . ." I look down sheepishly. "I thought you died in your time and I'd never see you again."

"Yeah, sorry about that." He winces. "I was playing football with some of the guys out in back of the manor, and I fell pretty hard on my ankle." Alex looks down at his plastered limb. "It turns out I broke it. I was told to stay off it for a few days, but I've been here."

"Ouch. Are you okay? I mean, are you in pain? Do you need to sit down?" I look around the room, pointing to any of the seating arrangements I have no idea if he can see or not.

"I'm fine. Really." He looks down, then rakes his hand through his hair once again. "I was hoping I would see you while I was laid up."

"You did?" I ask, feeling giddy.

"Yeah, and I was thinking how stupid that was because you were a ghost. You were dead. I mean, I thought you were dead . . . you know what I mean." He pauses as if debating whether he should say something else. "There was no possible way I could be with you, and yet I couldn't—I can't—stop thinking about you."

"You can't?" I squeak, hating myself for sounding so needy and hopeful.

"No." He sighs. "Not that knowing you're from the future is that much better. I mean, what does that even mean? Am I a ghost? And if I'm not dead, and we can meet, I'm like"—he calculates in his head—"twenty-five years older than you are in your time."

I sit heavily on the window seat, the only place I know exists in both time lines, and exhale noisily. "You're right. I don't know what to make of all of this either."

"Emma!" I start when I hear my name being shouted from down the hall and look down at my watch.

I hiss and call loudly, "Coming!"

Turning back to Alex, I whisper, "I have to go. I'm supposed to be meeting my boss."

"It's okay. I don't think we have much time anyway," Alex alleges, his hazy figure growing dimmer. "Tonight? At seven in the Long Gallery?"

I smile. "I'll be there."

"Me too. And you can tell me what a google is."

"What?"

"Google. You said you googled apoplexy. What does—"

Then he's gone. And that's when I realize that whereas Alex is now free to say what he wants about the past, I apparently still have to watch my mouth.

Chapter 14

I meet with Alex, and we ask a few more questions we were too polite to ask when we thought the other was from the nineteenth century. Alex is twenty-six. He was born in Hillfield in 1967. He went to boarding school in New Hampshire, CT.

"But why the US?" I ask.

"You know, everything that happens here is normal to me. I didn't even consider that it wasn't normal until I said something about a ghost and the other kids at school looked at me funny. Then . . . well, something happened, and after a while, I didn't want to be here or anywhere where people knew who I was, so I asked my parents if I could apply to places over there. And when I got accepted, I went. All of high school."

"What happened?"

Alex rakes his hand through his hair. "I . . . Do you mind if we don't get into that right now? I'll tell you . . . someday, but not right now, okay?"

I nod, and we sit in awkward silence for a few moments.

"So, what really brought you to Hillfield?" he asks, a little too brightly.

"Like I said, I'm typing up all the journals, but I've always been fascinated by this place." I tell him about my summer visits, my interest in the paranormal, and the article I read about Hillfield. "At first, when I met you, I just couldn't believe I was talking to a ghost. But now . . . I'm really glad I met you, Alexander Eason."

"I'm glad I met you too," he says with a smile. "Who knew writing in those stupid journals would pay off?"

With everything that has been said swimming in my head, I hold on to a random thought. "Wait. If I'm the one copying the journals, and no one outside of the family has seen them before me, how is Georgianna Eason quoted in a newspaper article I read?"

"Let me guess. It was something like, 'It has become such a common occurrence that I dare say neither the family nor the servants, save a few of the newer maids, bat an eyelash upon her sudden arrival or just as sudden departure.'"

"Well, I'm not sure it was word for word, but yeah. How did you know?"

"We give a tour of the house, and we go into the paranormal a little. The tourists love it. Probably everything in that article is something that could be learned from taking the tour."

"Bartholomew Eason—I'm working on his journals now—believed that time isn't linear, that it overlaps and folds onto itself. According to him, you're not a ghost."

"Glad to hear it. I don't feel like one. And for the record, I think he's right."

I smile as he makes himself comfortable. "Think about it. Throughout history, people have claimed to see ghosts, and some people seem to have more awareness of them than others."

"Why would people only start seeing the ghosts here when the Easons bought the house?"

"Well, it's possible the Cenas kept it quiet, or maybe they couldn't see. As for anyone who worked here, think of the time. They would have been thought of as witches, burned at the stake. I would have kept my mouth shut too. Even now, when people talk about ghosts, you're bound to see a few eye rolls. I can tell you when I'm out and about, it's not something I readily talk about."

"True. But why this house? What makes it so special? There are lots of old houses, but you don't see the number of ghosts you see here, if any."

"I don't know. I've been trying to research a few things like limestone foundations and ley lines—"

"Oh! *The Da Vinci Code*!"

"No, I haven't heard of Da Vinci's code. He was a brilliant man, though, so I wouldn't put it past him to think of some—why are you laughing?"

"Sorry," I say, his look of confusion making me laugh harder. "It's a book by a guy named Dan Brown. It's also a movie. It has nothing to do with what we're talking about except the mention of ley lines. I won't spoil it. Pretend I didn't say anything."

"I'm going to have to create a list of things to do and see in the future."

"It's so hard!" I bite my lip. "I keep forgetting my reality is not your reality."

We're quiet for a moment, and I collect my thoughts, thinking through everything that has been said so far. "Do you think *all* the people who are ghosts to me are just living their lives in a different time? You don't think they're actual *ghost* ghosts?"

"I think some, no, many of the people we talk to no longer exist in our time, but at the time we're talking to them, or see them, they do."

The implications suggested in his response hit me suddenly, and my light mood fades. "So then, you really are a ghost."

"Hey, I'm not that old. I'm like, what, forty-seven in your time?"

"And if that's true, why haven't you come to see me? Why haven't I been able to find any information on the internet? Then there's the article. It says—"

"Shh! Don't say anything." His hand comes up to cup my mouth, and I shrink back as the webby sensation engulfs my face. "I think there's a reason people don't see their own future. Let's say I find out I die in two years. Will I spend that time truly living, or will I cower in fear? Will I be so confident in the *when* of my demise that I create unnecessary risks for others?" He shakes his head. "I don't want the responsibility of that knowledge."

"And what about me? I *have* that knowledge. Should I impart it or keep it to myself, knowing that I could potentially prevent an event from occurring?"

"It has already happened, right? That's why it's history."

I frown. "No. Now you're contradicting Bartholomew's argument about time, the one you said you agreed with."

Alex opens his mouth to say something but closes it once more, his brows furrowed. "I don't know. Can the two ideas coexist?" He glances at his wrist. "But speaking of time, I have to go. I'm meeting my friend Louis. There's a new pub that's opened, and he says we *have* to go. Between you and me, I'm getting too old for this." Alex rolls his eyes, but he's smiling. He stands, and so do I. "I like how you challenge my mind, make me think," he says. "Are you free tomorrow for lunch? One o'clock?" At my nod, his smile grows bigger. "I'll see you later, Emma."

"Bye, Alex." As he walks toward the door, he grows more and more transparent until I can no longer discern his image. And because I can't see him, I don't know if he's left the room yet, but I wave anyway, just in case he looks back and can see me.

Chapter 15

Today, I can't wait for lunch. I continue typing up journal entries and compiling them in the database, but my thoughts are definitely not on the work at hand. He said he liked me. I'm twenty-two years old, and here I am, acting like a teenager—not that I acted like that when I was one.

A smile tugs at my lips, and I blush at the memory of Alex leaning in toward me. I wish he could have followed through—allowed me to feel his lips against mine, feel the touch of his fingers as he ran them through my hair. I know it's not possible, but that doesn't stop me from imagining what it would have been like, what it could be like, if only.

Keeping my mind occupied doesn't seem to be helping. Each hour of work seems to drag by, and I'm frustrated when I get several pages of a journal typed up, only to realize just a quarter of an hour has passed. The words are a blur in my mind. I'm not even paying attention to what they are saying and focus solely on getting them down correctly. Here's my chance to learn all the Eason family secrets, and instead, my mind is preoccupied by one of the Eason family members.

It's only when I find myself messing up on one of the lines that my mind starts processing the words I see before me on yellowing, fragile pages. This particular journal belonged to Bartholomew, but it's filled with so much sap I find it hard to read. It's after the entry where he lists all the things he loved about Marie. The devotion on his part was truly there—to the point of provoking nausea. Every detail of her being, from physical characteristics, such as the size and shape of the scar on the index finger of her left hand to the way she cocked her head—complete with how her hair framed her face while she was at it—was too much for me. And that's pretty much how all the entries are, except for this one. Deleting the words I had written in error, I read over the entry as I carefully type what I read.

We found a most extraordinary room. I don't think anyone else in the family knows about it, as it was closed off and in disarray. Marie was with me, and to tell the truth, the fact that we found a secret room in a house where I have lived for over three years now, while exciting and confounding, isn't even the amazing part.

Marie is real.

In the room, she's as corporeal as I am! And she allowed me to kiss her hand. It's terribly cliché, but oh, to be a glove upon that hand that I may be next to it often!

I don't understand how the room works or why it is only there where we can truly see one another, but I must find out. If there is any way to make the effects permanent, I mean to ask Marie to be my wife. There is nothing I would like more.

We are to meet there tomorrow. I fervently hope none of this was a fluke. I hardly dared leave her for fear of it, but I promised Eugene to help with one of the copious tasks a manor like this entails. Blast it!

I read through the entry again, growing excited as the extent of what it says dawns on me. A secret room. There's a secret room at the manor, as well as the possibility that I could actually get to see Alexander in the flesh, to touch him.

I hastily scan the rest of the entries I typed up today, but I don't see anything regarding the room or where it could be located. There's no mention of where Bartholomew walked or where he was in the habit of meeting Marie. As much as I dislike the idea, I'll have to go through all the entries again, searching for any clues that might help in locating the room.

I can't wait to tell Alex. Maybe he already knows about it. Bartholomew said the room was in disarray. Did he then tell his cousin and his cousin's wife about his discovery? Did he keep the room a secret? Bartholomew disappeared over two hundred years ago. Has the room been opened since then? It's possible it became common knowledge and incorporated into another room. I wonder if the original house plans and more recent plans would show any differences.

Typing through the rest of the entries in this particular journal, there are three more references to the secret room.

The room is small and has one window overlooking the interior courtyard. Because of its location, it's one of the few windows that hasn't been boarded up. The fireplace from the adjacent room keeps it nice and warm. I managed to find a small settee that won't be missed as well as a small table and lamp, and I've cleaned it up so that at least I'm not coughing and sneezing from the dust...

I worry sometimes that others will find it, so often do I find myself looking toward its location when on that floor...

The room has something to do with time, a suspension of it perhaps? Or a coalition of all time in one small space. That has to be it. It has to be the reason. What else is there?

An interior courtyard. In my meanderings around the manor, I've noticed windows being uncovered, but with the work going on, I've never wanted to get in the way, so I've never gotten close enough to have a good look at any of them, let alone to see what is on the other side of them.

I glance at my watch, tempted to stop working to go take a look. Instead, I jump from my seat. It's time to meet Alex. I hurry to save my work and put everything away and lock up. I don't have to dress up in period clothing anymore, and I feel a bit naked without all the billowing cloth, but instead of running up to my room, I dash into a bathroom to make sure I'm presentable before going to find Alex. Now, on top of wanting to see him for his company, I'm filled with questions about the secret room that maybe he can answer. And if he can't answer them, then maybe we'll be able to find the answers together.

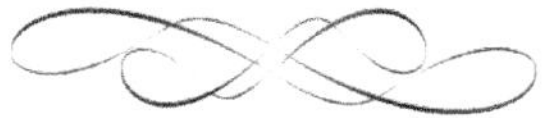

I find him in the Great Hall, hazy and not quite solid, sitting at one of the long tables. It's strange seeing him without his nineteenth-century garb. The clothing almost became a part of who he is to me, so it takes me a moment to get this new version of him straight in my mind. Yesterday, he was in jeans, and it looks like he's wearing the same pair again to accommodate the cast on his leg. Instead of a plaid shirt, he's wearing a nice dark blue turtleneck.

When he looks up, his expression creases with confusion before clearing, a bright smile coming to his lips. "I'm not used to seeing you in your clothes," he says.

"You know, I could sue you for sexual harassment, if I can sue a ghost," I tease and then laugh.

Alexander reddens. "That's not what I meant at all, and you know it." He smiles.

"Yeah, I was thinking the same thing about you." Then it's my turn to redden.

"Now who can sue for sexual harassment?"

I clear my throat and take a seat across from him. The room is surprisingly void of people. I was expecting workers to be finishing up their own lunches. "You're different as a twentieth-century man than I thought you were as a nineteenth-century man."

"Better, right?" Alex grins. Then he says, "I have to say I'm relieved. I felt so restrained. I didn't know how to talk to you. I didn't know how to tell you *when* I was from, if you would understand what I meant. I didn't want to scare you because I enjoyed—I enjoy—talking to you. It's nice that I can tell you everything and you'll understand what I'm talking about."

"I feel the same way," I say. "I wasn't sure how I was supposed to act as a nineteenth-century lady. I wasn't sure if some of the things I was saying were relevant to the time. I wonder how long it would have lasted if you hadn't broken your ankle."

"I'm glad we don't have to find out." Alex moves his hands and looks as though he is pantomiming taking a bite out of something.

"You're actually eating?" I ask. "I don't see anything."

"Ham and cheese sandwich." He takes another bite as I watch in wonder. "So," he says as he swallows, "you're really from 2014? What's that like?"

I wonder if I have the right to tell him everything that will happen in his future. Would there be some sort of butterfly effect?

"It's not that different, I guess. Technology has advanced, probably more than I realize, having gone through it, but people are still people. The music's better," I taunt.

"Have you ever seen the movie *Back to the Future* with Michael J. Fox? Actually, there's a second one that just came out a little while ago. Have you seen that?" I nod. "Is it anything like that?"

"You mean, do we have hoverboards and flying cars that run on garbage?" I laugh. "No. Can you imagine? It would be cool to have a time machine, but those don't exist either. I can tell you there will be a third *Back to the Future,* though."

"I already knew that. They already have trailers out for it. For someone from the future, you're not a very good source of information," Alex quips.

"Trust me, with technology today, I could blow you away with the amount of information I have at my fingertips."

"Want to put your money where your mouth is?"

"With inflation, it's worth quite a bit more nowadays," I say as I take my phone out of my pocket. If I can't see his sandwich, I'm pretty sure he won't be able to see what I'm doing. Anyway, it's a harmless way to have a bit of fun. "Okay, what's your question?"

"Okay, tell me this. What was the top song in 1989?"

"Phil Collins, 'Another Day in Paradise,'" I say after a few moments.

"Who said, 'If you build it, he will come'?"

"Oh, come on! I don't even have to look that one up. *Field of Dreams* is a classic! Next."

"How much for a gallon of petrol?"

"1.88."

"I pay 1.92."

"You're getting screwed."

"No, really. I'm not." He smirks. "Which stocks should I invest in?"

"Nice try."

"Worth a shot. You really have all of that information right there in whatever it is you're holding?"

"It's amazing what you can do with phones nowadays."

"You're holding a phone?"

"They're basically mini computers now. It tells the time, takes photographs, lets me look up information, and even tells me where I am if I'm lost and gives me directions to get to where I need to go."

"Wow, that's amazing. I know mobile phones exist, but all they do is call the person you want to talk to. I've never heard of one giving directions or taking photos. I wonder if it could take a photo of me."

"That's a good idea," I say as I put my phone on camera mode. "We have no idea what's going on here. I can see you very well, but I couldn't see the sandwich you were eating."

"And I can't see this phone you're holding. Go ahead. Take a picture. Let's see what happens."

Capturing Alex's image in the frame, I take a picture and immediately review the image. He's there, but he's so overexposed, it's hard to see any particulars. I can see his dark hair, bits of his eyebrows, and can tell he's wearing a blue shirt, but other than that, it looks as if he's been captured in a blinding white light. The table at which we sit and the part of the room behind him, though, are all clearly defined and aren't affected by whatever happened to Alex.

I take another shot, but the same thing happens. Just like all the photos I've seen provided as proof of ghosts.

"I have to ask you something."

"No, I don't have a girlfriend, and I'm not married. Being with you has been the closest I've been to being on a date in a while."

I smile. "That's not what I was going to ask, but why? You're not exactly ugly, and we've already established that you're nice to talk to."

"I don't know. I hate how people can be so fake. The women I talk to play coy and bat their eyelashes, and I'm just not interested in that. I want something real, and the sad thing is, the closest thing I've come to something real is by being excessively polite, on the cusp of being fake, with a girl I thought was a ghost and who I can't even touch."

He rests his hands on the table, and after looking at him for a few moments, I reach out and attempt to touch his hands with my fingers. What feels like electricity is the first thing I notice, a tingling sensation that reminds me of when my hand would fall asleep after having it in an awkward position for too long. It's not uncomfortable, so I add more pressure. That's when I pull away. Like the first time we ran into each other, the distinct feeling of spider webs spread across my fingers.

"That's what I wanted to talk to you about actually," I said after a moment. "I wanted to ask you if you know of any rooms in the house that used to be secret."

Alex's eyebrows raise. "Uh, secret rooms? Secret passageways, yes, but there are no secret rooms that I know of. Where is this coming from?"

"Well, I signed a confidentiality agreement stating that I couldn't talk about anything I've found in the journals, but since you're a member of the Eason family . . . you are, aren't you?"

"I swear to you that I am directly descended from Eugene and Georgianna Eason."

I bite my lip. This was all such a good idea when I was copying the journal, but now I'm not sure if I should say anything. What if, by saying something, I alter the course of history? But then, it's all history to me, and there has been no talk of secret rooms. Taking a deep breath, I forge ahead and ask Alex if he knows about Bartholomew and Marie and Bartholomew's subsequent disappearance. When he nods, I continue with my story.

"Bartholomew wrote about a secret room he found with Marie. I have the journal right here." I take the journal, wrapped in a plastic bag, out of the bag in which I have my lunch and the white gloves I'm required to wear when handling the journals, which I also remove.

Alex gasps when I uncovered the journal. "I can see it!" he exclaims. "It must be because it exists in both our time frames, you think?"

I nod as I put on the gloves and open the journal. "I was hoping it would be the case."

"Ok, so tell me more about this secret room."

I show Alex the three entries I found about the room. After reading them, he sits back and shakes his head. "That's amazing. I've lived here my whole life and have hidden in every nook and cranny that I ever found. Like I said, I know about a few secret passageways—"

"Like the one connecting the library to the room next to it?"

Alexander looks surprised and nods. "Oh, you know about that one, huh? Have you found the staircase from the second floor that bypasses the first and leads you straight outside?"

"No! Really? I'll have to look for that one. Are there others?"

"Maybe, but we're not talking about passageways; we're talking about rooms, and I have no knowledge of any."

"Do you think it was maybe opened up before you were born?"

"I used to listen to stories from my grandfather. He would tell me things about the house that his grandfather had passed down to him. Never did I hear him tell me a story about a secret room being discovered." Alex asks me to flip through the entries once more and stops at the second entry. "Take a look at this. It says the fireplace in the room next to it keeps the room warm. That at least narrows it down. It also says 'when on that floor.' That has to mean it's either the first or second floor."

"That's how it sounded to me too, and if that's the case, it narrows down the number of rooms we have to search even more."

"I don't know about any inner courtyard, though. I know windows were boarded up to avoid paying tax way back, but my family has done a good job of hiding where those windows were. I guess I could think about the layout of the—"

"No need. The refurbishing company that's here has been uncovering the windows. They're trying to get

Hillfield back to its original state, only with the added convenience of modern technology."

"So, why do you want to find the room? Just curiosity, or do you think there's treasure in there or something?" Alexander teases.

Puzzled, I search Alex's face before realizing I never showed him what was so special about the room.

My eyes widen. "I didn't tell you!" Quickly but carefully, lest I tear a page, I open the journal to the initial entry I found and turn the book so Alexander can read it more easily. I watch as his eyes scan the passage before stopping to scan it again. Upon finishing, a smile grows on his face, and his eyes widen as he looks up. "We'd be solid to each other? You wouldn't look like a ghost?"

"That's what the man says!" I grin.

Alex looks down at his wrist and what I suppose i a watch. "I have to go. I have to give a tour in about fifte minutes. Can I meet you later tonight, maybe in the Lo Gallery at seven? We can search through the second fl and work our way down, see if we can find the room."

"Ok, and I'll look for floor plans of the house, s there is maybe a room that looks like it should be bi or to see if anything looks out of place."

Alex nods as he and I stand up together. It was then that I could hear the work going on in one of the rooms of the house. Not only could I hear the di sound of a drill, but I could also hear a radio going in the background. I must have tuned them all out, so focused I was on Alex and our conversation. Not once were we disturbed. Even stranger, this is the longest conversation we've had. It's almost as if, now that our true times have been determined, the veil between our times has decided to be more lenient.

"I wish I could ask you out on a real date. Take you out to dinner, hold your hand as we walk through one of the gardens," he confesses, his hand running through his hair in what I had come to know as his telltale sign of frustration. Brooding, he stares off into the distance before his eyes focus on me again. "But we'll find the room," he assures me, and then with a twinkle in his eye, he adds, "for it would give me great pleasure to kiss your hand, milady."

I walk back to the library, sit at the desk, and once e put the white gloves on my hands, I take the journal t of the plastic bag once again and thumb through the ges. I have to read through it a second time, not only to ke sure my copying was accurate but also to see re is anything else I was too preoccupied to notice. B n't concentrate.

When and for how long I meet with Alex is a mysterious thing. Except for two occasions, when we had first agreed to spend lunch together and when he had broken his leg, he's always there when we set a meeting place and time. And, not that I'm complaining, he always stays visible longer than Annie ever has. Plus, the fact that we were able to tell each other the years in which we are living still lingers in my thoughts. Why with him but not with Annie? I know he lives at Hillfield Manor, so the fact that I never see him outside of our appointed times makes me curious.

I grab my laptop and backtrack to the Great Hall. Whereas it's true I spend most of my time in the library, I do find myself drawn to other rooms from where I'll work if the library feels too confining. Now is one of those times. Plus, Alex said he had a tour starting soon, and although I'm not sure where it would start, the Great Hall is one place where it is certain people would gather. Hillfield is a large estate. It's quite possible he and I are just never in the same location at the same time.

Besides when I thought he died, I've never actually gone in search of Alex, taking for granted that I would see him at our appointed times, but the fact that we had run into each other when we first met is enough to assure me that it's possible to do so again. Sitting at one of the two long tables in the room, I face the main doorway and wait.

I have some work to do, which is why I brought my laptop, but I find myself ignoring it in anticipation of what I believe to be Alex's impending visit.

After fifteen minutes or so, I begin to pace the room, always facing the door, and after a half hour, I'm about to give up when I see the first transparent figure enter the room. I can tell the shadowy form is a man due to his height and build, but I'm unable to pick out any specific features. Other figures begin entering behind him. Some are less transparent than the first, but none of them are as clear and concrete as the last man who enters the room: Alex.

While the group of shadows looks around the room, only Alex picks me out immediately as being incongruous to the setting. Without hesitation, he flashes me a brilliant smile before turning to talk to the people who had come in with him.

"This is the Great Hall. Built in 1642, the Great Hall was the main room of the manor. This is where everyone would come to eat and get all of their gossip. Over there"—he points to the far side of the room—"you'll see the dais, where the high table still sits. This is where the main family members would be seated. That way, they were in view of all their guests."

His voice gets lower. "Some of you are here for the architectural features of this estate, and some of you are perhaps just curious, having driven past Hillfield on your way to one place or another. And then there are those of you who are here for the supposed ghosts that are said to wander the halls."

"Have you ever seen a ghost?" I hear someone ask. I'm not sure from whom the voice comes, and to my ears, it sounds delicate, just above a whisper.

Alex looks at me and winks. "I have seen ghosts." He nods. "Keep your eyes open, and maybe you'll see one too."

That's when I decide to move. Up until this point, I've stayed relatively still since the first person in the group entered. Now, I move toward the huge fireplace at one end of the room, being careful not to touch anyone as I walk. Everyone except Alex is oblivious to my movement. I look at him and shrug. He shrugs too and holds a finger up, making sure no one is looking at him, and then draws his eyebrows together before throwing his arms up in the tradition of monsters on television. A shadowy form moves toward him, and he quickly shifts, pretending to stretch.

I smother a laugh. He wants me to scare them.

As he speaks to who I think is a small, older woman, her image so faint I have to squint to make her out, he glances at me over her shoulder. I shrug again and nod. It's ridiculous, but it would be fun to give everyone the scare they had probably come for.

Lifting my arms, I start to moan and move around the room. I see one or two people cock their heads as if listening, so I moan louder, but if anyone hears me, they're very good at ignoring my presence. At this point, I look at Alex, who has his hand over his mouth to cover his huge grin. I jump up and down as I make my way over to him.

"We'll stay in here a few minutes more, so if you would like to take photographs, please feel free to do so now." Alex walks over to a corner of the room, motioning me to join him. He keeps his hand up over his mouth, pretending to play with a nonexistent beard as he speaks to me.

"That was absolutely priceless." He chuckles.

"They didn't even see me! I wonder why. *You* can see me. Am I so transparent?"

"Literally or figuratively?" He chuckles again when I glare at him. "No, you're not transparent," he amends. "At least, not to me, you're not, but as you know, not everyone can see ghosts."

"Yeah, but in a group this size?" Not willing to let it go, I walk up to one of the figures, the man who was the first to arrive, and wave my hand in front of his face. No response. Thinking of the icky spider web feeling, I tentatively hold out my finger and poke him.

Nothing happens. I try poking the man again. It's as if I'm touching air. He notices nothing, and although I can see my hand going through his arm and waist, I feel nothing either. Turning to Alex, I notice he's been observing the whole exchange. He shrugs and shakes his head and then motions for me to try another person.

The next person I try to touch is a young woman no more than my age. She's with another girl, and both are giggling as they look around the room, pointing to one person or another. Like with the man, I poke her right arm just above the elbow. This time, I feel the spider web stickiness clinging to my finger. And she feels it too. With a sharp intake of breath, her left hand shoots up and covers the spot where I poked her. Removing her hand, she looks down to see if there is anything there. Seeing nothing, she looks around, her eyes wide.

It's mean, but I can't help myself. I poke her again, only on the opposite arm. Again, I hear her gasp, only this time, she grabs her friend's arm and starts to back up toward the main entrance of the room.

"What? What is it?" her friend asks.

"Something touched me!" the woman says, the tremor in her voice more than apparent.

"You're a terrible actress. I'm not falling for it." She pulls away from the woman's grip on her arm, intent on carrying on with the tour.

So, I poke her too.

Her eyes widen in alarm, and she lets out a muffled squeak, steps back, and grabs the woman's hand. "Okay, I believe you!"

Turning, I look at Alex triumphantly. With a grin and a shake of his head, he motions for the group to follow him. "We're going to go out this way, ladies and gentlemen," he says. The two women, though, have already dashed out the doorway leading to the foyer, and it isn't long before I hear the front door slam.

"I really didn't mean to scare them that badly," I say guiltily. "I guess I was a little overzealous since that guy didn't even feel anything." Alex and I traipse alongside the wall with the fireplace in the Long Gallery. Since the room takes up the entire floor, there's no use looking for any secret rooms on the length of the room with the windows. As far as the sides of the room are concerned, a large staircase and the upper landing occupy the space on one side, whereas a smaller staircase, most likely used by servants, and a small room take up the other side. With it being useless to investigate three sides of the room, the wall with the fireplace is the only one left to us.

"I wouldn't worry about it. They'll think about it, talk about how cool it was, tell their friends, and then they'll all come back another day," Alex guesses as he studies the wall. He's looking for hidden panels. "I don't think we're going to find anything here, and with all the windows opposite, I doubt there were any on this side looking over an inner courtyard."

"I still want to look a little more. I want to make sure we hit everything so we don't have to double back," I say, knocking on the wall in different locations in hopes of finding a spot that sounds hollow.

I feel my phone vibrate in my pocket and pull it out to see who's calling. My mom.

"I have to take this," I say as I move away.

"No problem, looks like I'm leaving anyway," Alex says, giving me a fleeting smile and a wave. He disappears before my eyes as I put the phone to my ear.

"Hi, Mom. You'll never guess what I'm—"

"Emma," she sobs. "It's your . . . your father. You have to come home."

The despair and urgency in her voice sets my heart beating triple time. "Mom? What happened?"

"H-he," she starts, but she can't continue and lets out an anguished moan.

Tears pool in my eyes and overflow, my own breath as ragged and staggered as hers. "I'm on my way," I whisper, gripping the phone and holding it tightly against my ear as if by doing so I'd hear laughter instead of sorrow.

"Mom, I'm going to catch the next flight out, okay?" I say louder, steeling myself. "Can you hear me?"

"Y-yes, yes. Come home, Emma. Come home, come home."

By this point, I'm tearing through the manor, making my way to my room to grab a bag large enough to throw a few outfits and my passport into. "I'm on my way," I repeat. "I love you."

Chapter 16

***"She looked so small as** she lay in the bed." Isn't that what people say when they see loved ones in the hospital who are weak and dying? If anything, it was Mom and Dad who looked smaller, more fragile than I had ever seen them look before. Mom didn't even get up from my sister's side, but she waved me over to her after I had given Dad a long, tight hug, and after giving me an affectionate squeeze, she resumed holding Eve's hand while she clutched one of mine with her other.*

When I fully rested my gaze on Eve, she looked the way she always looked. She had bruising and scratches on the parts of her body I could see, her arms and face, and yes, those were new, but other than that, even though we were told she was in a coma due to a depressed skull fracture and the associated swelling, she looked like she could wake up at any moment. For a while, I let myself believe she would. I guess that's why Mom, Dad, and I tiptoed around the room and whispered. That or maybe we were afraid that any little thing we did would have a ripple effect and Eve would leave us, because, at that point, we still had hope.

I'm not sure when hope left me. It was definitely after I watched Mom, tears running down her face, holding Evie's hand, praying to God to take her instead. She swore she'd do whatever He wanted, promised to suffer anything, as long as her little girl was okay. And it was after Dad, usually a stoic man, openly sobbed, his shoulders shaking as he covered his eyes with his hands.

Yeah, I think hope was still with me even then. For the most part, I was numb, observing things as if everything was on TV and I was just a passive viewer. What was happening was sad. What these people were experiencing was devastating—waiting, praying, hoping. These poor, poor people. But it didn't really register. At least, not everything. I heard the beeping of one of the machines and acknowledged a nurse when she came in to check on Eve's vitals. At one point, I was staring at my sister and I could have sworn she moved, the flair of her nostrils, the bend of a finger . . .

I wondered what she was thinking. If she was thinking. Did she hear Mom talking to her? Did she understand what was happening? Was she fighting as hard as we were willing her to fight to come back to us and open her eyes?

I think I started to lose hope when they brought the crash cart in. There are medical interventions and there are miracles, but at that point, I knew what was happening was beyond those, especially when a gray-haired doctor arrived, grim and tight-lipped, and ordered the nurse to charge the defibrillator to 200.

Someone pushed Mom out of the way, and I wanted to yell at them. How dare they? She just wanted to get close to her child, be there, help Evie make the hurt go away. But I also knew they were trying to give Eve every chance they could. And to do that, they needed access, and when it came to saving her life, Mom was just in the way.

I lost hope when they charged the paddles to 300. Eve's body jerked off the bed as if she became attached to the sticky pads they attached to her, and her mouth fell open. That's when she didn't look like herself. She wasn't my sister, her body just the shell of someone who had already said goodbye.

When they charged the defibrillator for the final time, that's when Dad knew. I could see it in his eyes; it was almost as if he lost a little of his own life at that very moment. The strength he always exuded lessened in a second.

And when they called the time of death, after they pushed the crash cart away and turned off all the monitors, that's when Mom knew.

And when she let out a long, anguished wail—well, that's when the rest of the floor knew.

My dad is in the same hospital. I thank God he's on a different floor and in a different wing. As distraught as my mom was when I spoke with her the first time, I think it would have pushed her over the edge to have to face the same doctors and nurses less than a year later.

Instead, she is surprisingly calm when I speak with her the second time, once I've landed and made my way into the airport. As I make my way to Passport Control, I listen as she tells me what happened: my dad had suffered an ST-elevated myocardial infarction, a major heart attack. Doctors performed an angioplasty and now he is resting comfortably, or as comfortably as can be expected. After asking her how she is holding up and for the room number, we hang up with my promise that I'll go straight to the hospital from the airport.

I close my eyes and heave a huge sigh of relief. I lean against a wall for a moment and allow my tears to fall. He's alive. After talking to my mom at Hillfield, I braced myself for the worst. But my dad is still with us. I'll have a chance to—I shake my head, willing myself to get the macabre thoughts out of my mind. He isn't Eve. *But he's older than Eve*, my mind argues. Hastily, I wipe my face with my fingers before getting into one of the queues. I need to tell him I love him. I told Eve—at the end, and I was certain she knew it regardless of whether she heard me, but with my dad—I need him to *hear* me.

As I inch my way forward, I remember the devastation Eve's death brought to my parents. How my mom rocked herself back and forth in Eve's old room, night after night, as if it might miraculously bring her back. How my dad stared blankly as he sat at the kitchen table. How I went back and forth between them, trying to be strong and carry the load so they could grieve. But I didn't feel strong. I constantly ran to my room, where I would break down and throw punches into the mattress, or the bathroom, where I would sit in the shower until the scalding water ran cold just so I could feel something other than my pain and my tears could be hidden by the rivulets of water running down my face.

I didn't want to go to the funeral. Although I had watched my sister die right in front of me, a funeral has always been, in my mind, what is final. In college, I went to the funeral of a girl two years ahead of me who died too young from cancer. All the mourners, the depressing music, the somber lighting, whispers, crying, agonized faces. I swore then that I would never go to another funeral until it was one of my parents' turn. I thought I had a lot of time. I didn't think—I *never* would have thought—I would be saying goodbye to my sister first.

The day was sunny and warm. We were on one of Eve's favorite beaches. There were about twenty chairs, but more people than that came, so people stood in small huddles, moving from one to another silently as they whispered words of condolence, shook hands, and gave hugs. I wondered where they came from. Eve had a close set of friends, but I had no idea she affected so many lives.

It didn't get past me that the boy whose life she had saved and his parents were also in attendance. There was nothing wrong with him. No scratches, no cast, and no limp of any kind. No one would ever know by looking at him that he had fallen into the water, had almost drowned, and caused, even unintentionally, someone else's death. I hated him, envied him, and forgave him all in one breath. He was alive because of my sister. My chest puffed with pride. I wanted to walk up to him and tell him that he better do great things with his life, that he better not screw it up. "Don't make my sister's death be in vain," I wanted to say. And I would have had I not seen the haunted look in his eyes, the maturity that had probably not been there the week before.

His parents kept touching him as if he would disappear, and I knew my mom would be doing the same thing if Eve was with us because she was doing it to me. She kept me in her line of sight, hugged me every chance she got, and reminded me how much she loved me.

Eve's urn sat on a small table placed in the sand. A large easel was beside it with a picture of her, her full name underneath—Evelyn Rose Beckett. Scattered across the rest of the easel were smaller pictures of Eve. Her with friends, with my mom and dad, with me. There was one where she stood on the very same beach. The sun was setting behind her and she stood with her hand on her hip, looking young, happy, and carefree in her bathing suit. Her hair, still wet, framed her face in dark, wavy tendrils. That was Evie in her element.

I felt myself tearing up and fought against the barrage of feelings I didn't want to face. Jerking my hand free from a well-wisher, I abruptly turned away. If I heard one more "sorry," if I unleashed one more tear, I wouldn't have been able to stop. I would have sunk to my knees, dissolved into a puddle, and been swept out to sea to be with my sister.

I vowed right then to never let another person in. The pain of loss was too great. I'd constantly be on pins and needles. If they were old, I'd worry about their health. If they were young—and that was worse—I'd worry about disease or cancer or, hell, drowning. Even if the person was an accomplished and perfectly capable swimmer. I'd be on the constant lookout for loss. That's what I learned.

So, what did I go and do? I fell for a ghost I have no chance of a happy ending with. And even if I find him alive and well in 2014, he'd be twenty years older than me. Maybe we'd have fleeting happiness, but at an age slightly younger than my parents, how long would that last? After all, here I am, standing in a Passport Control queue waiting to get my little book stamped so I can go tell my dad I love him before it's too late!

After talking with the guard and having my passport stamped, I stumble forward, eager to get to the hospital. I only have my carry-on, so I bypass the baggage claim area and make my way to the front of the airport where taxis usually wait.

As I get to the automatic doors, which open in anticipation of my walking through, I feel the vibration of my phone. My heart clenches, and I silently pray it isn't my mom telling me I'm too late. In a second, I deliberate checking to see if it's her, and if so, if I can pretend that not answering, refraining from knowing any more right now, will save me from heartache. I can continue believing that, although serious, my dad is stable. I'll get to the hospital and he'll still be there; maybe he'll even be awake and give me a tired smile.

I have to answer, just in case, but I refuse to look to see who's calling.

"Emma."

I lift my eyes upward in thanks. It's not my mom. I'm not sure who it is, though, and in my stressed state, I can only acknowledge that I answer to that name. "Yes?"

"Emma? It's Louis Wade, darling."

"Mr. Wade, hi." I glance at my watch. It's 10 a.m. Eastern Standard Time. "It's awfully early for you to be calling. I'm sorry, but I'm not working today. I'm not even at Hillfield. I—"

"Hush, child, I know. Marie told me. I'm calling to see if there's anything you need. We're all worried about you on this side of the pond. I volunteered to check up on you and offer any assistance we can provide."

Tears spring to my eyes once again. I'm so overtired and emotionally wrecked that I stand in silence for a moment, just gulping lungful after lungful of air.

"Thank you. That's very kind," I say once I've gotten my bearings. I tell him I've spoken to my mom and offer an upbeat prognosis. It rings false in my ears, but I hope it will satisfy him. It doesn't.

"Oh, you poor dear."

I draw in a long breath. "Look, I'm sorry to cut this short, but I'm just leaving the airport now. I know this causes a delay with the journals, and I—"

"No. Stop. Go be with your parents. Some of the Hillfield journals have lasted hundreds of years. I'm sure they can survive your absence. They'll be here when you return."

"Thank you."

"You're very welcome. And, Emma?"

"Yes?"

"Take as much time as you need. Please don't feel obligated to rush back. The job is yours. Okay?"

I take a breath as tears swim in my eyes once more. *Damn it!*

Blinking furiously, I hail a taxi as I speak into the phone. "Thank you, Mr. Wade. And thank everyone for their concern. Please pass on the news."

"I'll do that. I'll be in touch."

My dad being the patient instead of Eve is the only difference I can discern when I walk into the room. It's a different room, but the setup is the same. And my mom is perched next to the bed just as she had been with Eve, her hand clutching the pale hand of my father, her eyes taking in every minute detail in case one might make a difference. My dad's eyes are closed.

Dim light filters in through the window on the other side of the bed, accentuating the muted blues and greens of the room. The colors are supposed to be calming. In a hospital, though, I've only ever found them to be depressing. I don't think a hospital room has ever been cheery, except maybe in the maternity ward.

My mom doesn't get up. She doesn't even look at me, but she holds out the hand not grasping one of my dad's for me to come to her. Only when I squeeze her fingers does she bother to glance my way.

"You made it," she says.

"I did."

"It was awful, Emma, watching him go through it." Her breath is ragged on her next inhale. "I just felt so helpless. There was nothing I could do." She's silent for a moment. "I'm so glad I wasn't there when Eve went into the water."

"Mom..."

"Watching your dad, being there and not being able to do anything, I feel like *I* was the one dying. If I had been there with Eve, I think I would have."

"Have the doctors said anything else?"

"They're optimistic. He'll spend the next few days here. If all goes well, he'll be able to come home by the end of the week."

I sag against my mom. "Oh thank God."

"I'm sorry I dragged you here, honey. I was just so—"

"Mom, no! Don't you dare apologize. I want you to call me for stuff like this. You *better* call me for stuff like this!" I say, raising my hand in a fist and swinging it in a mock threat.

Two things happen then. My mom laughs, and my dad opens his eyes.

"David!" my mom exclaims, her attention fully on him. "How are you feeling?"

"Like I had a heart attack," my dad deadpans.

"Badum tish," I said, moving my hands like I'm playing the drums. "He'll be here all night, folks."

"Don't make me laugh," my dad says as he smiles. "It hurts."

"I love you, Dad. You know that, right?"

"Oh, sweet pea, I love you too."

After my dad woke, my mom felt a little better about going home for a couple of hours to get some things before coming back, especially since I'll be here to stay with him while she's away. The hospital staff is essentially allowing her to sleep over by looking the other way when it comes to calling hours. There's a medical chair in the room, which is padded, comfortable, and reclines, and my mom was adamant that it would be just fine for her, especially when she brought a small footstool from home to prop her feet on.

While she's gone, my dad and I watch a little TV, but for the most part, he sleeps. I'm dozing off myself when my phone buzzes. It's Marie.

"Hi, Emma. How are you doing?"

"Hi, Marie," I say quietly, touched by the concern shown by everyone. "Thanks for calling. I'm good. *We're* good. My dad's in stable condition and should be able to leave the hospital in a few days. How are you?"

"Oh, I'm so glad! James and I are fine. We've been reminded of our ages, so we've made appointments for checkups."

I smile into the phone, but before I can say anything, Marie continues. "Look, I don't want to keep you, so I'll make this quick. You asked me to look for Alex to tell him where you've gone. I looked in the Long Gallery and the Great Hall—that's where you said, right?"

Alex. My mind immediately moved to him once I knew my dad was in stable condition and my mom was okay, and my stomach flips at hearing the mention of him. "Yes, but don't worry, Marie. I shouldn't have—"

"No, it's fine. We're all worried about you, and *we* can pick up the phone," she says. "He can't. It must be terrible for him, wondering where you've gone, not knowing, being anchored to this house. But it's only been a little over a day, so he shouldn't be too worried. Regardless, I haven't seen him. You've been keeping him a secret, honey!"

"I'm sorry, I—"

"I'm just pulling your leg! Anyway, let's just say no one has answered to that name. Of course, we've been working quite a bit as well, so there's a very good chance I missed him."

"It's okay. But if you happen to see a guy with a cast on his right leg and maybe he's looking for someone . . ."

"I'll be sure to let him know. Do you need anything else? Is there anything we can do on our end?"

"No! Marie, you and James have been great. Mr. Wade too. I'm very lucky to have ended up at Hillfield."

"Aww, you're a peach. We're lucky to have you too," she says, a smile in her voice. "Okay, I'm going to hang up before this call costs an arm and a leg. I'm going to call you in a couple of days! You take care. Bye, honey."

"Bye, Marie."

Sighing, I put my phone on the table next to me.

Alex. I miss him. Picking up my phone again, I search for him on social media. Although there are quite a few men with that name, none of the ones with pictures are of him.

I try to assure myself that it doesn't mean anything. He could have moved, lived in an area I never would have thought of. Plus, there are lots of people who don't use social media. But he seems like the type of guy who would. He's so curious about everything, and it runs deeper than the whole paranormal aspect of our relationship.

Of course, he could have changed as he aged, or I may not have been looking on the correct social media sites, so I look for phone listings, but I soon realize that looking for Alex will be like looking for a needle in a haystack. And the fact that I can't find him begins to worry me. As I continue the search, this time focusing solely on the Easons and Hillfield Manor, I still come up empty. My worry escalates.

But that's the thing. Alex living in a year different from the year I originally thought he was living in makes him no less a ghost than he was at the beginning. He's still partially transparent. I still can't touch him. When I met Alex, he was a ghost I was curious about. After spending time with him, he became a man I found myself attracted to. The fact that he isn't somewhere I can physically touch scares me.

My dad sighs in his sleep, and I look over at him, my gaze softening when he absently touches the bed next to him, most likely searching for my mom.

Love is wonderful. I feel it when I look at my parents, when I looked at Eve. But it also hurts. There are too many variables, too many things that can go wrong. People leave or they die . . . or they never really have a chance in the first place. And after what happened to Eve, and with what my dad is going through, I don't know if I have it in me to bring anyone else into the picture. If being scared and worried all the time is what it means to care for someone, I don't want any part of it.

Unfortunately, I'm afraid I'm already in too deep.

Chapter 17

My room seems a lot smaller, even though I'm pretty much the same height and weight I was when I last slept here. It's a nice room, not too young and girly. That phase fizzled out when I turned twelve and got a bedroom makeover. After pouring over paint samples and new bedspreads from catalogs, I ended up with what is in the room. Moss-green walls, an old dresser my parents had, and a bedside table, both painted cream, and a beautiful oak desk found at a garage sale. The only things, really, that have changed since then are the bed, which went from a single to a double when I turned sixteen, and the person I am now.

My mom is at the hospital with my dad, who is resting comfortably, and I'm exhausted. But I can't sleep.

Maybe it's my nerves, all tied in knots still. Or maybe it's because the house is so quiet. Moving over to the desk, I open some of the drawers, wondering if my mom has looked through them. They're all, for the most part, empty. Even if half the stuff would have been better off dumped in the trash to begin with, I had dutifully packed up everything of mine when I moved out to go to college.

In the top, right-hand drawer, I find the article about Hillfield, the one that got me excited about its reopening. The one I shared with Eve. So much has happened since then. Sitting at my desk, I read through the article once more. One paragraph stands out.

Sadly, misfortune saw fit to continue its visitations upon the walls of Hillfield Manor. In 1976, the current Lord Eason's eldest son, Christopher Bartholomew Eason mysteriously disappeared without a trace at the mere age of nineteen, and most recently, under the shroud of yet another unexplained, yet unconfirmed, disappearance, this time of the Easons' remaining child and sole heir, the manor which had been used as a museum and tourist attraction since the 1920s, was closed in September 1993.

Alex. My mind furiously works through all the possible implications. Where could he have gone? What if we find the room and something happens to him there? Is it possible it's dangerous? Should we even be looking for it? I skim through the article again. Bartholomew went missing, and Christopher, Alex's brother, went missing as well. They have to be connected. How could one family have so many disappearances?

Then I remember what Mr. Wade said. Something about being friends with the owner's son who died . . . No, he said no one knows what happened to him, that the same thing happened to the first son.

It has all been in front of me this whole time. Mr. Wade knew Alex. Alex would be about the same age as Mr. Wade. Louis! Alex mentioned going out with him to a pub. I shake my head. Wow. The surreality of it all hits me with a sudden force, and I stare blankly at the article, my thoughts a twisted muddle.

One thing is for certain, though. I need to talk to Mr. Wade. If he's willing to talk, maybe I can learn something that might help, and then maybe I can stop Alex from disappearing—at least from his time.

Chapter 18

Yesterday, I arrived safely at the airport after staying two weeks with my parents. My dad is still a little weak, but both my dad and my mom assured me that everything is fine. I think they saw how anxious I was to get back, believing it's my job, which I do enjoy, I wanted to rush back to. They don't know about Alex. How could I explain? And what would I say anyway? *Hey, there's this guy I like, but he lives in 1993.*

Because I arrived late, I stayed at my grandmother's house instead of returning right away to Hillfield. It was probably for the best. I missed my alarm and ended up sleeping later than I intended. Damned jetlag.

But I'm back at Hillfield now, and after a warm reception from James and Marie, I've put my things in my room, and I'm ready to find Alex. On my way, I run into Annie.

"Emma! I've been wondering when I'd see you again. I was beginning to believe your work here was done."

"Annie! Hi. No, I'm not finished yet. There was a family emergency."

"Oh, I do hope everything is well now." Although her words form a statement, her eyes ask a question, and I have to smile at her concern.

"Everything is fine. Thank you. How are you? You're right, it has been a while since we last spoke."

Annie is a newlywed, and she has told me all about her husband. From what I can tell, she's a practical woman, but when she talks about him, she seems to morph into a schoolgirl talking about her first crush. She speaks of him now, and as I listen, I can't help thinking about my grandma. She used some of the same expressions.

"Annie, I want to hear all about it, but I have to go find someone."

"Your young man," she says, a soft smile on her lips.

"How did you—"

"I've seen you with him a time or two. Be careful, Emma. You're from two different times. I don't want to see you get hurt."

Looking down, I bite the inside of my lip. I don't want to see me get hurt either, but if my feelings are any indication, I suspect it's the only logical conclusion. I open my mouth to tell Annie exactly that, but, of course, by the time I look up, she's already gone.

"People come and go so quickly here," I mumble, quoting Dorothy from *The Wizard of Oz*. While I was home, I watched the movie one night when it came on one of the classic movie stations, and I felt a kinship with her. After all, meeting a talking scarecrow or tinman couldn't be any stranger than meeting and talking to ghosts.

I check the Long Gallery, the room next to the chapel, the Great Hall, all the rooms where we've met in the past. It's clear a lot of progress has been made by Marie, James, and the workers. Some of the rooms are completed; others just need the addition of furniture and decorations. Still others, that had been untouched when I left, have started having work done on them. I'm impressed by everything that has been done but a bit ashamed of myself for not noticing more of it before I left. And although I want to appreciate the rooms more, Alex isn't in any of them, so I move from one to the next until I've run out of places.

Sighing in frustration, I glance at the time on my phone. Not quite eleven. It would be great if I had a way to contact him. *Like with a phone*, I think as I shake mine. I could search all the rooms again, but I have a feeling it'll yield the same results.

Halfheartedly, I look through a couple more of the rooms as I make my way to the library. Lunch is only an hour away, and since I've met Alex in the Great Hall for lunch before, I'm hoping he'll be there today. If not, I could always come back to get my laptop and one of the more recent journals and go back there to work in case he gives a tour.

The library door is open. It's never open unless I'm in there. A sliver of alarm runs through me, and hurrying forward, it's Mr. Wade I see standing in front of one of the French doors.

"Mr. Wade?"

"Emma," he says, turning toward me. "You've made it back. How is your father?"

"He's well. Thank you." Mr. Wade and Marie both made a point to call during the last two weeks. They talked about the weather here and the work that has been going on, but I knew they were making sure I was all right. Their concern endeared them to me all the more. And whereas I wanted to talk to Mr. Wade about Alex, it didn't seem right to ask him about it over the phone. But the thought of talking to him about Alex now has set my stomach fluttering.

"I didn't expect to see you here today," I say as I move to the desk.

"Nor did I expect to be here, but I finished one meeting early and have another meeting in the neighborhood, so I figured I'd drop by on the off chance of welcoming you back." He smiles. "I guess it wasn't such an off chance as I believed."

I smile too. "Thank you. And thank you for your concern and your patience. I hope the Easons aren't too bothered by the setback."

He waves a hand in the air. "It's fine. You've made remarkable progress as it is, and I've no doubt you'll continue to do so. When I spoke to Mrs. Eason, all she was worried about was whether you'd be back to finish. When I assured her you were due back today, she asked me to send you her regards."

"That was nice of her." I take a deep breath because this seems like as good a time as any to segue into talking about Alex. "You know, from the journals I've read, most of the Easons seem to be nice people."

Mr. Wade smiles. "From my experience, I can tell you the Easons are wonderful people."

"You mentioned you were friends with someone who used to live here."

A more reserved look comes over his face. "Yes."

"Can you tell me more about him?"

Mr. Wade sighs and closes his eyes. "Why would you want me to dredge all of that back up, Emma? It was a sad time."

"I know. I'm sorry. It's just, Mr. Wade, I've met Alex Eason."

He gives me a cold stare, and it's moments before he speaks. "It's very unkind of you to say such a thing, Emma. I realize you're under a lot of stress with what happened to your father, and if you need more time away, that's perfectly fine, but to come back and make these wild accusations...I thought it was beneath you.

"Mr. Wade, I know it sounds—"

"Impossible. Because that's what it is, Emma. Alexander Eason is dead."

"But he wasn't in 1993. That's what year it is for him now."

Mr. Wade sits heavily on the couch. "You see him here?"

"Yes."

"And you've had conversations with him?"

"Yes. And I know you said the same thing happened to his brother—that he disappeared. The same thing happened back in 1798 too, and I'm just wondering if you can tell me anything so that maybe I can stop this disappearance, Alex's disappearance, from taking place."

Mr. Wade wipes his hand across his face, and when his hand comes away, he looks tired and worn. "It has been so long since I've seen him." His eyes narrow. "Are you certain?"

I tell him about how Alex and I met and how we came to giving the time periods we are in, and Mr. Wade chuckles. "Yes, I never understood why Alex enjoyed giving those stupid tours. He has a law degree, for goodness' sake!" He stands and paces the room. "I'll help you. I don't know how much good it will do. The past is the past. What's done is done, but I don't want it said that I didn't do everything I could."

He takes a seat once again. "The last time I saw him was in September 1993. I remember him becoming extremely interested in the house around that time, maybe some months before. When I asked him about it, he said he was working on a project. I couldn't get anything else out of him. We'd go out a few times, but he always seemed distracted, and when I asked him what was on his mind, he'd say, 'The less you know, the better, old friend.'"

"He didn't say anything else?"

Mr. Wade frowns. "At one point, he was talking about taking an extended trip. I jokingly asked where we were going and he got very serious. 'It's somewhere I have to go on my own,' he said. 'If I can get there. But I'll see you again.' That stayed with me. Then, about a week later, he was in a sour mood. Said he wasn't going anywhere, that he was stuck here. He spit the word 'stuck,' like Hillfield had something to do with it."

Where was he going to go? For a moment, I allow myself to believe he was possibly planning to visit me, but I was only months old in September 1993. So why would he be stuck? Stuck as in not being able to leave? Like a ghost might be? I file it in my mind to ponder another time. I want to mention the secret room and see if Mr. Wade has heard of it, but there's no way for me to do so without him getting suspicious, especially if Alex never mentioned it to begin with. "You said he was working on a project and was interested in the house. What do you mean?"

"I'd come over and find him tapping on the walls and looking up into chimneys, stuff we used to do when we were kids when looking for secret passages."

"But he never mentioned finding one?"

Mr. Wade laughs. "You could be a lawyer yourself, Emma, with all your questions, but no. Most likely, all the passages there are have been found, and we explored all of them when we were boys. I'm sorry. That's all I can tell you."

"Thank you for talking about it with me, Mr. Wade." I glance at my phone. It's after noon. "I'm about to go see if Alex is having lunch, if you'd like to join me."

Mr. Wade looks down at his watch and then at me. "I wish I could," he says. "But I have a meeting I must get to, and unfortunately, I never had the sight."

"Wait. You can't see them? But you said you used to see Marie—"

"Exactly. I saw *Marie* talking to what to me looked like thin air. Alex could see them, though, and he'd tell me what they looked like. At first, I thought he was lying, that they both were, but I've witnessed enough people experience them to know he was telling the truth."

He closes his suitcase, his fingers resting on the closed lid. "Emma," he says, his voice quiet, almost a whisper. "If you do see him again, tell him hello for me, but if you don't mind, I'd rather not hear any more about him." He looks up at me, his eyes sad. "He was my best friend, like a brother to me." He turns to the door. "It was hard when I lost him, and I don't want to do that again."

Chapter 19

"Emma!" Alex hurries toward me, his cast making his gait awkward. "You're here! I thought I lost you."

I stand when I see him, a huge smile on my face. He looks even better than my memories of him, and I've been known to embellish. I take a few steps in his direction, and he reaches out a hand. I hold mine up to it, willing to feel the spiderwebs as if they're further proof he's here in front of me. The energy of our reunion is electric. We don't say anything—we don't need to. Just being in his presence is enough.

The world around us melts away. It's only us, lost in the touch of each other's hands. When we drop our hands, Alex looks deep into my eyes, and everything feels right. It's like everything is exactly the way it needs to be, which is strange because of our situation, but I hold on to the feeling. When I'm finally able to speak, the words come out in a rush.

"Alex, I'm so sorry. I tried to get word to you, but—"

He shakes his head in a gesture to stop. "I understand. This"—he waves a hand between us—"makes it a bit difficult. But what happened? Where were you?"

I tell him what happened, and he closes his eyes. "Oh, Emma. I'm sorry. But he's okay now?"

I smile. "Yes. He's much better and on orders to take it easy."

"Good. I know it's not your fault, and please don't think I'm blaming you, but I was getting really worried. I thought . . ." He lowers his head. "It sounds silly now, but I thought maybe we had tempted fate and landed on the wrong side."

I take a seat once more, thoughts of his disappearance flitting through my mind. "Alex, you said you wouldn't want to know about the future, but—"

"Don't tell me."

"I *have* to tell you! I can't *not* tell you. Alex, you disappear."

Although he's hazy, I can still see the color draining from his face, and he sits heavily across from me. "What?"

"It was something I read before, but I forgot about it because it was all in the past and didn't concern people I knew—or so I thought. But I found that article I told you about, and it talks about your brother's disappearance and then goes on to say that you disappear too—in September 1993."

"That's only a few months away."

"I know. So then I was thinking that maybe the room has something to do with it." I study Alex, who's staring past me, a haunted look in his eyes. "Maybe it's a good idea if we *don't* look for it."

Alex's attention snaps back to me. "No. No, Emma, don't you see? That means we have to find it all the more."

My brows draw closer together in confusion. "What?"

"If the room has something to do with disappearances, then that's what happened to my brother, and if that's the case, maybe I can find some evidence of where he went."

Sighing, I close my eyes. He's right. And if the same had happened to Eve, I would have wanted to do the same. Opening my eyes, I take another breath and say, "Then help me find the room, but don't go in. I'll look for you."

He cocks his head and lifts an eyebrow. "No."

"Come on, Alex! If it's the common denominator, we could prevent you from going missing."

"And what if it's a way for me to find Christopher?" Determination sets his features, and he shakes his head.

"With or without your help, Emma, I'm going to find the room."

I jump up and start pacing the room. I don't know why I thought this would go differently. In my head, I thought he'd see the logic. In my head, he—

"I've already got it narrowed down to five places. I've just been waiting, hoping you'd come back to find it with me."

I stop pacing, Alex's words interrupting my thoughts, and turn to him. I don't want anything to happen to him, but I'm also curious about the room. Before I can say anything, he stands and walks toward me.

"You said September. That gives us some time. We can still find the room, and I just won't go in there in September."

I nod. What else can I do? He'll search for it with or without me, and at least if I'm there, maybe I can help in some way. "Narrowed down to where?"

Alex smiles. "I've missed you."

Alex and I meet in the music room. He tells me there are pictures on the wall, but in my time, they have all been removed and placed under a tarp in a corner for painting and other work to be done. Everything else has been removed and put in storage for the time being.

The walls are solid. There are no discerning cracks whatsoever. The fireplace is the only thing that stands out with its marble mantel atop a dark wooden surface and its depths reserved for firewood. Alexander bends to study it and peers inside the firebox itself. "I wouldn't think they would put the entrance to a secret room in here. Totally unsafe, but that doesn't mean there is no lever or something."

"It would probably be easier to see with a flashlight," I point out, ready to take out my phone to aid him before I remember he can't see the phone so most likely wouldn't see the light it can provide.

"It just so happens I brought one, Miss Smarty-Pants," Alexander replies with a smirk as he takes out a small flashlight from his pants pocket. He presumably shines the light into the clean fireplace. "No one has had a fire in here for over fifty years. The ventilation isn't the greatest, and my family doesn't want to take chances of ruining the pictures."

As Alex speaks, I wander over to a bunch of portraits leaning against the wall under a tarp for protection. Slowly lifting the tarp, one portrait in particular draws my attention. The colors in the painting are vivid and bright despite its age, and the brushstrokes are precise and intricate. It's an oil-painted portrait of the original Easons. Mr. Eason sits in a chair with a regal bearing, his gaze fixed on the painter in front of him. Mrs. Eason stands tall at his side, her arm loosely draped upon his shoulder. There's another man on Mr. Eason's other side, only instead of looking at the artist like the other two subjects, he is staring off to the left, his face purposely pointed away, almost in profile.

"Hey, Alex, do you see a picture of the Easons? He's seated, she's standing, and a guy is looking away?"

Alex turns his head, studying the walls. He moves to stand next to one, his eyes apparently roving over the portrait.

"Yes, this portrait has always intrigued me. The man looking away is Bartholomew."

"*The* Bartholomew? The one who wrote about the room?" I ask. I bend next to the portrait to get a better look just as Alex steps closer to the portrait on the wall.

"Yes, that Bartholomew. It's a strange picture, isn't it?"

"It makes me wonder what he's looking at," I say as I try to get a closer look.

We both turn in the direction Bartholomew is facing, based on the placement of the picture in Alex's time, and regard the side of the house. We've already established that a large staircase and its upper landing compose that side, but Alex hobbles over to investigate anyway. "It's true there's a staircase here, but there's no way a staircase is going to take up the whole side of the house. Look here. See? This room takes up a bit of the side of the house. It's possible that between this room and the staircase, or between the room on the other side of the house and the upper landing, there's a secret passage. Remember I told you about the secret passage that is basically a staircase leading outside? I wonder if there could be one leading to another secret room."

"Wait! They're not in this room. Look at the background. The fireplace in here is pretty impressive. Wouldn't the artist want to capture something like it if it was created here? Plus, Bartholomew says it's a room *next* to one with a fireplace, but even if the picture has been moved from one wall to another in *this* room, it isn't possible." I point to each wall as I talk. "There are windows along that wall. This one has the staircase, as you said. That one has the hallway on the opposite side, and this one has the fireplace."

"You're right." Alexander examines the picture some more. "I'm trying to think of what room they're in." Practically clawing his fingers through his hair, he gives an exasperated sigh. "It could be any of them."

"Well, we're narrowing it down. We know it's not this one. We know it's a room next to one with a fireplace—"

"Wait."

"What?"

"Look here. This isn't a custom-sized door. All the common rooms have custom-sized doors to accommodate the large parties of people that would gather. It was part of the prestige, I guess. Anyway, the only rooms without custom doors are the bedrooms, which all have fireplaces. I highly doubt these three would pose in one of the bedrooms, but they aren't in any of the common rooms either."

"They're not?"

"No. The door is standard."

"But the journal said that the secret room backs up to a room with a fireplace. Are there any rooms that were reserved for the family that weren't bedrooms but have fireplaces?"

Alexander's eyes grow large as he remembers something. "Yes!"

"Yes?"

"If you weren't a ghost, I'd kiss you right now." He grins at me before turning and hobbling toward the smaller staircase.

"For repeating everything you've said in question format? I ask as I follow him without delay.

"There are rooms that were used as family rooms that have fireplaces," Alex says as he eases his way down the stairs, his cast making them difficult. "Two. The chapel and the library."

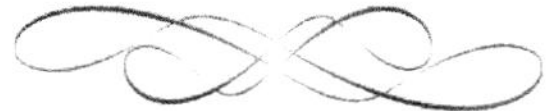

Coming out of the small chapel room, Alex and I look at each other. The excitement we had felt upon entering is dimmer, but there is also an edge to it. With only two viable options to start, we're now down to one, and although it's getting late, I won't be able to sleep until the last one has been thoroughly searched. If the secret room isn't in the room next to the library, we'll have to start from scratch.

Wanting to move forward but afraid of disappointment, we hesitate in the corridor and stand looking at one another. I feel myself leaning toward him. All I want is to rest my head on his chest for a moment, just one moment of physical closeness.

Alex's breath hitches and his nostrils flare as his eyes linger on my mouth. "What the hell, Emma?" he whispers, his gaze shifting to my eyes. "We have to find this room soon. I don't know how much longer I can stand not being able to touch you."

"What if we don't find the room?"

His beautiful hazel eyes close momentarily, and when they open again, they are filled with longing, with bitterness, with sorrow. "We can't go on like this."

"I know."

"We're going to have to move on."

Chapter 20

We slowly and wearily make our way back down the hallway. Could it possibly be the room where the journals will be kept in the future? It has already been established that there is a secret passage leading there from the library. But then, there's the other room next to the library. It's a smaller room that I've looked in a time or two. Right now, the room is empty, waiting for paint and furniture to be replaced. It doesn't have any nooks or crannies that I can think of.

I'm focused on the door of the library when I notice something I never took notice of before. My eyes widening, I increase the speed of my walk. Alex keeps up and looks over at me, his brow raising in question.

"I think I know where it might be," I say. With mounting excitement and anticipation, I run the rest of the way to the library. Standing just outside the entrance, I scan the walls.

"Tell me what's going on in your head," Alex says once he's next to me, and I glance briefly over at him before studying the wall once again.

"It's not symmetrical," I say. "I would think the door would be dead center, but instead, there's more space to the left than the right."

Alex nods and steps up to the wall. "There's nothing here. There are no seams to indicate a door, and I don't see any levers, not even close to the floor."

"What about the room next door?"

"The gentleman's room?"

"Yes, the—wait, what? Seriously?" I roll my eyes.

Alex shrugs. "That's what it was called."

"Fine. Let's go in *the gentleman's room*," I say with as snooty of a voice as I can muster. I walk past Alex as he chuckles and turns left into the room. About three feet inside the room, on the right-hand wall, there's a small door about half my height. "There!"

"That's just a storage cabinet. Instead of having to carry cleaning supplies and the fireplace tools from room to room, in the rooms that were used frequently, they would hide them away in little storage cabinets like this one. It saved time."

Just the same, I open the cabinet and squat to peer inside. It's wide and tall enough for me to fit into, and I hunch over and crawl inside. But it's as he said. Just a small cabinet, now empty.

Disappointed, I sink to the floor and bang my head against the back wall. "Damn."

Alex squats as best he can with his cast just outside the cabinet door. "We'll find it, Emma."

"The room behind the library bookshelves, did it always have the other door on the other side of the room? Maybe it once was hidden, but they opened it up?"

Alex frowns. "It's always been there, as far as I know. Do you want to check it out? We'll know soon enough if it's the one Bartholomew was referring to."

Could it be that simple? I nod and hoist myself up to scoot out of the cabinet but almost instantly turn back around when my arm hits one of the walls.

"Did you hear that?" I ask Alex, who is stooped just far enough away that the spiderweb feeling doesn't happen.

Alex shakes his head and gives me a grin. "But then, sometimes I have trouble hearing you, let alone what's going on around you. Do it again."

I pound my fists against the walls of the cabinet, and the one on the right, as I'm facing outwards, reverberates with a hollow sound. With bated breath, I search the wall for any sign of a secret latch, my fingers trembling as I trace the edges. In a moment of serendipity, my fingers catch onto a small lever at the top, and with a sharp tug, it gives way. This is it! My heart thumps wildly in my chest, and I turn to Alex with sparkling eyes. With one last gasp of excitement, I push open the door and step inside.

Chapter 21

By the light of my phone, I can see that the room is small, no more than an eight-by-eight-foot cell. There is an old settee against one wall, discolored with age and dust, and a small table set in the middle of another wall. It has a candle firmly ensconced in its mirror-backed holder, a small pile of candles, and a small box, which I can only imagine is a tinderbox, used to create a flame before matches, next to it.

Alexander walks over to the latter, lifts it, and shakes his head, putting it down once again. Patting the leg of his jeans, he retrieves a lighter and uses it to light the candle in the holder. It isn't much, but it gives off enough light that we can see each other and the rest of the room, which is bare except for the thick layer of dust that covers everything.

On all the occasions I have been with Alex, we have been alone, but now, when being alone together means so much more, I suddenly feel shy. We stand there, eyeing one another as if we are seeing each other for the first time. In a lot of ways, I guess we are.

Alex's hands hang loosely from his pockets as he looks at me, and under his gaze, I feel like the most beautiful woman in the world. From a mere foot away, his stare caresses me from head to toe, appreciation and a sense of wonder shining brighter than the candlelight reflecting in the mirror-backed holder.

And Alex. Well, he is magnificent. The intensity of his gaze in those almond-shaped eyes; the way his lips almost curl up into a smile; the way his hair stands up, slightly ruffled; the way his shirt fits him in all the right ways, showing off the definition of his muscles in every way that is right, sends my pulse racing.

My mouth feels dry, and I wonder what to say to him. I want to touch the ever-present stubble on his face, run my hands across the broad expanse of his chest. I hadn't allowed myself to think about him like this. Not seriously. But now, my world has changed. This room exists, and he is right here in front of me, wholly, fully here.

And then he steps closer, his hand straying toward my hair. "I want to know what it feels like," he whispers, staring into my eyes. He tugs on the band holding my hair up in a ponytail, and my hair falls around my shoulders. Pushing my hair aside and exposing my neck, he slowly bends forward. Every hair bristles in anticipation, raising to his lips as they barely graze my skin. He proceeds to massage the tense muscles with his fingertips, and I close my eyes, groaning in contentment.

"I want to know all of you." His voice is rough as he tips my head back and his lips touch mine with a restraint he is barely able to contain. My restraint, however, is gone. My hands seem to move of their own volition, so powerless I feel against the onslaught of sensations. They reach up and my fingers are suddenly entwined in his hair, pulling him closer to me. He deepens the kiss, his tongue exploring mine.

Gasping, I pull back, breathing heavily. His eyes burn into me, and he tentatively nudges my nose with his, a question. *Yes. Oh hell, yes*, I think as my lips once again seek comfort from his.

We move deeper into the room and toward the settee, our steps an awkward dance since we refuse to let go of one another. So focused I am on the feel of Alex's body next to mine and the tension building at my core that I don't readily notice the crunch underfoot or feel a cool breeze against my heated skin.

It's only when my foot lands on something that slides, causing me to slip, that I once again become aware of my surroundings. Alex's arms tighten around me, preventing my fall, but our lips part and I look down at my nemesis, a piece of glass.

Frowning, I glance at the window. It has been shattered. Jagged edges remain in the frame, but the wooden cross that once held the panes of glass together in the middle has been torn away, a thin piece of wood the only thing letting me know it was once there. Shards of glass glitter and sparkle on the floor and settee from the candlelight.

"Emma, what's wrong?" Alex's arms ease as he releases me.

"The window's broken. Probably not a good idea to sit on the couch with all the glass," I say.

"It's broken?" He steps away from me and crosses to the window, lifting his hand to touch the frame.

"Stop! I rush over to him and hold on to his arm. "You're going to cut yourself."

"Emma, the window's not broken."

"It's not broken?" I whisper, confused. "Of course it is." I bend over and pick up a shard of glass from the floor, holding it up to show Alex.

He glances at the fragment in my hand and then at the window again as if it is a complicated puzzle.

"It's not broken for me," he says softly, his brows furrowing.

"I don't—" My mouth locks, and my brain doesn't seem to be working. "H-how is that possible?" I stutter.

Alex huffs and gives me a wry smile. "With everything we've seen, you're seriously asking that?"

I return his smile. "Okay, fine. If the window is broken for me and not for you, it had to have happened between our times, but if we can touch each other—"

"And kiss," he interrupts, leaning over to brush my lips with his.

"—and kiss," I amend with a grin, "then why do we each see something different with the window?" I ask as I gingerly lean over the sill and look down into what looks like a small inner courtyard.

Alex shakes his head. "I don't know." He pulls at the lift and jiggles the window from left to right a little before it starts to go up. I giggle as I watch his attempts to open the window because it looks weird to me. It's almost as if he's miming trying to open a window I can't even see. He raises an eyebrow and gives me a smile that says he's going to humor me, before stooping and leaning over the sill as well. "I can close the shutters to try to keep the draft out. You still see shutters, right?"

"Yeah, they're there. I'm going to run to my room and get some blankets." I turn to leave but just as quickly doubled back to Alex.

"You're still going to be here? This is real?"

Alex pulls me to him and brushes my hair back with his fingers. "You're going to come back? I'll still be able to hold you like this?"

I smile. "Those are pretty much the same questions I was asking."

He wraps his arms around me and holds me for a few moments. "I'll be here, Emma," he whispers. "I'm not going anywhere."

As I turn away and walk out the door, his words comfort me—until I remember our circumstances and that his going somewhere, disappearing, is one of the things I'm afraid of.

We lie on the small settee quietly. Alex rests against the arm of one end, with his cast-ed leg stretched out the length of the couch and the foot of his other leg resting on the floor. I sit between his legs, with my back against his chest, my head nestled between his neck and shoulder. His arms are around me, mine resting on his, and he looks down at our hands as his caress mine in the flickering light of the candle.

"I don't know what this is," he says quietly. "It's like I've known you forever but not at all at the same time." He kisses my neck, and I tilt my head, allowing his soft lips more exposure.

"I know," I whisper, not wanting to break whatever spell has come over us.

"It's incredible. Unbelievable. Technically, I should be an old man right now—"

"You dirty old man," I tease.

"I meant, of course, distinguished gentleman," Alex says as he nips at my ear before becoming serious once more. "I just don't understand the point of all this. There has to be some way where one of us can cross over, right? I mean, what would be the point of having a room where we can be together if we can't ultimately be together?"

Shifting positions, I lift myself off of Alex and turn. Putting my hand under my chin, I rest my elbow on the arm of the settee. "I don't know. It doesn't make sense. I'll keep going through the journals, but I've already typed all the ones belonging to Bartholomew in hopes of finding this room. Maybe he did find a way and told someone else. And if he left a clue as to the whereabouts of this room, maybe he left one somewhere about how we can go backward or forward in time."

"Would you come back here?" Alex asks, reaching for a strand of my hair and avoiding my eyes. Sighing, he looks up. "I would be willing to go forward. If that's the only way, I'll go."

"I can't go back." I shake my head. "I couldn't do that to my parents. They've already lost Eve, and I can't imagine what it would do to them . . ." Tears threaten to fall and I blink a few times, willing myself to calm down and breathe through the pain.

"I'm sorry. That was thoughtless of me. Of course you can't."

"Unless . . ."

"Unless what?"

"If there's a way to go back, do you think I could warn my sister? I mean, I don't know how it would affect everything if I am there as a child growing up and there as an adult. Can I even be in the same time as myself? Isn't that a paradox or something?" I'm silent for a moment. "I'd want to go see them, and I wouldn't be able to, not until a day or two before—" I cut myself off, and Alex pulls me against him so that my ear is against his chest. I listen to his heart as my thoughts race. "It would be close to twenty years until I saw her, and she might not even recognize me at that point, but if I could warn her, she'd never get on the boat, and then she would be here for my parents, and I'd—"

"And what if your sister didn't listen to you? Your parents would still lose two daughters, and one—you—they wouldn't even know. You'd be close to fifty years old, and sure, they'd have some time with you, but they'd lose watching you get married, having kids, getting your first gray hair."

"And what if I die somewhere between my time and yours? Then you'd be stuck in the past alone."

We're both silent. "It's all hypothetical anyway," I say after a while. "Maybe all that's to this room is what we've discovered already—a way for us to be together. If there is a way for one of us to go forward or backward, maybe we should see which is more beneficial. Also, is it a one-way ticket?"

"Are you getting bored with me already?"

"No!" I butt my forehead against his playfully. "But if one of us is going to forever change timelines, maybe it would be best to discuss all the potential ramifications."

Alex sighs, his chest rising and lowering, and after snuggling against him a minute longer, I sit up fully. It's late, and Marie and James are probably wondering where I am. Plus, I promised to call my mom. I shiver. The room is chilly when I'm not nestled up to Alex, and I look down to make sure my shirt is buttoned correctly.

"You sure you don't want to get a couple more blankets?" Alex asks huskily, a lascivious twinkle in his eyes. It's tempting, and an internal debate is warring in my head when Alex kisses my shoulder. "No, you were right. I wouldn't want you to get glass splinters."

"A couple of splinters might be worth it," I say, leaning against him.

He smiles. "Plus—he looks around the room—"this isn't the right place. It's cold and dusty."

"And this couch could collapse at any moment," I say solemnly.

Alex smirks and shakes his head slowly. "And we couldn't have that."

"No," I whisper.

We stare into each other's eyes, and Alex leans forward, brushing my lips with his before touching his forehead to mine. A low growl escapes his throat as he tucks an arm around my waist and hoists the two of us to standing. "You have to go. Now. Or I'm not going to stop. I won't be able to," he says, his hands coming up to frame my face as he kisses me once more.

"Okay, okay. I'm leaving," I say, wanting to stay and for this night not to end. We hold hands until we get to the door and then pass through one at a time. The sensation of spiderwebs overwhelms me and, even though I know it's not real, I let go of Alex's hand.

When I look at him again, he's just an echo of the strong and solid man I left in the room. My heart stutters, and I try to remember how to breathe. I knew this was what would happen once we crossed the threshold, but it's still a cruel reminder that no matter how real and corporeal he is in that room, outside of it, he's almost as transparent as the air.

"Hey," he says, his voice a low rumble.

"Hey." I can barely speak.

He takes a step closer, and I take a step back.

"You okay?" he asks, his voice tight, his face a mask of concern.

"Yes." That's all I can manage.

He starts to say something and stops, shifting his weight. "I just," he says, looking everywhere but at me. "We'll figure this out, whatever this is."

I nod, refusing to use my voice for fear it won't come out over the lump in my throat.

He lifts his hand as though about to stroke my cheek, but then lowers it with a sigh instead. "You're not a game to me, Emma." He drags a hand over his face and stares at his feet before meeting my eyes again. "I just need you to know that."

I nod again. Already he's growing fainter to my eyes, our time evidently up.

"Tomorrow," he says.

"Tomorrow," I respond, and before I can backtrack and tell him he's not a game for me either, because all of a sudden it's extremely important that he knows, he's gone.

Chapter 22

It's difficult to put into *words how I felt when, rounding the corner of the observatory, I discovered her standing directly in my path. Like the others, she was visible but clearly not corporeal. Because I'd frightened her—imagine* me *frightening a ghost—I begged her pardon, feeling like a complete idiot as the words left my mouth. As if it was beyond her expectations, her eyes widened, and she absently tucked a strand of hair that escaped from her bun behind her ear. "It's I who should beg pardon, sir," she said. That's when I blustered and blathered for a moment, partly because she has the most melodious voice I've ever heard even though it sounded muted, as if from a great distance, and partly because I heard it to begin with. She responded* *to a question I'd asked. It's utterly fascinating. How is it possible? I believed spirits, should I ever encounter one, would be dumb due to that most tedious of reasons—death. They go through the motions, echoes of who they were in their former lives, but nevertheless, are irrevocably dead and therefore unresponsive to introduced stimuli. I was wrong. It took moments for the shock to wear off, and before I had my wits enough about me to engage in further conversation, she disappeared.*

—Bartholomew Eason, 1878.
Eason Family Estate Library

Time . . . folds here. I don't know how else to describe it. It just does. People can talk to and touch those who should be long dead and buried. For what purpose? It's as if Nature herself asked what was impossible that she could make possible. God, well, now God created all men to die—there is a time and a season and all that, but Nature . . . she has a sense of humor. Look at goats in Morocco, for example. They climb trees. Trees! Or what about that lake in Tanzania? A bird swoops down because it's thirsty, and it gets calcified. What about the lake where you can't drown? There's so much salt in it, you float. Why wouldn't she be able to do this too?

—Emma Beckett, 2014.
Personal journal

The nights are cooler here than in upstate New York, which makes the sitting room off the kitchen that much cozier with a small fire going in the enormous fireplace that dominates one wall. It's Friday night. The lights are off, and with the fire and a few candles lit here and there on tables around the room, it's quite easy to imagine it as it was two hundred years ago.

Homecomings worked their magic in here first. Exposed beams on a ceiling have always reminded me of old and worn bones peeking down through a base of plaster. Here, though, they are a work of art. Brought back to their original luster, the large square beams bring my eyes up and across the length of the room, allowing me to see the quality of the workmanship not only on the ceiling but with all the woodwork. Like the beams, the door frames, window frames, and wooden floor are all polished. The walls, a pale yellow, contrast with the rich, warm oak tones throughout the room. Cream-colored curtains keep the room bright on a sunny day but soothing and warm on cool nights like this one.

About two feet from the stone fireplace face, a large red antique Oriental rug lies, ready to capture some of the chill that will surely pervade the manor during the winter months. Above, on the mantel, a key wound clock strikes the hour before the pendulum resumes its quiet staccato beat.

I lazily sprawl on an oversized chair and enjoy the company of James and Marie, who sit kitty-corner to me on a well-cushioned loveseat. After a long day of work, the peace and quiet of the darkened room is a welcomed treat. Lifting my tumbler of Irish cream, I take a sip and let the taste roll over my tongue before swallowing.

I take a deep breath, trying to push the worries from my mind and enjoy the moment. I look up at James and Marie as they chat quietly about their day. Their conversation is calming and carefree, a stark contrast to my own tumultuous thoughts.

Alex was with me earlier in the evening, and his presence was like an electric shock to my system, sending sparks of longing through every nerve ending. He looked so handsome in the dim light of the secret room, his eyes shining with an emotion I'm afraid to name. Staying at Hillfield Manor, near him, will be my downfall. How can I stay, knowing our time together grows shorter with each passing day, knowing we're no closer to understanding why or how he disappeared? But then, how can I leave when my heart is here?

So I sit, enjoying my visit with Marie and James but wishing for Alex's company instead. We both need space to think, but it doesn't make it any easier to be apart from him.

I take another sip of my Irish cream and let out a sigh. It's going to be hard to look at things objectively now that my emotions have become so involved. How can I possibly separate my feelings when they go so deep? All I know is that tonight, despite the underlying sadness of my circumstances, the distance and being with Marie and James has helped.

"I imagine this is what it must have been like," I say. "Way back when."

James nods slowly as he regards the fire. "This old house has definitely had its share of quiet evenings. Imagine a harpsichord sitting over there"—he points to a corner of the room—"with a small cushioned stool just behind it. And over there"—he points again, to the left of the instrument—"just under the window there, a Demilune table made from Mahogany..." James's voice trails off. His head is bent so I can't see his face, but his shoulders shake a few times. I keep silent, realizing he's struggling with something, but I don't know what to do.

Marie lowers her head so it rests on his shoulder and rubs his back. After a few moments, she lifts her head and whispers in his ear. He nods, clears his throat, and nods again as if collecting his courage before speaking.

"So, I told you when you arrived that I would sit down with you and tell you about the ghost I met and spoke to." He's looking down and rubbing the back of his neck, and when he glances at Marie, she pats his leg.

"It's a good story," she says, glancing over at me and smiling before her eyes return to James once more and she nods encouragingly.

I look from one to the other, at James's nervousness and Marie's reassurances, then put my glass down on the table in front of me and lean forward, my arms on my knees. "You don't have to tell me if you don't want to," I say, noticing James's reluctance.

"Well, you've told us about Alex . . . I think it is only fair that I should share my story with you." James chuckles but sobers quickly.

I didn't tell them anything about the room or what was written in the journals, but the other night, after they asked me where I go off to so often, I broke down and told them I spend time with Alex, hold his hand, and talk without the worry of fading away.

"The way you both looked at me and then away, I thought you believed me to be a raving lunatic." I sit up in the chair, my lethargy forgotten in this revelation.

Marie laughs. "No, we didn't think you were crazy. We just didn't know how much to say."

"What do you mean?"

"Well," James says. "The ghost I saw was Marie."

What?

"And the ghost *I* saw was James."

I sit still for a moment, studying the two of them. They remain silent as I absorb their words. Then James stands up and bows deeply before me. "Bartholomew Edward Jameson Eason, milady, also known as James Gale. It's a pleasure to make your acquaintance."

I shake my head. It isn't possible, yet everything between Alex and me proves that it must be. I tap my face a few times, attempting to rid myself of my stupor.

"Okay," I say. "Okay. This is good." Hope begins to spring within me, and I start to feel giddy. "No," I amend, "this is freakin' amazing!" I jump off the chair, do a couple of twirls around the room, and then hug both James and Marie, who are looking at me with amusement. Then I sit back down, take a couple of deep breaths, and lean forward. "Please, tell me everything."

"I don't know where to start. I suppose you have read the journals? I sounded like a lovestruck fool."

"You were," Marie interrupts, a smirk playing on her full lips.

"Yes, perhaps I was. Perhaps I still am." He pauses and looks fondly at Marie before turning to me.

"I came here in 1878. I was helping my cousin, Gene, around here with the accounts. He wasn't that well, you see, and Georgie was a complete fool. Don't get me wrong, she was nice enough, but she had no business sense whatsoever. Had the manor been left in her hands, we wouldn't be standing here today.

"Anyway, everything revolved around keeping the place running, and I was pretty involved with it. In the course of a few years, we saw plight and plague. It wasn't a pleasant time. Anyway, not long after I arrived, I encountered this woman. I had seen other ghosts around the estate and heard the gossip about them, but until that point, I had never heard my cousin, his wife, or any of their kids ever mention them.

"One night, I decided to ask them. I remember we were sitting right here, as a matter of fact, and I brought up the subject of ghosts. It got pretty quiet at first, but afterward, both Gene and Georgie admitted to having seen ghosts on the estate. I was flabbergasted. I had no idea. And I never thought Georgie the type to keep something like that to herself. I found a new sense of respect for her that night...

"Anyway, I determined that I was going to find the lady I saw and try to communicate with her. I swear I must have spent a month roaming the halls trying to find her again—"

"I was out of town, visiting family," Marie interrupts.

"Then, there she was. One day, after I had pretty much given up hope of ever seeing her again and almost had the feeling that maybe I had never seen her in the first place, there she was. She was walking in one of the rooms off the Long Gallery on the third floor. She paused to look out the window, and I called out to her. I don't think she heard me, for she didn't turn around, so I walked up to her and tried to tap her shoulder. My hand went right through her.

"She must have seen me in her peripheral vision because at that point she practically jumped and spun around quickly with her hands up in the air like she was about to grab my head and smash it like a watermelon."

Marie laughs. "I was about to do just that. I took a self-defense course."

James shakes his head at her before turning to me, his eyes still holding the disbelief he must have felt at that time.

"Can I continue the story?" Marie asks, and James waves for her to continue.

"It was 1976 for me. I was twenty, and I was in love with this place, not unlike you. I would roam the gardens and pretend that times were different, simpler. When I came inside the manor, it was all I could do to keep my wits about me. The place was well cared for, and it was obvious the Easons wanted to preserve the original character of the manor while at the same time having modern conveniences, such as indoor plumbing and electricity. The first time I came here, it was for a party. A friend of mine thought it would be like, far out, so fab!" I laugh at the slang she uses. "Anyway, her father knew the

Easons and asked for a solid, so we were able to boogie down in the hall and—"

"Can you stop with that disgusting language now? I didn't understand it then, and I don't understand it now, and why anyone would want to talk like that is truly beyond my comprehension. You sound like a pudding-headed—"

"Oh, take a chill pill, dude." She holds up a hand as if talking in confidence. "I truly only talk that way to annoy the hell out of him. If it works, I know he's still listening."

Her eyes sparkle as she continues the story. "Anyway, we were all asked to dress in Elizabethan attire, and I truly felt the part. I had wandered away from the rest of the party and that's when I ran into James for the first time. I have to admit, I thought I had one too many to drink. Here was this man in front of me, but I could see through him. A friend called for me at that point, and I went back to dance with her.

"The next time I saw him was about a month later. As I said, I went to visit my grandparents, and when I came back, the manor was hiring cleaning staff. I found out I would get to be here all the time, and I would get to dress up in period clothing. I was in heaven. It was my third day on the job, and I was on my break when he accosted me." She winked.

"What did you do?"

"Well, when I saw that I couldn't touch him and he couldn't touch me, it went a lot toward my relaxing about the whole thing. He wasn't scary to look at. He was quite the opposite, actually, and there was just something about him that made me know I could trust him. Does that make sense?" Marie eases back onto the cushion.

"Anyway, at first, I had to strain to hear him, but once I did, it didn't take long for my ears to sharpen. I asked him what the year was, and he was hesitant to tell me."

"I thought I was dealing with a ghost who didn't understand she was dead," James says. "I didn't know what to say to her, but at the same time, I thought, if I could help her to move on, maybe it was for the best. I told her the truth."

"How did you take it?" I ask, looking at Marie.

"Well, I already figured he was a ghost, so I told him the truth too: 1976. He couldn't believe it. He *wouldn't* believe me. I mean, look at the way I was dressed, but then I showed him my shoes—"

"And she came one day dressed in jeans and a T-shirt. I had to believe her then." James turns to Marie. "I went about it all the wrong way. We could have saved so much time—"

"Don't beat yourself up over it, honey. Who's to say what is the right way to go about doing something like this?

Had you ever heard of it before? I hadn't. There are movies and books, sure. I had years to go before *Back to the Future* came out, and even then, it wouldn't have helped."

"So, what happened then?"

"We talked . . . a lot. Every day, we would walk up and down the halls, and we would find different rooms to talk in. I could see him just fine except for a slight haze, but it seemed other people couldn't make him out as clearly as I could. When people called for me, he couldn't hear it, nor could I when someone was talking to him on his end."

"I think people thought I was crazy at first," James says. "I already told you Gene and Georgie had seen ghosts in the manor before, but they never said anything about standing and talking to one for hours on end."

"Then one day, we were talking and . . . we found a room. It was quite by accident, really. I was supposed to be cleaning—"

My eyes widen. "The secret room!"

James closes his eyes and nods in confirmation. "So, you do know about the room?"

I nod. "We found it—with the help of your journals and the portrait of you and the Easons."

James sighs. "It was well hidden, don't you think? I don't believe anyone in the house knew of its existence. Why the Cenas had it built that way alludes me. The only thing I can think is that they didn't realize what it could do and had built the room just for those things they didn't want getting into the wrong hands. I never found any records, and no one has ever stepped forward with any explanations. Needless to say, I never asked any questions either."

"So, you were able to see each other? I mean, you were solid to each other?"

"As solid as we are now, yes."

"We wanted to tell everyone," Marie said quietly. "I mean, do you understand what we found? It's a gate to time travel!"

"So, the room *does* act as a portal of some sort? Alex and I have been wondering about that." I look over at James. "You never wrote anything about it in your journals."

"By the time I knew, it was too late. When we found the room, we weren't sure exactly what it was. Was it an instrument of evil, there to tease us, to tempt and torment us, maybe drive us mad? People will go to extraordinary lengths when driven by a deep-seated desire, an irresistible urge. Was it a test of some sort? By writing everything down, would I somehow be leading others into a trap into which I, too, had fallen? I just didn't know. So I kept it quiet. I tried to be cryptic with my wording, never giving an exact location."

"Cryptic or not, you left clues."

"I did. Call me a romantic. It was most likely dangerous if my journals fell into the wrong hands, but I couldn't help hoping someone else might have the chance that we had."

"And you found a way to be with Marie." My eyes look from one to the other.

"It's more like the way found us." James's eyes shift from mine, and Marie, too, looks away as she gently rubs James's back.

"Can you tell me what you know? Please?" I look from one to the other, wondering what they're keeping from me.

"It's something only the room can share with you."

"What?" I ask incredulously. "What are you saying?" I go over to James and kneel before him. "Please, you have to help us. We'd like to have what you have, or at least be given that opportunity."

"It's not that we don't want to help you, dear," Marie says. "We're here telling you our story, aren't we? It's just we *can't* tell you because we don't *know*."

"So, then, what happened? One minute you were in the room and then the next"—I snap my fingers—"you were in a different century?"

James nods, frowning. "That pretty much sums it up. I don't remember much except for a lot of wind. That was my experience."

"That's where the Gale surname comes from," Marie chimes in. "Like in *The Wizard of Oz*. I think he must have hit his head or something because he wasn't able to tell me much else either when I found him. All I can say is, whatever blew this man from his time to mine, I'm thankful. I'm so thankful every day."

Frustrated, I get up and pace the room. I glare at them, wanting to lash out but knowing they're not the ones at whom I'm angry. It's the whole situation. How does it all work? *Why* does it work? James and Marie's eyes follow me as I pace. Suddenly, another question comes to mind. "Did you go back?"

James startles. "Go back? You mean to my time? I thought about it. I thought about it for quite some time. How could I not? I thought about seeing this house as it was back then again, seeing and living the 1800s firsthand again . . ." His voice trails off, and it's obvious he is lost in his memories of his parents and his sister, and maybe even of Eugene and Georgianna Eason. I remain silent, the ticking of the clock and the crackling of the fire the only noises within the room. He hasn't answered my question, though, and I'm curious whether the room offers a return journey.

Arduously, I walk up to him and kneel before him once again. "Did you ever try to get back?"

James sits silently for a moment more. The fire crackles and a log, burned more on one end than the other, tumbles from its precarious perch on high. Hesitantly, he begins. "Back when I was eighteen or so, I walked out on my family. My father wanted me to go into finance as he had. I didn't. My mother didn't want to go against my father and urged me to do as he wished, and I tried, but I just didn't take to it.

"I went to America for a while. New land, new opportunities, I thought—it doesn't matter, really. Anyway, eventually, I went back home. I missed my mother and my sister, and I wanted to try to make things right with my father. I practically skipped up the steps. I was so happy to be home, to see everyone again. And it was just as I imagined it would be. My mother cried." James smiles fondly at the memory. "And my sister bustled all about. Even my father shook my hand. But after that first day—no, after a few hours—I could tell things were different. I was a visitor in the house I grew up in. I was a stranger walking in halls I knew like the back of my hand.

"That's when I came here to work for Gene. He was my father's nephew, and when I told her I was going to leave again, he encouraged me to help Gene out—probably for the sake of my mother. I knew she just wanted me to stay relatively close. They only lived about a day's journey from here. Today, you could easily get there in an hour by car.

"I loved my life back then. I loved who I was, and I loved my family." He looks at me then. "But after meeting Marie." He shakes his head. "It was like a light switch clicked on in my head, which was extraordinary, seeing as we didn't have electricity." He chuckles at his own joke. "When I came back to the house I grew up in, I found out I couldn't go *home* again, but then I found a new home, a wonderful and warm and loving home, and it was where this woman right here was." He looks at Marie, and I see the love they have for one another shining in their eyes. Then he looks at me and says, "From that day to this, I have not once been in that room. There is no way I would chance being swept away with no guarantee of being able to come back."

My footsteps echo off the walls as I trudge back to my room, trying to unpack all that James and Marie revealed to me. My mind races with the information they shared, and although I tried to probe them for more, they had no answers. As I reluctantly bid them good night, they asked me to keep the truth to myself, which I will, of course. But I did ask to share it with one other. Alex. The only reason they could have for letting me know James's true identity was to give me a spark of hope. And though the future remains uncertain, I now carry a sliver of possibility—maybe Alex's disappearance leads him to me after all.

Chapter 23

Alex isn't too long behind me, and as he stands in the doorway of the room, my steps quicken until I'm in his arms, my heart swelling with joy. We luxuriate in the moment, content to hold each other without words. I breathe in the scent of him, feeling the warmth of his touch radiating through my skin. It feels surreal and beautiful, and it crushes me that this room is the only place I can hold him like this.

Alex slowly releases me and reaches out to take my hand in his. His skin is soft and warm, and I feel a surge of electricity as our fingers intertwine, making me look up. We stay this way for moments, hours—I can't tell—our eyes locked, our breathing in sync, until Alex pulls me over to the settee and sits next to me.

"You have something to tell me." His voice is soft and full of certainty.

My eyes widen. "How do you know?"

He kisses my nose, then smiles. "I just do."

I explain everything I heard from Marie and James, starting with the secret room and ending with James's true identity. Alex listens without saying a word, his expression shifting from surprise to understanding.

When I finish, Alex sits in silence for a moment before exhaling sharply and turning his gaze away from me. He seems to be processing what I've said, and I wait quietly for him to respond. Finally, he looks back at me and says, "James went forward. I don't think anyone can go back."

"Why not?"

"You'd be going to a time before you existed. I was thinking about it last night. Once you exist, you are a part of the world. Everything that happens from that moment on is partly because you were there."

"That's a bit far-fetched."

"Your car won't start in the morning, so you ask a friend to drive. She's on her way over, and because she doesn't go the way she normally goes, she gets into an accident that she never would have gotten in had she gone to work the way she normally does. She's paralyzed. The guy who slammed into her car feels so guilty that he starts drinking. He loses his job, and his wife ends up leaving him and marrying someone else. They go on to have two kids she wouldn't have had had she never left the man who hit your friend. One of those kids grows up to create a new drug that cures cancer. Great, right? Wrong. There's a side effect that goes unknown for years. Sterility. The thing is, they've decided to give everyone the drug as a childhood vaccine. A whole generation of people is lost because your friend decided to pick *you* up when your car broke down."

I nod. "Yeah, the butterfly effect. But what does that have to do with me going back? It's still *my* future, even if I'm in the past."

"It is, and it isn't. It's your future in a past that already happened before you got there."

"That's not necessarily true. Who's to say I wasn't meant to be there? Who's to say that when I jump back, I'm not integrated into the whole space-time continuum? If all time can coincide at once, and I think we know that much to be true just from being here, then why not be able to go back?"

"Everything moves forward. You don't see people growing younger. You can't reverse the day and make it start again. If you went back, you'd have knowledge of a future that hasn't even happened, and that means, the future can never exist the way you remember it because you altered it just by going in the past—hence, you can't go back because the circumstances that led you to go back in the first place would never have taken place."

I shake my head. "Okay, stop. My head hurts." I laugh. "The fact is, we have no idea what will happen. I'm no astrophysicist, and the last I heard, *you* have a law degree."

"Okay. You're right. But it seems a bit coincidental that you found out I potentially disappear, don't you think? It's just hard not to consider all this stuff when we're living it."

"Yeah." I lean back against him, and he puts his arms around my waist, pulling me closer and cradling me in his embrace. I drop my arms over his and sigh contentedly.

Silence fills the room as we lose ourselves to our own thoughts. It's a relaxed silence borne of two people who are completely comfortable with one another, and I close my eyes, happy in the knowledge that, at this moment, there is nowhere else I want to be.

After a while, Alex clears his throat.

"There are no signs of Christopher here."

My eyes pop open, and I stiffen before pulling out of his embrace, sitting up, and turning to face him. I nod and lower my eyes. "I know."

Alex looks toward the window vacantly and nods.

I touch his arm, willing him to look at me, and when he does, his eyes are clouded with sadness. "Will you tell me what happened?"

Alex sighs and his focus strays to once more to the window. "Christopher was older than me. A lot older. Ten years. It's not like we were like you and your sister. If his friends were over, I was practically banned from the room." He huffs. "But when it was just the two of us"—he smiles—"we were thick as thieves." His smile widens at a memory before he shakes his head. "Maybe that's just how I remember it. Anyway, one day when I was eight, he wasn't there anymore. He was arguing with my parents quite a bit at that point. He was nineteen; he wanted one thing, and they wanted something else. My parents were not the type of people you say no to—not then, anyway."

Alex reaches for my hand instinctively. "They looked everywhere, hired investigators, launched a massive search, but they never heard a word. It was like he dropped off the face of the earth. The authorities were no help. He was nineteen, an adult. They said he was allowed to do what he wanted. There was no evidence of foul play, so they pretty much considered him a runaway." Alex sighs. "It has been eighteen years." He nods slowly, as if coming to a realization. "Deep down, I always thought he'd come back for me, let me know how he was, what he was doing. That's not going to happen."

I wrap my arms around him. "I'm sorry, Alex. I . . . I didn't realize—"

"That I could possibly understand what it is you're going through?" He smiles sadly. "I don't like to talk about it. After he left or disappeared or whatever, my parents changed. They became shells of their former selves, especially my father." He shakes his head. "I remember them being so big." He looks at me, and I nod, remembering my own parents in a similar light. "They had such huge personalities too. And they could be demanding. Very demanding. But after Christopher . . . It was as if they disappeared too. I started seeing them less and less. They'd take more trips away, and then they sent me to boarding school in the States. It was as if I reminded them of what they didn't want to be reminded of."

"That must have been hard."

"It was. I was a kid who needed my parents, and they weren't there." He gently pushes me away from him before standing and going to the window.

"Back then, I hated them, and I hated myself. I thought if I had been more like Christopher, then maybe they would have wanted to spend more time with me."

I shake my head, frowning. "No! I'm sure that wasn't—"

Alex turns my way and smiles grimly. "I know. I know that *now*, after a few therapy sessions. But I was a kid. Anyway, now I wonder what would have happened if they had continued to be the way they were, or if Christopher's disappearance would have made them even worse, their grip that much firmer on *my* life. If they had, who knows if I'd be sitting here with you today. Maybe I would have run away as well."

I think about my parents. They've changed since Eve's death. They're quieter, more fragile physically and emotionally—but then, I am as well. "I'm sorry you and your family went through that."

Alex gives me a small smile. "Emma, I'm telling you this because even though you've faced an undeniable, agonizing loss, there's one thing you have that I don't: closure. You know what happened. And right now, I thought all the outcomes would be bad, but now I have hope. If what happened to James happened to Christopher, he's out there. He's living and breathing. And that can't be a bad thing, right?"

Would knowing Eve was out there where I couldn't see her or contact her give me a sense of peace, or would I worry more, not knowing if she was lonely or hurt and suffering? I don't have any answers. I stand and walk over to Alex and squeeze his hand.

Alex sighs and squeezes back. "I'll write a letter to your parents, warning them about Eve."

I turn to face him, my eyebrows raised and my heart speeding up in my chest. "What? Alex, you don't have to do that. I never asked you to."

He huffs. "I know you didn't ask me to. I *want* to." He shrugs. "It's for science."

I grin. "It's just for science, huh?"

"Well, maybe just a little bit for you."

I hold his stare for a moment, noting the sparkle in his eyes and the upward tilt of his lips. "Thank you," I whisper, leaning in to nuzzle my nose with his before I kiss him.

Chapter 24

"What can I help you with, Lucas?" I say, my tone evident that it's the last thing I want to do.

"It's more how I can help you," he says, his eyes sweeping over me and sending a shiver down my spine. He sets a book on the desk, and I recognize the cover as the journal about the secret room. My eyes blaze with disbelief, and I gasp as I look at Lucas. His face is solemn, but I can tell he knows the importance of this object. "Where did you get this?" I ask, my voice tight with emotion.

Lucas waves a hand in the air and ignores my question, asking one of his own. "Have you ever thought about telling anyone about what goes on here?"

My heart thuds in my chest. I didn't even realize the journal was missing, which doesn't look good, considering it's my job. But here it is, back in my hands, though the questions remain. How did Lucas get a hold of it?

I set my pen down, reach for the journal, set it on the desk in front of me, and then study Lucas. His body, perched upon the edge of the desk, is relaxed, but his fingers give away his agitation as he fidgets with a pen, switching between tapping it against his thumb and clicking it open and closed. "Not really," I say, deciding to play dumb. "People already know about the ghosts. That's why people always came when it was opened, right?"

"That's not what I'm talking about, and you know it," he says, tapping the book with a pointed finger. "All the proof is right there."

"Is it proof, Lucas?" I ask, standing. "Is it really? Because all I see are a bunch of words on old paper. Anyway, I signed a nondisclosure."

Lucas sneers. "You and that damned disclosure! You know as well as I do that everything in that book is worth more than any nondisclosure you signed. Seriously, what could happen? What's the worst they said they would do? Take away your salary? Do you realize how much money you could make with this information?" He picks up the book and shoves it in my face.

Narrowing my eyes, I take it from him and walk to a table across the way where I set it gently on the table.

"What can I help you with, Lucas?" I ask again, turning toward him and crossing my arms.

"I always knew there were secrets about this place. Growing up, I'd hear Marie and James whisper about it. 'Hillfield . . . disappearances . . . secret room.'" Lucas stands and walks around the desk toward me. "They'd always change the subject whenever they caught me. I'd ask, but they'd act as if they didn't know what I was talking about. Made me think I was crazy. The only thing they *would* discuss? The fucking ghosts—as if *that* isn't crazy."

He points to the book and then points at me. "You could help me by telling the truth when the time comes. Hell, say you signed a nondisclosure, for all I care. That will help my case all the more. But stop acting like a hoity-toity prig when you *know* you want this information to come out just as much as I do."

I shake my head. "I'm sorry, Lucas. I don't know what you're talking about. Thank you for returning the journal." I hold up the book, the evidence he needs to prove his case.

He smirks. "Aww, that's cute. You think it's the original."

I look at him sharply before looking at the book in my hands closely. He's right, it's too new. My face pales as I open it and skim through the pages it's now obvious to me are only scans of the original. "Where is it, Lucas?"

"Why, whatever are you talking about, sweet Emma?" he says, his eyes wide with mock innocence.

"Where's the book?" I growl, my concern at the implications of it being in his possession growing with each second. Because of the nondisclosure agreement, I've been fastidious about locking the door whenever I'm not in the library, making sure all the journals I work on remain in the room, but I don't care what this could do to me or my credibility as a professional. This is about Alex and his family. *What would happen to them if word of the secret room and what it could do got out?*

"I don't know what you're talking about." He chuckles and walks closer. "Why are you so upset? You have the book."

"Cut the shit, Lucas!" I slam the book down on the table and step away. "Where is the original?"

"I'm just a worker here. I don't have access to the originals, not like you do." He chuckles again and steps closer until he's standing only inches away and reaches for the journal. "I'll give it back to you, but you have to promise me you'll show me where the room is." He takes the fake journal in his hand and turns it over a couple of times. "I'll give you some time to think about it." He pats my cheek and steps away, throwing the book on the table.

"It was so nice talking to you, Emma. We always have such interesting conversations, don't we?" he says, and moments later, the library door clicks shut behind him.

I sink into the closest chair. My hands are trembling and I take a few deep breaths, trying to calm down and think. I have to tell Alex, but we're not supposed to meet until later this afternoon. Marie and James. They should know too.

Getting up, I grab the journal before racing to the door, making sure it's securely locked behind me. Then, constantly scanning my surroundings to make sure Lucas isn't following me, I follow the sounds of the work being done on Hillfield and find Marie and James overseeing some construction in one of the anterior rooms.

Marie glances over and waves, but when she studies my face, she taps James on the shoulder. He glances first at her and then at me before turning to one of the construction workers and saying something. Moments later, they're both by my side.

"We have a problem," I say, my voice hoarse. "Is there somewhere private we can go for a minute?"

James nods, looks once more at the work being done, then guides us out of the room and into the next, securing the door behind him. "What's this about, Miss Emma?"

"Lucas found the journal about the secret room," I say, wringing my hands and pacing before them. "I don't know how he got it; I lock the door behind me all the time."

I stop pacing and face them. "He came to see me today and gave me a copy." I hand Marie the book in my hand. "He says he's keeping the original unless I show him where the room is."

James slams his fist against the wall. I've never seen him angry, but he is now. "Blast that boy!" he exclaims, his face a mottled red. He slams his fist against the wall once more and then takes up pacing himself. "I knew we shouldn't have offered him the job here, but I kept hoping he'd changed."

Marie is quiet, her eyes downcast, but she nods in agreement.

"What should I do?" I ask. "I'm going to tell Alex, but I won't see him until later, and I'm sorry to put this on you. Really, I am, but I thought maybe you'd have some ideas."

"No," Marie says, putting her hand on my arm. "We're glad you told us."

"Well, he's fired, that's for certain," James says. "We can't have him wandering around, searching."

"But he has the journal." I look from one to the other. "If that gets out, what could it do to the Easons?"

Marie holds up her hand. "Wait." She takes a step forward, her eyes darting around the room as she thinks. "James, remember the silk flowers?" She nods as she lifts her head to James. He, too, nods, a soft smile touching his lips. "It might work," he says. "It's something that was around in his time as well as hers."

"What are you talking about?"

"She'd have to take him to the room," Marie says.

"But he can't see them," James responds, his smile growing. "Once he leaves, we'll take away his privileges to be here."

Tired of not understanding, I throw my hands up in the air. "Will you *please* tell me what you're talking about?"

"Sorry, Emma," Marie says. "Once, when James and I met in the room, he brought me a bouquet of silk flowers. It was winter, but he wanted me to have something beautiful." She smiles at the memory. "Anyway, when I left the room, I took them with me, not even thinking of it, and when I did, they became insubstantial in James's time. He only saw them as he saw me outside of the room."

"What?" I ask, my eyes widening. "How is that even possible?"

James chuckles and looks at me knowingly. "Must you ask?" he says. "So what we're thinking is that you take Lucas to the room, making sure he has the journal with him. He can't see Alex outside the room, so have Alex waiting just outside the door. Get Lucas to leave the journal inside the room, even if just for a few minutes."

Marie's eyes are lit up with anticipation as she continues. "Once Alex sees you come out, he can go in and retrieve the book, and once you see *him* come out, journal in hand, you can part ways with Lucas. It won't matter if he goes back in the room because the journal will no longer be there."

I shake my head, my brows furrowed. "Are you sure it will work?"

James sighs. "There are no guarantees. I remember we remarked on how strange it was with the flowers, but we never tried it again."

Marie nods. "It wasn't long after that when he jumped forward," she says. "And even if it doesn't work, he'll have given you the journal, so if you'd like, after Alex leaves, you can go in and ensure it's gone. If it's not, take it with you."

"We'll not be too far," James chimes in. "We'll be just in the hallway. Then, when we see him, we can inform him that his services will no longer be required. He'll be escorted off the property and won't be permitted back on the premises."

Marie sighs in resignation. "I hate to do it to him, my own flesh and blood," she says, a frown creasing her brows, "but he's had a nasty streak in him ever since he was a teenager." She shakes her head and smiles sadly. "He used to be a very sweet boy. When my brother- and sister-in-law died in a car accident, we were Lucas's guardians." She takes James's hand in hers. "At first, we thought his anger was grief and hormones, but as the months turned into years, he grew more and more sullen."

James clears his throat gruffly. "The day he turned twenty, he moved out, rarely a phone call or a visit, so when he came here inquiring about a job, we thought maybe he was trying to make amends. We thought wrong."

I grab one of their hands in each of mine. "I'm sorry."

Marie closes her eyes and pats my hand with her other. "It was a long time ago, and we'd hoped it was water under the bridge."

I lean forward and hug Marie. "I'm sorry just the same."

"Marie, dear," James says, concern for her etched in his eyes as he takes her in, "I should get back out there. Are you going to be all right? Do you need me to stay?"

The love she has for him shines brightly as she smiles. "I'll be okay. I'm right behind you."

He leans in, placing his hands on her shoulders, and kisses her on her forehead, his lips lingering for a few moments. When he's standing straight once more, he looks at me. "Let us know when. We'll be there."

Once the door is shut behind him, I look once more at Marie. "I really am sorry. If I had been more careful with the journals—"

Marie waves her hand in the air in dismissal. "It wouldn't surprise me if he went in there and stole it right out from under your nose while you were there." I let out a gasp of surprise and she chuckles. "I love my nephew.

He's the son I never had. But I also know what he's capable of." She eyes me shrewdly. "And I imagine this wasn't the only incident you've had to put up with." She takes a step closer and lowers her voice. "Emma, be honest with me please, has he ever tried to hurt y—"

"No!" My response is immediate. Lucas is a Grade-A piece of crap, but he's never done anything more than bully and intimidate.

Marie sags and closes her eyes, looking much older than her fifty-odd years. She sighs in relief. "Good. Good. I didn't think he would, but my faith has been shaken." She opens her eyes once more and straightens her spine. Giving me a tired smile, she grabs onto the door handle. "Let us know." And with that, she walks out the door.

Chapter 25

When it's time to meet Alex, I check that I've logged out of my computer and that the door is locked behind me, just as I do each time I leave the library. Now, however, I check twice. I have no idea where Lucas is, and the last thing I want him to do is get his hands on another journal. As I make my way into the next room, I slowly make a complete circuit around the space and then stick my head out of the door to see if I've been followed. It's not Lucas I run into, though, and I back up, my face scrunched, as the sensation of spiderwebs overwhelms me.

"Nice to see you too," Alex says with a grin. "Were you waiting for me?"

"No, but that would have been nice of me, wouldn't it?" I give him a cheeky smile before walking around him and looking down the hall again. "I have something to tell you. Wait until I go in and make sure I'm not followed, okay? If I am, don't come in."

Alex rakes his hand through his hair with a frown. "What's going on?"

"I'll tell you when we're in there," I say, nodding toward the small closet before making my way over to it.

I'm pacing back and forth in the small room for far too long before Alex comes in.

"Was someone looking for me?" I ask when he finally appears.

"Tall guy, blond hair, perpetual frown? Someone you want to tell me about?" he says as he stops before me.

"That's him," I say, crossing my arms over my chest and glaring at the door. "He's such an asshole. What did he do?"

"Honestly, not much. He knocked on the library door, and when there was no answer, he jiggled the knob a few times, probably checking to see if it was locked. Then he walked into the room below us and glanced around before leaving. I watched him walk down the hall and turn the corner before I came up here. Who is he? An ex?"

I bark out a laugh. "Hardly. That was Lucas."

"Lucas?" Alex says. "As in Marie and James's Lucas?"

"The very same. It turns out he somehow got a hold of James's—Bartholomew's—journal, the one talking about *this* room."

Alex sinks to the couch. "Shit," he breathes out. He wipes his hand across his face. "I'm assuming there's more."

"He's basically holding the journal hostage, threatening to show it around unless I show him where this room is," I say, falling onto the couch next to him.

"No! Hell no!" Alex's eyes flash with warning. "Emma, don't you dare, not even a hint."

"But, Alex, he's threatening to expose your family. He's got the journal. People are bound to figure out the clues like we did. Then what?"

Alex bounds from the couch and paces the room as I did minutes before. He rubs his hands over his face, takes a long breath, and then seems to calm down. He stops and stares at me. "What else?"

"Well, I spoke to James and Marie, told them what Lucas was threatening to do, and they have a plan that I think could work."

"Okay," Alex says, coming to sit by me once again. He sighs. "Okay. I'm listening."

I tell Alex everything that James and Marie told me, about the silk flowers, the plan where he comes in and grabs the journal after Lucas leaves it here, and their plan to fire Lucas once we have the journal back.

"That might work," Alex says when I'm finished. His brow is still furrowed with concern, but he looks more relaxed, and his shoulders are no longer nearly raised to his ears. "But what if he doesn't carry out his end of the deal and doesn't take the book with him when he leaves? Then he has the book and the location of the room."

I nod. "I could ask Marie and James to have some of their workers ready to handle a thief if he gets past with the journal. Then there would be witnesses as well. Would that make you feel better?"

"How did he even get the journal anyway?"

I shake my head. "I lock the door behind me every time I'm out of the room. Marie said she wouldn't be surprised if he took it while I was there."

"So, they willingly let a thief into my home."

I close my eyes. I understand he's upset, but blaming Marie and James isn't helping anything. "Come on, Alex." I sigh. "Don't be that way."

"Emma, he threatened you. He threatened my family!" He growls and slaps his hand on his leg. "If he were in my time, I'd knock the crap out of him."

I can't help it. I laugh. All I can picture is Alex now, running after Lucas and ineffectually trying to go through him to get Lucas to feel the spiderweb sensation. I wave my fingers in the air. "Boooo, Lucas, I'm going to get youuuuu."

Alex smiles grudgingly. "It's not funny." He pouts. "I would too kick his ass."

"Yes, you would," I agree. "My big, strong man."

I lean in and give him a kiss. "We should have started with that."

Alex pulls me closer. "Yes, we should have," he says before kissing me again. And again. Then, abruptly, he breaks off. "Wait. If he made one copy, who's to say he didn't make another? He'll still have the information, and he'll still have the location."

"Well, so far, we've been in here quite a few times, and we've never seen anyone else, so if no one like you—"

"Or you," Alex interjects.

I roll my eyes and smile as I continue. "—walks in here, it's just another secret room. Lots of old houses have them, especially places this big. As far as the journal, if he only has a copy, he could have invented the whole thing. Plus—"

"Wait a minute. You just said it. Why not show him another secret room? Does he know about the one in the library?"

My eyes widen. I can't believe I didn't even think of it. "That's brilliant! Oh, but wait." I get up from the couch. "Can you come with me? We have to see if you'd be able to take a journal out of there . . . and out of here, for that matter, just to make sure."

Alex follows me out, and we make our way to the library. He walks through the door, but I have to unlock the door and open it in my time. Once I make it through, Alex is smirking at me over by the bookshelves hiding the adjacent room, his arms crossed in front of him.

"That's cheating," I say as I close the door behind me, lock it, and make my way over to him.

Alex laughs. "It kind of feels like it, but the library door on my end was open." He turns to the bookshelf. I see him touch the lever by the frame of the case, but although the door must open for him, it doesn't for me. Once he has passed through and I can no longer see him, I, too, push on the lever by the frame of the shelf. The new cases have been delivered, but the journals have not yet been placed within them, so they lie in neat piles on a few tables that have been placed there until the books can be sorted.

Alex looks from the journals to me. "I don't know what you're seeing, but for me, some of the journals seem to be floating on air." He walks over and touches some of them cautiously, as if they will fall. "It's so strange," he says. "When I'm not with you, I see everything the way I'm sure you see things. Everything has its place, but with you"—he steps up to me and smiles—"there's magic."

I smile too and, despite the dreaded feel of the spiderweb sensation, touch his hand with mine. I want to go back to the other room where I can touch him and feel the warmth of his skin, feel the stubble of new growth on his chin, but I know this is important.

With a sigh, I drop my hand and pick up one of the journals. “Shall we try this?”

“Just tell me what you want me to do.”

I set the journal down on the table next to us. “Okay. I guess just try to take this journal out of the room.”

Alex reaches for the journal, but his hand goes through it. He frowns and tries again. “I don’t get it. If the journal exists in both our times, how come I can’t touch it? I was able to touch Bartholomew’s journal.”

I shake my head. I don’t know. “What if you take the journal that Lucas has now and hide it someplace where he won’t find it?”

Alex nods, but he’s still frowning. “If I did that, though, wouldn’t that change things? Then you would never read the journal.”

“Yeah, but you’d be able to show me where the room is.”

He runs his hand back and forth through his hair, a tell that something’s bothering him.

“What is it?”

“Let’s just see what happens with the journal in the other room first. Okay?”

Taking the journal in my hand, I turn toward the door, glancing over my shoulder to see if Alex is coming. He still looks pensive, and it makes me curious to know what he's thinking.

I close the door, knowing he'll be able to get out in his time, walk through the library, and close and lock that door too before walking through to the next room. Looking around to make sure I'm alone, I enter the door to the secret room and place the journal on the table by the candles. Alex appears behind me by the time I'm done.

"You going to tell me what's wrong?" I ask.

Alex holds up a finger, suggesting I wait. Then he tries to take the journal. This time, his hand connects with the leather-bound book. He looks at me in surprise and grins before taking the book out of the room. I look at the table. It's definitely gone.

He doesn't return right away, so I figure he's taking the journal back to the library. Sitting on the couch, I stretch my legs and lean back. It's a relief that we'll be able to get the journal back from Lucas, but he'll still know the location of the room, which is why I don't understand why Alex doesn't want to bypass the whole situation by hiding the journal in his time.

Standing up, I pace the small room a few times, wondering where Alex is. As I turn once more to the door, ready to go find him, I almost run into him as he comes back in.

"I'm sorry," he says. "I took a little longer than I thought I would. Lucas."

I look up sharply. "What happened?"

"Well, somehow he has a key to the library."

"What?" I dig into my pocket and pull out the keys I have, showing them to Alex. "How could he have a key? He's not even supposed to be working in this section of the house!"

"I don't know how he got it, but he has it." Alex rubs his face and sinks onto the couch, grabbing my hand to pull me down with him.

"He must have gotten it from Marie or James—not that they willingly gave it to him."

"Well, he was snooping around in there when I went to return the journal. He looked through a couple, but the ones you have out are pretty recent, so he probably didn't think they were worth taking."

Because I was finished with the older journals, dating back hundreds of years, they have been placed in the adjacent room off the library, awaiting placement in their storage containers. He must wonder where all of them are, though. And if he does, I wonder if he has a key for that room as well. I don't even have a key.

"Well, it's good that this room works and you'll be able to get the journal back from him, but why don't you want to hide the journal in your time so Lucas won't find it?"

Alex's face reddens. "It's complicated."

"Try me. All you'd have to do is find the right one and hide it somewhere."

"It's not that simple, Emma."

"Why not?"

He pauses, swallowing. "I already told you. If someone found the journal between my time and yours, it could change the course of history."

"But that's what we're trying to do, isn't it?" I ask. "We'd still end up meeting. I just wouldn't know about the journal."

"And you're the one who told me about it. So, what? All the conversations we had, will they have even happened?"

I didn't think about it that carefully. Here, I'm always the one talking about space-time continuums and whatnot, but as I hear him speak the words, I realize I'm not the only one taking all of this into consideration.

"Emma . . ." He pauses. While he's choosing his words, he caresses my arm with feather-light touches, and goose bumps rise on my skin. "I like you. A lot."

When he raises his hazel eyes to mine, the truth of his words is there, and now I have goosebumps for another reason. "And part of what I like about you is what I learned from our time searching for this room. I don't want to remember things that you won't remember experiencing too. And I don't want to chance that hiding the journal could bring about more changes than we could ever possibly know."

I force myself to look away, blinking several times to keep the tears at bay. I can't help it. I've come to care for this man more than I'd like to admit, and it scares the crap out of me. Not only because what we have is hardly ideal, given the circumstances, but also because I very well might lose him—to time.

He plays with the fabric on my sleeve absentmindedly, his eyes scanning the small room. I can tell he's lost in thought, and I'm grateful for the reprieve, but then he smiles at me and I feel my insides clench.

"What's the smile for?" I try to sound casual, but I fail.

He laughs self-consciously. "I've scared you, haven't I?"

I touch his face, tracing his cheek, his jaw. "No. No, you haven't scared me. I feel the same. What scares me is this." I wave my hands in the air, suggesting the room, the house, our situation. "And wondering if I'll lose you like I did Eve. And there's not a damn thing I can do about it." My voice cracks at the end, and I look away from him. If I continue to do so, I'll break down.

"Emma," he says softly, and I can hear the tremor in his voice. "We'll figure something out. James and Marie did. And again, I go missing. It's probably because I'm there with you."

I hold his gaze, seeing all the emotions that must be reflected in my own—fear, confusion, but love and adoration too. My eyes become glassy, and I allow myself to succumb to the emotions I've been trying so hard to keep at bay. I burrow my face into his chest and let go.

He wraps his arms around me and holds me. He doesn't even try to placate me. He knows our situation. What is there to say?

I exhale loudly and pull away from him, wiping my eyes. "Anyway," I say, and my voice sounds hollow. I stand up and breathe in, trying in some way to give myself distance, trying to keep myself from falling into a deeper funk. "So, the journal works in here. Can you be free tomorrow?"

Alex stands as well. "Absolutely."

I drop my head, hiding the anguish I'm feeling, but my voice sounds strong as I say, "James and Marie will be around, and you'll be around. This will work. And I'll tell Marie about the key. We'll get it back from him and change the lock."

We go over everything once more and set the time we'll meet. I have to check with Lucas to make sure he'll be available, but his desire to know the room's location is bound to make him drop everything. Of course, his desire to be an asshole could cause him to make me wait it out as well. We have a contingency plan in place, though, in case Alex doesn't show—it's still random when he disappears outside of the room—or Lucas doesn't.

Alex has to leave for a tour group, but he kisses me before he goes. He opens his mouth to say something, but in the end, he just smiles. There's assurance in his eyes that everything will be just fine, and I pray he's right. This has to work. I may not be able to save him, but at least I can save his family from having to deal with the fallout of what Lucas is planning. And for right now, that'll have to be enough.

Chapter 26

I wander the library aimlessly, my feet moving from the window to the fireplace, to a bookcase and back again, as I wait for Lucas to arrive. He said he'd be here, journal in hand, at eleven, five minutes from now. While I wait, I go over the plan again in my head. I told Marie and James last night, and they plan on being in one of the rooms nearby, trying not to be too obvious.

There's a brief knock at the opened door before Lucas walks in. Foregoing any barbs or taunts, he comes right to the point. "How do I know this isn't just another secret room, that it's the one talked about in the journal?"

I hold out my hand for the journal he's holding and inspect it carefully. It's the original. Placing it on the desk in front of me, I try to lure Lucas out of the room.

"Nice try," he says, picking up the journal. "The room, then the journal."

Sighing, I guide him into the next room, open the small cabinet, and usher him into the secret room. He looks around the small room, unimpressed.

"So, again, how do I know this is the room Bartholomew talks about?"

"I've asked Alex to meet us here so you can see for yourself."

His eyes widen. "You did?"

"Come on, let's go see where he is. Just leave the journal on the table. We're not going far. Sometimes he waits for me just outside the door."

Lucas sets the journal down and follows me out of the room. Thankfully, Alex is there, and he gives me a wink, but I pretend not to see him and he moves past me to go to the room himself. Lucas, of course, is oblivious to everything.

My heart is pounding as I think of everything that could go wrong, but I fold my arms across my chest and turn to Lucas with what I hope is an impatient attitude. "He's not here yet." I tap my foot in mock annoyance. "He said he'd be here. Let's just give him a few more minutes."

Stalling for time, I ask Lucas what his plans are now that he knows the room's location.

"You're awfully interested for someone wanting nothing to do with this. Starting to come around to my way of thinking?"

"No. I still think you're a prick. Blackmailing me is a shit move, Lucas, and you know it, but I want to know that the Easons won't get hurt."

Lucas eyes me suspiciously and then tosses his head back. "If you're worried about your precious reputation, the less you know, the better, right?"

Alex reappears from the doorway with the journal in his hand, and he scurries toward the library to store it. I told him I wouldn't go back to the room until he gets back, so I have to keep Lucas talking even though all I want to do is walk away from him right now.

"Look, if there's some sort of personal agenda you've got going on, so be it, but don't drag down the Eason name. They've done nothing to you!"

Lucas's eyes turn cold, and he steps up so he towers over me. "You don't know shit," he says, his voice low, dangerous. He stares at me for a few moments before he backs away and glances around the room. "Looks like your boyfriend isn't going to show. I'm going back for the journal."

Alex walks back into the room just then, and when he nods, I know the journal is safe, so I raise my voice, the signal for Marie and James to come in. "We had a deal! I show you the room and you give me the journal. You can't go back on your word, Lucas." I go to block the door, but Lucas pushes past me, throwing over his shoulder, "Watch me."

Alex's fists are clenched as he glares at the cabinet through which Lucas disappeared, but he turns to give me an encouraging nod just as Lucas comes barreling back out through the door.

"What the hell did you do? Where is it?" he practically growls.

I widen my eyes and feign innocence. "What are you talking about? It's right where you left it."

"Do we have a problem in here?" James asks as he steps inside, followed by a few of the crew. They're a motley bunch. One is on the shorter side, but his arms are massive and he has a bright red beard and glasses. Another is tall, about six foot five, muscular, and bald. His eyes are dark, almost black, like the sky before a thunderstorm, and his mouth is drawn in a thin, tense line. The third, standing a little behind the others, is thin with blond, shoulder-length hair and wears a golden cross in his ear.

Lucas glances at them before turning back to me, murder in his eyes. "What are you playing at, bitch?" he says to me in a low growl, ignoring James.

I drop my arms and gape in stunned silence at the venom in his voice. It's so quiet I wonder if the others can hear, but when I see James's eyes narrow on Lucas, it's certain he at least can.

"You have no fucking clue who you're messing with."

Alex stands up straighter, his hands turning into fists as he faces Lucas with a dangerous gleam in his eyes. I glance at him, knowing he feels helpless, but there's nothing he can do. He slams his fist against the wall, but because he's no more substantial than a shadow, his anger goes unnoticed by Lucas, oblivious to his presence.

"Lucas," James says, stepping up to him, his eyes devoid of all humor usually found within. "Your services are no longer required. Please vacate the premises immediately."

Lucas curls his fingers into a fist, his arm shaking with repressed rage. He takes a step toward me, but two of the guys who came in with James take a step forward as well.

"Do not," James says slowly, "make me ask you again."

Lucas pauses, eyeing the two men who now stand on either side of him. He knows as well as everyone in the room that his best choice is to do what James asked. He rolls his shoulders in a shrug. "Fine." He starts to walk away, but suddenly, he's right next to me, his fingers digging into my shoulders and his mouth right next to my ear. "But this isn't over," he whispers, his breath against my skin sending a shiver down my spine.

He spins around, tossing a scathing look my way as he leaves.

James looks at me, silently asking if I'm okay.

I nod, and he turns to follow Lucas out, as do the crew members.

After they leave, all I can do is stare at the floor. I'm in shock. Lucas has always been a jerk, as far as I'm concerned, but I've never seen him so angry, so volatile. And the thing is, I still don't understand it.

Alex steps into my line of vision. His jaw is clenched, his anger apparent, and his hands are still balled into fists. If he could have pulled me up to the room, I believe he would have. Instead, he has to settle for asking me to go up with him, and when we do, he pulls me into a tight hug.

"Are you okay?" he asks, his voice tight.

I nod, burying my face in his chest.

"You're shaking," he says, pulling away from me enough to look down into my eyes. "Come here."

He leads me over to the couch and pulls me down so I'm seated on his lap with my legs on the cushion next to him. One of the blankets from my room is still there, and he pulls it over me, covering us both as he continues to hold me.

After a while, he says, "I'm sorry, Emma. If I could have done something—"

"It's not your fault," I interrupt, trying to keep my voice steady, and I open my mouth to say more, but I forget what I want to say as the scene plays over again in my head.

A knock at the door has us both instantly to our feet.

"It's just me," Marie says, standing at the entrance. Her eyes dart around the room nervously, as if she's afraid whatever happened to James here to pull him forward in time will happen to her as well. Since James doesn't remember what it was, I can't say I blame her. Strangely, I've never thought about it in terms of myself before now. *Could I suddenly be ripped into the past without getting a chance to say goodbye to my parents? Without them knowing what has happened to me?* It's a sobering thought, and I wrap my arms around myself, the trembling from the adrenaline still coursing through me, kicking itself up a notch.

"Are you okay?" she asks.

It's the second time this has been asked in a matter of minutes, and I almost laugh. Instead, I inhale shakily and nod.

"Lucas is gone. James took the key to the library. He had a key to the front door as well. We'll have new keys made and new locks installed, of course, but I wanted you to know he's not going to hurt you."

"Thanks, Marie. And I'll be down soon to thank James as well." I can see she's anxious to get away from the room, but I have to ask. "Marie, why is Lucas so angry?"

She sighs and closes her eyes. When she opens them again, they're resigned. "You know about Lucas's parents—how they died in a car accident."

I nod. This is something Marie has told me before.

"Well, the accident happened on the same night we told them about James. My brother had always been able to see ghosts—for lack of a better word." She looks at Alex apologetically. "And he kept saying James looked so familiar to him. That night, he recognized where he saw James, and he confronted us about it, so we told him. Laura, my sister-in-law, loved everything paranormal—kind of like you—and she was so excited about it."

"But how would Lucas know about that?"

"Lucas was with them. He heard the conversation. I thought he was too little to understand. He was only a little boy and had been playing with his cars when we were telling the story. I had no idea he was paying attention."

Marie steps backward so she's out of the room before her face appears once more in the doorway. "After the accident, sometimes Lucas would say something, allude to the conversation. James and I thought it best to tell him it was his imagination. The story is so far-fetched as it is, and we thought by telling him it was a made-up story, that he'd eventually forget about it. He'd say, 'But Mommy and Daddy were talking about it in the car right before . . .' But he'd never finish the sentence."

A sudden twang of pity for Lucas hits me. I picture him sitting in the backseat of a car as a little boy while his parents talk excitedly about what they've learned. Then, whatever happens to cause the accident throws his world into chaos, and he's left trying to make sense of what happened . . .

"He blames Hillfield for the accident," I say, my words whispered.

Marie shakes her head and shrugs. "Hillfield, me and James, I don't know."

"Why did you let him work here, knowing all of that?" Alex asks. It's the first time he has spoken since Marie entered, and his voice is tinged with anger.

"I'm sorry, Alex. Truly. We both are. The last time Lucas even mentioned Hillfield, he was about twelve or thirteen. We thought, finally, he had put it behind him.

"He is very good at what he does, and we debated whether *not* hiring him would make him question why and lead us right back to him thinking about what we so badly wanted him to forget."

"Instead, hiring him has had the same outcome," I say.

"Yes," Marie agrees. She glances behind her and leans into the room once more. "I'm sorry. I have to go back to James. We'll answer any other questions you have. We honestly had no idea this—what has happened—would happen."

"Thanks for telling us, Marie," Alex says. He steps forward and gives Marie a hug, and she gasps before smiling.

"It's so strange to see you just as you were when I worked here, Alex." Her smile fades. "You know, sometimes I question my memory. It has been so long. Was it just my imagination that James was once like you, that everything to do with this room wasn't just a story we concocted, a bit of fun to tell those who asked us how we met? It's hard remembering that when he was outside of this room, he was merely a shadow, but then, here you are—proof."

She grasps my hand and squeezes it before turning, leaving both Alex and me to stare after her and reflect upon her words.

Chapter 27

Dear Beckett family,

This is going to sound strange, and I apologize in advance for any distress I may cause with my words, but I have information I need you to hear. Your daughter, Evelyn, will be in a boating accident that results in her death on 12 July, 2013. I can't tell you how I know this. I don't even know if sending this letter to you will alter other important events in her life, in Emma's, or yours. I'm sorry for being so cryptic, and I'm sorry I can't offer you anything more. All I can assume is if all goes well, you'll know more about how all of this transpired after that date.

All my best to you and your family.

Alex

"I sent the letter."

"What?"

"The letter to your family. I sent it."

"You sent it?" Hope blazes in her eyes, and the haunted look that has been present ever since Lucas was dismissed finally takes a backseat for once.

"Yes." I smile.

Emma's so excited she launches herself at me. I hold my arms out, ready to catch her and hold her tight against my chest, only to remember at the last moment that that's not possible. I flinch as she goes through me, not just because of the feeling of spiderwebs but because I'm waiting for the sound of her fall. And I can't do anything about it.

She catches herself at the last moment and keeps to her feet, but I see her scowl as she tries to wipe off nonexistent webs clinging to her face and arms. I hold back a laugh, and she glares at me before grinning in return.

"When did you send it?"

"I just put it in the mailbox."

"Like, this morning? Or you just got back from dropping it into the mail now?" She sighs in exasperation at my lack of detail. "It makes a difference!"

"It does?"

"Well, yeah! I mean, maybe we have to wait until the letter is actually picked up because there's still the possibility for you to go back and get it. But, actually, once you made up your mind, it should be a done deal."

She looks at me quizzically, and I return her stare, uncertain of what she wants me to say.

"So, everything should be fine now, right? Everything you do is in the past for me, kind of, I mean, outside of when we're together in the room, because then it's the present for both of us, I guess, which is a total mind bender. But since you already put the letter in the box, that's the past for you, and for me, well, it's the past either way, so everything should be done now anyway, right?"

She's procrastinating. Hope and fear are radiating from her, and I want to pull her into my arms and assure her I've done everything I can to get her sister back to her. Apart from her parents thinking I'm crazy, I don't see how anything can go wrong. If I received a letter like that, I don't think it's something I could forget too easily. I'd probably memorize it, at least the date and the circumstance, keep the letter in a safe place and look at it every once in a while, and ensure that I did everything I could so whatever it was didn't come to pass.

I think about my parents and my brother and how different our lives would be if someone had sent us a letter with similar details. Maybe my parents wouldn't be so distant. Maybe my brother and I would be best friends despite how much older he was. But then I wonder if his being here now would change the course of my life. Would I still be giving tours of this house? Would I have moved on to different pursuits? There's no way to know.

A sudden chill moves down my spine. How much will that letter change the course of actions between Emma and me? She's obviously here and would be here regardless or else she never would have shown up to begin with. But will she be the same person? Will all the experiences she's had that made her who she is change? Will she grow up differently now?

I haven't been paying attention and shake my head a little to clear my mind and concentrate on what she's saying.

". . . her about all this, and she'll have no clue what happened. My parents won't either. You and I will be the only ones with this knowledge! It's so messed up. In a good way, obviously. But don't you think I should *feel* something? Like, shouldn't there be some sort of brain shift? I feel like there should be this, like, brain freeze as all the new information transfers and fits in with the information I remember. That's what happened on *The Butterfly Effect.*

Oh, but you don't know about that movie yet. You *have* to see it when it comes out. I think it's in the early 2000s. I'll look it up later."

I watch as she rambles, a smile on my face. I've heard of the butterfly effect but have no idea what she's talking about. Brain freeze? Whatever. The only thing I know is I haven't seen her like this in, well, ever. It makes me happy that I made her happy, and it's the best feeling in the world. I want to make her feel like this all the time.

"Emma."

"I'm using *like* too much, aren't I? I always do that when I get nervous. I can't help it, but why should I be nervous? This is Eve we're talking about here, and—"

"Emma, shhh."

"What?" She looks up at me, and even through her transparency, I can see the blush on her face.

"Ooh, my phone's upstairs. I'm going to call Eve right now! You want to come with me?"

I glance down at my watch. "I have a tour in about ten minutes. How about I meet you in our room in two hours, and you can tell me all about it then?"

She reaches for me again, and we both scrunch our faces as the feeling of spiderwebs creeps over us. I laugh and give her a smile. She beams back at me. "Alex, I . . . I don't know what to say. This is everything. I—you—I just want to smother you in kisses right now."

I wink at her. "Why do you think I suggested the room? Go. I'll see you in two hours. Keep that thought!"

Emma flashes me a grin before running out the door. A few moments later, I imagine that I can hear her tearing up the stairs. I want it like this always.

No. I want more.

The thought sobers me. I don't know how all of this is possible, and I'm so thankful for it, but damn it, I want more. I want more than seeing her mostly in shadow, more than a few hours of being able to touch her in a dusty secret room. I want sunshine and moonlit walks. I want to see the wind rustle through her hair. I want to see her around others, on a rollercoaster, at a restaurant. I want all of her, and it's getting to the point where it's not merely a want. It's a *need*.

My watch beeps, and I sigh. It's time for the tour. I straighten my waistcoat—such a pain in the ass—and head out.

Emma

My heart is pounding as I enter my room. *It has to work*, I keep telling myself. *It has to.* My parents aren't the type of people to disregard a letter of this magnitude, and even if they didn't have the letter, a date would stick out.

Hell, even if they remembered the year. "Eve, you can't go on a boat in 2013." End of story.

As I search for my phone, I keep waiting for memories to come to the surface of them mentioning something, anything, about a letter or staying away from boats. Maybe they didn't tell me and just told Eve? They would have told me too, though. Just in case. That's the type of people they are. They plan for things. My parents keep a will and update it. When I turned eighteen, I remember them talking about changing it again since Eve and I were too old to have guardians any longer. They were on top of details like that. And this would be something too huge *not* to keep a record of.

I find the phone on the side of my bed, and when I pick it up, I hesitate. In the last year, I've called Eve's number more times than I can count. Sometimes I just want to hear her voice again—*Hi, you've reached Eve Beckett. I can't come to the phone right now, but if you'll leave your name and number, I'll get back to you as soon as possible*. I used to tease her because she never seemed to have her phone.

"What's the point?" she asked. "Nobody calls me anyway."

"That's because everyone knows you never have your phone!"

She'd smile and promise to take it, and she'd do so for a day or two before forgetting about it again. That was Eve.

That is *Eve*.

With my breath coming faster, I dial Eve's number and wait for the call to go through.

Riiiinnng.

My hands, clammy and trembling, clutch the phone as I desperately pray for Eve to pick up.

Riiinnng.

There were always three rings before the call would go to voice mail.

Riiiinnng.

The phone picks up, and I collapse on the bed, my breath leaving me completely. It didn't work.

Hi, you've reached Eve—

It feels like my heart is being ripped out all over again, like I'm reliving her death a second time. Hanging up the phone, I dissolve into tears. It isn't fair. It's so unbelievably unfair!

The sound of my phone ringing makes me stifle my sobs. Wiping the tears from my eyes, I reach for it and check the screen to see who's calling. *Evie.*

My heart once again in my throat, I answer. "Eve?" And before I can get another word out, I dissolve into tears once more. "Eve," I mumble between loud, snot-filled sniffs. "Thank God—"

"Emma?"

"Yes! Eve! You don't know how glad—" I take another shaky breath, trying to calm myself down. "It's so good to hear your voice!" I burst into tears again. "You don't—"

"Emma." And then I hear crying on her end too. I want to assure her I'm okay, that hearing her voice makes everything so much more than okay, but as I listen, it takes a moment for my brain to register that it isn't Eve's voice at all.

"Mom?"

"Oh, Emma," my mom says, her voice filled with pain and sorrow.

"I thought—" I swallow, but the lump that has formed in my throat won't go away. I drop my head onto my knees as I hold the phone to my ear, the sound of my anguish mixed with that of my mother's the only sound for minutes. "I'm sorry, Mom."

"No, I'm sorry, honey. I don't know what I was thinking. I shouldn't have called from her phone. I was—" Her voice breaks again, and she's silent for a moment before continuing. "I guess there's no need to keep her phone charged, but I can't help myself. I was looking at the photos she has. She didn't take her phone a lot, but when she did, she always took photos."

"I know." I sound hollow, my words a choked whisper.

"Well, I'll call you soon. From my phone." She tries to laugh, but it doesn't work, and I can hear her swallow a sob instead.

"Mom? Did you ever receive a letter?"

"A letter? What kind of letter?"

"When Eve and I were little, did you ever get a letter warning you about Eve's accident?"

Silence reigns for a moment, and in that space of time, my thoughts wreak havoc. *They* did *get a letter—Wait, was that* this *year they were supposed to worry? Or they threw it out, thinking some wack job was trying to torture them. Or they turned it over to the police to get more answers. Or they gave it to Eve after extracting a promise from her to stay away from water on that date. Or—*

"Emma, where is this coming from? What are you talking about?"

Clear confusion comes through the connection. She has no clue what I'm talking about. *They never got a letter. Why would Alex make this up?* "Sorry, Mom. I just woke up," I lie. "I had a dream that you and Dad got a letter when Eve and I were little, warning you about what was going to happen."

"You have no idea how much I wish that were the case." She's silent for a moment. "Once, your grandma said something. She said, 'Eve died. You must tell her so it doesn't happen.' I asked her what she was talking about, but she just patted my hand. It was toward the end when she was taking so much medication. Sometimes, she would be so lucid, and other times, she would come out with such bizarre things . . .

"You know, I'd love it even more to have a letter telling us we didn't have to worry about you at all, that you'd have long, long, happy and healthy lives, dying well after we do. Your father and I would move heaven and earth to keep you two—you now—safe. That's the thing with parents . . . we raise you to the best of our ability, but then one day, we have to let you go. And it's like watching you walk and ride a bike and say your first words all at the same time."

She pauses and takes a shaky breath. I hear the longing in her voice, and it breaks my heart for the pain she and my dad have gone through.

When she's composed herself, she continues, saying, "We raised smart, capable, beautiful women, and we wanted to see you blow the world away with all you have to offer. That's how proud we were when each of you moved out. But it's also like watching your child walk away for the first time on her own or waiting for her to come back from a date. The world's so big, and so many things can happen. You just want to chain them up, force them to live at home, do whatever you can to make sure they stay as safe as they were when they fell asleep in your arms as a baby. If I could have the help in a form of a letter to tell me what I have to do to keep you safe, you better believe I'd keep that letter close."

"I love you, Mom."

"Oh, sweetheart, I love you! So, so much. Wherever you go, whatever you do, always know that."

After we say our goodbyes, I sit there on the edge of my bed for a long time. Thoughts fly through my brain in random order. Eve, Alex and what it means to us that he's literally living in the past, the secret room and what it offers, Lucas and his obsession and anger. Then back to Eve, to Marie and James, and why the room pushed James forward in time. I think about my job here and what I'll be doing afterward, my parents and how they're getting older, how my heart will be torn in two all over again when the time comes that I lose them as well. How can I stand to take any more loss?

It's not my intention to start a fight with Alex when I go to the room in search of him. I'm upset, angry, hurt, disappointed, and pretty much every negative emotion within me propels me forward with one unifying thought in mind: making as many of those feelings as I can go away.

I get there first, and as I wait, I allow my anger to build. *How could he possibly mess up sending a letter? Is there a reason he didn't want to send it but just told me he did to make me happy?* There is no good reason. None. And if there is, I'm not willing to listen to it, not when my sister is dead and life continues without her.

When he enters through the door, he has a smile on his face, and the joy there—joy for *me*—almost puts a lid on my anger. *Almost.* The thing with pain, though, is that it tends to make me lash out, even when ultimately I know my tongue lashings will most likely come back to bite me in the ass.

"Did you even send the letter?" I ask, each word dripping off my tongue with venom. My eyes narrow in accusation.

Alex's face turns into a mask of confusion as the smile that was fixed there melts off like decorative ridges of a candle. "What? Of course I did! What happened?"

"Don't you think the question is more like what *didn't* happen?" I ask. "She wasn't there, Alex! She's dead. *Dead!* She's still dead." I crumple onto the couch, my sobs the only sound that breaks the silence.

Alex drops to his knees before me. "Oh, Emma." He tries to wrap his arms around me, but I swat away his attempts. I want to remain angry. Anger is easier than the pain of sadness, and these are angry tears. I don't want pity or sympathy.

"Maybe it just takes a little time," Alex says as he pats my knee. "Maybe it all depends on the letter being in the system or something."

"No. Don't you get it? All that is in the past for me. By 2014, all of that has been done! It should have worked. I should be able to board a plane and go hug my sister instead of sitting here and talking to—"

"To what? A ghost? Someone who's dead or will be, or might as well be?" Alex stands abruptly and moves to the other side of the room. His back is to me, but I can sense his anger in the rigidity of his posture and the way he inhales and exhales deeply, as if holding back a cascade of spiteful words. "And who the hell made you an expert on time travel all of a sudden?" he asks, the dam holding back his arsenal of hurtful, albeit valid, points, bursting as he spins to face me. "You have a degree in quantum physics you've been hiding? You want to tell me how all of this"—he throws his arms up in the air to indicate the room—"is possible then, oh brilliant one?"

"Shut up." My retort is juvenile and ineffectual. I imagine a scoreboard with a point being drawn on his side in my head. That and the smirk on his face lead me to say something I probably shouldn't. "If someone could prevent your brother from disappearing, wouldn't you want every opportunity to prevent it?"

If I had a knife and plunged it into Alex's side, he wouldn't look any more surprised and hurt than he does now that I've uttered those words. Score one for me in the hitting-below-the-belt category. I've just dredged up all the pain and hurt he's been able to keep under control since his brother went missing. From his expression, I can see it's every gut-wrenching feeling I've been suffering since Eve's death, and whereas he's been trying to help me and has been nothing but kind and caring, I've thrown his grief in his face like a bucket of battery acid.

Alex's hands curl up into fists, and he pales. He heads to the door, and I know I need to apologize, but before I can formulate the words, he turns back to me.

"I understand your grief, Emma, and I've sent the letter. I can't make you believe me." He narrows his eyes. "But I don't appreciate being used. Do you even care about me, or is this all about getting your sister back?"

My eyes widen in surprise. Of course I care about him. I care too much! Memories flash through my mind of our meeting and getting to know one another. I think about how he made me feel even before we could touch. I think about how his very being is imprinted on my mind so I'll know what he looks like and smells like even if I never see him again. We've laughed, we've shared sorrows, we've talked about real events. He brings out the best—and worst—in me, and I love him.

While I sit reminiscing, Alex stares at me, waiting for a reply. My mouth opens, but words aren't forthcoming. *How can I tell him that my feelings for him are exactly why I need to get away from him?*

"We both know this can never work," he says softly. "You're there; I'm here. So, what am I? A way for you to get a do-over? What are you going to ask me to do next, mail you the winning lottery numbers? Christ, Emma!"

"No! No." This isn't what I had in mind. This isn't how I envisioned this conversation going. My anger and hurt spurred me to drive a wedge between us, but it was only so I could get away and lick my wounds. I didn't want to hurt him in the process. And that's exactly what I've done.

"Look, this isn't working," Alex says, his head bowed so he doesn't have to meet my eyes. "I'm stuck here, and you're . . . you're not living. It's like you're stuck with ghosts no matter where you turn—me, the others around here, the memory of your sister. You need to leave, Emma. You need to get out and never look back."

His words send a shiver down my spine. With him stuck here, it's what I was planning all along—if I could tear myself away—but now that the words are out, it's the last thing I want. "I'm sorry I mentioned your brother. That wasn't fair. I was angry and disappointed, and I . . . I say things I don't mean sometimes. I just want"—my lips tremble and my voice shakes—"I want her back so much, you know? But I don't want to lose you too."

"Emma, there's nothing more that I want than for us to be together, but you staying here..." He shakes his head. "You're going to end up resenting me. I'm just going to hold you back, and if . . . if something does happen to me, you'll be alone, even more than you already are." His face shows resolve. "I'm asking you to leave, Emma. I *want* you to leave. Finish your work and go."

Everything inside me begs me not to go, but there's nothing I can do. I do my best to avoid his gaze, but I see his eyes on me, noticing the pain, recognizing the same thing in me that's written all over him—sadness, longing, love. It's too hard, but I know he's right.

"Goodbye, Alex."

Chapter 28

It's Wednesday, but I don't care. I've stayed at Hillfield and worked over a few weekends, so I'm allowed to take a few extra days off. Anyway, I need them. After leaving the room, the finality of what happened between Alex and me pressed down on me like a load of bricks. What had I done? Perhaps it's for the best, but I can't shake the feeling that it's not supposed to end this way. How is that possible, though, when all we can do is squeeze in moments of physical contact in a stupid secret room? When I can't possibly tell anyone of my involvement with him without sounding crazy?

In spare moments, I've searched for him online, but I always come up empty-handed. Plus, Hillfield Manor has been closed for the last twenty years. If he was around, why wouldn't he be here, in his home?

I kept it together enough to tell Marie where I was going and call Mr. Wade to tell him of my plan for a long weekend, but then I got out of Hillfield as fast as possible. Now, at my grandma's house, I can't stop the tears from falling as the expression on his face etches itself deeper and deeper in my mind. I lashed out when I shouldn't have. I hurt him. And whereas I believe my anger and disappointment were justified, they weren't aimed at him. There's no one to blame. Life happens; people die. But it sure as hell doesn't make it any easier.

Shit.

I debate going back and groveling at Alex's feet, begging him to forgive me and take me back. But how long will it last? Do we have a month? Two? Is he meant to jump into my present? Every second with him would be a blessing tinged with pain, wondering when he would be taken from me.

I feel a slight chill as I sit on the hard wooden chair, my fingers brushing against the cold metal of a fork and knife sitting on the table. The chair creaks beneath me as I shift in my seat, and I can feel a slight roughness in the fabric of my clothes as they rub against my skin.

The kitchen has always been one of my sanctuaries at my grandma's. The scents of her cooking always filled the air, and people always congregated here to talk to her as she whipped up something or cleaned another. Her death hit me hard, not unlike Eve's, but I guess I always figured that she would die before I did. That eventuality had always been in my mind, especially in the latter years, when she slowed down and started to forget, and I wonder if that's part of the reason I have trouble moving past Eve's death.

Eve was young. We were supposed to grow old together, experience our weddings, watch our children play together, and mourn our parents when it was their time to leave us, but now I'm alone.

And I don't want to experience all of that stuff without her.

Tired and restless, I get up from my seat and begin looking through the rooms of the large house, its high ceilings and intricate details. I remember my parents' worried expressions as they tried to convince my grandma to leave behind a place that was clearly too large and difficult for her to care for alone, but she refused. My parents had to settle for closing the rooms upstairs and hiring someone to come in and clean once a week.

As I walk by each room, I see remnants and ghosts of the people who have come and gone. I run my fingers along the countless nicks and scrapes as I pass through, feeling the presence of all of them—my grandma, parents,

Eve, and even my own presence as a child echoing through the empty rooms.

Chuckling hollowly, I sink onto the window seat in the living room and stare absently out the window. Maybe Alex is right. I'm living in the past, if not with the ghosts at Hillfield, then certainly with my memories. And if that's the case, I'm *not* living.

I move to get comfortable and look down at the cushion. It has seen better days, and the cover could use a good wash. Sighing, I get up and take the cushion cover off. There are some stored in plastic under the seat, but I have no idea how long they've sat untouched, so before I put this one in the wash, I lift the seat to see if the rest will need washing too.

As I take each one from the plastic, shaking them out in vain to get rid of their creases from being folded, something falls to the floor. I ignore it, thinking it's a receipt, and continue removing the cushion covers. They could all use a good cleaning, so gathering them up, I also bend to pick up the receipt only to realize it's not a receipt at all. It's an envelope. Addressed to me.

Cushion covers forgotten, I throw them onto the seat and open the envelope. Inside are a couple of handwritten pages, and I immediately recognize my grandma's writing. Tears sting my eyes as I unfold the sheets, wondering as I do so when she could have written this and what she had to write me that she couldn't have just told me.

Dearest Emma,

Perhaps you were hoping for treasure? I hope I can offer that—if not in the form you imagine. Indulge an old woman for a few moments, please, while I explain.

One day, you were sitting by the window in the living room, and you turned to me and asked who had lived in the house before me. I told you Grandpa and I had bought the house from an elderly couple who had raised five kids in the house. "Do you think they're still here sometimes?" you asked, and I was startled. "What do you mean? Like a ghost?" (It was around that time you were fascinated by Hillfield Manor). "No," you said. "Like they're living their lives at the same time we are."

My heart nearly stopped. How could you be so young and yet ask such a profound question? I wanted to sit you beside me and tell you right then about my experiences, but I didn't want to scare you, and I knew your father believed it was all nonsense. When I had gathered my wits about me once more, you had left the window and were playing with Eve, so I said nothing.

I never forgot the incident, but it was shoved to the back of my mind. Then, in the summer of your fourteenth year, I heard a peal of laughter that brought back so many memories of a dear friend of mine. It was her laughter. I rushed into the kitchen, knowing it was impossible, but hoping all the same that my friend had somehow found me and had come for a visit. And there she was. Tears came to my eyes, and I bit back a sob as I took in her appearance. I hadn't recognized her before, so caught up I had been in seeing her with the eyes of a grandma, yet she had been visiting me for years—every summer.

I'm taking a chance that you'll never find this at all, and my words will fill this page just for the sake of allowing me to unburden my mind, but if you find this . . . Oh, Emma. I hope you'll be filled with a sense of wonder and satisfaction in knowing what has become of a dear friend. And I really believe you will find it.

I remember something my friend said once. It was after I found out I was pregnant with your father. I told my friend I would have to leave my position at Hillfield Manor. That I was with child and wouldn't be able to continue for much longer. "What? Really? Well, I'll go to the foot of our stairs!" she exclaimed. "If I could hug you, I would, but I'll do it later. You're going to make an awesome grandma!"

Emma, do you recognize me, dear friend? I never forgot you and was thrilled beyond measure to know that all this time, in what seems like a lifetime ago and in this one, we're even closer than I could have hoped. We're family.

There's no need to rehash it all here. You already know my story, but now you have an even better understanding. And to answer your 7- or 8-year-old self, yes. Yes, I believe they're still here sometimes. I'm with you now—as you read this letter and in my own time, in the same space.

Isn't it extraordinary?

PS I've told your parents and Eve about her accident. I can only hope I've somehow prevented it and you have no idea about that of which I speak. If, however, you do, and I was unsuccessful, well, there are no words . . .

All my love,

Annie/Grandma

A chill shoots down my spine. *Is it possible?* I read the letter again, a smile growing on my face even as tears course down my cheeks. Annie is my grandma!

I sit heavily on the window seat and allow everything I know about Annie to come flooding through. But of course! She always reminded me of someone, but I could never put my finger on it.

I knew my grandma's middle name was Annalise, but I'd never heard her referred to as Annie, and now that I know Annie and my grandma are one and the same, I can't believe I didn't recognize that her eyes are the spitting image of my father's. And her warm smile, which always made me feel so loved, is identical. Why had I never asked to see pictures of her when she was younger? I make a mental note to ask my parents to show me some the next time I see them.

I read the postscript again. I told Annie—my grandma—all about Eve, and she remembered. I think back to talking to my mom. *"She told me Eve died."* But that was already when my grandma was starting to lose herself to age. It must have been a lucid moment—just as it was when she wrote this letter.

I want to rush to Hillfield now and look for her, but then, just as quickly as my thoughts turn to the manor, I think of Alex. Deflating, I lean back against the window. I know if I return now, I'll look for him and apologize again, and it's something I need to do. He deserves that much at least, but maybe some distance would be best. He said he was a do-over, and initially, that's exactly what he was: a way for me to prevent someone else's death when I couldn't prevent Eve's. But the feelings I have for him now are so much more than that. So much more.

Still, I keep wondering if maybe this is all for the best. Sighing, I gather up the cushion covers and the letter from my grandma, hugging it to my chest. All these months, she's been with me, and I never knew. But, of course, she has always been with me—in my thoughts and memories. Just like Eve. I glance down at the letter again. Seeing as this conversation hasn't happened yet, I know I'll see her again, and that's what helps me with my decision.

I've already told Marie and Mr. Wade I'd be here for the weekend, so that's what I'll do. I'm going to sleep late, hang out with friends—living ones—and I'm going to try like hell to keep Hillfield in the back of my mind.

Chapter 29

***I flip up the lid of** my laptop, ready to Skype Eve, but she's already there, her face so close to the screen I can't make out her surroundings. I know this is a dream, just like all the other conversations I've had with her this last year, but it still feels real, and the pain I've felt ever since her passing courses through me afresh, even as elation at seeing her again steals my breath. I worry my questions will mean this will be the last time I see her as clearly as I do now. I don't want my memories of her, like the pictures in a newspaper, to fade and yellow with time.*

"I tried to bring you back."

Eve snickers. "From what I understand, it's always a one-way ticket. No returns."

"Why do you keep haunting me?"

"Haunting? No, Emma. Deep down, you know that."

"But you keep visiting. It can't just be my brain creating all of this, right?"

"Looks like we're keeping to our schedule of monthly lunches." She pulls back from the camera a little and nibbles on a sandwich. "Just remember, I'm the one who thought of doing our little video sessions. I wanted to check in on my baby sister."

That's right! The memory hits me like a jolt. Eve suggested meeting via Skype just after I moved to England. She said she missed me, and now it seems the roles are reversed. "I miss you."

Eve pauses to give me a brief smile before taking another bite, then chews thoughtfully. "I think it's a bit more complicated. What is it, Emma?"

I take a deep breath and then exhale slowly. "I want to know that when we die, it's not the end."

"You've always had that preoccupation. Isn't that why you're so obsessed with ghosts?"

I huff. "I'm not obsessed."

Eve studies her sandwich as if it's the most interesting thing in the world. "Why is it so important to you?"

"I need to know that this"—I wave my arms around me—"means something! That when people say 'there's a

reason' that there really is a reason! What's the point of living, of loving, if there's nothing at the end of it all?"

"You want reassurances."

"Yes."

"You want a cookie-cut answer to an age-old question that has never been conclusively answered."

"Damn straight!" Frustration seeps into my tone. "It's not fair!"

Suddenly, Eve is sitting in front of me, the laptop screen gone. It's just the two of us.

"I'm here, aren't I?"

My heart thumps wildly in my chest. "So, you're saying there is *something more?"*

Eve smiles, and I feel like she's talking to me as if I'm a small child who doesn't have the capacity to understand her. "I'm saying that even if there's nothing more, I'm still here . . . because of you. I live on through you. Maybe there is something more, and maybe there's a reason.*" She smiles again. "We don't have all the answers when we're alive."*

I want to pull her close to me. I never knew the last hug we had would be the last, and I'm mentally kicking myself for taking my moments with my sister when she was alive for granted.

She wraps her arms around me, and I swear I can feel them. I can even smell her favorite perfume. I cling to her and sob. I sob for Eve, whose life ended too soon; for my parents who had to outlive a child; and for me, who, maybe selfishly, just wants my sister back because I love her.

"There's no need to worry about me anymore, Emma," she says. She lets go of me by degrees, and when she's in front of me again, her brow creases in concern. "But what about Alex?"

My lids flutter open. She's right, and I hate that she is, or that my brain is. Whatever. I can't bring Eve back, but Alex is still here. Kind of.

Standing in front of the gates of Hillfield once more, I take a deep breath and pull out my phone to call Marie to let me in. The bell and intercom system has been turned off due to passerby buzzing in at all times to ask when Hillfield will be open once more, and after Lucas was found with the key to the library and front door, there was no telling what other keys he had, so all exterior locks had to be changed. Now, only Marie and James, and the Easons, of course, have access.

Marie comes bustling out the front door. She's quick on her feet, and she's standing next to the gate, with keys in hand, in record time.

"Did you have a nice break?" she asks, her eyes filled with sympathy. Although I didn't tell her what happened between Alex and me, my red-rimmed eyes were surely a sign of how I was feeling when I left.

I smile as she swings the gate open. "It was what I needed," I say. "How did everything go here?"

Marie's eyes widen. "You didn't hear? I was convinced you would have heard the story on the news or read it in the papers. We've had a busy few days."

I stop in my tracks. "What happened?" I was completely tuned out over my long weekend. Not wanting anything to interfere with trying to relax, I had decided not to follow the news or social media.

"You know the inner courtyard?" At my nod, she continues. "We had the grounds crew come in to start sprucing it up, and they found human remains."

"What! When did this happen?"

Marie closes the gate, and we start back to the manor at a slow gait. "Thursday afternoon. The grounds crew, as well as everyone inside, had to stop what they were doing immediately, and the police were called. The whole place was considered a crime scene for the rest of the day."

Some friends and I had gone out Friday night, and they hadn't said a word. Of course, I had sworn them not to talk about Hillfield. I told them I needed to get out of that headspace. Perhaps they thought I knew and that the remains were what I was referring to.

"Do they know who the remains belonged to?"

"No. I didn't see them myself, but apparently, it happened a long time ago. Forensics is going through everything. I guess they're going to run a DNA test and whatnot. Emma . . ." Marie's voice fades, and she glances around herself nervously.

"Marie, what is it?"

"It's possible the remains belong to one of the two Eason brothers that went missing."

I feel the color drain from my face as I take in her words, and I slump onto the front steps, my legs suddenly too weak to carry me. Alex! I close my eyes and try to control my breathing. Questions swirl through my mind, but I don't know which one to ask first. The window in the secret room faces the inner courtyard. But what happened? Was he pushed? Did he slip? I gasp as I think about the broken window that I can see but Alex can't. *What the hell had happened?*

"I . . . I need more information. Marie, you have to tell me everything," I say, my voice ringing with desperation. *If those are Alex's remains, then anything I do now won't make a difference, will it?* I drop my head between my knees and take deep breaths. I feel like I'm going to throw up.

Marie reaches down and takes hold of my hand, squeezing my fingers. "Hold on." She rushes into the house, and I remain seated on the front steps, trying to think, but it's as if I've suddenly been struck dumb. A part of my mind knows exactly what is adding up, but another part of my mind is refusing to even think about the possibility.

Marie comes back out of the house a few minutes later, a folded newspaper in her hand. Tentatively, she hands it to me. There on the front page, lower right-hand corner in bold letters, is the caption: Skeletal Remains Found at Hillfield Manor. I read on.

Male skeletal remains were found late Thursday afternoon on the Hillfield Manor Estate. A patrol unit was sent to investigate after a grounds and maintenance crew member, identified as Thomas Gerrow, called in the body. "With the owners coming back, we were asked to do a more thorough job on the landscaping. We were working on an interior courtyard that hasn't been maintained since the early 90s."

A homicide unit was dispatched shortly after.

The identity of the deceased male, as well as the cause of death, have yet to be determined. "At this point, we don't know if there was any foul play. We'll have to wait for official autopsy reports before we can make that kind of determination," homicide detective Jennifer Barret explained.

Speculations, however, are plentiful. In 1973, the high-profile mysterious disappearance of Christopher Bartholomew Eason made headlines. His whereabouts continue to remain unknown. Then, in 1993, Hillfield Manor abruptly closed its doors. Alexander Eason, Christopher's younger brother and sole heir to the Eason estate, has not been heard from nor seen since. Is it possible the remains belong to one of the Eason siblings?

When asked to comment, Thomas Gerrow could only add, "There's always been something strange about Hillfield, but a body is not something I thought I'd be digging up!"

Hillfield Manor only recently became occupied once again when the Homecomings refurbishing company was called in to update the interior for the reinstitution of Eason family members later this year.

The paper hangs from my hand limply once I'm finished with the article, and I stare blankly in front of me. *I have to warn him.*

I rise to my feet shakily and grab the handle of my suitcase, but it slips out of my hand. Cursing, I bend to pick it up, but Marie tsks, and her hand on my arm is firm. "I'll get it," she says. "Go find him."

Nodding, I give her a weak smile before rushing into the house. How do you find a ghost? Up to this point, Alex and I have planned when we would meet, either inside the room or within the main house, but no plans were made the last time we were together.

Pulling out my phone, I check the time. Usually, Alex leads a tour at ten o'clock. It's ten thirty now, and I can only hope I'll find him in one of the main rooms.

For the next few minutes, I'm running from room to room, squinting as I search for numerous faint outlines of ghosts that are not as clear as he is, a clue that he isn't too far away. I check the Great Hall and the numerous rooms extending off it. I check the Long Gallery, the conservatory, and the kitchen. Finally, I see him in the billiards room. He's in the corner, his arms waving as he points out one thing or another while speaking.

At first, the room seems empty, so clear he is to me, but as I glance around, the shadowy outlines of others become more apparent, until, after a few moments, I can see the hazy features of several of those on his tour.

I take a deep breath and try to focus on Alex's words. I can't hear him unless I'm concentrating, but right now, I'm too agitated to listen. I'm halfway through the room when he finally looks my way, and I can see when he notices me because he freezes for a moment, his whole body tensing, and his words cut off. Abruptly, though, he looks away. "Feel free to look around this room and take pictures," I hear him say. "I'll be here if you have any questions."

"Alex," I say once I'm standing next to him, "I need to talk to you."

Alex doesn't acknowledge me. Instead, he nods to a particularly clear apparition. She's not as clear as Alex, but I can see her long dark hair and the way she's eyeing him like he's a piece of Halloween candy she's ready to gobble up.

"Alex, I'm sorry! Okay? I'm sorry, but even though I wanted to say that, there's something else that's more important."

Alex's eyes flick my way, and I gasp. His expression . . . It's so . . . There's anger there, and hurt and disappointment, and I hang my head because I know I'm the one who put those emotions there.

Closing my eyes, I swallow a lump in my throat, then say, "Please, will you meet me in our room after the tour?"

The brunette who was eyeing him—who is still eyeing him—walks up to him and says something flirtatious in a husky voice. I'm not paying attention to the words. I'm too busy watching his reaction to her. Alex turns her way and smiles one of his winsome smiles, one of the smiles I thought was only reserved for me. One that made me feel like the most beautiful girl in the world.

A sob catches in my throat, and I turn away. I want to run out of the room, run all the way to my grandma's, and forget I ever met Alex Eason or heard of Hillfield Manor. But he means too much to me for me to walk away now, even if he *is* acting like an ass. I'm almost to the door, wiping the tears from my cheeks, when I hear him.

"I'm sorry," he says loudly, looking at me pointedly before he turns to his tour group. "Ladies and gentlemen, our time in this room is up." He turns back to me. "I'll meet you," he says, then turns once more to his group, "in the next room, right through those doors. We have about twenty minutes left on our tour."

He says that last part for my benefit, and I nod and exit the room. I make it about halfway down the hall before I have to lean against the wall to keep from falling into a heap on the floor. Taking deep, steadying breaths, I close my eyes and tilt my head against the wall. This can't be happening. Alex's disappearance. This is what happened. A terrible hope that it's Christopher instead fills my head, and I instantly feel guilty, especially when the hope intensifies for a brief moment before I think again of the window. It was broken for me, not for Alex, which can only mean it was Alex who died.

I sit in the darkened room, my gaze drawn to the door as I wait expectantly for Alex. There is an air of tension in the room as I sit and wait, hearing only the faint sounds of the house as it settles now and again. But as Alex enters the room, everything seems to still. My eyes are drawn to his tall and muscular form, his dark hair, and his piercing gaze, and we are left with only each other's breathing and the rustling of our clothes as we shift nervously. The quiet persists for a few moments as our gazes hold, locked in an intense but silent exchange before it is ruptured by a sudden intake of breath.

"I did it to hurt you," Alex says with no preamble. "Smiling at that girl—I did it to hurt you."

I close my eyes and sink lower on the couch. "It worked."

Alex comes over and sits next to me. "I'm sorry," he says, barely a whisper. "It was stupid and petty—"

I lift my hand to his mouth to silence him. "I did the same thing by talking about your brother. I'm sorry. I know you've done everything you can to help me." I inhale deeply and let my breath out slowly. "I was just angry at the situation, and I took it out on you. It wasn't fair, and . . ." I shake my head. "I'm sorry."

Alex's eyes are soft and warm as he gazes at me. His hand appears steady as he gently brushes his fingers over my cheek, his touch tender and gentle. His gaze never leaves mine, and I feel myself getting lost in the intensity of his lingering stare.

I don't realize I'm leaning toward him until our lips are only inches apart and I feel the warmth of his breath on my face. But then his lips are on mine, and all of my doubts and fears move aside. His kiss is gentle, yet filled with a deep passion that sends tingles racing through my body.

I wrap my arms around his neck, pulling him even closer as our kiss grows more and more urgent. I have never experienced anything like it, the overwhelming feeling of desire and longing that fills me as I lose myself in Alex's arms.

We stay like this for what seems like seconds, minutes, an eternity, our kiss growing deeper and more intense with every moment. I never want it to end.

Alex's hands move across my body, and I shudder in delight as they grip my waist, pulling me on top of him so I'm straddling him. I can feel him, hard and thick, pressing against my leg, and I want more than just his lips.

I pull back, panting softly as, once again, the reality of our situation hits me. This can't happen. Not here. Not like this. I remember the article I want to show him, and it's like a punch to the gut. This will most likely never happen for us.

Alex's eyes search mine before closing in resignation. Moments later, they open and he leans toward me until our foreheads are touching. For a moment, I can't look away, but I force myself to take a deep breath in an effort to regain my composure, or at least to appear like I have some control, and when I do, I slowly, reluctantly peel myself off him and sit next to him.

"There's something else," I say. I'm afraid to look at him. Once I tell him, there will be no chance for us. How could there be?

Alex frowns. "What is it?"

"A, uh, a body was found—well, skeletal remains—were found in the inner courtyard"—I point toward the window—"Thursday. There's speculation that they belong to—"

"Christopher!" Alex bows his head, and a hand comes up to cover his eyes. I see his chest rise and fall like a sea swell. Then, suddenly, he looks at me, devastation written over his face.

I tell him what I can from the article I read and what Marie told me. All the while, he stares blankly ahead, and once, I see him wipe a tear from his eye hastily.

After I've told him everything I can remember, Alex sits back. "Those remains could be my brother's. And if they are, what does that mean? It opens so many more questions. But if they're not his, then where the hell is he?"

My mouth hangs open, my eyes wide and unblinking. "Alex! Yes, those remains could be your brother's, but it's just as possible they're yours! They were found out there." I point to the window again, my finger practically jabbing the air. "And the window, at least in my time, is broken."

The two of us sit still and quiet, our expressions thoughtful as we process the implications of what has been revealed.

"Emma, why exactly are you telling me all this?" Alex asks, his voice soft, hesitant.

Tears instantly spring to my eyes. "Because we can't come here anymore. I don't want anything to happen to you, Alex."

He grabs my hand and squeezes it. "Emma . . ."

"Alex, I only have about a week left, anyway. Seriously, what were we planning to do when it's time for me to leave? The doors will be locked to me. I can't visit. And let's say I could. Let's say I stay on. Then what? I wait for something to happen to you? It's already almost August. We know the house closes in September in your time, so that means whatever happens to make you disappear happens between now and then."

"That's why we should keep coming to this room," Alex says, his voice smooth and persuasive. "I'm sorry, Emma. Call me selfish, but I want to spend every moment I can with you, especially knowing how little time we have. Plus, you keep saying I'm going to die. Stop. You don't know—"

"But if you're still alive during my time, wouldn't you have come to see me? We've been talking about this room and about our different timelines. Even if you didn't come to see me, why not write a letter or an email and give a hint about where this room was or . . ."

"You've seen *Back to the Future*, right? You can't mess with the timeline. Maybe it has something to do with that. Maybe I can't be in two places at once, just like your future self can't come back and tell you the same information."

"But you're *not* in two places at once. Not really. In this room, yeah, okay. But out there—" I point to the door "—you're just a shadow. And as far as the timeline, wouldn't we be screwing that up either way?"

"No, not really. If I come forward, I'm not changing anything.

"That doesn't make sense. You are changing something because you would no longer be in your timeline. That's a big change."

"The way I see it, my timeline seems to be cut short anyway. You can't find any records of me so far, and as you just mentioned, I haven't come knocking on the door. The way I see it, I'm supposed to come forward."

"But someone was just found, Alex! A body was just found. I don't *want* you to try to come forward—hell, we don't even know how it's done! What if you trying to come forward is exactly why you end up"—I choke on a sob—"dead?"

"If that's what's meant to happen, then that's what's supposed to happen. I'm not going to let the what-ifs be the things that stop me."

"No!" I get up from the couch, stand in front of him, and shake my head. "No. Alex, we've both lost people. You know what it feels like to be the one left behind. Don't make me lose you too. I can't."

Alex stands too and grasps my shoulders. "Look at me, Emma." But I don't want to. He can't be asking me to take a chance with this. It's too much of a risk.

His sigh is deep and heavy, and he draws me to him in a tight hug. I cling to him, breathing in the familiar scent of his cologne. I hold him, savoring the feeling of his strong arms around me, knowing it might be the last time I will ever get to feel this way.

"I'm sorry," Alex whispers, his voice thick with emotion. "I don't want it to end this way."

Tears fill my eyes as I think of everything we could have had together. I know Alex feels the same way.

"It's not your fault," I say, my voice breaking as I try to keep the tears at bay. "We just weren't meant to be together."

Alex pulls back slightly, looking me in the eye. I can see my emotions reflected at me, anguish and heartbreak, and loss.

"I will never forget you, Emelia Beckett," he says, pain evident in his voice. "Never."

Tears stream down my cheeks as I realize that this is it. Our relationship, however unconventional it is, is over, and there is nothing I can do to change that. But even as the tears flow, I'm grateful for the time we've had together. It was more than I could have ever asked for.

"I'll never forget you either," I say, my voice barely a whisper.

Alex strokes my face with his hand, and he leans down to kiss me. It's soft and lingering, and I know he's just as reluctant to let go as I am.

I lean into him, savoring the feeling of his lips against mine, and I let out a soft sigh as I kiss him back.

When we finally break apart, Alex leans his forehead against mine. We stand that way for a bit, holding one another, not wanting to let go. We both know this is it. This is the end.

"I'll miss you," Alex says. He turns away from me abruptly, and in a few steps, he's at the door, where he pauses, his face away from me. I wait, my breath held, hoping he'll turn around and come back to me while at the same time, for both our sakes, hoping he won't.

He grips the edge of the door, but he doesn't turn around. He doesn't say a word. All I can see is the back of his head, bowed, and the rigidity of his spine as he stands next to the door, his expression hidden from me. After a few moments, he slams his fist on the door.

And then he's gone.

Chapter 30

As I sit outside today, basking in the warm sunlight and enjoying the rich fragrance of the blooming flowers, I can't help but feel a slight lift in my spirits. The world seems to be swirling around me in vivid colors and hypnotic scents, trying to pull me out of the foul mood that has been weighing me down.

But even as I revel in the peace and tranquility of the moment, I know I must keep my head down and focus on my work. I have to keep pushing forward. I have a lot to do, but I'm finding it hard to continue. I'm trying to get it all done as quickly and efficiently as possible while dreading the end because then I'll have to leave.

I have a few more journals to copy, but I can't take them outdoors, and since I needed to find a place where it is highly unlikely for me to run into Alex, I'm sitting on a small bench on a terrace in one of the gardens. The database I'm working on is, for the most part, up to date, but I want to make sure I've recorded everything as it's supposed to be. This one has nothing to do with the journals, another thing I needed to distance myself from, and deals solely with all the rest of the books in the Eason's collection.

As I work, I feel pressure building up inside of me, and the dread I've been feeling since Alex and I said goodbye moves to the forefront of my mind. It's as though I have a heavy weight in the pit of my stomach and a tightness in my chest. The day after tomorrow is my last day, and the closer it draws, the more I want to stay.

I don't want to see Alex—that would be torture. But just being here makes me feel close to him. I know he's here.

I keep imagining what it will be like when I leave. Maybe I'll be sitting in my grandma's house, and there's a knock on the door. When I open it, there's Alex, older, probably looking more like Mr. Wade, but there, alive.

He'll tell me I was right, that he wanted to call or text, but something always kept him from doing so until I was out of and away from Hillfield. We'll figure out that had I stayed, the room would have found a way to move him—with deadly consequences. He'll tell me I've saved him, and then—

And then what? For over twenty years, Alex will have been living his life. During that time, he'd probably meet someone, fall in love, and get married. Will he have kids? What could there possibly be between us? He'll only be a few years younger than my parents. So much will have changed. Will it be an issue?

I look up from my laptop, realizing I've been sitting here with my fingers hovering over the keys for the last few minutes. Here I am acting like this will be what happens, and in a lot of ways, I hope it will because then there will be closure.

Standing, I set my laptop on the table in front of me and stretch. I can't concentrate and hope a walk around the manor will give me some motivation. Grabbing the laptop, I move through the doors into the lady's parlor before making my way to the library, where I deposit it on the desk before locking everything up once more. As I make my way to the front of the house, I can't resist stopping in the great room, my eyes roaming over the room in search of Alex, the one person I want to see the most. He's not there, and my heart drops in my chest. I know it's for the best, but it still hurts.

Just as I'm about to turn away, something catches my eye, and it's clear I see her before she sees me. Annie, my grandma. I can't help the smile that bursts on my face as I see her and all the things I never noticed before: the smile like my dad's, little mannerisms that I've seen her make hundreds of times as my grandma but never noticed as Annie, even the way she wipes off a table.

She scurries over to me, a smile like my dad's on her face. "Emma! I've been looking for you!"

I know why too, but I quickly school my features. I'm not supposed to know. "Hi, Annie. How are you? Everything okay?"

"Emma, I wanted to find you. I was afraid you'd already left Hillfield."

I lose some of my excitement. "No, I'm leaving the day after tomorrow."

She steps closer. "Then it won't be so hard to say what I have to say. Today is my last day." Her eyes are twinkling and she's practically bouncing where she stands.

I feign ignorance. "You're leaving? Why?"

"I'm expecting! I wanted confirmation before I said anything, and then I didn't see you, but Edward and I are thrilled. Can you believe it?"

"What? Really? Well, I'll go to the foot of our stairs!" I say with a laugh, an expression of surprise I learned from her.

For a moment, I forget and lean in, my arms outstretched to give her a hug. At the last second, though, I drop my arms. "If I could hug you, I would, but I'll do it later. You're going to make an awesome grandma!"

Annie's face twists into a look of confusion and bewilderment, and she furrows her brow in deep thought. Her eyes are wide and her mouth is slightly agape as she tries to grasp the meaning, but then her face clears and she shakes her head. "The way you talk. A grandma! I'm not even a mother yet, but I'm going to be!" She hugs herself and bounces once again on the balls of her feet.

"I'm so happy for you; that's wonderful news," I say, but then I realize that this is the last time I'm going to see her—ever. Sure, I'll be in her future, but she'll no longer be in mine. My smile falters. "I'm going to miss you."

"Oh, Emma," she says, her voice softer than I've ever heard it. "Hasn't this house taught you anything? No one ever goes away. Not really."

I reach out to grab her hand, hoping to make a connection. I expect to feel spiderwebs, but instead, I feel nothing. My hand goes through hers. Looking up, I see her smile at me. "I'm going to miss you too."

Afraid I might cry, I glance away to compose myself, and when I look back, she has already faded away.

Chapter 31

I settle my bags on the front porch, then make my way to the sitting room where I'm meeting Mr. Wade to sign off on the work I've done here over the last eight months. I run into Marie and James in the hallway, talking to a contractor, and Marie holds up her index finger, asking me to wait.

As they listen to whatever it is the contractor has to say, I look around me. A shadowy figure walks into a room across the way with a backward glance, and I smile, but she doesn't stop. It's amazing how familiar to me the shadowy figures have become. I have none of the fear I had at the beginning, and I'm going to miss their presence—one in particular.

"So, you're all set to go?" Marie asks, approaching me with James right behind her.

I smile sadly. "Yup.

"You made sure you've got everything? Do you need anything for the road? I can make you a sandwich or—"

I pull Marie into a hug. "I've got everything. I'm going to be staying at my grandma's for the next few days anyway until my flight home to visit my parents."

Marie nods, tears in her eyes. "Oh, this is silly!" she says with a huff. "You'd think I was never going to see you again. You will come and visit, won't you?"

"I promise." Marie and James will be wrapping up everything on the manor within the next week. They've been commissioned for another estate not far from this one that will begin in a couple of months. I've already sworn to visit them there after I've found a new job, and even if that new job is in the States, I'll come back. Marie and James have become family.

"Of course you will," James adds, coming over and putting his arms around Marie. "You've made working here each day a delight, Miss Emma. We're proud to know you, and we're looking forward to hearing about where life takes you."

"I don't know if I'll get used to *not* seeing ghosts turn up randomly in rooms," I try to joke, but the thought of Alex has me choking on my words.

Marie grabs my hand. "I'm sorry things didn't work out for you and Alex. If we could tell you how the room works, we would. We'd never knowingly—"

I shake my head. "No. It's okay. I know you wouldn't." I take a deep breath. "Well, I better get to the sitting room. I'm meeting Mr. Wade to sign off on everything."

Marie nods and pulls me into another hug. "Oh, have you seen Lucas?" she asks, pulling away. "I heard he's around here somewhere. Someone let him in when they were entering. He didn't realize Lucas had been fired. We've got some people looking for him, but I'm sure he'd want to say goodbye," she says with a twinkle in her eye.

I refrain from giving a laugh of derision. If anything, Lucas would only want to say goodbye to try to weasel out any other information he could get on the secrets of Hillfield Manor. "No, I haven't seen him."

"Well, send word if you do," James says, coming up behind me. "We don't need any more trouble from him."

"What about the room?" I ask. There's no one around us, but I lower my voice anyway. All the journals have been locked in the room off the library. Even the bookcase leading to it has a lock on it, thanks to Mr. Wade hearing about Lucas's attempts to take a journal. He doesn't know about the specifics of what was written in it, but after he told the Easons, he was told to take precautions. Some people came by yesterday to install the new coded switch. It's more obvious than what was there but hides behind some books so isn't readily seen.

James nods. "Don't worry about that. I have someone stationed over by the library, and, as Marie said, we have a couple of people looking for him now."

I turn to James. "Can I give you a hug too, Bartholomew?"

"That's just between us, you know," he says with a wink as he wraps his arms around me.

"I only told Alex with your permission," I say, giving him a squeeze.

James nods and pulls away, a smile warming his face. "Everyone deserves to be happy, Miss Emma. You'll get your happiness too. I can feel it in these old bones."

I smile. "Thank you, James." I give his hand one last squeeze.

With one final farewell, I turn and leave Marie and James behind. I'd like nothing more than to tell them I want to stay, but I need to move forward or else I'm just going to get stuck in the past for good.

I walk down the hallway, heading for the sitting room, and I'm almost at the door when I hear a loud chuckle to my right.

"Well, what an interesting development."

I turn around, a frown already lining my face. I'd know that voice anywhere.

Lucas.

Stepping out of one of the rooms he's been hiding in, he's grinning at me, and I can see the wheels turning in his head as he thinks of some dig or another to make. A part of me wants to walk away, ignore him. At the same time, I'd like nothing better than to smack that grin off his face.

"What do you want, Lucas? How did you even get in here? Couldn't let my last moments at Hillfield be joyful, could you?"

He tsks. "Oh, but you're not happy, are you, sunshine?" he says with an exaggerated frown. "Tell me, have you seen your imaginary boyfriend around?" I bristle at his words and he smirks. "I don't know what's sadder, an imaginary boyfriend or a boyfriend who's a ghost. The first one is just in your head, which makes you just plain crazy, and the second is dead. Either way, you don't get a lot of action, do you? No wonder you're so uptight."

I turn on my heels. "Your such an asshole, Lucas," I say over my shoulder, but then I turn and face him. "And just for the record, either way, he's more a man than you'll ever be. Have a nice life."

"That's the best you can come up with?" he calls after me. "Man, if that's all you've got of an imagination, your boyfriend must look like a stick figure!" I hear his chortles as I enter the sitting room, and I close the doors behind me to block out the sound. With my hands in fists,

I count to ten, praying I'll have the strength to keep from going back out there and knocking him on his ass. He's headed right for James and Marie, though, so I figure he'll get what's coming to him anyway.

I take a deep breath and turn to the room, hoping Mr. Wade isn't here and didn't witness Lucas's taunts. He isn't on the sofa in the middle of the room where I expect him, and I close my eyes in relief, but then I hear a quiet cough coming from the corner of the room where two low armchairs are nestled for quiet conversation. An older lady peers over at me from one of the chairs. As I step forward, she stands up.

"You must be Emma," she says. "I'm Marilyn Eason, Alexander's mother. It's very nice to finally meet you after all these years."

I lick my lips and swallow, trying to moisten my suddenly parched lips and throat. "You're Alex's mom? I . . . He's . . . It's a pleasure to meet you as well," I finally manage. Alex told her about me? When? "Uh, I was looking for Mr. Wade. I have some papers to sign."

Mrs. Eason waves her hand. "Don't worry about that. I was in the library earlier and looked through some of the online logs. It's obvious you've done a thorough job."

I nod, and we both stand awkwardly for a few moments before I get up the nerve to ask, "Where . . . How is Alex?" I have no idea what she knows and what I don't.

She shakes her head, her eyes downcast. "I had a hope that he'd be here." She smiles sadly. "That's why I decided to have the renovations done." She must see my confusion because she takes out a book from her bag. "This is Alexander's journal. When I learned that he had disappeared like Christopher did, well, I was beside myself. I wondered if there were any clues he might have left to say where he was going, and I found this." She sets the journal on the small coffee table in front of her and takes a seat, motioning for me to take the seat opposite.

"I've learned a lot about you, a lot about *him,* through this journal." She sighs heavily. "I didn't realize how isolated he felt from his father and me, although I should have . . . We were so consumed with finding his older brother that we didn't even consider . . . Anyway, Alexander wrote about the room you found and what it does. He didn't say where it is"—she gives me a sharp look—"and I don't want to know. It's caused enough heartache as it is, but because he dated his entries, with yesterday's date being the last one, we hoped this is where we'd find him. We even made contingencies in case we didn't make it this long. His father didn't." She sighs again and places her bag on the floor next to her.

"He wrote about the remains," she murmurs before looking at me. "And I prayed I'd never hear about them myself. I even wondered if I should start the renovations. Is doing that what started the whole thing in motion? What about hiring you?" She laughs bitterly. "It was a classic 'which came first, the chicken or the egg' scenario." She shakes her head. "I kept telling myself that if he knew about the remains, he'd have given up the nonsense of trying to find a way forward. I hoped that maybe he had gone away for a little while to clear his head. But one month became two, then six, then a year. No word, nothing. Then, well, as you know, the remains were found."

I bow my head to hide my shock. So that's it, then. The remains are his. If his mom doesn't even know where he is, that's the only outcome. But how did he find a way to jump? And why did he do it, knowing the consequences? I'm silent as I school my face and bury my sorrow, at least for now.

I lean toward Mrs. Eason. "When I first met Alexander, I thought he was someone from the distant past. I found a journal with his exact name, and with the way he was dressed, I assumed he and his namesake were one and the same." I fold my hands in my lap. "I lost my sister a while ago. I couldn't save her, and I was thinking, 'What if I can save him?'" I give a self-deprecating laugh. "And then I found out he was living in 1993, and I came to know him better, and he was smart and funny, and he made me feel good about myself." I look into Mrs. Eason's eyes. "We never found a way to jump."

I pause and let my words sink in. She doesn't say anything, but her expression tells me she understands what I'm saying.

"As far as I know, he'd given up trying to find a way because of the remains." I look away because I can't bear to see the pain etched on her face. "I wish"—I pause, tears threatening, and take a deep breath—"I wish things could have been different."

Mrs. Eason wipes her cheek with a tissue and then pats my hand. "I read about Evelyn. I'm sorry."

It's so strange to hear my sister's name on the lips of a woman I just met that I stare before nodding. Alex has her eyes, and when I focus on them, it's him I see.

"One of the things that will stick with me was what he said to me the last time I saw him. He said, 'I love you, Mother, but I can't be here for you anymore. I have been trying to be the son you lost and the son who remained behind, and I can't.'" She breaks off and sniffs. "Then he said, 'I'm sorry I've been a disappointment. I'm sorry I wasn't enough to keep you home after Christopher disappeared, but I have to stop being sorry, stop living for you, and start living for me.'"

She blows her nose, sniffs, and dabs at her eyes again. "My biggest regret is that I never told him that he *wasn't* a disappointment. Not in the slightest. He was my baby boy, and I loved him. I wanted him to know that if anyone was a disappointment, it was me. He deserved a better mother." She looks at me, her eyes pleading for understanding, for forgiveness that isn't mine to give. "If anything, my sin was that I loved my older son too."

My eyes tear up again, and I blink rapidly. If Alex were here, he'd have his mother in his arms in a heartbeat. Everything would be forgiven. He'd smile and say something like, "We're here now" or even simply "I love you, Mother." And it would all be okay.

Mrs. Eason grabs my hand. "I'm telling you this because I don't want you to blame yourself for this. Ever. You were trying to save Alex, and I think I know my son well enough to recognize that he can read people as well as he can read all those journals you typed up. He knew you cared for him, that you were scared. And even if I didn't know my son so well, he made it clear enough in his journal," she says, pointing to the book on the table. "Which reminds me, I believe I have something that belongs to you." She rummages in her purse and produces an envelope that she hands to me. "That's your family, isn't it? The letter came back, address unknown."

I take the envelope from her. This is the first time I've seen Alex's writing, and I swallow a lump in my throat over the fact that it'll be the last. I take a look at the address. Two of the numbers are inverted. He sent the letter as promised. Did he remember the address wrong?

Had I mistakenly given him the wrong one? I lived in that house when I was little, after all. Does any of it matter?

We sit in silence for a few moments, both of us lost in our thoughts. Mine are of Alex, the way he looked when I first saw him, the way his voice, deep and rich, seemed to touch my very core the first time I truly heard him, the way his hand felt, warm and strong on mine.

"If you don't mind," I say, "I'd like to go to the room one last time before I leave."

Mrs. Eason pats my hand again. "Take your time. The commissioner is supposed to be meeting me here shortly to go over the forensics report." She takes a stuttering breath. "I know what he's going to say, but I keep praying it won't be the case. I'm almost tempted to tell him not to come. There's too much finality in it."

I rise from a chair and take measured, deliberate steps as I make my way to the door. My movements are slow and steady, with my gaze cast down toward the ground in front of me. My body seems to move with an air of quiet determination, as if I am preparing for some great challenge ahead.

"Emma."

The way she says my name has me pause. It's the way my mom says my name when she wants me to pay attention, and I turn to face her.

She hesitates, her gaze on my face, before she says, "I know what it's like to lose someone you love. I also know what it's like to want to push out any other potential pain, even if it means losing out on knowing and loving someone so—" she swallows heavily— "extraordinary. Don't make the same mistakes I did. Don't ever push away the possibility of love because you're afraid. If you do, then *you* are the ghost; you're not living."

I slump where I stand. The weight of her words is so heavy that it takes some effort to breathe. They're an echo of what Alex said, and there's truth to them, but it's excruciating, and I don't know if I can stand the pain. I give her a watery smile and nod. I'm too choked up to use words. Turning, I exit hastily.

The room is empty when I barrel through the door. There's a stillness about it, as if it hasn't been used in years, neglected and forgotten. Silence hangs heavy in the air. I turn in a circle, my eyes roaming over every surface. He's everywhere in this room. He's on the settee, where he and I sat so many times, laughing, dreaming, learning more and more about one another. He's by the window, next to the table, lighting a candle, walking in through the door. I can hear his laugh, rich, deep, and full; feel his arms around me, strong and comforting; and smell his cologne, a scent I only know because of him.

Moving to the settee, I crumble upon it and sob. It's not right. I want to scream at God, the universe, this stupid house. What is the point of it all? Why let me fall in love with someone just to take away any possibility of us being together? Why give me the knowledge that he's going to die? Is it some sick joke to give us the capacity to care, to love, just to take away the people we love? Eve, my grandma, Alex, my parents some day?

Batting away my tears, I punch the cushioned seat of the settee. Then I punch it again, and again. Punching it through my pain and my sorrow, punching it through the anger that courses through me, my helplessness and vulnerability. I get up and kick it, then punch it some more.

This is for taking my sister away from me. Bam! Whack!

This is for giving me the capacity to love. Bam. Bam.

This is for giving me Alex and then taking him away from me. Bam. Bam. Bam!

"Son of a bitch," I choke out, my words aimed at no one and everyone. I fall onto the settee once more and pull my knees to my chest. The room is still again, the silence pressing in on me, and I weep once more as an overwhelming feeling of despair consumes me.

When the tears stop falling and I'm staring into space, my eyes puffy, my head aching, and my heart sore, I realize I'm not wishing I had never known them. It would be easier, so much easier, but no. I'm wishing I had more time. They brought me light and laughter, people to confide in, people who cared.

With Eve, there was nothing I could do. But I pushed Alex away when I could have had more time. I could have had more memories, more togetherness—just more.

After a few long moments, I steady my breath and push myself up from the settee. I have to go. I have to get as far away as possible because, even though it'll take some time, I've got people to meet and memories to make. A life to live.

Taking a letter I've written for Alex out of my back pocket, I prop it up on the settee. He'll never read the words now, but they're the words I need to say. My goodbye.

As I survey the small, neglected space a final time, it's Alex's laughter—the soft, deep rumble he'd make during our quiet times—that I hear, his heated gaze I see, and I smile, swallowing over the lump in my throat. Loving him was worth it. It was worth it all.

Leaving the room, I walk a few steps and stoop through the small door one last time. I close it and secure the latch before closing the cabinet door that has kept my whole world a secret. My bags are already on the porch, and I've already said my goodbyes to Marie and James. There's nothing left for me here at Hillfield Manor.

Moving from room to room, I notice the changes that have taken place over time. Some rooms are bigger, back to their original size. Others have restored windows—once covered to save money—ceilings, and woodwork. There are fresh coats of paint, new window treatments, and gleaming floors. The space seems transformed, renewed and revitalized by these modifications. So much has changed here during my time. Including me.

I step out the door, close it behind me, and leave Hillfield Manor.

I don't look back.

Chapter 32

The living room couch is soft and deep, so much so that Mom and Dad complain and threaten to get rid of it. Mom has problems with her hip and Dad has knee pain. It's getting to the point where, although it gives me comfort, the couch is bringing them too much pain, but because they don't come here too often and they know how much I like it, they've kept it. Before the next time they come, I'll splurge on a loveseat for them, and then, when I decide where I'm going, I'll happily take the bigger couch off their hands, even if it means I'll have to ship it back to the US with me.

Different English and American accents reach my ears as I flip through the channels—sports, cooking, music, news. There's nothing in particular I'm looking for, just hoping for a distraction. One I can't seem to find.

Sitting up, I flip off the television and sigh. My plane leaves late Thursday night, still a couple of days away. I'm in limbo, waiting for what's coming next. My resumé has been updated and applications have been sent out, both here in England and in the States. They're all great places. I'd be lucky to get any one of them, but the one I really wanted, a job as estate manager and tour guide at Hillfield Manor, was offered to me via email yesterday.

My heart fluttered when I saw the subject line, excitement flowing through me for a moment before I remembered. It used to happen all the time after Eve died, that momentary forgetting, that second where all is right with the world. If it weren't for Alex and the memories of him I have, it would have been ideal. The salary offered was a good one, and the hours would have allowed me to work on becoming a freelance genealogist, something I found I want to pursue. But expecting to come upon him around every turn would be my downfall. It's still tough walking around without Eve, but somehow it would be worse without Alex.

With Eve, I know the only place she now resides is within my heart—okay, and maybe the folds of time. Life at Hillfield Manor has made it impossible to discount that possibility. But with Alex, would he still appear as a true ghost? Would he continue to become corporeal in the room? And how would that be fair to me? I'd be stuck in a literal dead-end relationship, never being able to move on because the dead man I am in love with would be there as a constant reminder.

Already the what-ifs and maybes run rampant through my mind at night, when I'm alone and vulnerable to their corrupting influence on my sanity. During the day, though, during the day, there has to be something to make me not lose the plot.

My phone buzzes and I reach for it to look at the text. *On my way!* It's my friend Bec. Even though we keep in touch through email and social media, I haven't seen her or had a real conversation with her since before I moved to England, just before Eve's death. Although she lives in the States, she's here on an annual business trip and thankfully has a bit of free time.

"Hey, woman!" she says, pulling me into a hug the moment the door is no longer a barrier. "Oh, it's been too long." She rubs my shoulders as she pulls away and looks me in the eye. "How have you been?"

Instead of falling into easy conversation, which is what I want, I fall apart, losing myself to uncomfortable sobbing.

"Oh, Emma." She hugs me again, one of those tight hugs that lets me know she's not planning on going anywhere until I'm ready. When I finally pull away, wiping under my eyes and my cheeks with my fingers, she holds up a hand, telling me to wait. "I was going to bring this in anyway," she says as she opens the screen door and leans over to pick up a bag. "I just wanted to hug you first. I had no idea you were going to come undone on me." She smiles to soften her words, and I'm grateful she doesn't hold my breakdown against me. "I'm assuming this isn't about Eve."

I shake my head.

"Then it's a man." She pulls a bottle of rosé out of the bag and grins.

I grin too and grab the bottle and her hand and lead her into the kitchen.

"Where's Mom and Dad?" Bec asks, all too aware that if they were here, they'd be in to say hello and give her a hug.

After seeing how close we all were, Mom insisted Bec call her Mom too. "The more the merrier," she had said. "Especially when I don't have to clothe and feed you." Dad agreed, so Bec found she had gained a bonus set of parents. She has called them Mom and Dad ever since.

"They're still in Corning"—I glance at the clock on the wall—"most likely at the doctor's," I say, setting the bottle on the counter, getting a corkscrew out from one of the draws, and pointing to one of the cabinets over the counter. "Just a checkup."

Bec nods. "So, I have a few hours. Is that enough time for the full or the abridged version?" She goes to the cabinet I pointed out, where we keep the wine glasses, and takes two out.

I give a bark of laughter and shake my head, unsure of what to say. Will she even believe the story to begin with? I open my mouth to speak, but the doorbell goes off before I can say a word. I sigh and wipe under my eyes. I probably look like a mess, just the type of gossip to give whomever it is at the door.

Bec gestures for me to stay. "I'll get it. Peppermint Patties or the peanut butter kind?" she asks as she's walking out of the room. I snort. "Peanut butter!" I yell into the air, even though Girl Guides here in the UK don't sell cookies.

I'm attempting to find a place for the bottle in the fridge when I hear his voice. It's faint like it normally is when we're not in the room, and I hate my brain for making me remember so vividly what it is I never wish to forget.

"Emma?"

This time, the voice is accompanied by a scuff of shoes. It's too real, too distinct, to be my imagination, and I freeze. I want so much to turn around but am so afraid of the disappointment I'm sure will follow.

A hand, warm and heavy but comforting in its solidity, is placed on my shoulder, squeezing me, and a gasp escapes my lips. "Alex?"

Turning, I look up and into his eyes. He's here. He's here! Suddenly, I'm touching his arms, his chest, his face. He's here, and he's solid and warm and real, and I can't get enough of him.

Breathing him in, I pull him into me, his bright eyes and warm smile the last thing I see before I'm wrapped in his strong embrace.

"How are you here?" I ask, my voice shaky. "And you're not an old man." I touch his cheek and he laughs.

"No, I'm not." He kisses me, then pulls me into a tight hug once again. "It was the room. I don't know how, or why, but the room worked."

"It worked?" I realize it's a stupid question as it leaves my lips. He's standing right in front of me. Of course it worked! But I'm fully stunned and my brain seems to be two steps behind.

He releases me and smiles that radiant smile that eclipses the sun. "It worked."

I can't stop staring at him, taking him all in. "And your cast is off."

Alex smiles. "They removed it yesterday."

Then we're laughing and hugging and kissing. I swear I'm dancing at one point, and all the while, I keep at least one hand on him at all times.

Winded, we calm a little. "How?" I ask.

Alex takes my hand. "We need to talk."

Bec, who must have been hiding in the hall, comes in at that moment with a smile on her face. "I think I'm going to take this as my cue to leave. Tell Mom and Dad I said hi, and call me! I'm sure I can get away tomorrow or the next day." She looks at Alex and then back at me, raising her eyebrows suggestively before giving me a wink and sailing out the door.

When I turn back, Alex is looking past me and to the door through which Bec disappeared. "Your sister? It worked?" he asks. And when he turns back to me, his eyes are filled with happy confusion.

I smile sadly and shake my head. "No. That's my friend, Bec. She's known me and my family for years, and she always said my parents treat her as if she's one of theirs, so she adopted them as a second set."

Alex pulls me in for a hug. "I'm sorry."

"No, *I'm* sorry. I never should have doubted you, and then, it turned out to be all my—"

"Stop," he whispers. "It's in the past—literally."

I grab his hand and pull him out of the kitchen, through the hall, and over to the couch in the family room. "Sit," I say, and when he does, I straddle him so we're face to face. "I want to hear everything. When did you get back? What happened?"

"I got back Saturday, the day you left."

My eyes widen. "What? Why didn't you get my number and call me? I was here! I could have—"

"I wanted to, I did, but my mother was there, and then the police were there. And I started to wonder if maybe you didn't want me to contact—"

"Of course I wanted you to contact me!"

"Emma, the way we left things . . ."

I nod. "I know, but—"

"Let me talk. Please."

I nod and he takes my hand, dropping his eyes to it as he rubs the flesh between my thumb and index finger. "I know we left things . . ." He sighs and gives me a rueful smile. "There's a lot to say, Emma, and we don't have to figure everything out today. I think we'd be idiots to believe we could, but the way I feel about you—" He breaks off, gazes at me intensely, and gives me a soft smile. "I hated how we parted. If I could have taken away the pain and sadness, I would have. And if you'll let me, I'd like to try."

The sincerity I read in his expression brings tears to my eyes—again—and I pull him to me, marveling at his warmth, his strength, how *here* he is.

I nod. "I don't want you to end up hating it here and resenting me," I say and bite my lip. "And, okay, fine, I'm scared I'll care too much and lose you one way or another."

"I think that's one thing we both understand, huh?"

I sigh. "But I promise I won't be clingy either." I look down and let go of his hand, laughing sheepishly at how tightly I was gripping his fingers. "Sorry."

He laughs with me. "I don't expect you to be clingy." His eyes widen. "But *I* might be. At least for a little while as I get used to this century."

We smile at one another, and I'm so happy he's here that I lean forward, bringing my lips to his. Our first kiss is almost shy, tentative. An agreement of sorts. The second is exploratory as we test the boundaries of this new life where touch between us is no longer hindered by location. Alex groans, and with one hand on the back of my neck and one on my lower back, he pulls me against him, deepening our kiss. "I missed you," he whispers huskily, breaking away.

I smile. "I missed you too. I love you, Alex," I whisper, looking into his eyes.

His smile is instant, lighting up his entire face and holding the promise of warmth and affection. It's seductive too. His eyes darken as they linger on me, and his nostrils flare slightly. He exudes an irresistible allure that calls to me, drawing me in with his intoxicating charm, and his lips find mine once more. "I love you too, Emma. I think I always have, even before I met you."

"You know what? We're not in the room anymore," I say, my voice breathy. There's a suggestion there he picks up on immediately.

He groans as he grounds against me. "I want you," he says, his voice rough.

Staring into his eyes, I reach down between us, and my eyes close as my fingers trace the outline of his length through his jeans.

"That can be arranged." My voice is soft, filled with lust and exhilaration. Sitting back, I tilt my pelvis forward. Through our clothes, unwanted barriers, his hardness presses against me. My hands move to his neck, then his shoulders, his chest. I work to unbutton his shirt, craving not only his touch but the feel of his skin against mine. As I do so, he slides his hands to my thighs, tugging at my skirt. Pulling me against him with a low growl, he moves underneath me, then flips me over so he's on top of me and I'm lying lengthwise on the couch.

Breathing heavily, I put my hand on his chest. "Not here. Follow me."

He allows me up, and I grab his hand. As he follows, he slides his hands around my waist from behind. Gently, he pulls me against him, peppering kisses along my neck. I tilt my head, moaning as the soft stubble along his chin tickles my skin. Turning to face him, I entwine my fingers in his hair, tugging his head down. His kiss is hungry, urgent, and he pushes me against the wall, his hardness a constant pressure against my lower stomach. I lift my leg and press against him, and we both moan at the friction.

"Wait," he says. His eyes are closed and he rests his forehead against mine, trying to slow his breathing. "You're beautiful," he says quietly. "Here"—he motions to my face and body—"and here," he says as he touches his finger to my chest over my heart. "I thought it every time I saw you and every time I wasn't with you and wondered what you were doing. I don't think I ever told you, and that was one of the things I would have regretted if I never saw you again."

"Come on," I murmur breathlessly, once again taking his hand in mine. We move through the house eagerly, toward my bedroom, and as we enter the room, I turn around and bring my lips to his, pulling him toward me. He picks me up, and I wrap my legs around his waist. I nuzzle my nose against his before our lips meet once again. This is where I'm supposed to be. I close my eyes as I luxuriate in the rightness of this moment.

Chapter 33

Alex is caressing my arm when I wake, his fingers soft as they move up and down unhurriedly. With my head on his chest, I'm content to listen to the beating of his heart as his chest rises and falls.

"This is nice," I say.

He nods against my head.

"You never told me what happened in the room."

Alex sighs and moves abruptly to the edge of the bed. "Come on, get up. Let's take a walk."

There is a resignation in his voice that has me lifting my head to face him. "What's the matter?"

Alex frowns and swings his legs to the side of the bed. I know he's debating what words to use, but I don't want to wait. His change in demeanor has me on high alert, and I sit up. I don't think he's changed his mind about us. He wouldn't have said what he did if that was the case, but my thoughts go there anyway. "Alex?"

He leans over and touches my face, sensing my thoughts. "I'm not going anywhere, but what I have to say . . . I need to be walking."

I frown as he picks up his boxers and puts them on. Locating my underwear and a pair of jogging pants, I put them on in a hurry, then grab my bra off the floor. By the time I have my shirt on and turn around, Alex is fully dressed and is tying the laces on one of his shoes.

"Alex? Just say it. Is this about the room? What happened?"

He pauses before tying his other shoe and standing to face me. His eyes are shadowed and his jaw is tense. "The body . . . Emma, it was Lucas."

My eyes widen. "What?" My voice is strangled, and I shake my head in disbelief as I think of Marie and James and the heartbreak they must be feeling. "No, wait. Come on." I grab a zip-up sweatshirt and open the door to my room. In a few minutes, we're out of the house and walking down the driveway. The afternoon sun has faded to a gray evening glow, and the trees are tall shadows all around us. The whisper of cold air tingles my skin, and I pull on my sweatshirt.

"Okay. Tell me," I say grimly as I look up at him.

Alex rakes his hands through his hair. "I'm sorry. I should have told you when I got here, but I—"

"Hey," I grab his hand. "Stop. Just tell me what happened."

"He was in the room," Alex says. "I went there in the morning, hoping to see you once more before you left. I understood your concerns, and I have to admit, the remains scared me more than I was willing to acknowledge at the time. But I wanted to let you know how I felt, tell you that I'd never forget you." He squeezes my fingers. "I'm glad it didn't end that way."

"Me too," I say, and we continue walking in silence for a few moments.

"Anyway, I don't know how he got into the house again, but as I was sitting there, Lucas walked in. He started at first. I'm sure he wasn't expecting me, and then he got that cocky look on his face. 'So, you're Alex,' he said, and he laughed and rubbed his hands together. 'I *knew* there was something to this house! I was starting to think the whole room thing was bullshit, but I can admit I was wrong,' he said. Then he asked me how everything worked, how he could jump. I was totally honest with him, told him I didn't know, said I wasn't going to look into it anymore and that the remains found on the property dashed that hope.

"Then he got this gleam in his eye. He said it didn't matter because the room would still make a mint if only for the fact that he could see me, whereas, in the rest of the house, he couldn't. 'Do you know how much money can be made here, man?' he asked. I told him it didn't matter, that it wasn't his house to make decisions about, regardless. It didn't faze him one bit. He started talking about blackmailing my family, saying that now that he knew the secret, he was sure my family would pay 'a pretty penny' to keep it out of the tabloids. 'How much do you think it's worth?' he asked."

Alex lets go of my hand and puts both of his on the back of his neck, rubbing away tension as he leans his head back and looks at the sky. He takes a few deep breaths. "At that point, I was pissed," he says. "I figured since I was in the room, I could get in a solid punch or two, so I got up and walked toward him. But then . . ." He shakes his head and stops walking. "It was the weirdest thing. It was like a lightbulb was turned on and kept getting brighter and brighter. Then, I don't know how to describe it. It was like I could see the room in 1993, and I could see the room as it is today. The glass in the window was intact, as I remember it, but it was broken too, with shards of glass on the floor."

Alex starts walking again. "Lucas grabbed onto me, and I just remember staring at him, my terror reflected in his eyes. The light got even brighter. I had to shut my eyes. I covered them with my hands"—Alex raises his hands, mimicking the actions—"but it was like my hands weren't even there. The light was so intense. I felt Lucas grab on even tighter, but then he was wrenched away, and I heard the shattering of glass. I tried to turn to the sound, but it was everywhere and nowhere at the same time. I can't even tell you if I was able to move or not because I don't know if I did. I don't know how long it lasted—maybe twenty-five years." He laughs sardonically. "And then, eventually, I was able to open my eyes, and when I did, the window was shuttered, this"—he pulls out the letter I wrote to him from his back pocket—"was on the couch, and Lucas was gone."

"Wow" is all I can manage to say.

Alex nods. "I didn't even look out the window. I immediately left the room and went looking for you, but I found my mother instead—I'll tell you about that later—and not even a couple of minutes passed before Marie came in with a police officer."

We start walking once more, and I lead us in the direction of the neighborhood playground.

"Marie recognized me, and she grasped my arm and whispered, 'Welcome back.'" Alex smiles softly, but then he sobers. "We were all in a good mood, but Mother mentioned that the police officer was there to give her his findings on the body found in the yard. My mind went to

Lucas, of course, but how would that have been possible? They found *skeletal* remains. There was no way Lucas's body could decompose that quickly. The officer said forensics had been able to trace the DNA, but before he told us more, he wanted to understand something about the case. He found something extremely strange and wondered if maybe we could give him a plausible explanation."

"*Which* strange thing was he referring to?" I ask, somewhat amused.

"Well, that's the thing. You know as well as I do that there are a number he could have been talking about, but this one was new even to me. From the state of the remains, the body had been lying there for close to three decades, and forensics determined the remains belonged to a male of approximately thirty years."

I frown and then smile in confusion while shaking my head. "Okay . . . But that doesn't mean it was Lucas."

"Well, dental records determined the remains as belonging to a man who had only *recently* turned thirty, a man who hadn't even been reported missing."

"Ah," I say, my voice a whisper.

Alex meets my eyes with his and dips his head.

Having made it to the playground, I sit heavily on a swing, and Alex sits on the one next to mine. "So, what,

Lucas somehow jumped from today back to 1993 where you were?"

"All I know is that his body was found in the courtyard. Somehow, there must have been some sort of transference or something, and maybe the charge was so intense it blew him out the window, and because no one knew of the secret room, even if there was some chance of saving him, no one would have known where to look, especially with all the windows boarded up and covered."

I shake my head. "You've said before that you don't think people can go back in time, but this proves it's possible. I wonder if the consequences of going back are always so dire."

"I have no idea, but now I have almost zero doubt Christopher's disappearance had something to do with the room. He never confided in me, but what else could it have been?"

I place my hand on his knee. "Well, I haven't heard of any other remains being found, so that's a good sign he made it to wherever he jumped, if that's what happened."

We're silent for a few moments, and while I'm sure Alex is thinking of his brother, I think of Marie and James. *How did they find out?*

"Then what happened?"

"Well, the officer saw that Mother was anxious, so he got on with the report. He said initially they suspected the body to be mine."

I nod. "It makes sense. That's what we were thinking too."

Alex smiles. "You should have seen his face when Mother pointed to me and said, 'How could that possibly be Alexander when he's sitting right here?'"

I laugh along with Alex. "I can picture her saying that."

"Yes, Mother told me she met you. I have to hear your side of the story."

I nudge him. "Later. You have to finish this one first."

"'Alexander Eason? Your son, the man who went missing in 1993?' the officer asked. 'Does he look like he's missing?' Mother replied. He looked like he wanted to argue, but Mother continued. 'We never reported him missing, young man, because he wasn't. Regardless, it's neither here nor there. It wasn't Alex, so who was it?' And that's when he asked us if we knew a Mr. Lucas Lloyd." He drops his head. "Poor Marie had been standing in the room the whole time, as curious as the rest of us were. There was a crash as the plate she held in her hand fell to the floor before she followed right after."

I gasp, my hand coming to my mouth. "Oh, poor Marie."

"I immediately yelled for James, who luckily wasn't far, and then helped the officer get Marie situated on the couch."

"Is she okay?"

"She's fine—as well as can be expected. It was just the shock of it all."

"I need to go see them. They had their share of issues with him, but they loved him like a son."

Alex looks at me. "And you?"

"What do you mean?"

He sighs and looks away before turning to me once more. "Somehow, I got it into my head that there might be something more between you and Lucas."

My eyes widen in surprise. "What? Why do you think that?"

"Well, he whispered something to you right before James kicked him out, and then you were acting a bit strange afterward. And now, when I told you it was his body . . . I guess I just assumed there was more between you two than you were telling me."

I smile and reach over to grab his hand. "I promise there was never anything between me and Lucas." My smile falters. "He could have been a nice guy if he had put the past behind him." I think of how I had been warned to do the same about Eve—and Alex—and almost hadn't listened. It's one thing to think fondly about memories but quite another to not let go and move on.

"Do you think you'll ever be sorry you came forward?" I ask, fearful that Alex may be having doubts.

He turns in his swing and grabs onto the chains on either side of mine so we're facing one another, then he leans in and gives me a kiss. "Never."

The conviction in his voice is palpable, and it gives me the courage to face whatever is in store for us, regardless of how much time we have. Because time is unpredictable. Unpredictable and ephemeral. I squeeze Alex's hand and then sway back and forth on my swing, pumping my legs to gain momentum and lift me higher.

A wide smile appears on Alex's face as he also glides off the ground. We silently swing back and forth, our eyes focused on the future ahead of us. No matter how much time we have left, whatever time we do have, we'll make it count.

Epilogue

I finished yesterday. Alex asked me to write everything I could remember down. Another journal to add to all the others within these walls. And who knows, maybe it'll help someone else in the future. Alex says I should think about getting it published, turning it into an e-book, and perhaps get some readers. I think he just wants more visitors.

Alex loves our "company," the many people we meet each day looking for a thrilling story or hoping to catch a glimpse of a ghost for themselves. We have a steady stream of people from all over the world from the moment we open the doors in the morning until the time we close them late afternoons, and we've found more than a handful of individuals hiding in one room or another, hoping to spend the night and conduct séances. Some of them see our ghosts, and some of them don't. The skepticism on both sides is real, and that is part of what keeps some of them coming back time and again.

For myself, I feel honored to see them. I've come to realize the ones dressed up in period clothing are always smiling and polite. Maybe it's because they know the secret, that as long as time exists, no one is ever dead, not in the grand scheme of things anyway. I've also come to realize that time runs concurrently as well as chronologically, and although we can't jump back to the past or open a door to the future at will, we're all ultimately headed in one direction—toward personal fulfillment.

One thing Alex and Marilyn agreed upon was closing the room. It has caused a lot of heartache for their family, even if it brought happiness too. But they've made it possible to exit the room from the inside, just in case someone happens to show up in the future.

Marilyn doesn't live at Hillfield. She says it's too big, too much for her eighty-year-old body to handle. Plus, although she won't admit it, I think she's still searching. Now and then, she'll leave the comfortable flat she bought to go on what she says is an adventure, but I know it's a lead she is pursuing. She will continue to look for Christopher until her dying day.

Alex searches too. He's become a master of all social media platforms, and sometimes when he thinks I'm sleeping, I'll watch him as he's bent over the computer, the back of his head a silhouette against the glowing screen, examining the faces of individuals who might be his brother. And who can blame him?

But that doesn't mean he's put his life on hold. He's studying to retake the bar exam—there have been more than a few changes since 1993—but while he's studying, he enjoys giving tours of his house, meeting new people, and living life to the fullest. And every day, he makes sure I know how grateful he is that I'm there to share his journey. I'm grateful too and try not to take any moment we have together for granted. Life's too short for that.

So, yes, it has been a year since Alex traveled and ten months since we reopened the house for tours. Mom and Dad have decided they'll stay at Grandma's house for half the year and in the States for the other half. I'm glad. It'll be that much easier to visit them regularly. I also see Marie and James occasionally. They were here for the grand reopening, and I, of course, went to Lucas's funeral. It was the first I'd been to since Eve's, and it brought back a lot of memories, but I had to be there, thankfully with Alex by my side.

I still miss Eve every day, but it's getting easier to laugh at memories without the accompaniment of tears. Whenever I think of something we did together, I smile, the memories in my head mini reenactments of events that I now know will take place over and over again, ad infinitum. Why? Because once here, no one ever goes away. Not really.

I've learned to take comfort in that.

Acknowledgments

Whew! Like *The House on the Lake*, there were times I did not think *Within These Walls* would get done, and it had nothing to do with the story itself and everything to do with procrastination. Why? I'm not sure. The question whether you, dear reader, would enjoy this tale definitely flitted through my mind on more than one occasion. And with that said, I'd first like to thank *you*! Thank you for liking the cover or blurb enough to purchase *Within These Walls*. I sincerely hope you enjoyed Emma and Alex's story, and I would be grateful if you took another moment of your time to leave a review.

Thanks to my students who, with what sounded like genuine sincerity, wanted to listen to a scene from *Within These Walls*. I'm sure it had nothing to do with an actual interest in my story and everything to do with getting out of five minutes of literature analysis, but it made me feel good nonetheless. Plus, you all gave the appropriate "That sounds really good!" response, so you all pass! Haha.

Even more thanks go to my beta readers, Monique Seelen, Judy Cross, and Lindsey Pogue. You read more than a scene and couldn't be bribed with good grades! Thank you fo your input. You gave me some great pointers, and your enthusiasm when I asked you to read was heartwarming.

I'd like to thank my ARC readers as well. Some of you have read my stories before and others are reading my work for the first time. I hope this story doesn't disappoint!

Finally, I want to thank my husband and my boys. I wouldn't be the person who wrote this story without you, so you made it possible. Pi!

About the Author

Holly Hill Mangin is an English literature teacher at a prestigious lycée in the South of France, a freelance copy editor at Fresh as a Daisy Editing, and the author of *The House on the Lake,* which won a gold medal in the Wishing Shelf Book Awards. Holly lives with her husband and their two kids a stone's throw away from the French Riviera, and she finds that reading and writing go a long way in procrastinating learning French.

Other Books by Holly Hill Mangin

The House on the Lake
Le Maison sur le lac (French edition)
Nora: A Savage North Chronicles Fanfiction Novella

Printed in Great Britain
by Amazon

27159593R00235